Faith Map

Resources for children based on the Sunday readings

Year B

Written by
Maurice Billingsley
Rachel Denton
Yvonne Fordyce
Jill Ormondroyd
Moire O'Sullivan
Ian Smith
Stephanie Thornton
Kathryn Turner

Edited by Yvonne Fordyce
Design by Active Noise
Illustrations by Louise Hilton

Published by Redemptorist Publications in 2005
Alphonsus House, Chawton, Hampshire, GU34 3HQ UK
Tel: +44 (0)1420 88222 Fax: +44 (0)1420 88805
email: rp@rpbooks.co.uk, www.rpbooks.co.uk
A registered Charity limited by guarantee.
Registered in England 3261721

ISBN 978-0-85231-304-6

Printed by Butler Tanner & Dennis Ltd

Contents
Roman Catholic

Advent and Christmas

Lent, Easter and Pentecost

Ordinary Time

Solemnities and Feasts

Contents

Anglican

FaithMap follows the Catholic Lectionary. Often, the readings on which the text is based are the same as those given in the *Common Worship* lectionary. This list, therefore, only indexes those Sundays on which this happens. On occasions when the Catholic and *Common Worship* lectionaries do not match up, the user may wish to consider working from the Catholic provision for the day.

Advent and Christmas

Lent, Easter and Pentecost

Ordinary Time

Sundays after Trinity

Principal Feasts and Festivals

if earlier than the Second Sunday before Lent
* if after Trinity Sunday

Introducing FaithMap Year B

FaithMap is interactive, fun and engaging for children of all ages and abilities. It is a valuable resource for anyone involved with Children's liturgies, Sunday schools or children's groups. It can also be used in primary schools for assemblies or class teaching and by parents who want to explore the Gospel message at home with their family.

Designed for a range of ages, **FaithMap** offers a choice of two approaches: "Young Ones" and "Juniors", plus additional suggestions for children with learning difficulties.

FaithMap is based on the Catholic Lectionary for Year B (on the majority of Sundays this coincides with the *Common Worship* Lectionary) covering all possible Sunday celebrations in Year B. Each week the Sunday Gospel is explored through 5 sections.

1. **Introduction** to the theme of the day with a Leader's Reflection.
2. **Arrival:** Gather around a focal point, which reflects the theme of the day. The Sunday Gospel is read from the Lectionary or the Children's Lectionary.
3. **Response:** Suggested questions for discussion to find out what the Gospel is asking of us. A story or real-life experience follows, to link up with the Gospel and to help the children understand its message.
4. **Activity:** A practical section with a photocopiable template and suggestions for activities suitable for a range of abilities. Tips for those with learning difficulties are included.
5. **We Come Together** to share, pray and sing, offering the opportunity for parents to join in the group's activities. TheGospel message is highlighted, and work from the activities shared in a short prayer time to end the meeting.

There is also a photocopiable **Family Sheet** for each week, which the children can take away with them and use during the week. This takes the learning experience home, back to the heart of the family for ongoing discussion and daily prayer. It includes a weekly thought for parents, and a picture symbol to mark/colour each day when the suggested action is completed.

It's a rich resource giving you all the information, ideas and material you need to run successful sessions with children. Use some, or all of the sections, and feel free to add your own ideas to help bring the Gospel message alive.

We hope that you and the children in your care will enjoy using **FaithMap.**

1st Sunday of Advent

1. Introduction to the theme of the day

Aim: To recognise that we are at the beginning of a new liturgical year – Year B – and to turn our eyes to Jesus, who created a whole new beginning for the world when he was born as a baby in Bethlehem.

Leader's Reflection: Although we begin to use Mark's Gospel this week, we do not use it in earnest until after Christmas. This week's reading is, in fact, taken from almost the end of the Gospel as Jesus prepares his disciples for his death and the struggles that they will soon be facing.
He knows that one of the biggest dangers in the spiritual life is to become complacent and encourages his disciples (including us) to maintain a spirit of alertness and awareness. It is easy to begin to drift and to lose the cutting edge of our faith, yet it is our enthusiasm and delight in it that can be our greatest evangelising tool.

2. We arrive

We sit in a circle ready to listen to the Gospel.
Remind the children that we are looking forward to something that is quite close – what is it? And how do they feel about it?
Talk about the new church year and that we are entering the Season of Advent, which is all about looking forward to Jesus' coming.

Focus

Purple cloth and candle.
Advent wreath.

Gospel: Mark 13:33-37

Read from the Lectionary or Children's Lectionary.

3. We respond

What is the Gospel asking of us?

Work in age groups if appropriate. Alternatively, choose the discussion ideas, story and activity most suitable for your group.

Young ones

Invite the children to think about times when they have been too excited to sleep: Christmas/birthdays/getting ready for holidays and so on.

Story (read with help from the children)

Gordon was driving his mum up the wall.

Tomorrow was to be his birthday and he was going to have a bonfire party with fireworks.

But he was just too excited and his mum was beginning to wonder why she had suggested it.

"Gordon, I know you're excited but you still have school tomorrow so...

All: **"Go to bed, Gordon!"**

Gordon hopped from one foot to the other – he was too happy to be cross at being told off.

"Come on now," said his mum. "Get into your pyjamas."

Gordon found his pyjamas but decided to use the top as a cape and play Batman.

Mum said warningly, "Gordon..." so he stopped playing Batman and put on his pyjamas.

He managed to brush his teeth without too much trouble and then Mum said,

All: **"Go to bed, Gordon!"**

They went upstairs and he and his mum said their prayers – asking God for a nice evening tomorrow, and that he would bless Nanny, Uncle Joe, Auntie Mary, the hamster, his friend Alec's goldfish ... and ... suddenly Mum realised that Gordon sounded as if he was going to ask God to bless everyone in the whole world and this could go on all night! "That's enough now – God has plenty to be going on with. It's time to...

All: **"Go to bed, Gordon!"**

Gordon got into bed – Mum kissed him goodnight and turned out the light.

A few minutes later, Gordon switched on the light.

All: **"Go to bed, Gordon!"**

Gordon switched off the light and got back into bed.

A few minutes later he tiptoed to the door and opened it.

"Where are you going?" asked his mum.

"Oh, just to the bathroom," said Gordon.

"Well, hurry up and...

All: **"Go to bed, Gordon!"**

Gordon went back to bed.

A few minutes later, he got up and went to the door.

"Mum, I'm thirsty"

His mum got him a drink and said,

All: **"Go to bed, Gordon!"**

Gordon went to bed. He tossed and he turned. He tried lying on his back. He tried lying on his side. He tried lying on his front. He tried to count sheep. He sang all his favourite songs in his head. He thought about his friends – but that just made him all excited again. He was awake even after his mum went to bed. He just wasn't going to get to sleep that night, he decided.

Then – just as if only a few minutes had passed – he heard his door open and realised that he had gone to sleep after all. There was his mum with a big smile on her face.

"Happy birthday – I'm amazed you aren't downstairs already! It's time to...

All: **"Get out of bed, Gordon!"**

Juniors

Talk about waiting for Jesus to come: how the Jewish people expected the Messiah and longed for his coming; how Jesus comes to us today in his word and in communion; how Jesus has promised to come again.

Story

Isaiah was always unusual. He spent a lot of time thinking about things and talking about how God might feel about the way people were living.

His family knew that people were not living as God wanted. They also knew that Judah was under threat from their neighbour Assyria.

Isaiah did not agree. He insisted that the people had to grow strong in trust again and to be obedient to God's Law and then the country would be safe. He put his thoughts into writing and, though it made him unpopular with some people, others agreed with what he said. It was not that he thought things were hopeless – just that people had their priorities wrong.

What the people of Judah had feared did eventually happen – Assyria overran their country. Many of its people were sent into exile in Babylon far from home – among people who did not believe in God. They began to see where they had gone wrong but thought that they would never be able to return home and put things right.

Friends of Isaiah had kept his writings and began to add to them. They promised the people that God would bring them home – and that they would be allowed to start again. They encouraged the people to have faith and trust in God.

What they promised would happen came about – and the people were allowed to return to Jerusalem. The prophets reminded them that they had learnt a hard lesson – and now was the time to live as God had always wanted his people to live: acting justly, being loving and merciful and walking humbly with their God.

Encourage comments relating the story to the Gospel.

4. Activity

The activities over the coming weeks are based loosely on the Jesse Tree – this will extend into the Christmas period. During Advent, use a branch in a pot of sand. The branch should be large enough for the children to hang the fruits of their labours from for the next four sessions.

Young ones

Use the template to cut out enough candles from card for the group. The children can colour them in – or, if time and resources permit, use sequins and ribbon to decorate them.

Juniors

Activity as for the younger children but the children could write "Happy New Year: Year B, Year of Mark" on the candle.

Tips for learning difficulties

Have the candles ready to decorate. Ensure that there are bright colours for the children to use.

5. We come together

Parents can be invited to join in at this stage.

Focus

Invite everyone to become still and to look at the Advent wreath. Remind everyone about the special season we are beginning.

Light the first candle and sing the first verse of "Christmas is coming, the Church is glad to sing" (John Bell) or another candle-lighting song.

Gospel

Jesus wants his friends to be ready for his coming. We meet Jesus today in his word and in communion. He wants us to be alert and ready to welcome him with open hearts.

Prayer

Jesus, this special time of year reminds us that we can meet you every day.

Keep us awake and alert so that we recognise you in your word, in Holy Communion and in other people. Amen.

Share

Talk about what happened in the session – what the children have learnt. Invite the children to hang their candles on the branch – perhaps with a reprise of the candle-lighting song.

Sing

"Christian children, Advent bids you"

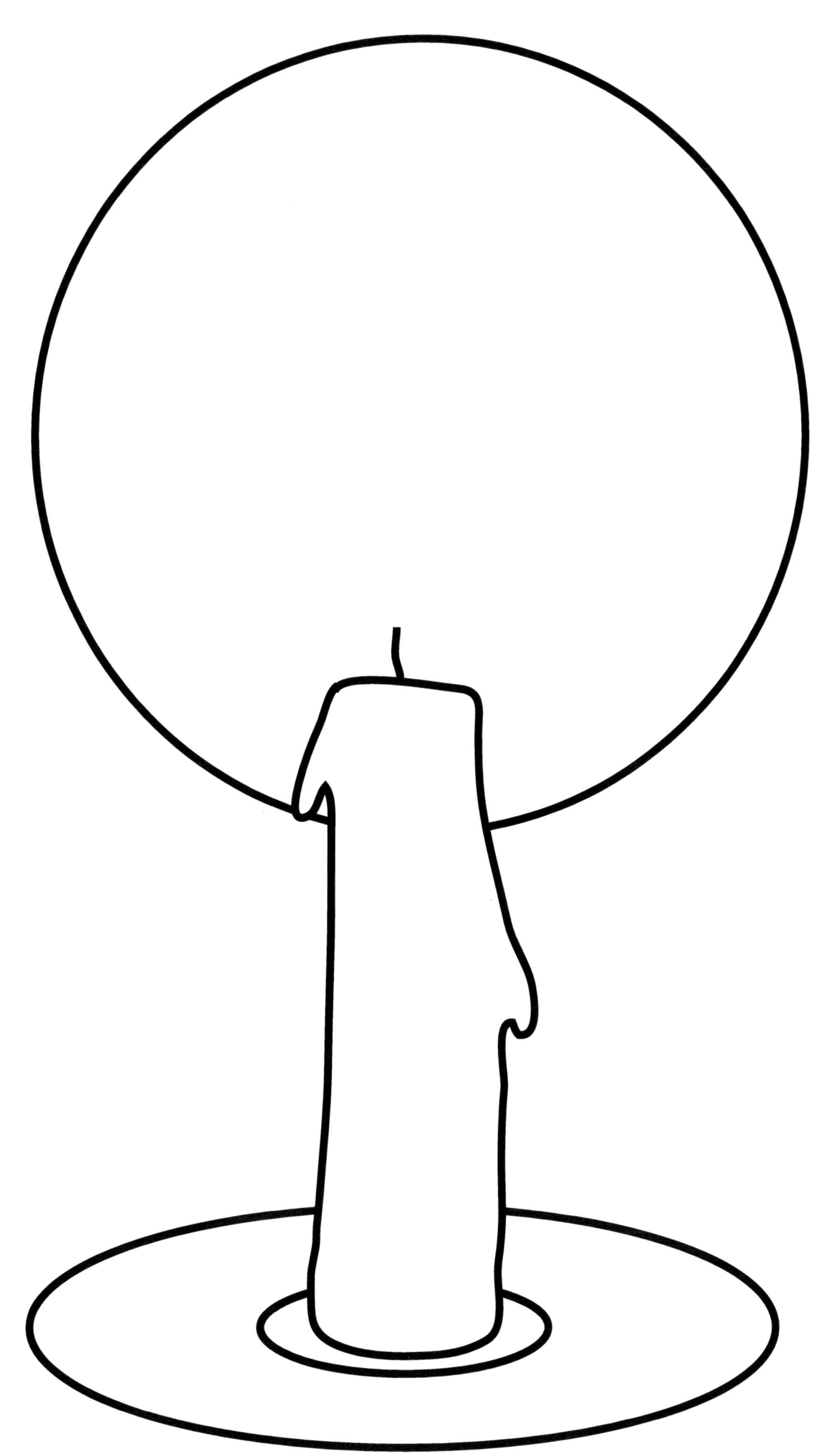

2nd Sunday of Advent

1. Introduction to the theme of the day

"Prepare a way for the Lord"

Aim: To introduce John the Baptist as a prophet: the one who prepared the way for Jesus.

Leader's Reflection: The life of a Christian can often feel like being John the Baptist – a voice crying in the wilderness. In our ministry, however, we can take his work as our model and ethos. We are working to prepare a way for the Lord – making his paths into the hearts and minds of those we work with open and ready.

John's sense of proportion offers useful reminders too. He was a great man with many followers but he knew that his work, like the work of all prophets, was constantly to point people towards one who was still greater and who, two thousand years later, has millions of followers.

2. We arrive

We sit in a circle ready to listen to the Gospel.
Has anyone anything they would like to tell us about stars they saw last week? What good things did people see?

Focus

Purple cloth.
Advent wreath.

Gospel: Mark 1:1-8

Read from the Lectionary or Children's Lectionary.

3. We respond

What is the Gospel asking of us?

Work in age groups if appropriate. Alternatively, choose the discussion ideas, story and activity most suitable for your group.

Young ones

Have the children seen people making roads or laying paths? What sorts of things do such people have to do? Think about: clearing the ground, bringing in the materials, hard work and so on.

Story (read with help from the children)

Leonie was looking forward to the weekend. Last summer, Dad had built her a playhouse and she had had a great time with her brother and sister and all their friends. They had had picnics in there nearly every day.

When autumn came they could still play in the playhouse but by the winter, the ground was so soggy that they couldn't get to the house to play any more. Dad had promised that, when the fine weather came again, he would make a path for them – and next weekend was when it was going to happen.

It was much more complicated than Leonie had expected. Before they even started, Dad took her out and asked her to show him how she got to the playhouse. Leonie thought this was a silly question until Dad said, "Well, you don't walk through the pond, do you? And what about the washing line?"

So Leonie showed her dad how she came out of the door, walked past the dustbin, onto the grass, round the pond, past the washing line, round behind the tall shrubs and into her house.

Dad had a long think.

"Hmmm," he said.

Leonie knew that "Hmmm." Dad loved building things and had brilliant ideas. He could make amazing things out of things that other people threw away. Mum was always saying:

All: "Now what's he up to?"

"Right," he said and off he went.

When he came back, he had some bags of concrete-mix, a few bits of metal fencing and some bits of old wood.

All: "Now what's he up to?"

First of all, he made different shaped moulds using some of the old wood and poured concrete in. Then he fixed the two bits of metal fencing to a strong piece of wood. Then he disappeared into the tall shrubs with some more of the wood. And then he said, "That will do nicely for one day."

The next day, he took the wooden moulds from the concrete and Leonie could see that he had made arrow-shaped ones and house-shaped ones. He laid them like stepping stones in the grass – straight towards the pond.

All: "Now what's he up to?"

He called her mum out to help and together they carried the strong piece of wood with metal railings onto the garden and manoeuvred it across the pond! "I'll use the other metal pieces to make guard rails either side", Dad said to her mum.

He carried on laying the paving – past the washing line – and straight towards the tall shrubs

All: "Now what's he up to?"

Dad disappeared into the tall shrubs. "You wait there," he said.

All: "Now what's he up to?"

Leonie could hear clipping and then sawing and hammering and her dad reappeared with twigs sticking up out of his hair. "Just the last slabs now," he said.

An hour or so later, he had fixed the last bits of metal fencing to those across the pond. "Now," he said, "show me how you're going to get to the house."

So Leonie went out of the door, walked past the dustbin, onto the stepping stones, across the bridge over the pond, past the washing line, under the arch through the tall shrubs and into her house.

Dad came and joined her. "Not a bad weekend's work," he said. "Wonder if I could do something to make Gran's garden path a bit straighter for her... Hmmm."

"Uh-oh," thought Leonie,

All: "Now what's he up to?"

Juniors

What do the children understand about making a way for the Lord? What sorts of things help to prepare people to meet Jesus and to get to know him better: the Gospel stories, people's actions – showing love and kindness.

Story

St Ignatius Loyola was born into a wealthy Spanish family. As a young man, his life would not have been seen as preparing a way for the Lord as he used his money to buy extravagant clothes and kept bad company.

Eventually, he became a soldier. He was seriously injured by a cannon ball and endured a terrible recovery which included operations without anaesthetic. His bravery amazed those who looked after him. During his long recovery, he read about the lives of the saints, and realised that he wanted to become a different kind of soldier: one who used his courage to speak up for Jesus. He had visions which helped him to see that he had made the right choice, but also many trials and fears.

From these he learned a new way to be strong and brave – a way that attracted other men – and together they founded a new order called the Society of Jesus, or Jesuits. They travelled far and wide, teaching people the Good News about Jesus.

Today, they are often found on the side of the poor and vulnerable – using their gifts and talents in practical ways and helping people to come to know Jesus through them.

Invite the children to respond to the story of St Ignatius. Do they know of other people whose lives help people to get to know Jesus?

4. Activity

Young ones

Use the template to cut out enough prophets from card for the group. The children can colour them in – or, if time and resources permit, use cloth for clothes and wool for hair and beard.

As the children work, explain that the prophets told the world that a special person called the Messiah was going to come to make the world a better place. We believe that person is Jesus.

Juniors

Activity as for the younger children but the children could be invited to write on the scroll something good that they would like to prophesy for the world. Talk about possibilities as they work: people who are hungry will be fed; those unjustly held in prison will be freed. Also encourage them to think about the part they might play in this – now and in the future.

Tips for learning difficulties

Have the figures ready with cloth clothes and woollen hair ready cut. Help the children to draw a smiley face on the prophet – explain that a prophet is someone who tells people how much God loves them and wants them to be happy.

5. We come together

Parents can be invited to join in at this stage.

Focus

Light two candles in the Advent wreath and sing the first two verses of "Christmas is coming" or another candle-lighting song.

Gospel

Jesus did not come unannounced. God planned his coming and sent messengers called prophets to prepare people to meet him. John the Baptist was the last and greatest of the prophets. The coming of the Messiah was imminent.

Prayer

Lord Jesus, we want to be your messengers.
Help us to live in ways that help people to see what being a Christian means.
Teach us how to prepare the way for you.
Amen.

Share

Talk about what happened in the session, and what the children have learnt. Hang the figures of the prophets on the branch, perhaps singing the candle-lighting song again.

Sing

"The King of glory comes"

3rd Sunday of Advent

1. Introduction to the theme of the day

"Witness to the light"

Aim: To reflect on our call to be witnesses to the light of Christ.

Leader's Reflection: John the Baptist again takes centre-stage in the Gospel. His charisma has attracted a great deal of interest and some have begun to speculate about who he might be.

It is tempting to see the questioning as doubting or trying to catch John out but, in fact, questioning and trying to get to the truth of the matter is something that it is helpful to cultivate.

We respect the questions of those we share the Gospel with. If we ourselves have questions it is important to explore them – even if we do not find completely satisfying answers. God gave us intelligence to learn more about him – though he desires that it is tempered with a humility to accept that sometimes we have to fall silent in front of the mystery that is God.

2. We arrive

We sit in a circle ready to listen to the Gospel.

Has anyone anything they would like to tell us about last week's Family Sheet? Did anyone try the "as the crow flies" activity?

Focus

Purple cloth.

Advent wreath.

Gospel: John 1:6-8. 19-28

Read from the Lectionary or Children's Lectionary.

3. We respond

What is the Gospel asking of us?

Work in age groups if appropriate. Alternatively, choose the discussion ideas, story and activity most suitable for your group.

Young ones

Being afraid of the dark is very common – talk to the children about this fear and the ways in which families help them to cope with it: nightlights, things to cuddle and so on.

Story

"Basil, you cannot be afraid of the dark. You are a nocturnal animal. We sleep during the day and we hunt at night. It's what bats do."

Basil's mum was exasperated. All her other children had been perfectly normal bats. They had been born, grown strong, and had gone out at night to hunt for insects. What she had done to get a bat like Basil she would never know. To make matters worse, because he wouldn't leave the nest to hunt for himself, she was still having to bring food home for him. This could not go on.

"Basil," she said, "just what are you afraid of?"

"Dunno," said Basil.

"That doesn't help. Come on now – what is it?"

"Just don't like it."

"How do you know you don't like it if you've never tried it? It's dark in the nest – you don't mind that!"

"'S diff'rent. It's inside dark not outside dark."

"Dark is dark," said his mother. "Well, if you want to stay here and be silly that's fine – but I am off to enjoy the evening. I'll be back later – but don't expect me to bring any treats home. You'll have to be satisfied with midges – if you want juicy moths you'll have to get them yourself."

Basil was left alone. He had to admit that midges were getting very boring – but his mum wouldn't bring him anything that was too heavy to carry. He was also getting a bit fed-up of being told off and embarrassed about being the only bat ever to be frightened of the dark. He wondered if he should try to look out of the nest and see what the outside dark looked like.

He peeped through a crack and saw that it was actually lighter outside than inside.

"That's odd," thought Basil. "How can outside dark be lighter than inside dark?"

He crept quietly along the roost. He was the only one there anyway – but he did not really want anyone coming back to see him.

He stuck his nose around the exit hole of the roost. It definitely was lighter outside than inside but he could not see why.

He put all of his head outside the hole to try and work out why – but could not see.

He put the top half of his body out – but still couldn't see.

There was nothing for it: he crawled out and perched by the hole – and he still couldn't see.

In a flash he decided what to do. He spread his wings wide and thought, "I'll fly out – take a look – and fly back."

So, for the very first time, Basil flew in the outside dark. And to his surprise, there, high above him, was a gigantic silver ball and glitter stuck to the sky. It was so beautiful that he suddenly became very curious and started to fly higher and higher to see what the ball was...

But he never found out – because on the way he met hundreds of very juicy moths and decided that they were much more interesting than silver balls in the sky.

Invite the children to respond to the story – why was the outside dark lighter than the inside dark? How did that help Basil?

Juniors

We take electric light for granted now. We walk into a room, flick a switch and the light comes on. A man called Thomas Edison is the person we have to thank.

Edison was an inventor and produced wonderful new ideas for using electricity. Perhaps his most famous invention was the light bulb. Until then, people had some electric lights but most of them used gas lights. Unfortunately, gas lights had open, flickery flames and were dangerous.

Developing the light bulb was not an easy job. The hardest part was finding the right material for the filament (the little wire inside the light bulb). Edison filled more than 40,000 pages with notes before, in 1879, he finally had a bulb that survived a 40-hour test in his laboratory. He tested more than 1,600 materials including coconut fibre, fishing line, and even hairs from a friend's beard, until he tried carbonised bamboo which proved to be a winner.

Obviously, an electric light bulb that only worked in a laboratory was not going to be a lot of use and so Edison went on to work out how to make a lighting system where power was generated and sent along cables to light bulbs in people's homes.

What we take for granted was like a miracle to the people at the time!

Discuss the difference that having electric lighting has made to people's lives: in homes, offices and workplaces, camping and outdoor pursuits, lighthouses and so on.

Draw out the benefits of being able to see things that were hidden, being safer, being able to explore things.

Help the children to link that to the light of Christ: his light helps us to see the difference between good and evil; shows us the way to live our lives; shows us the good hidden in others. In his light we can feel secure.

Talk about the role of the witness – one who has seen and heard and who tells others. How can we witness to the light of Christ we have seen and heard? (e.g. talking about it/setting a good example)

4. Activity

Young ones

Use the template of John the Baptist to cut out figures for the children. The children can colour them in or dress them – furry fabric would be ideal for this.

Juniors

Use the template of John the Baptist but add a speech bubble in which the children write “Witness to the Light”.

Tips for learning difficulties

Have the figures cut out ready to glue on ready-made clothes and hair.

5. We come together

Parents can be invited to join in at this stage.

Focus

Light the third candle in the Advent wreath and sing the first three verses of “Christmas is coming” or another candle-lighting song. Invite those gathered to become still – to look at the wreath and to listen to the summary of the Gospel.

Gospel

John the Baptist is such an important figure that we hear about him two weeks running! He came as a witness to the light he knew was coming into the world – the light of Christ. He puzzled many people – but they all recognised him as a man of God and, though they did not understand, were attracted to what he had to say.

Prayer

Jesus, you are the light of the world.

Help us always to walk in the safety of your light.

Amen.

Share

Talk about what happened in the session – what the children have learnt – and hang the figures on the tree – perhaps singing the candle-lighting song again.

Sing

“Lord Jesus, come”

4th Sunday of Advent

1. Introduction to the theme of the day

“Gabriel’s mission to Mary”

Aim: To show how Mary’s obedience to the will of God changed the world.

Leader’s Reflection: The story of the Annunciation is so well known that it is easy to miss its significance. It is, however, one of many similar encounters between humans and messengers from God – not all of which are recorded or possibly even recognised. God is intimately concerned with the lives of his children and strives always to lead us on the path which leads to fullness of life. Each person has a destiny – but whether they choose to accept the challenge is always up to them. God never imposes – though he can make it hard to say “no”. Obedience to God and the willingness to accept our destiny will never be easy options. Like Mary, we ask “How?” or “Why me?”
Like Mary, it is unlikely that we will know fully whether we have succeeded until the day we encounter the risen Lord and know that he is truly alive – and so are we.

2. We arrive

We sit in a circle ready to listen to the Gospel.
Has anyone anything they would like to tell us about last week’s Family Sheet? Did anyone find out what time the sun rises on their birthday?

Focus

Purple cloth.
Advent wreath.

Gospel: Luke 1:26-38

Read from the Lectionary or Children’s Lectionary.

3. We respond

What is the Gospel asking of us?

This week, there is one story which is likely to appeal to all ages. Younger ones will simply enjoy the story; older ones may appreciate the humour and understand the biblical allusions. Work in age groups, if appropriate, for the activities.

Story

Muriel was an apprentice angel. She had been an apprentice angel for a very long time – though as the other angels said, "We don't have time in heaven, we have eternity." Muriel knew that, of course, but the facts were the same, she just wasn't making any progress towards being a fully qualified angel.

"You're trying too hard," said her friend Nathaniel.

"It's all right for you," said Muriel, "you've been a proper angel for two thousand three hundred and seventy-six human years. You've been on loads of solo missions from God. I still have to go with an experienced angel until I can prove I won't mess things up."

She blushed slightly as she remembered her last effort. She had gone with Gabriel to talk to a man called Zechariah about his wife, Elizabeth, who was going to have a baby – even though she was quite old. This baby, God said, was going to be a great prophet who would prepare people for the birth of the Messiah. It had all gone really well at first. But then Gabriel had said, "Your wife will have a son", and Zechariah had said, "That's impossible!" and then Muriel had said – well, what she had meant to say was, "You can't speak to Gabriel like that" – but she had only got as far as "You can't speak" – and now Zechariah couldn't – speak, that is.

Gabriel had just sighed and said, "Once the baby's born, he'll be fine but Muriel, please ... oh never mind."

Nathaniel had laughed when Muriel told him about it – but Muriel said, "It's OK for you to laugh – but how is he going to tell anyone that the baby's name is to be John?"

What made matters worse was that Muriel was supposed to be going on another baby-announcing mission – with Gabriel!

And he was on his way over to them at that very moment.

"Hello, Nathaniel. Ready, Muriel?"

Muriel got up slowly.

"All you have to say is, 'Do not be afraid'. Best start practising now, I think?"

Muriel practised saying "Do not be afraid" in as many different ways as she could all the way to Nazareth.

They entered the house and there was a young woman busy getting a meal ready.

She turned, saw the two angels, and dropped her cooking pot on the floor where it smashed into pieces.

Gabriel poked Muriel in the back. "Now," he whispered out of the side of his mouth.

Muriel could not say a word. The young woman looked so shocked and upset as she looked from the angels to the broken cooking pot and back again that Muriel felt really sorry for her.

She went over to the pieces – and the young woman backed away.

Muriel looked at Gabriel who smiled and nodded and Muriel carefully picked up the pieces, asked God for a kind gesture, and then handed the mended pot back to Mary and said, "Don't be afraid."

The rest of the mission was easy. Mary had said "yes" and God's plan could go ahead.

Best of all, Gabriel had told Muriel that she was going on another mission – around the time Mary's baby was born.

She had to practise saying, "Do not be afraid" again and would have to join the angel choir to learn how to sing "Glory to God in the highest" – but now she would be doing it as a fully qualified angel.

As Gabriel had said, this was the most important mission an angel had ever had to do – and Muriel had pulled it off.

Young ones

Invite the children to respond to the story. Have they felt like Muriel – as if they were always getting things wrong? Do they know who Mary's baby is going to be? And what was Muriel's next mission going to be?

Juniors

Invite the children to respond to the story. What are the similarities between Gabriel's announcements to Zechariah and to Mary? What are the differences? Draw out the fact of Mary's reflective obedience.

What difference did her "yes" make to the world?

As a matter of interest – can the children tell you how Zechariah communicated his baby son's name when the time came? And what is Muriel's next mission going to be?

4. Activity

Young ones

Use the template to cut out figures of Mary. Use colouring pens/felt tips or fabric and wool.

Juniors

Use the activity as for the younger children but add a speech bubble in which the children can write "yes" or "let what you have said be done to me".

Tips for learning difficulties

Have the figures ready cut out with any fabrics or other materials prepared and cut to size.

5. We come together

Parents can be invited to join in at this stage.

Focus

Light the fourth candle and sing the four verses of "Christmas is coming" or another candle-lighting song. Invite those gathered to become still and ready to listen.

Gospel

God sends the angel Gabriel to a young woman, Mary, to announce that she is to conceive the one God has promised for so long. It was the dream of many young Jewish women but God chose one who was filled with grace and without sin. Her obedience changed the course of human history. It led to the birth of Jesus, the Son of God and Saviour of the world.

Prayer

Hail Mary, full of grace,
the Lord is with thee.
Blessed art thou among women
and blessed is the fruit of thy womb, Jesus.
Holy Mary, Mother of God,
pray for us sinners now and at the hour of our death.
Amen.

Share

Talk about what happened in the session – what the children have learnt. Hang the figures of Mary on the tree. Admire everyone's handiwork.

Sing

"Lord Jesus Christ"

The Nativity of Our Lord (Christmas Day)

1. Introduction to the theme of the day

Aim: To help the children to add a spiritual element to their Christmas festivities and to look at the characters who appear in the Christmas story.

Leader's Reflection: This could be a special session on Christmas Eve – helping the children to focus again on the spiritual dimension to Christmas. It could also give parents a useful extra hour to finish off shopping!

By the time we get to Christmas Day, many of us are exhausted by shopping, cooking, office parties or frantically trying to get things finished before the Christmas break. Coupled with the fact that in the northern hemisphere we are in the darkest days of the year with several months of wintry weather to come, it is easy to feel jaded and lacking in enthusiasm.

It is here that the "magic" of Christmas helps. We may be feeling Scrooge-like as we enter Christmas but the familiar carols, the warmth of greetings as we come together, and, for those of us who work with children, an infectious joy and excitement, all serve to melt the wintriness and remind us what Christmas is all about.

For many people, Christmas Day marks the end of Christmas – for us, it is the beginning of twelve days of celebration as we remember the holy night when God entered human history as a vulnerable baby, born into poverty but destined to save the world. Like Mary, it is unlikely that we will know fully whether we have succeeded until the day we encounter the Risen Lord and know that he is truly alive – and so are we.

2. We arrive

We sit in a circle ready to listen to the Gospel. Greet the children with a Happy Christmas. If meeting on Christmas Day, invite them to tell you about one of their presents and why it was so special. What did they give to their family and friends – and why did they choose those presents? If meeting on Christmas Eve, ask them what they would hope for – and, in strict confidence within the group, what have they prepared for others?

Focus

White/gold fabric. A crib. Gold or sparkly candle. An attractively illustrated version of the Christmas story.

Gospels: Matthew 1:1-25 (vigil); Luke 2:1-14 (midnight); Luke 2:15-20 (dawn); John 1: 1-18 (day)

Read from the Lectionary or Children's Lectionary.

You may like to use a summarised version so that the whole story can be told.

3. We respond

What is the Gospel asking of us?

It is likely that the group will be quite small – though there may be young visitors if families have come together for the festival. On this occasion it might be useful to have all the age groups together. Use the ideas as appropriate to your group for this session.

Young ones and Juniors

Story

The Christmas story is part of the greatest story ever told so instead of a story, the children will be encouraged to explore the original more deeply.

Have the children been in a Nativity Play in school or in the parish? What parts did they play? Can they tell you about it?

Think about the Christmas story and the people who appear in it. How did Joseph feel when the angel told him that Mary's baby was God's baby? How did they feel about having to go to Bethlehem? How did the innkeeper feel? And the shepherds? It can be interesting to invite the children to sit on a "hot seat" and speak in their own words about being a character in the story. For example:

"I am Joseph and ... I was very upset when Mary told me about the baby. Then the angel came in my dream and I knew that God wanted me to bring up his Son. I couldn't believe it, but said I would."
"I am a shepherd..."

Help the children to think about the impact the birth of Jesus had on the people around him ... was it all happy? Remind the children that people had waited thousands of years for this baby and had thought he would be a king born in a palace. The shepherds were people on the fringe of society – it shows us that Jesus came for the poor. How can we follow Jesus' example of caring for the poor – especially at this time of year?
Explain to the children that our Christmas story is taken from Matthew and Luke's Gospels. We have joined the two versions of Jesus' birth together to get a fuller picture. Mark has no "infancy narrative" and John's version of Jesus coming into the world is a sort of cosmic poem – some children may enjoy the language even if they cannot fully explain its meaning. Matthew was writing for Jewish people and he actually wrote a long family-tree for Jesus. Some children might be interested in seeing how far it goes back into history, right back to Abraham... some of the names are interesting to play with. Do the children recognise any of the names, e.g. Jacob and Joseph, David, Solomon?

4. Activity

Young ones

Cut out the template of Joseph, Mary and baby Jesus in the manger and paste onto card. Colour or use fabric and wool to make into decorations to hang on a Christmas tree.

Juniors

Collect pictures of cribs from around the world. Show the children how they reflect the country of origin. A huge selection can be found at http://www.udayton.edu/mary/gallery/creches.html
Explore the idea that Jesus came for everyone in the world and cribs are a good way of reminding us of this.

Bring the crib up to date. Explain that the first cribs were made by St Francis of Assisi. He wanted to show that Jesus was born into poverty and used a real stable and ox and ass to convince people that it was a very harsh place to be born. Invite the children to think about what would make a good example in our day. Have things like cardboard boxes, pieces of old cloth, newspapers and create a new setting for the crib figures – baby Jesus in a cardboard box with shredded newspaper and old cloths to keep him warm, etc.

Make a retablo. A retablo is a South American tradition – figures set in a box illustrating a Bible story and especially the crib. Any shallow box will do but a circular cheese box is attractive. Have the children cover the back with plain paper; on the inside, cover with dark blue paper and add silver stars. Use the outlines of Mary, Joseph and the baby in the manger and have the children cut them out of felt adding features to their faces. Use a sticky-fixer to fix them in the retablo to give a 3-D effect. Add string to hang it from the tree.

Tips for learning difficulties

Tell the Christmas story and point out details from the illustrations. Help the children to make the card figures or retablo – encourage them to enjoy the different textures and colours of the fabrics/stars/card, etc.

5. We come together

Parents can be invited to join in at this stage.

Focus

Light the candle. Invite those gathered to become still. Today we remember the great gift that God gave to the world when Jesus was born in Bethlehem. We take a few minutes to be still in the busyness and enjoy being together at this special time.

Gospel

Over two thousand years ago a baby was born in Bethlehem. His mother had had to make the long journey there with Joseph her husband because they had to be counted for Roman taxes. When they got there, they had to stay in a stable because there was no room for them in the inns.
When the baby was born, shepherds watching their sheep on the hillside heard angels singing and were told to go and worship the child. Most people did not hear anything – most people did not know that anything special had happened. But we know that on this night our Saviour was born: Jesus, the infant King.

Prayer

Loving Father, today we remember the day when Jesus was born.
Help us to enjoy this feast,
enjoying giving and receiving gifts
which remind us of the greatest gift of all –
your Son, Jesus.
Amen.

Share

Invite the children to show their parents the things they have made.
Christmas is such a busy and exciting time of year. It is easy to forget why we are celebrating – but today gives us a chance to remember that this is the day when Christians celebrate the birth of their Saviour, Jesus. We do not know the exact day of Jesus' birthday but in the dark days of December it is good to remember the birth of Jesus who is the Light of the World.

Sing

If time permits, allow the children to choose a few carols to sing – many will know them by heart. Or have a selection on transparencies to put up for everyone to join in.

The Holy Family of Jesus, Mary and Joseph

1. Introduction to the theme of the day

"Jesus' first visit to the temple"

Aim: To foster a sense of Jesus' place in Jewish history and tradition and the importance of older people in maintaining continuity and stability then and now.

Leader's Reflection: Jesus was born into an ordinary Jewish family who followed the customs and laws that their ancestors had followed for generations. They were part of what is sometimes known as the "Remnant" – a small number of people who held fast to the promise that God would send a Messiah. Simeon and Anna belonged to the Remnant too – long after it was fashionable or seemed likely any longer that a Messiah would appear. It was only to be at the end of very long lives that they would set eyes on an infant child and have the wisdom to see that this was the One God had promised to send. Linked through them into Jewish history and following the purification customs of his people, Jesus is revealed as a Jewish baby who will be brought up in accordance with the Law and who will, in time, be its fulfilment.

2. We arrive

We sit in a circle ready to listen to the Gospel.
Is everyone having a good Christmas? Take time to share the news of the week.
Has anyone anything they would like to tell us about last week's Family Sheet?

Focus

White or gold cloth.
Candle.
Crib.
The branch used in Advent is replaced by a Christmas tree on which the Advent figures have been hung.

Gospel: Luke 2:22-40

Read from the Lectionary or Children's Lectionary.

3. We respond

What is the Gospel asking of us?

Work in age groups if appropriate. Alternatively, choose the discussion ideas, story and activity most suitable for your group.

Young ones

Story

Christopher did not know much about anything that was going on around him. To be honest, even though it was nearly Christmas, all he did was sleep – wake up – feed – get changed – and go back to sleep again. Ciara thought it must be a really boring life – especially at Christmas when there were so many exciting things happening. Mum said that Ciara had been just the same at his age. Christopher was four weeks old.

Because he was born so near to Christmas, Gran and Grandad had invited the family to go to stay with them over Christmas and had asked Ciara and Christopher's aunties, uncles and cousins too. Ciara was looking forward to it.

When they arrived, everyone had a look at Christopher, who was fast asleep. Ben, who was the same age as Ciara, soon lost interest and said, "It doesn't do much, does it?" Ciara agreed – but said "It's not an it, it's a he." She was, after all, Christopher's big sister.

Grandad came over and took a look. He saw that Christopher was waking up. He undid the straps and lifted Christopher out. He took off his snowsuit and his hat and held him. Ciara was a little bit jealous – she would have liked a cuddle too. "But," she thought, "Christopher does look sweet with Grandad holding him." Somehow he looked even tinier than when Dad held him.

Grandad was talking to Christopher. "I remember holding your big sister when she was your age. She was so beautiful and such a good baby. I said to your mum, 'You can be very proud of this young lady. I bet when she's a bit older she'll make a very good big sister.' I think you're a very lucky young man to have a big sister like Ciara."

Grandad turned round and smiled down at Ciara. "I was right, wasn't I?"

Ciara smiled back. "Christopher's a very good baby too, Grandad. What do you think he'll be like when he gets bigger?"

"Let me see now," said Grandad. "Let's go and sit down with him and have a think about that."

And so they did. Grandad, Ciara and Christopher sat together on the sofa and Grandad and Ciara talked about what the baby would be like when he grew up.

Christopher did not know much about what was going on around him. He had gone back to sleep.

Invite the children to respond to the story. Did any of them see their grandparents over Christmas – or are they planning to go and see them/have them to stay?

Encourage them to talk about their grandparents – what do they especially enjoy doing with them? Do grandparents have special things that only they do (e.g. special words or treats)?

Juniors

On this occasion, give the children time to think about a story they would like to tell you – about their grandparents. Do their grandparents tell them stories of when they were young?

Be sensitive to those who might not be in contact and ensure that no one feels that they have to contribute. Encourage the children to value the special relationships that they may have with their grandparents.

Talk about Simeon and Anna. They were not Jesus' grandparents and were probably old enough to be his great-grandparents. Why did they recognise Jesus when other people did not? Draw out that they were not as busy as other people – that they were wise – that they took the time to look properly. Help the children to see that older people today have the same gifts – often undervalued but still precious.

4. Activity

Young ones

Use the template to make the members of the Holy Family. The children can colour them in or "dress" them with pieces of fabric. Stick them onto a piece of card ready to hang on the tree.

Juniors

As above but allow scope for greater creativity: the children could colour in a background for the card – the stable at Bethlehem or the temple, for example.

Tips for learning difficulties

Have the materials ready cut to size and shape. Help the children to choose which they want to use for each character and to stick them in place.

5. We come together

Parents can be invited to join in at this stage.

Focus

Light the Christ candle in the wreath. Invite those gathered to become still – to look at the candle and think about this special time of year. We have looked forward to Christmas for so long. Remind the children that each of the four Sundays of Advent is represented by a candle.

Gospel

We have celebrated the birth of Jesus. He was born into a Jewish family and they followed the customs laid out in the Law and took Jesus to the temple to follow the purification rituals that the Law required. There, he and his family were met by two elderly and very devout Jews, Simeon and Anna, who saw something very special about this family. They recognised that Jesus was going to grow up to be very great – that he was the one they had waited all their long lives to see. Simeon realised that the greatness would be costly and that Mary would suffer deeply. However, both saw God's hand at work again in human history and gave praise and thanks that they had lived to see it.

Prayer

Loving Father, thank you for the gift of Jesus. Thank you for our families who love us – and especially today for our grandparents and great-grandparents and all the older people we know who love us and who are wise and kind. Amen.

Share

Talk about what happened in the session – what the children have learnt. Hang the Holy Family images on the tree.

Sing

"Go, tell it on the mountain"

Solemnity of Mary, Mother of God

The 1st Sunday of Christmas

1. Introduction to the theme of the day

Aim: We remember that Jesus was God, even when he was a baby, even before he was born. That is why we call Mary "Mother of God".

Leader's reflection: Today we celebrate Mary, Mother of God. This is Mary's most authoritative title, and demonstrates clearly that the particular honours due to her are derived solely from her relationship to her son. Today, in celebrating her motherhood of God, we are also celebrating the fundamental truth of the Christian faith: Jesus, God and man.

2. We arrive

We sit in a circle ready to listen to the Gospel.
Has anyone anything they would like to tell us about last week's Family Sheet?

Focus

A lighted candle, white fabric,
baby clothes, baby doll or similar.

Gospel: Luke 2:16-21

Read from the Lectionary or Children's Lectionary.

3. We respond

What is the Gospel asking of us?

Work in age groups if appropriate.
We think about how God was born as a baby – Mary's son.

Young ones

Story

Mary was very tired. It was hard work having a baby! She had been there when Elizabeth gave birth to her little boy, John, so she knew what it was like, but even so she hadn't expected it all to be quite so busy and crowded. It wasn't really Joseph's fault, he had never been at a birth before, so she had sent him off to try and get some help, but she really hadn't expected him to bring back half the countryside with him. Well, the innkeeper's wife had been really helpful and Mary was grateful for that, but what those four shepherds were doing there she really didn't know.

Mary frowned to herself. It was all over now, and she had a job to do. When the angel came to tell her she was going to have a baby, he had said that Jesus would be the Messiah, the Son of God. God's Son! Mary hadn't told anybody, but all the time she was waiting for Jesus to be born, she had been just a little bit worried. If he was God, wouldn't that show in some way, make him different somehow, all shiny or something? Nobody had said anything yet, in fact the shepherds had all said he was quite adorable – but maybe they were just being polite. Very carefully Mary unwrapped the baby Jesus from his swaddling clothes. Ten fingers, ten toes, a bit squidgy looking, but all new-born babies looked like that. No, he just looked like any ordinary baby.

Mary smiled to herself and wrapped him up again and hugged him in her arms.

Juniors

Story

Imagine God: the ruler of the universe. Imagine God who not only created the universe, and then filled it with himself, but now rules over it all as well. Imagine God, bigger than the universe.

Imagine a human being. Imagine how small they are compared to the universe. Imagine a girl. Imagine the tiny space of her womb. Imagine the Whole of God, concentrated in that tiny space.

That is what happened when Mary agreed to be the Mother of God.

Mary knew that Jesus was the Son of God because the angel told her: "He will be called the Son of God" (in those days, if you were called something it was the same as being that thing), but it took over 400 years for the Church to officially say that Mary was the "Mother of God".

The way it happened was as the result of an argument about who Jesus was.

The argument was between two men called Cyril and Nestorius. Nestorius was Archbishop of Constantinople in 428. He believed that Jesus was God and that Jesus was human (which is right), but he believed that the "God" bit of Jesus and the "human" bit of Jesus could be separated. We sometimes hear about people who are "possessed" – they are taken over by another spirit (usually bad), and then that spirit goes away, and they are just themselves again. That is what Nestorius thought Jesus was like – that he was "possessed" by God's Spirit (which is good), but that when God's Spirit went away, you would be left with just Jesus.

Cyril was Patriarch of Alexandria. He said that Nestorius was wrong. He said that Jesus was God and Jesus was human, just the same as Nestorius said, but Cyril said they couldn't be separated. He said that if you took away the God bit of Jesus, then Jesus wouldn't exist any more, and if you took away the human bit of Jesus, then Jesus wouldn't exist any more.

The Church had a big debate about it at the Council of Ephesus. They decided that Cyril was right. Jesus was God and human, both of them, all of the time, and that they couldn't be separated, even when he was a baby, even before he was born. To prove how important it was, they made a new title for Mary – "Theotokos", which means "Mother of God", because even before she gave birth to him, Jesus was both human and God.

4. Activity

On the template page is a picture of Mary. You can see from her shape that she is pregnant.

Young ones

You need to colour in Mary's clothes so that she is warm and happy whilst she is waiting for Jesus to be born. Use lots of bright colours – her favourite colour is supposed to be blue.

Juniors

You will need a separate piece of paper. On it draw "God: Ruler of the Universe". Use your imagination. When it is finished, fold it up very small, and use glue to hold it in the space of Mary's womb (make sure you can still unfold it!)

Tips for learning difficulties

Make a collage of God from magazine pictures: stars, big countryside, mountains etc.

5. We come together

Parents can be invited to join in at this stage.

Focus

Gather around the candle and the baby clothes.

Gospel

After Jesus was born, shepherds came to the stable and told Mary and Joseph what the angels had said: "Today a saviour has been born and he is Christ the Lord." Mary thought about what they said. Her son, Jesus, was Christ the Lord. He was God.

Prayer

Mary, when your son Jesus was born, you knew that
he was the Son of God. You thought about
him, and about what that might
mean for the whole of your life.
Think about us now, and help us to
be good people like Jesus wanted.
Amen.

Share

In pairs, you can show the work you have done today.

Sing

"Mary had a baby, yes Lord"

2nd Sunday after Christmas

1. Introduction to the theme of the day

"Who is Jesus?"

Aim: We begin to find out more about Jesus, not just as a baby at Bethlehem, but as the most significant baby ever born. Today we learn that he existed even before time itself.

Leader's reflection: The next four weeks set the scene and the context for Jesus' active ministry. Today we listen to John's Gospel identifying Jesus with God himself before time began; during the week we celebrate the Epiphany – the revelation of Jesus to humankind. In the River Jordan next Sunday, Jesus embraces his manhood – fully God, fully man. At Cana he is identified as the one to bring unbounded joy to the lives of people, and finally, towards the end of January, as the fulfilment of the Old Testament scriptures.

2. We arrive

We sit in a circle ready to listen to the Gospel.
Has anyone anything they would like to tell us about last week's Family Sheet?

Focus

A lighted candle, white fabric for Christmastide. A globe or a picture of the world or of the stars.

Gospel: John 1:1-18

Read from the Lectionary or Children's Lectionary.

3. We respond

What is the Gospel asking of us?

Imagine a time before you were born, your parents might sometimes talk about those times. They might say, "before you were even thought of!" It is difficult to think of the world without ourselves in it. Now imagine a time before your parents were born, before anybody that you know was born. Imagine a time before anybody that you had ever heard of was born, before anybody at all was born, before the world even existed. St John tells us that, even then, the Son of God existed and loved us.

This week there is one story for all but work in age groups, if appropriate, for the activities.

Young ones and Juniors

You can prepare the youngest children for this week's story by asking them how old they are, how old their parents are, who the oldest person they know is. What about before all of those people were born – did people still exist? How do they know? Did the world exist before there were any people? What is the oldest creature they know? Did the world exist even before dinosaurs? The effectiveness of this story will depend on how it is read. Look through it beforehand to decide where you will pause, speak softly, sing out etc. It will work best if the children are lying down with their eyes closed.

Story

Close your eyes. It is dark. We are going to go right back to the beginning of time, before you existed, before I existed, before anything existed. It is dark. There is nothing at all, just darkness. Imagine nothing. Imagine the floor beneath you isn't there. Imagine yourself falling through it, falling through nothing, falling through darkness, through silence. Nothing at all.

Then God spoke!

Whoosh! For a split second, everything stops, everything freezes. Every nerve in your body tingles, the hairs on your head stand on end ... then ...

Hallelujah! Suddenly an explosion of light and warmth. The sound of that voice hits you like a thunderclap. Your body is thrilling with energy and you are swept along on a sea of happiness. Around you the tiniest bits of matter whirl and radiate light too bright for you to look at. Whirling and darting past you, under you, above you, all around you. And you want to sing!

That was the beginning. In the beginning God spoke.

As you watch, the tiny particles begin to find each other, to stick to each other. Slowly small lumps of shining matter are forming, sticking together like magnets, growing, getting bigger and bigger. It takes six billion years for the earth to form. At first a dark knot of molten lava, then, as it cools and the waters begin to gather, a shining jewel of green and blue.

You are set down on the dazzling earth by a lake in the cool of the shade under the trees. Even as your feet touch the ground, you can see fish beginning to form under the water of the lake. Shyly at first, then with more confidence, they come scrambling out of the water to look at you. More sure of themselves, they grow tall and wide and begin to strut across the land. You are walking with dinosaurs!

You watch from the shelter of a bush as more animals are formed; soon the air is filled with the rainbow flashes of birds on the wing, and across the ground swarm and patter and gallop creatures of every description and none. You recognise some of them, admiring the strength of the horses, and laughing at the antics of the monkeys; wondering at the beauty of the butterflies and trembling at the roar of the lion.

Then you see a creature that you know well. He stands upright with his head held high, and he grins at you. 3000 years before Christ and 5000 years before you were born, the first human walks on the face of the earth. All is well in the world, and God rests in his heaven.

4. Activity

Young ones

The young ones can help the juniors by providing them with pictures of dinosaurs, or of themselves, to attach to the timeline at the appropriate point.

Juniors

Use the information on the template sheet to make a timeline from the beginning of our universe to the present day. You will need a 15-metre length of string or strip of paper. Mark off each billion years (1 metre on the string) then attach it around the wall of the place you meet. Draw the events and attach them at the right place on the string. Compare the time before Jesus was born with the time since. Imagine God existing all that time, knowing that he was going to be born into the world he was creating, as a tiny baby.

Tips for learning difficulties

These ideas would be most suitable for those with quite severe learning difficulties. They aim to heighten the sensory experiences in the creation story. Before God speaks, cover the head of the child (and a helper, for reassurance) with a dark cloth. Pull the cloth off and throw a small amount of glitter into the light of a torch to represent the whirling atoms. As each animal is announced, produce a picture or a toy version. Use a mirror to show the child the "first human".

5. We come together

Parents can be invited to join in at this stage.

Focus

Gather together around the globe and candle. If possible have the rest of the room in darkness.

Gospel

This is the very beginning of St John's Gospel. He calls Jesus by a different name. He calls him "The Word". In our reading we shall use the name that we know best, "Jesus".

In the beginning was Jesus;
Jesus was with God.
And Jesus was God.
He was with God in the beginning.
He made everything.
He gave us life.
He came to live with us
And we saw that he was God.

Prayer

Dear Father, even before the world began, you existed. In Jesus, you made everything that exists. Thank you for sending him to live with us, so that we can know about you. Amen.

Share

Select a person from the group to tell everybody the story of the timeline.

Sing

"He's got the whole world in his hands"

Time	Distance on time line	The history of Evolution The story of Creation
Around 15 billion years ago	15 metres	Beginning of the Universe The very beginning of *Genesis* *God created the world*
Around 10 billion years ago	10 metres	Universe cooled down to the temperature of the sun
		Stars and galaxies start to form
5 billion years ago	5 metres	Earth formed
4 billion years ago	4 metres	The oldest rocks we can find on earth date from around this time
3 billion years ago	3 metres	Life began
500 million years ago (1/2 billion)	50 cm	First vertebrates (fish) were formed
250 million years ago	25 cm	Dinosaur era
65 million years ago	6.5 cm	The dinosaurs disappear and other land animals begin to develop
5 million years ago	5 cm	First apes
2 million years ago	2 cm	Apes stand up – the beginning of the human era
		The story of Adam and Eve. God created man and woman
5000 years ago	1/2 cm	*The story of Abraham*
3500 years ago		*The story of Moses*
3000 years ago	3 mm	*The story of King David*
2000 years ago	2mm	*Jesus was born*

The Epiphany of the Lord

1. Introduction to the theme of the day

"We saw his star and have come to adore him"

Aim: To show that the coming of Jesus was God's gift to the world.

Leader's Reflection: The story of the three kings is, of course, one of the best-known elements of Nativity plays and children delight in the rich costumes and gold card crowns. However, a closer reading of the Gospel shows that there is only one king mentioned – Herod. The three wise men – for that is how Matthew refers to them – were astrologers. In our day, astrology is seen as a fringe activity but astrologers were the scientists and thinkers of the time. They studied the skies and ancient writings and interpreted astronomical phenomena as signs of events of world-wide importance. Their interpretation of the star as announcing the birth of a Jewish king led them naturally to Herod's palace – but their expectations were confounded when the new king was to be found not there but in far simpler surroundings. The birth of Jesus was announced by a star – obviously visible even in Jerusalem, yet there is no evidence that any Jew saw it and registered its meaning. It was scholars from Gentile countries who read the signs and undertook a potentially hazardous journey to find the one they were to recognise as the Christ. Their preconceptions were challenged – but their intellect and years of study and contemplation predisposed them to recognise that things are not always as they seem. Sometimes, a change of mind and more especially of heart and soul is needed to glimpse the creative ways in which God is at work in the world.

2. We arrive

We sit in a circle ready to listen to the Gospel.
Has anyone anything to tell us about their Christmas – or about last week's Family Sheet?

Focus

White or gold cloth.
Candle – perhaps one with stars on.
Three "gifts".

Gospel: Matthew 2:1-12

Read from the Lectionary or Children's Lectionary.

3. We respond

What is the Gospel asking of us?

There is one story this week with suggested discussion ideas for each age group. Work in age groups if appropriate.

Story

Kiran and Usha were excited. A messenger had just arrived to say that, at last, their uncle Roshan was on the last stage of his journey home.

Their uncle had been away for many months on an important journey. He had gone to see a king!

Uncle Roshan had many scrolls and heavy books and spent most of his time in the day reading or in the night gazing at the stars and writing notes by the light of a candle.

A few months ago, he had got very excited. He took the children out and pointed at a star.

"We think," he said, "that the star up there means a king has been born far away in a place called Judaea. We're going to go and see him!"

He and two of his friends had gone – and they had been gone so long that everyone was beginning to worry that something might have happened to them all.

Then the message came – they were coming home!

Two days later, Kiran and Usha were watching and waiting and suddenly caught sight of him. "Uncle Roshan! Uncle Roshan!" they cried as they ran to meet him.

He whisked Usha into his arms and rumpled Kiran's hair. He put Usha down and picked up his bags.

"Come on, let's go and find your mother."

Over their meal, Uncle Roshan told them stories about his adventures.

"But did you meet the king?" asked Kiran.

"I met two kings," said Uncle Roshan. "One lived in a great palace with lots of servants – but he wasn't the greatest of the kings I met."

"So how big was the other one's palace?" asked Kiran.

"And how many servants did he have?" demanded Usha.

"Ah! Now that was the strange thing," smiled Uncle Roshan. "He didn't have a palace. And the only servant he had was his mother." He glanced at the children's mother and gave her a huge wink.

"So – how did you know he was a king?" she said.

"We just knew. He was only a baby – but the star had rested over the house he was in ... and we just knew. We gave him the gifts we had taken. It had seemed odd to give gifts like frankincense and myrrh to a baby – though I think the gold would come in useful. But, even looking at him and touching his little hand... we could feel the power that is growing in him."

Kiran and Usha looked at Uncle Roshan. He looked serious but very happy too.

"And," he said, "the first king didn't give us anything. But the little king's mother gave us something. He had lots of curly hair and she cut off some of the curls. She said, 'We have very little that you could take back with you – but this will remind you of my son. Take it – and remember us. Perhaps one day you will hear of him again.'"

He took some small packages out of his bag and put it on the table. When he opened them, the children and their mother saw several soft, dark curls nestling in the wrapper.

He gave one to each of them and said, "I thought it would be good to share them – so we all have one. I thought we could have lockets made to keep them in. I think having this gift from the baby king with us will be a blessing to us."

Kiran and Usha reached out and touched the hair – and imagined the baby who gave it fast asleep in his mother's arms.

"Perhaps one day we'll meet him too," they said.

"Somehow, I think many people will meet him... and I think even more people will hear about him... even people in our own country, so far away. This king could become the king of the whole world."

Kiran and Usha looked at Uncle Roshan. He looked serious but very happy too.

"Yes," he said, "the king of the world."

Young ones

Invite the children to respond to the story. Who are the kings in the story? What present would they take if they went to see baby Jesus?

Juniors

Who are the kings mentioned in the story? Why does Roshan think that Jesus is greater than Herod? The characters' names are Sanskrit – from the Indian sub-continent. Talk to the children briefly about the cultural heritage of India, Arabia and China – that their civilisations are steeped in hundreds of years of learning and the search for knowledge and understanding. You may also like to add that St Thomas is reputed to have taken the Gospel to India – explore the idea that real-life people like Roshan, Kiran and Usha did, in time, hear more about the baby king.

4. Activity

Young ones

Have a selection of small boxes (e.g. large matchboxes), gift wrap and sticky tape ready.

Invite the children to draw a picture of Jesus or use the outline provided and draw in his features.

Help them to fold the paper up and put it in the box. Wrap the present up and add thread or ribbon for hanging. Stick on a ready-made label: "To the world with love from God."

Juniors

Have the materials listed above available. Invite the children to think about something Jesus did or said that showed he was God's gift to the world (e.g. a healing) and ask them either to write or draw it on the paper.

The children can then fold the paper, put it in the box, wrap it up, write out the gift label and attach thread or ribbon for hanging.

Tips for learning difficulties

Use a baby Jesus model from a crib and help them to wrap him up as a present in a box and attach a ready-made label and thread for hanging.

5. We come together

Parents can be invited to join in at this stage.

Focus

Light the candle. Invite those gathered to become still.

Gospel

Before Jesus was born, the Jewish people thought that the Messiah was just for them. God knew better. When Jesus was born, a star appeared and wise men from far-away countries understood that it meant that someone very special – a king for the Jews – had been born. They travelled to Jerusalem – but the new king was not born in splendour and power. Instead, they recognised him in a small baby sitting with his mother. They honoured him and gave him gifts: gold, frankincense and myrrh.

Prayer

Lord Jesus, we honour you just as the wise men did all those years ago.

We know that you came to us as the greatest gift that God could give to the world.

Help us to respond to the gift by growing more and more like you each day.

Amen.

Share

Talk about what happened in the session – what the children have learnt about Jesus being God's gift to the whole world. Invite the children to hang their gifts on the tree.

Sing

"We three kings"
"What child is this?"
"The first Nowell"

The Baptism of the Lord

1. Introduction to the theme of the day

Aim: To see Jesus' baptism as the starting point of Jesus' earthly ministry.

Leader's Reflection: The majority of people have no recollection of their baptism and even witnessing a baptism does not always convey the significance of what is happening. It is a sacrament rich in symbolism and affirms our place as adopted children of God. Jesus was, of course, the Son of God and had no need of baptism. Yet, he sensed that it was necessary – perhaps as a witness to others. It may also have served a purpose for Jesus in marking the end of his life as a carpenter and the start of his ministry of preaching the Good News and healing. As a human being, Jesus would have needed to mark the turning points of his life – to find ways of marking the move from one way of life to another. On this, the last Sunday of Christmas, we mark a turning too – from reflecting on the birth of Jesus to beginning to engage with a man with a mission; a mission he has called us to continue.

2. We arrive

We sit in a circle ready to listen to the Gospel.
Has anyone anything they would like to tell us about last week's Family Sheet?

Focus

White cloth.
Candle.
Christmas tree with symbols from previous weeks.
Bowl of water.

Gospel: Mark 1:7-11

Read from the Lectionary or Children's Lectionary.

3. We respond

What is the Gospel asking of us?

Work in age groups if appropriate. Alternatively, choose the discussion ideas, story and activity most suitable for your group.

Young ones

Story

It was a very busy weekend because at church on Sunday morning, Christopher was going to be baptised. Mum and Dad had invited Gran and Grandad and all their families and friends to come to church with them and then to come to the house to celebrate Christopher's big day.

On Sunday morning, Mum and Dad had checked everything was ready and they set off for church. Christopher was wearing a long white dress – but Mum said it was not a dress but a "Christening Gown". She also said that Ciara had worn it when she was baptised and, when Ciara said that she had never been small enough to fit into it, had shown her photographs of her baptism. Ciara was amazed.

"And you slept through all of the party too!" said Mum.

It was just as normal at first – except that they sat at the front. After the Gospel, Father Michael asked them all to go and stand at the font. He told everyone in the church that today was a big day for baby Christopher – that he was going to be baptised.

Mum held Christopher over the font. Father Michael poured water over his head and said, "Christopher James, I baptise you in the name of the Father and of the Son and of the Holy Spirit." Christopher looked a bit puzzled but he did not cry.

Then, Father Michael put oil on his head, and wrapped him in a white shawl and then gave him a candle – though he asked Mum and Dad and the godparents to hold it for him.

And then he turned to the congregation and said, "Let's give our newest parishioner a big welcome to God's family" and everyone clapped.

Later on, back at the house, Christopher was sitting on Grandad's knee and enjoying all the fuss and attention. Ciara had helped Mum to put out all the cakes and sausages on sticks and cheese and pineapple on sticks and jellies. She was proud to be Christopher's big sister.

Invite the children to talk about any baptisms they have attended. What did they see and hear? Was there a party?

Juniors

Melech was reading and struggling to understand a scripture passage written by Isaiah. As he looked out of his chariot, he saw a Jewish man walking along. The man introduced himself as Philip and said that he was on his way to Gaza. He asked what Melech was reading and Melech showed him the passage that had given him so much trouble.

Philip asked if he had understood it. Melech said, "No, how can I understand it without someone to explain it to me?"

Philip looked at the scripture and said, "I know who this is talking about – I was one of his disciples!"

"So it was not Isaiah then. But then – who was it?"

"A man called Jesus," said Philip. "I was a disciple of his. He was a great prophet and healer – a wonderful man to know."

"You say 'he was'. Is he dead?"

Philip laughed. "Well, he was – but he certainly isn't now!"

"Although he was a good man," he went on, "he ran into real problems with the Jewish and Roman authorities. He was actually arrested and tortured – that is the part about 'he was humiliated' that Isaiah mentions here. And his trial was a charade – that's the bit about 'justice was denied him'. But this bit, where it says 'his life on earth has come to an end' – that's the bit where it gets really amazing. You see, his life did end – on a cross."

Melech was horrified, "Crucified – a common criminal! But you said..."

"Yes," said Philip. "He was a great and good man but he was crucified just like a common criminal. But – and you may not believe this – he rose from the dead. I saw him – I spoke with him – I touched him – I even ate with him!"

Melech did not know what to think. This was incredible, but Philip was obviously perfectly sane. And somehow, deep down, he realised that he knew that Jesus was still alive and he knew even more strongly that he wanted to be part of this great story.

The chariot came to a lake and Melech ordered the driver to stop.

"Will you baptise me? Here. Now."

Philip knew that Melech's faith was beginning to grow so he smiled and said, "Of course!"

Melech went into the water. Philip said, "Melech, I baptise you in the name of the Father and of the Son and of the Holy Spirit."

Melech was filled with the Spirit and went on his way rejoicing. Philip continued on his own way preaching the Good News and baptising those who had come to know Jesus.

Invite the children to talk about any baptisms they have attended. What did they see and hear? What are the symbols used in baptism – and what do the children think they mean? If possible, have the words of the prayers used for each symbol and use them to convey the specialness and dignity that baptism confers on us.

4. Activity

Young ones and Juniors

Role-playing baptism. This activity is suitable for all the children to do together – though if your group is very large you may wish to split it into the usual age groupings.

Gather together the things used in baptism and have a doll ready to be "baptised". Help the children to decide who is going to be the priest, the mum and the dad, godparents and so on. Adults can take a role too!

Lead the children through the rites of baptism – explaining what each symbol represents or inviting them to suggest things themselves.

If time permits, a "post baptism" party of a biscuit and drink might be appropriate.

Tips for learning difficulties

Some children may prefer to be with a friend in the background, others may wish to take a more active role. Allow the children to participate as far as they are willing and able to do so.

5. We come together

Parents can be invited to join in at this stage.

Focus

White cloth, bowl of water, oil, lighted candle. Invite those gathered to become still.

Gospel

This Sunday, we leave Christmastime behind us and look ahead to a New Year. Jesus was leaving behind his old life and starting a new one teaching people about God. He wanted to mark the change and so went to John the Baptist and asked to be baptised. John realises that he is the one that he has told people about – the one whose sandal John does not feel worthy to undo. Jesus insists and, as he emerges from the water, the Spirit of God comes upon him and God declares that Jesus is his beloved Son.

Prayer

Lord Jesus, you were baptised and God said you were his Son.
Thank you for sharing your life with us in our baptism.
Help us to grow strong in faith and love
and to be worthy of the name Christian.
Amen.

Share

Talk about what happened in the session – what the children have learnt.

Sing

"All over the world the Spirit is moving"

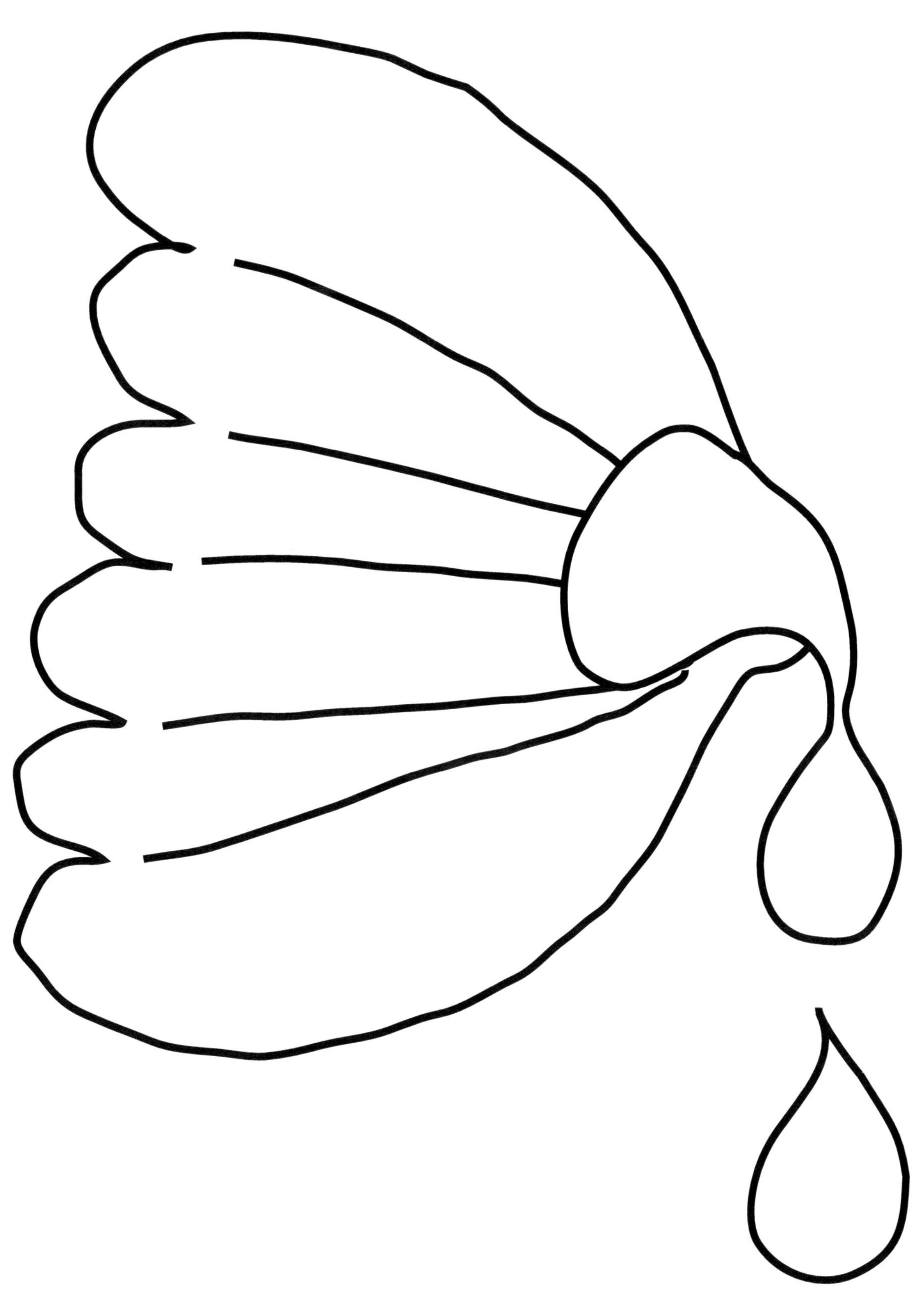

1st Sunday of Lent

1. Introduction to the theme of the day

"The kingdom of God is close at hand"

Aim: Jesus tells us that, with God's help, we can make his kingdom happen now, in our own families and communities.

Leader's Reflection: It is apparent from their writings that the apostles and the very early Church believed that the "second coming" of Jesus and his kingdom were events to be expected within their own lifetimes. Two thousand years later, our expectations have become a little more long-term. We believe that these things will come about in the fullness of time, but our understanding of "close at hand" is possibly a little more imminent even than that of the earliest days of the Church. The kingdom of God can happen here and now, when and where we let it.

2. We arrive

We sit in a circle ready to listen to the Gospel.
Has anyone anything they would like to tell us about last week's Family Sheet?

Focus

A lighted candle, purple fabric for Lent. A decorated crown.

Gospel: Mark 1:12-15

Read from the Lectionary or Children's Lectionary.

3. We respond

What is the Gospel asking of us?

Talk with the children about the kingdom of God. What do they think it will be like, what will we do, how will people behave?
Remind them that today is the first Sunday of Lent. Lent is a time when we try particularly to live in God's kingdom, here and now. We try to live in the way God wants us to live. Work in age groups if appropriate. Juniors, particularly, might want to do something special, or to concentrate on one way of living more closely to God's way.

Young ones

Story

Henry the honey-bee was excited. The time had come again to choose a new Queen bee in the hive. Each year a new princess-bee hatched out of an egg in the nursery, and each year the bees had to choose between the old Queen and the new princess. Some bees always chose the old Queen, because they didn't like things to change. Others always chose the new princess, because she was usually very pretty – as all princesses are. Henry liked to listen to their ideas about the hive first, and then choose the one he thought would make the best Queen.

Everything and everyone was a-buzzing. The day for choosing had arrived. The old Queen made her speech first. She stood up and adjusted her crown.

"Fellow bees," she said in a distinguished and haughty voice, "fellow bees, I like things the way they are. We have an easy life, plenty of honey and plenty of time for sleeping." She yawned. "Now I think it is time to go to sleep again." And she lay down on her back and dozed off.

The bees all applauded politely, several followed her example and promptly fell asleep as well, but Henry was not impressed. He waited impatiently for the princess to speak. She was a little bit shy and fiddled with her tiara as she looked around at all the bees.

"Erm, fellow bees, erm ... I am very young, and I don't know much about the way things were. But I think there is more to life than sleeping. I want to have adventures, and to explore new flowers, and to fly high in the sunshine. If you want me to be Queen then your life might not be quite so comfortable," she looked around nervously, "but it will be a lot more fun!" And with that she sat down again, blushing furiously.

Now was the time for voting. Which one to choose? Henry was thinking hard about everything he heard so that he would choose the right one.

Which one do you think he chose? Which one would you choose?

Juniors

Story

St Casimir is the patron saint of Poland.

Born on 4 March 1484 in Cracow, he was the son of King Casimir IV and Queen Elizabeth, the second of seven brothers. All the boys were taught by monks and priests instead of going to school, so Casimir listened carefully to everything his teachers had to say and then began to behave in ways which were very strange for a prince of Poland.

He liked to pray instead of sleeping, and would spend all night kneeling outside the church because he couldn't get in to say his prayers. When he did go to bed, he slept on the floor instead of his soft and comfortable royal bed. He gave away all his fine clothes, and liked to spend his time talking with the workmen around the palace and the poor people waiting at the gate. He would tell his father, the king, about the things which were worrying these people, and persuade him to change the laws so that they were better looked after.

When he was only thirteen, the noblemen of Hungary decided they wanted a new king, and asked Casimir if he would come to rule them. He was not very happy with the idea, but agreed to try because he thought that was what God wanted. By the time he got to Hungary, though, the people had all changed their minds and decided to keep their old king. The soldiers who were with him were frightened by the fierce people and they all ran away, but Casimir was unharmed and returned to Poland, very relieved.

The king was not very pleased with what had happened in Hungary, and sent Casimir into exile, but he soon realised that Casimir was a good man and a just ruler, so he called him back to Cracow. Now when the king went away to sort out his affairs in other states, he could leave Casimir in charge of his kingdom. By now the people had got used to his strange ways, and began to admire him for his holiness instead of laughing at him.

Casimir was only 23 when he died from lung disease.

How did Casmir help God's kingdom to grow on earth? What can we all do in our lives?

4. Activity

Each child should make a paper crown and decorate it by colouring, cutting and sticking the jewels from the template; juniors can write or draw on the jewels anything special which they will be doing during Lent.

Have a chair ready prepared as a throne. In turn, each child can sit on the throne and describe what it would be like in their kingdom if they were king or queen.

Tips for learning difficulties

Have the paper crowns ready made for decorating.

5. We come together

Parents can be invited to join in at this stage.

Focus

Gather in a circle with the crown in the centre, a lighted candle and purple fabric for Lent.

Gospel

When Jesus grew up, he was a carpenter. When he was thirty years old, he went into the desert for forty days to pray and to talk with God. When he came back, he did not go back to being a carpenter, he became a preacher instead. He told the people, "The time has come for God to be King. Make yourselves ready."

Prayer

Pray together for God's kingdom to come. Each child can put their crown into the centre and use this prayer:
"Jesus, in your kingdom I pray that ..."

Everybody responds with:
"Your kingdom come."
Amen.

Share

Talk about what happened in the session. What have the children learnt about how we can bring about God's kingdom on earth today?

Sing

"Go tell everyone"

2nd Sunday of Lent

1. Introduction to the theme of the day

"Jesus is transfigured; we see him as God"

Aim: We can spend all our lives getting to know God – through prayer, through other people, through our church and through all our other experiences. But in the end we can never know him completely. God will always be a mystery to us.

Leaders' Reflection: In both the story of Abraham and Isaac and in the story of the transfiguration, the people involved must have left the scene somewhat bewildered and shaken. The events were unexpected and we must adjust our private image of God in light of them. Such transformations of our relationship with God must occur regularly if rather less dramatically throughout our lives, as we grapple with new experiences and new ideas all of which speak to us of God.

2. We arrive

We sit in a circle ready to listen to the Gospel.
Has anyone anything they would like to tell us about last week's Family Sheet?

Focus

A lighted candle, purple fabric for Lent. Pin a large question mark to a tablecloth.

Gospel: Mark 9:2-10

Read from the Lectionary or Children's Lectionary.

3. We respond

What is the Gospel asking of us?

Work in age groups if appropriate. Alternatively, choose the discussion ideas, story and activity most suitable for your group.

Young ones

God sometimes seems to do very strange things which we do not always understand. Try to give some examples from your own life. Encourage the children to give examples. These may be sad, happy or simply strange. Resist the temptation to try to give any answers.

Story

Use the story of St Joseph and the strange things that happened to him, from the Juniors' section, adapting it to the younger age group as you see fit.

Juniors

"God's ways are not our ways." "God works in mysterious ways."
We do not always understand the way God works. Try to give some examples in your own life of strange things that you did not understand at the time. Encourage the children to give examples. These may be sad, happy or simply strange. Resist the temptation to give any answers, emphasising complete trust in God.

Story

19 March is the feast day of St Joseph. St Joseph was a carpenter. We do not know the names of his parents or much else about him, except that he was a very ordinary man and a very good one. He lived in a small village called Nazareth, went to the synagogue every Saturday and said his prayers every day. He worked honestly, never cheating his customers. Everybody who knew him said he was very kind and generous. And of course, he was in love with a girl in his village called Mary.

Joseph was very excited about getting married. He was looking forward to having his own home and to raising a family. Mary was a good girl, and she would make a good wife and mother. All the preparations for the wedding were going very well, until ...

One day, Mary came to see him and told him something quite shocking. She said she was going to have a baby! Joseph was very upset. He knew the baby wasn't his, because he wasn't married to Mary yet. But nor was anybody else! So who was the father of the baby? Mary told him a strange story about an angel that had come to visit her. She said that the baby was from God. Joseph didn't believe her: whoever heard of God having a baby?

Joseph was beginning to think twice about marrying Mary. Maybe she was secretly in love with somebody else, although Joseph didn't think so. Or maybe she was mad, crazy; seeing angels and things like that. It would be difficult to look after a mad woman for the rest of his life even if he did love her. Joseph went to bed that night a very worried man.

Whilst he was asleep, Joseph had a dream. In the dream an angel came to him and told him not to worry, that the baby really was God's baby, but that God wanted Joseph to marry Mary and look after Jesus.

When Joseph woke up, he didn't feel much better. He had learnt a lot about God from his parents and at school and in the synagogue; God wasn't supposed to behave like this. God having a baby! It didn't fit Joseph's idea of God at all. And now he was going crazy, dreaming about angels and things. But he decided to marry Mary after all; if they were both crazy, they might as well be crazy together, and you never know, the angel might have been telling the truth.

Nine months later the baby boy was born in a stable in Bethlehem. Shepherds came down from the fields to see him, they said that angels had spoken to them as well and told them where to find the baby. Later, three strange visitors came to visit and left very expensive gifts. It was all very unusual.

That night Joseph had another dream: more angels! They told him to leave Bethlehem and go to live in Egypt for a while. They said it was dangerous for him to take Mary and the baby back to Nazareth. By now Joseph was beginning to believe in angels so he packed their bags and they left the next day. God seemed to be in control of everything, although Joseph had never heard of these things happening before. Maybe he didn't know God quite as well as he thought.

4. Activity

Young ones

God loves to surprise us. Collect a number of "surprises" – pop-up books, Jack in the Box etc. Let the children play with them. They can make their own surprise pop-up card using the template. They can choose a picture from an old greetings card to stick inside and decorate the front themselves.

Juniors

God is a mystery to us. He made our world and the universe and each one of us, so it is not surprising that we still do not understand it all. Working in pairs, make a list of really difficult questions – things that you do not understand, but would like the answers to. Choose one of them to ask in the sharing session at the end.

Tips for learning difficulties

Some large cards with questions: Why does...? What do...? Where is...? Who is...? could help to start the children off.

5. We come together

Parents can be invited to join in at this stage.

Focus

Gather together around the candle, the purple fabric and question mark.

Gospel

Jesus went up the mountain to pray. He took with him his friends Peter and James and John. While they were praying together, Jesus began to glow with a white light, so bright the apostles could hardly bear to look at him. Moses and Elijah – two of the holy people from the Old Testament – appeared next to him and he began to talk with them. The friends were all amazed at what was happening and wanted to talk about it, but Jesus told them to keep it a secret for now.

Prayer

Jesus, today we see you in a different way, in a mysterious way. Thank you for surprising us. Amen.

Share

Young ones can share their surprise cards; juniors can ask the questions they have thought up. The adults present can try to answer them!

Sing

"We behold the splendour of God"

MAKE YOUR OWN CARD

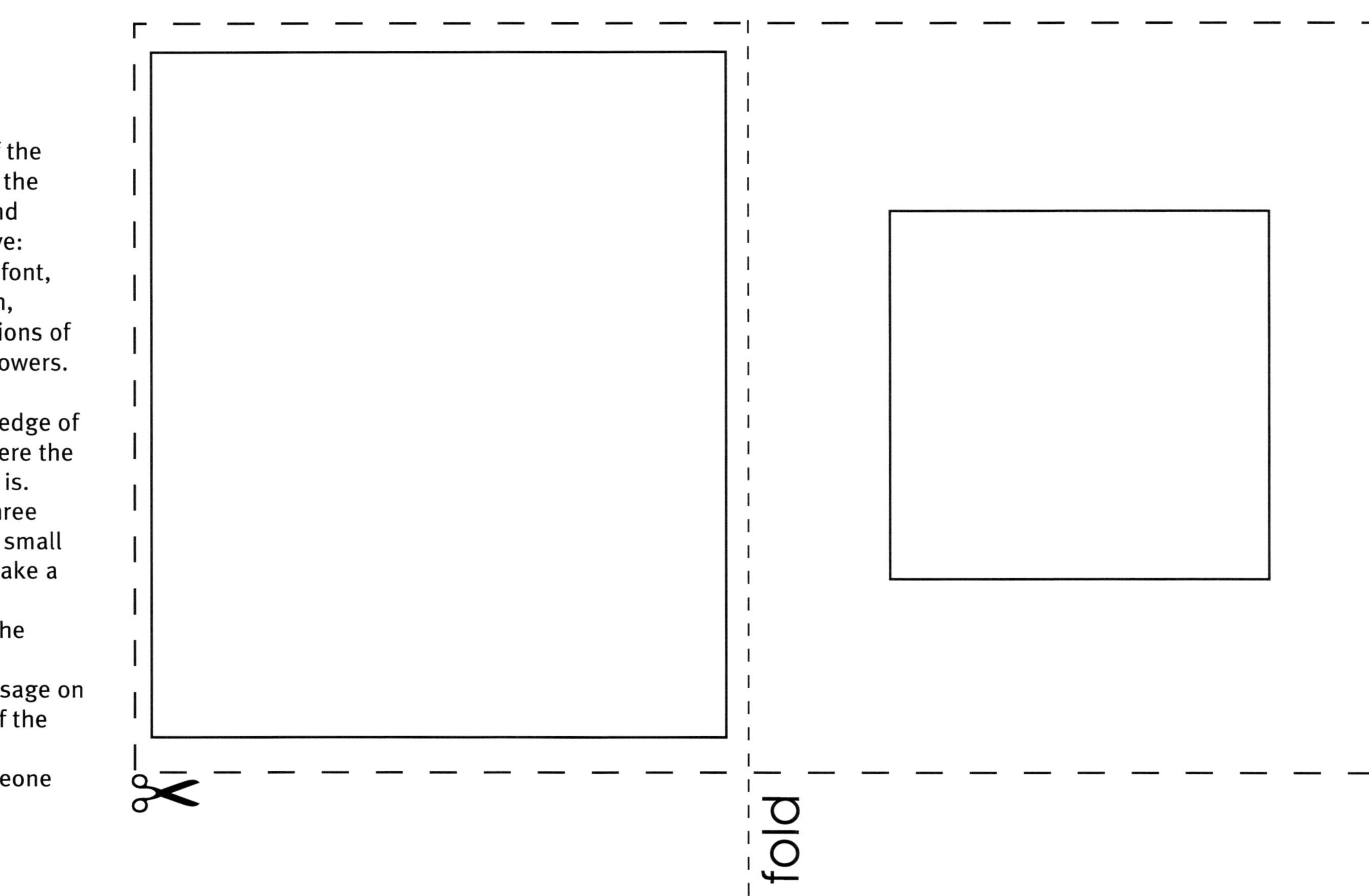

1. Draw two of the following in the rectangle and square above: Tabernacle, font, altar, lectern, candle, stations of the cross, flowers.
2. Colour in.
3. Cut out the edge of the card where the scissor icon is.
4. Cut along three sides of the small square to make a door.
5. Fold along the dotted line.
6. Write a message on the inside of the card.
7. Give to someone you love.

3rd Sunday of Lent

1. Introduction to the theme of the day

"My Father's house is a house of prayer"

Aim: We remember that every church is a special building. It is a place where we can come to be quiet, to pray and to meet God.

Leader's Reflection: We approach the house of God with reverence. This is quickly learned by children from the example of the adults around them; however, it may be worth focusing on some points of behaviour e.g. quietness, the sign of the cross, genuflection, and practising these with the children; also spending some time thinking about the things which the children encounter in the church. Some, like candles and flowers, will have similar and familiar uses at home. Others like the tabernacle and font will be more specific to the church.

2. We arrive

We sit in a circle ready to listen to the Gospel.
Has anyone anything they would like to tell us about last week's Family Sheet?

Focus

A lighted candle, purple fabric for Lent. If using the photographs or drawings of artefacts suggested under learning difficulties, these could be pinned to the cloth, or propped up as a display.

Gospel: John 2:13-25

Read from the Lectionary or Children's Lectionary.

3. We respond

What is the Gospel asking of us?

Work in age groups if appropriate.

Young ones

Discuss with the children why Jesus was so upset in the Temple. What did he find there? Why did he mind? Think about your own church. How do people behave when they come in?
Why do they behave in that way? What sort of things are there in the church which help us to think about God or to talk to him? What would Jesus think if he came to your church?

Story

Maggie the mouse was visiting her friend, Caroline. Caroline lived under the floorboards in a church. Caroline had told her there was a party in the church every Sunday, and Maggie was very excited.

On Sunday morning they got up very early. They cleaned themselves, brushed their fur until it was quite shiny, and went to sit up at the back of the church to watch. At the other end was a stage, with a big table on it. Caroline told Maggie that was the altar.

Maggie noticed that as the people came into church they were bowing or genuflecting in front of the altar. That was because the altar was God's special place, Caroline explained; they were really bowing to God. Maggie had not bowed when she came into the church, so she bowed right down until her nose touched the ground so that God would know she was bowing to him.

The people in the church started singing. That was great fun and Maggie joined in with her squeaky little voice, until a man walked to the altar wearing a long purple dress. "That is the priest," Caroline whispered. "When he speaks everyone else is quiet."

Then a story was read from a very big book. It was a lovely story about a man called Jesus, who made people better.

The priest prepared some bread and wine on the altar and shared it with everybody. Then everyone went very quiet. Maggie asked what they were doing. "I think they are talking to God in their heads," said Caroline. "We cannot hear what they are saying, but God can."

Behind the altar was a little box with a door on it. It was called a tabernacle. Maggie learned that it was a place to put any bread left at the end. "So none for us?" she whispered to Caroline. "Oh no, I think the bread is very special, so there are never any crumbs left over.

But don't worry; I have a lovely dinner waiting for us under the floorboards." And bowing to the altar again, they both scurried away to eat their own very special meal.

Juniors

Discuss with the children the use of the Temple and Jesus' reaction. Think about your own church and the special behaviour required there. What sort of things are in church that help us to think about God or to talk to him? What would Jesus think if he came to your church?

Story

Blessed Sibyllina Biscossi was a very special person. She was an anchorite in the thirteenth century.

In those days, if you went into a church, particularly large churches in town centres, you were quite likely to find an anchorite. An anchorite is a person who has decided to spend the rest of their life living in the church and praying. Special cells were built into the church walls for this purpose. They were tiny, and once the anchorite was inside, the doorway was walled up as a sign that they would stay there for the rest of their life. Usually the cells had two windows. One looking into the church so the anchorite could follow Mass, and one looking outside so people could come and speak to the anchorite about God.

Sibyllina was an orphan and blind. She was taken in by the local Dominican nuns, and when she was only twelve she became a nun herself. Because she was blind she could not work like the other sisters, and so she prayed for them instead. She prayed particularly to St Dominic, and believed that he would cure her blindness. On his feast day, she prayed particularly hard, and waited all day for her sight to return. By evening nothing had happened, and she tried not to be disappointed, but during her night prayers Dominic appeared to her and, taking her by the hand, led her through the darkness into a place of wonderful light. "This is heaven," he told Sibyllina. "You will see the glory of God when you get here, but not before."

So Sibyllina understood that she was to stay blind for the rest of her life.

Once she had realised that the special work God had called her to was prayer, she decided to be an anchorite. At the age of only fifteen she was walled up into a tiny cell in the local church, and stayed there for 67 years.

4. Activity

Young ones

Enlarge a symbol of a church onto an A4 piece of paper. Discuss with the children the sorts of things that people can do in church. Draw these on the sheet of paper in and around the church.

Juniors

Using the template, explain all the artefacts. They can write about them in the space provided, and draw them in the box. Alternatively, visit the church to locate the artefacts.

Tips for learning difficulties

Use photographs/drawings prepared of the artefacts to attach to the template. These could be prepared with flaps, the tabernacle opening to reveal a host; the font, to reveal water; the wick of the candle could lift to reveal a flame; the altar, a "pop-up" priest, and the book on the lectern, the word Gospel. You may even be able to find a large model of a church.

5. We come together

Parents can be invited to join in at this stage.

Focus

Gather around the candle. Take time to let people really settle and to talk to God quietly in their heads. Place the picture of the church in the centre, on the purple fabric.

Gospel

Jesus went into the Temple in Jerusalem. It was filled with people selling things as if it were a market. Everybody was shouting out and laughing and talking. Jesus became very angry and sent everybody who was not praying quietly out of the Temple. "My Father's house is a house of prayer," he said.

Prayer

Use the children's rhyme with hand actions.

"Here is the church, here is the steeple, open the doors and here are the people."

Each time the doors are opened, ask one of the children to nominate one of the people to pray for. Finish each prayer with "Amen".

Share

The work from the activities.

Sing

"Build, build your church"

"God and man at table are sat down"

Tabernacle

Font

Altar

Lectern

Candle

Stations of the cross

Flowers

4th Sunday of Lent

1. Introduction to the theme of the day

"Heaven is our real home, with God"

Aim: Many of the stories in the Old Testament are about the people of Israel living in exile. This means that they had to live away from their homes, in strange countries. Our real home is with God in heaven. Because Jesus came to save us, we know that one day he will take us back there.

Leader's Reflection: The Old Testament is the story of a people in exile. Although the Jewish people did spend periods in the land that God promised them, many of the books talk of their longing to be there, or foretell a time of exile which is imminent. Our time on earth can also be viewed as a time of exile from heaven – we are a pilgrim people, journeying towards God's heavenly kingdom.

2. We arrive

We sit in a circle ready to listen to the Gospel.
Has anyone anything they would like to share from last week's Family Sheet?

Focus

A lighted candle, purple fabric for Lent, a small tent.

Gospel: John 3:14-21

Read from the Lectionary or Children's Lectionary.

3. We respond

What is the Gospel asking of us?

Work in age groups if appropriate. Alternatively, choose the discussion ideas, story and activity most suitable for your group.

Young ones

To live in exile means to live away from your home. Discuss with the children why somebody might choose to leave their own home and live in exile. What sort of things would change – language, job, schools, shops, friends etc.?

Story

At the bee election held a few weeks ago, the old Queen won! Henry had voted for the young princess, but as she had lost, she decided to leave the hive. Henry and some of the other bees were leaving with her.

Henry was sad to leave the hive. He said goodbye to his friends and packed up his honey pot before joining the other bees that were leaving. Everybody was nervous. The hive was lovely and warm, and they did not know where they were going. They would have to sleep outside until they found a new home.

Taking a deep buzz, they all set off into the sky looking for somewhere to settle for the night. They found a hole in the trunk of an old tree and landed there. It was very tiring, buzzing around and settling the baby bees, and Henry knew he would have to get up early to collect the nectar for breakfast. He thought longingly of the stores of honey back at the hive, but they could not go back now. Everything will be fine, he told himself, trying to believe it.

The next day the bees set off again. Some flew ahead and came back to tell the others what they had seen. It was all very exciting, so many things they had never seen before. Then one bee came back with the news they had all been waiting for. He had found a new hive, and it was clean and dry and empty.

Everybody rushed to have a look. It was different from the old hive. It had a red roof, and was round instead of square, and the flowers nearby were different as well. But everybody was very happy. It might be different, but it was going to be their new home. Hoorah!

Juniors

Discuss with the children why somebody might choose to leave their own home and live in exile. What sort of things would change ... language, schools, jobs, shops, friends? It is possible that children will know refugees in their own school. Reflect with them on the difficulties these children might have had in coming to this country.

Story

Imagine you and your family have just arrived in ----. You and your family are refugees from ----. Why did you leave that country?

Your best friend, Pedro, still lives there with his family. Think about Pedro now, what does he look like? What did you enjoy doing together?

You are in bed thinking about tomorrow – your first day at your new English school. You do not speak any English. How do you feel? Before you go to sleep, say a prayer to Jesus for tomorrow.

Driiiiiing. The alarm clock wakes you up. You must get dressed quickly, put on that strange school uniform, tighten up your shoes, brush your teeth, then downstairs for a quick breakfast. Next thing you know, you are on the path leading up to the school with your mum. Everybody around you is laughing and shouting and playing and fighting. How do you feel? Can you see anybody in the playground that you think will be a friend? Anybody you don't like the look of?

You walk to the school office with your mum. They point to chairs nearby and you sit down. Other children are passing and looking at you. How are they behaving? Do they seem nice?

A lady arrives and speaks to your mum. Your mum hugs you and tells you to go with the lady. You follow her down a long corridor. There are noisy classrooms on either side. What are you thinking? The lady stops at one of the doors and goes inside. It is suddenly quiet. Everybody is looking at you. You wish Pedro was with you. What would you say to him now? The lady says something and you recognise your name. Everybody looks at you again. How are they behaving? Is anybody smiling? Is anybody being silly?

The lady shows you a desk and you sit down. Who are you sitting next to? They seem friendly and are trying to talk to you using actions instead of words. What are they saying? How do you feel?

For the first lesson, the teacher writes some words on the board. It is the start of a letter. You decide to write to Pedro. Imagine what you will write.

4. Activity

Young ones

People who live in exile or who are refugees cannot live in their own houses any more. In some countries they often have to live in tents for a while. Let the children use curtains, tables and chairs to make a tent. Discuss with them where they will cook, sleep, wash, use the toilet etc. Or, using the template, draw these activities in and around the tent.

Juniors

Get the children to lie down quietly. Read through the story slowly, giving plenty of time for the children to imagine themselves in the situations. If there is time, they can write the letter to Pedro telling of their first day at school.

Tips for learning difficulties

The story could be acted out physically instead of in the imagination. Children can draw a picture or make a tape to send to Pedro instead.

5. We come together

Parents can be invited to join in at this stage.

Focus

Gather together around the tent, the purple fabric and lighted candle.

Gospel

God loves us all so much, that he sent his only Son, Jesus, to be our friend, so that he can bring us all back to our best home with God.

Prayer

Jesus, we pray for people who are refugees. They have to live away from their homes.
They cannot always live with their families or friends.
Bless them all and keep them safe. Amen.

Share

Each child can sit in the entrance of the tent in turn, and say a thank you prayer for their own house, or an asking prayer for people who are refugees.

Sing

"At the name of Jesus"

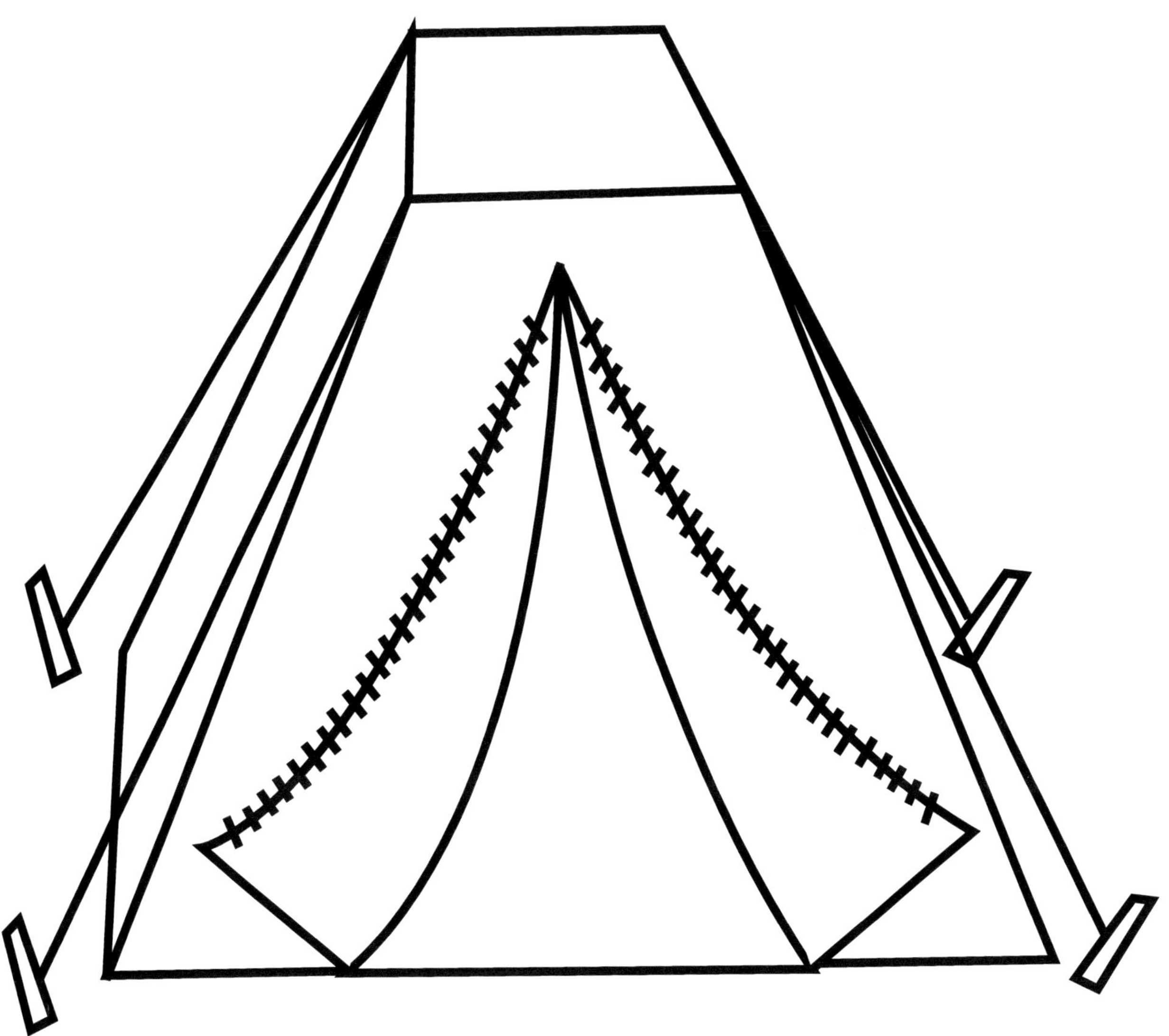

5th Sunday of Lent

1. Introduction to the theme of the day

"The grain which dies yields a rich harvest"

Aim: To reflect on the idea of sacrifice as something which gives life and bears fruit.

Leader's Reflection: Sacrifice has become an unpopular concept – seen as a negative "giving up" of things we enjoy. In a time and a place where many people want things instantly, it can be hard to convince children that going without – or deferring a pleasure – is not the end of the world. To them, it may simply seem unfair when "everyone else" gets things straight away. And yet, from the earliest days of encounter with God, deep in our Judaic roots, the idea of sacrifice as part of the life of a believer has been very strong. It is not in the wanton destruction of something that new life is born – but in the offering back to God what God gave us in the first place. In a mysterious way, we then receive back from God much more than we could ever have dared to believe or imagine... but the trustful sacrifice comes first. Things are not always as they seem. Sometimes, a change of mind and more especially of heart and soul is needed to glimpse the creative ways in which God is at work in the world.

2. We arrive

We sit in a circle ready to listen to the Gospel.

Has anyone anything they would like to tell us about last week's Family Sheet?

Focus

Simple purple cloth, a candle, packets of seed.

Gospel: John 12:20-33

Read from the Lectionary or Children's Lectionary.

3. We respond

What is the Gospel asking of us?

Work in age groups if appropriate.

Alternatively, choose the discussion ideas, story and activity most suitable for your group.

Young ones

Have the children ever planted anything – or watched parents or grandparents do so? Was it worth "losing" the seed and getting the tools dirty? Why? What happened?

Story (read with help from the children)

Millie had been given a "Young Gardeners' kit" from Grandad at Christmas. He loved gardening and wanted to help Millie to learn how to enjoy it too.

It was beautiful. A little trowel, a fork, a little watering can and some packets of flower seed – and all wrapped up with cellophane and a big green bow.

Millie had put the set in her bedroom and looked at it every day – but she never opened it.

All: **Not the way to make the seeds grow!**

Mum had given up telling her it was time to open the package and plant the seeds. It was no good just looking at the seed packets and keeping the tools nice and clean... As she said:

All: **Not the way to make the seeds grow!**

One spring Sunday, Grandad came to see them.

"Where are your baby plants, Millie?" he asked.

"Errm – well – they're still safely tucked up in their packages. It's very cold and wet outside. I don't want them to get spoilt."

"Hmm," said Grandad.

All: **Not the way to make the seeds grow!**

"My seeds are all planted – and have leaves now. Let's take a look at those packets," said Grandad.

Millie went and got the kit – undid the bow very slowly and took out the packets.

"As I thought, just the right time to plant these. What we'll do is sow the seed and then pop them on the window-sill indoors until it gets a bit warmer. But honestly, Millie, if you leave them in the packet they will just die and never be what God wants them to be."

Millie thought that was a good plan. Her little plants would be safe from the cold until she had helped them to grow big and strong enough to go outside and look beautiful in the garden.

Invite the children to respond to the story. Can they understand how Millie felt?

Juniors

Johnny Appleseed did not have a home or a family. He believed he had a special mission to travel throughout the United States – and to plant orchards. He never really understood why – but he knew that he was to plant apple pips wherever he found good soil. He then tended the little plants and, as soon as they were strong enough, he left that place and went to another – and started again.

Johnny never saw his trees bear fruit. By the time they did, he was long gone and far away.

But the people who came after him, looking for somewhere to settle and bring up families, came across the orchards Johnny had planted. When they saw them, they knew that here was good soil for them to grow their crops and the promise of sweet apples to help their children to grow strong and healthy in their new home.

Invite the children to respond to the story. What did Johnny Appleseed sacrifice (give up) to take up his mission? How do you think he might have felt about that? What reward did he receive in his lifetime? What was the even greater gift he left with other people?

4. Activity

There are many colourful plants that can be sown now with a fair degree of success. Make a selection of hardy annuals and decide where to sow them. Younger children may well like to plant a few seeds in a pot to take home. Older children may be happy to work in a small part of a church garden – or plant up tubs or window boxes. If the latter is chosen, it might be wise to be prepared to have a quick "plant-check" over the next few months – to keep plants watered (and to replace any losses!)

It may be interesting to leave a few seeds unplanted and compare the progress of the planted and unplanted ones during the summer.

Young ones

It would probably be wise to have the compost in the pots already. Use fairly large seeds (e.g. sunflowers) which the children can press gently into the soil. Have a sticky label ready on which the children (with help where necessary) write their names and, if time permits, decorate with pictures of flowers. Put the label on the pot. The picture from the template page can be coloured in at home or used as an alternative activity in the session.

Juniors

Follow the activity as with the younger children but this age group should be able to add compost very carefully themselves. Disposable gloves with newspaper underneath would act as added precautions.

Tips for learning difficulties

Have the pots with the soil ready and help the children to sow the seeds. Have the labels with their names on ready and encourage them to decorate their label before sticking it to their pot.

5. We come together

Parents can be invited to join in at this stage.

Focus

Light the candle. Invite those gathered to become still – to look at the candle, and the pots of seeds, and think about the time of year.

Gospel

Jesus said,
"Unless a grain of wheat falls on the ground and dies,
it remains only a single grain;
but if it dies, it yields a rich harvest."

Prayer

Jesus, you gave your life for us.
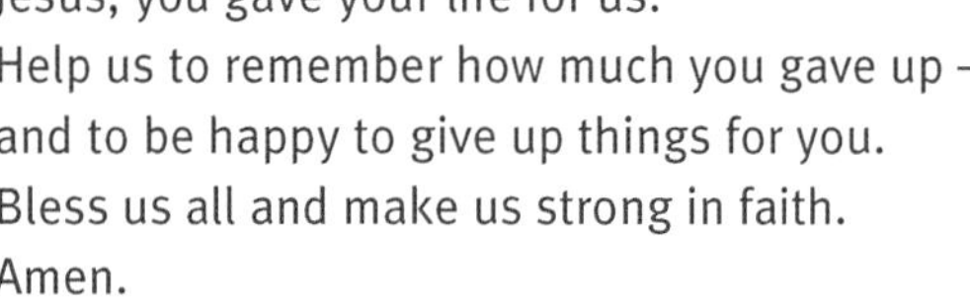
Help us to remember how much you gave up –
and to be happy to give up things for you.
Bless us all and make us strong in faith.
Amen.

Share

Talk about what happened in the session – what the children have learnt. Explain that we have used seeds to show what Jesus' words meant. Some seeds have been planted – what will happen to them? And what do we need to do to help them?

Sing

"In the earth the small seed is hidden"
"The farmer comes to scatter the seed"

Passion Sunday (Palm Sunday)

1. Introduction to the theme of the day

Aim: To remember and celebrate Jesus' triumphant entry into Jerusalem – but hint at the sense of foreboding about what was to happen at the end of the same week.

Leader's Reflection: In some ways it is sad that the event of Palm Sunday is so quickly overshadowed by the events of the Passion. This was the moment when Jesus could have claimed it all – and yet, even now, comes as a humble king on a colt, fêted by children.

In the crowds who, in disillusionment, would be baying for his blood, there would surely have been the simpler souls who were actually wiser than the rest. Jesus would not have preached a kingdom which would have led to the destruction of Israel by the Romans. His kingdom was not of this world and it is the children and unlearned who see that most clearly. It is our children who see that most clearly – and who need to be affirmed in their love of the Redeemer King who suffered the little children to come unto him. Today, we are called to nurture the deep and simple love children have for Jesus.

(Note: Hosanna was a word of acclamation but also a cry for deliverance: "Save us, please".)

2. We arrive

We sit in a circle ready to listen to the Gospel.

Has anyone anything they would like to tell us about last week's Family Sheet? What did the children "sacrifice" last week to make someone else happy?

Focus

Red cloth with palms and a candle.

Gospel: Mark 14:1 – 15:47

Read from the Lectionary or Children's Lectionary.

3. We respond

What is the Gospel asking of us?

As it is likely that numbers will be few this week, one story is offered for all. Work in age groups, if appropriate, for the activities.

Story

Deborah was so excited. Her friend Jesus was coming to Jerusalem!

Jesus often came to her house for a meal and he was always taking the children out to play and getting into trouble for getting them back late!

Her mum and dad didn't seem so excited – in fact they seemed worried.

But Deborah thought it was wonderful that Jesus would be coming to spend Passover week with them. Apart from Tobias, Miriam, and Rufus, Jesus was the best friend she had.

Jesus had promised to let them know that he was on his way and, sure enough, John (his youngest disciple) ran into the house to tell them that Jesus was just outside the city. Jesus had asked him and one of the others to go and get a colt for him to ride.

"But he always just walks," said Deborah's mother.

John grew more excited. "There's a prophecy that the true king of Israel will come into the city – riding on a donkey!"

Deborah was thrilled. Her friend Jesus – a king. "He would be wonderful," she thought. "No one would be hungry – or sick – or sad ever again."

John took her hand. "Would you like to come and greet him?"

"Oh yes!" said Deborah. "Can we call for the others on the way?"

"Of course we can!" said John, his eyes shining with excitement.

"John," Deborah's dad said, "I'm not sure... Will it be safe?"

John said, "Of course it will be safe. I promise, if it looks as if there is going to be trouble we'll come straight back. But the people are all on Jesus' side – no one would dare do anything."

"All right – but we'll come too. We'll meet you by the gates."

Deborah could not understand why her parents looked so worried. When Jesus was king everything would be perfect.

People were pouring out of the gates to see Jesus. Deborah and the others could see how proud the disciples were but Jesus just looked pleased to see his friends.

Everyone started cheering, "Hosanna! Hosanna!"

They threw down palm branches to make a carpet for him. Some people even threw their cloaks in front of him.

Everyone was wild with excitement and Deborah waved her palm branch furiously, "Hosanna! Hosanna!"

"Blessings on the one who comes in the name of the Lord!" shouted Tobias.

Jesus turned to see where their voices came from and waved to them. "See you later," he called.

People followed Jesus into the city and on to the Temple.

Later, Jesus came to Deborah's house. The house was crowded with people coming to see Jesus and talking about what might happen.

Jesus looked uncomfortable with all that he heard around him and seemed happy when Deborah squeezed over to him with a cup of wine and a piece of bread.

"It's not much, sorry," Deborah apologised.

"It's perfect," said Jesus with a smile. "Do you think we could round up the others and nip outside for a while? It's a bit too noisy in here."

Deborah was delighted – she had thought Jesus would be too busy with the adults to want to spend time with the children.

For a while they all just walked and talked as Jesus ate his bread and drank his wine. Then they had a game of chase – which Jesus always let them win – and then they played hide and seek until it was too dark to find anyone.

At last Jesus said, "It's time to go home. Deborah, tell your parents I'm going to the Garden of Gethsemane to pray. I'll be back later."

When they went in, Deborah passed on Jesus' message. Her parents glanced at each other worriedly.

"Off to bed now," they said.

"Don't worry, Jesus will be fine," said Deborah.

But her mother and father did not look quite so sure.

Young ones

Invite the children to respond. What would they have done if they had been there? Can they imagine Jesus playing games with them?

Juniors

Invite the children to respond. What do they think the crowd was expecting? Why were the disciples so proud? Why were Deborah's parents worried? Draw out the events of the week to come.

4. Activity

Young ones

Have the palm leaves ready for the children to colour in and add "*N*... says 'Hosanna!' for Jesus!"

Juniors

On their palm leaves, the children could write the words "Hosanna! Hosanna! Blessed is he who comes in the name of the Lord. Hosanna in the highest!" Talk about where in the Eucharistic Prayer they hear those words.

Some may like to create figures of Jesus and a crowd to make a collage.

Tips for learning difficulties

Have the palm leaves ready to colour and add their name. Where necessary, have the child's name ready-written in bubble writing to be coloured in.

The palms could be pinned to a board to resemble a carpet. If used, add the figures.

5. We come together

Parents can be invited to join in at this stage.

Focus

Light the candle. Invite those gathered to become still – to look at the candle and palms.

Gospel

On Passion Sunday we have two Gospels. Today, we have looked mainly at Jesus' entry into Jerusalem and how excited everyone was. They threw palm branches down and shouted, "Hosanna! Blessed is he who comes in the name of the Lord!"

Prayer

Holy, holy, holy Lord,
God of power and might,
Heaven and earth are full of your glory.
Hosanna in the highest!
Blessed is he who comes in the name
of the Lord!
Hosanna in the highest!

Share

We know that despite the great happiness of Jesus coming into Jerusalem, the week ended very sadly – and that Jesus was to die. Today, though, we remember the hope and joy of the people in Jerusalem who wanted Jesus to be their king and celebrate the kind of king Jesus will be for us in heaven.

Sing

"Sing Hosanna"
"Shine, Jesus, shine"

Easter Sunday

1. Introduction to the theme of the day

"Alleluia! Jesus is risen"

Aim: To celebrate the Good News that Jesus died and is risen to eternal life. To celebrate that his resurrection opens the way to eternal life for us too.

Leader's Reflection: In the same way that the bare branches and dead foliage of winter give way to days of increasing light and warmth, after Lent, we begin to do the same. We allow the warmth of the risen Christ to percolate our very beings – to germinate the seeds of new life in us – to turn away from things that feel dead or life-sapping and look forward to new possibilities, to new horizons that become visible in the light and life of Christ.

2. We arrive

We sit in a circle ready to listen to the Gospel.
Has anyone anything they would like to tell us about last week's Family Sheet?

Focus

A white or gold cloth, candle, flowers, a bowl of water with small flowerheads.

Gospel: John 20:1-9

Read from the Lectionary or Children's Lectionary.

3. We respond

What is the Gospel asking of us?

This week, one story is offered for all. Suggestions for discussion are offered for both age groups. Work in age groups if appropriate. Alternatively, choose the discussion ideas and activity most suitable for your group.

Young ones

What did Mary find when she arrived at the tomb? Whom did she tell? Look at the Paschal candle in church. Who is the familiar person in the story? How did Deborah feel when Jesus died? What about now he is risen?

Juniors

Reflect on the Gospel. Try to imagine what the disciples were thinking as they ran to the tomb. Talk about new life, then read the story or allow children to take reading parts. Talk about Deborah's feelings during the story. Have the children experienced anything like that? (Note: Sensitivity is needed but it can be useful to explore some of the emotions of grief with children and for them to know that it is sometimes necessary to be angry with God.)

Story

Deborah had hardly stopped crying for two days. On Friday evening, her mother had explained very gently that their friend Jesus had died.

Deborah could not believe it. They had had supper with him the night before and he was perfectly well then. He couldn't be dead. But the tearstains on her mother's face told her that it was horribly true.

Deborah had asked how Jesus had died – but her mother's eyes filled with tears and she would not say. Later, Deborah overheard her mother talking to her friends. "He didn't even have a fair trial. I just can't believe that they would ... they would crucify Jesus."

Deborah put her hand over her mouth. It was even worse. Her best grown-up friend had been crucified – but he wasn't a criminal or a bad person. How could this have happened? Why didn't the grown-ups stop it happening?

She became angry with her parents and Jesus' disciples and everyone. They should have done something. Now Jesus was dead and it was all their fault. She could see they were upset – but was too angry to care.

It became even worse when her father said, "We're going to have to stay indoors. People know Jesus came to meals with us. They might – well... just to be on the safe side, we'll stay indoors and keep the doors locked."

So now she couldn't even see her friends. It was just not fair.

Between crying and feeling angry, Deborah had a miserable time. She even began to feel angry with Jesus for getting killed and with God for letting it happen. She managed to join in "O God, why have you abandoned us?" when her family prayed together that evening – and she really meant it.

On Sunday morning, she woke to loud banging on the doors. Her father told her to stay where she was, picked up the large stick he had left by the door – and called, "Who is it?"

"It's John. Let me in – something has happened!"

Deborah's father opened the door and locked it quickly behind John.

"Pull yourself together and tell us what this is about," demanded Deborah's father.

When John had got his breath back he said, "The tomb is empty!"

Deborah's mother gasped, "So they have stolen his body?"

"We don't think so," John replied. "Everything else was there. We think that – that Jesus is risen from the dead. Don't you remember? It makes sense. He kept telling us and we just didn't understand. Don't you see?"

But Deborah's mother and father did not see – and John left unable to convince them of what he knew.

Deborah went out into the courtyard angrier than ever. Now she couldn't even visit Jesus' grave and put flowers there as her mother had promised.

She walked over to the tree where Jesus had counted to a hundred in hide and seek the previous week – and gave it a hard kick.

"Ouch," said the tree.

Deborah looked up from her sore toe and nearly fell over with shock.

Peeping out from behind the tree was a very familiar face.

"But... but... everyone says you're... errm..."

"Dead?" said a familiar voice.

"Errm..." said Deborah, nodding.

"Do I look dead?"

"No," said Deborah slowly. "Are you a ghost?"

"No – not a ghost. My Father raised me as he promised he would. That's all."

"That's all?" cried Deborah. "That's all? If that's true then it's the most wonderful thing that's ever happened in the whole history of the world!"

"It's true," said the familiar voice as the familiar person came from behind the tree and whisked Deborah into the air.

Deborah squealed with glee.

The familiar person put her on the ground and took her hand.

"Oh," Deborah said. "Your poor hand. What..."

And she realised what it meant – it was where a nail had been.

"It's all right, Deborah, honestly. It had to be this way – but it really doesn't hurt... honestly."

Deborah took the hand and walked with the familiar person into the house.

"Mum... Dad... someone wants to say 'Hello.'"

4. Activity

Young ones

The children can decorate the Easter person opposite by colouring in or using fabric, etc.
If funds permit, the "Alleluia" could be coloured in with gold pens or glitter.

Juniors

On the reverse side of their figure, children can draw and colour in a face which expresses sorrow/grief... the Good Friday person.
Then, on the printed side, decorate in a way which expresses an Easter person.

Tips for learning difficulties

Have everything to hand with any fabrics to be used pre-cut to size.

5. We come together

Parents can be invited to join in at this stage.

Focus

Bowl of water, a flower head for each child and a white cloth. Light the candle. Invite those gathered to become still – to look at the candle and think about the time of year.

Gospel

When Jesus died, his disciples thought it was the end of the world. Then early on Sunday morning, Jesus' friend Mary went to the tomb and found it empty. She ran and told Peter and John and they went to look. It was true the grave clothes were there – but no Jesus. At last they understood what Jesus meant when he said that he would rise from the dead.

Prayer

Fill our hearts with your love so that we may tell the whole world about you.
Amen.

Share

Talk about what happened in the session. The children have heard a story about a young girl who heard her friend had died and was sad and angry. But then she met him again and her sadness was turned to joy.
This is the promise of Easter. While we sing, we will put flowers onto the bowl of water to remind us that in baptism we died with Jesus – but will share his risen life for ever.

Sing

"New daytime dawning"
"We are the Easter people"
"Alleluia, alleluia, give thanks to the risen Lord"

ALLELUIA

2nd Sunday of Easter

1. Introduction to the theme of the day

Aim: To recognise that we are people who have not yet seen Jesus face to face – but who still believe.

Leader's Reflection: The Gospel offers comfort to those of us who struggle with belief at times. Thomas has known Jesus – knows the disciples to be, by and large, sane and sensible – but cannot make the leap of faith to believe that Jesus is risen. Jesus does not condemn his lack of belief but offers the tangible proof Thomas needs. He acknowledges the difficulty of believing and honours those who, despite having yet to meet him face to face, still persevere and nurture the faith they have.

Our role is a precious one in helping children and adults to meet Jesus in the scriptures and through the sacraments so that their relationship with him is fostered. It is not all one-way though – very often, we find that our love of God is deepened by seeing how he is at work in others.

2. We arrive

We sit in a circle ready to listen to the Gospel.

Has anyone anything they would like to tell us about last week's Family Sheet?

Focus

White cloth, candle and flowers. You may wish to use a bowl of water as a feature during the whole Easter period.

Gospel: John 20:19-31

Read from the Lectionary or Children's Lectionary.

3. We respond

What is the Gospel asking of us?

Work in age groups if appropriate. Alternatively, choose the discussion ideas, story and activity most suitable for your group.

Young ones

What did Jesus do when he first appeared? How do we offer each other the peace of Christ?

Story (read with help from the children)

Henry had had chickenpox and missed two weeks of school. It was very strange going back. Almost like the first day, he thought.

His class was really excited.

"We had a puppet show while you were away," his friend Sam told him. "It was really good. Shame you missed it."

Henry looked round. He could not see any signs of a puppet show.

All: **I don't believe you.**

Sam said, "It's true. Kirsty, you tell him."

Kirsty said, "There were two puppeteers and lots of puppets – all different shapes and sizes. They were really clever."

Henry said, All: **I don't believe you**

Michelle came over and said, "They did the story of Cinderella and the one about the Three Little Pigs. It was really funny."

But Henry said, All: **I don't believe you.**

Paul leaned over and said, "I liked the bit where the wolf was blowing the house down and we had to shout out 'By the hair of my chinny chin chin I will not let you in.' It was really loud."

But Henry said, All: **I don't believe you.**

At that moment, Miss Wilson came into the room. "Hello everyone. We have some visitors who want to hear what you thought of their show last week." And in walked two puppeteers with a big box of puppets.

Henry nearly fell off his chair.

The puppeteers said, "So what did you think?"

Everyone shouted out: "Really good." "Clever." "Funny." "Loud."

And Henry whispered to Sam.

All: **Now I believe you!**

Juniors

Discuss the Gospel. Invite the children to tell you stories of times they have not been believed and then have been proven right. And times when it's been the other way round.

Talk about what makes someone believable – trustworthy – genuine – truthful.

Story

Tell the story of the boy who ran to his village shouting "Wolf, wolf" and getting a response the first few times but, when the villagers had been tricked one time too many, they stopped responding. What do the children think happened the next time – when there really was a wolf?

What does this tell us about the importance of being truthful and reliable when we speak to others?

4. Activity

Young ones

Use the template to make simple finger puppets of the children in the story. Invite the children to colour them in and to act the story out using their puppets.

Juniors

Find pictures of characters from film and television that the children are likely to know. Categorise them into the ones whose word the children would trust and the ones whose word they would not trust. Help them to work out why they have made the choices as they have. How do these choices relate to people they might meet in real life?

Talk about the importance of balancing implicit trust with thinking for oneself. Thomas may have doubted the others – but at least he was thinking for himself and not just going along with them for a quiet life.

Tips for learning difficulties

Have the finger puppets ready prepared for the children to colour in. Help them to retell the story of Henry and his friends.

5. We come together

Parents can be invited to join in at this stage.

Focus

Light the candle. Invite those gathered to become still – to look at the candle, the flowers and to think about Easter.

Gospel

Jesus appeared to his disciples and said, "Peace be with you."
Unfortunately, Thomas was not with them and refused to believe.
Jesus came back the following week and showed his hands and his side to Thomas who fell at his feet and said, "My Lord and my God."
Jesus said, "You believe because you have seen me. Happy are those who have not seen and yet believe."

Prayer

Risen Jesus, we ask you to bless our faith –
to help us to believe when it is easier to doubt –
to believe when people make fun of our belief –
and to look after the faith of each other
so that we grow strong together in faith, hope and love. Amen.

Share

We have talked about the importance of believing people who are our friends and whom we can trust... but remembered that not everyone deserves our trust and that it is important to make up our minds for ourselves. Jesus is completely trustworthy and so we can believe his Word and follow his example and know that he is with us always – even though we cannot yet see or hear or touch him.

"Bind us together"

When coloured in, cut out the rectangle and wrap the paper around the child's finger. Fix with sticky tape.

3rd Sunday of Easter

1. Introduction to the theme of the day

"Remember the words I spoke to you"

Aim: To realise that death is not the end. Rather, those who die live on and stay very close to us in our everyday thoughts and memories.

Leader's Reflection: Death is something feared by many. Whether it is the death of a loved one or our own personal death, we often do not want to think about it, inevitable though it is. But death too can be befriended. When a friend or family member dies, it can be an opportunity to reflect on that person's life in greater depth. When someone dies, we can see how much that person meant to us, how we had good times together and how much that person made us into who we are today. Death can provide that unique opportunity to remember and to give thanks.

2. We arrive

We sit in a circle, ready to listen to the Gospel.
Perhaps we want to talk about something from last week's Family Sheet?
We are God's people, living in his light. Pray together, holding up a candle:
"The light of Jesus be in our hearts."

Focus

In the centre of the circle, place a lighted candle on white cloth for Easter time, with some spring flowers.

Gospel: Luke 24:35-48

Read from the Lectionary or the Children's Lectionary.

3. We respond

What is the Gospel asking of us?

If appropriate, work in age groups but join together as one community at the end of the session.

Young ones

What did Jesus say to the disciples to make them less frightened? What did Jesus do to show that he was real? What did he ask his disciples to be? What does he ask us to be?

Story

One night, Jane began to dream. In her dream, she saw herself floating through white, fluffy clouds, way up high in the air. Soon she came to a big gate, where a man stood with a big book.

"Hello Jane", he said, "my name is St Peter and I see that you have come to visit us here in heaven. Come in and have a look around. Make yourself feel at home," he said with a big smile. Jane thanked St Peter and then wandered through the gate.

Soon she saw big, beautiful angels who were dressed in white and flew around using their feathered wings. "Jane, Jane, welcome, welcome!" they were singing. Jane felt very happy that everyone was being so friendly and that they were so happy to see her. She continued on and saw other people: men, women and children all smiling at her. She waved at them and they waved back cheerfully.

Then she came to a beautiful chair where an old man was sitting. He opened his arms wide and Jane ran up to him and gave him a big hug. "Jane," he said, "we are so happy that you have come to visit us. Any time when you want us to be with you, just tell us and we will come to visit you."

"Thank you," Jane said.

And with those words, she woke up!

Juniors

How did Jesus reassure his frightened disciples? Make the sign of peace with each other. Jesus wanted his disciples to be his "witnesses". What did he mean? We can be his witnesses by living God's way, as Jesus showed us.

Story

Mary was a kind, little old lady who lived at the end of the street. She was loved by many of her neighbours because she was always smiling and would joke and laugh a lot. One night, as Mary was sleeping, the angels took her away to be with God in heaven.

Her neighbours, family and friends were very sad that she had gone. They all went to church to say goodbye to Mary at her funeral. The priest, who had known Mary for many years, said many nice things about her during the sermon. Then they brought Mary to the cemetery and laid her to rest.

Back home, everyone met together for tea afterwards. They started talking about Mary, remembering all the good things she had done. People heard stories about Mary that they had never heard before and were surprised about all the things they learnt about her. One man told a funny story about when Mary had dressed up as a clown for the children at the local school. Everyone laughed and began to feel very glad that they had been able to know Mary.

Even months and years after Mary left the street, people would still remember the little old lady and would talk to her as they used to before. They knew that Mary was beside them in spirit and was in fact closer to them now than she had ever been before.

4. Activity

Young ones

When people die, they go to heaven.
Who lives in heaven? (God, Jesus, Mary, saints, angels etc.)
Do you know anyone who lives in heaven?
Can we talk to people who live in heaven? What can you say to them?
Colour in a picture of heaven (see template) and draw in some people who live there.

Juniors

Does anyone know of someone or something that has died — a friend, relation, pet, famous person?
How do you feel when someone or something you love dies?
What do you remember about that person or pet?
Where are they now? Are they close to you?
Write the name of someone who has died or whom you have not seen in a long time and write three memories about him/her.

Tip for learning difficulties

Ensure that they understand what it is to remember someone, perhaps using the following questions:
Point to the part of the body where you remember things. (In your head) If you do not see someone for a long time, do you remember them? What do you remember about them? (Their face/voice/words)
How do you feel if you see them again? (Happy/sad)

5. We come together

Parents can be invited to join in at this stage.

Focus

Place the images of heaven around the lighted candle, and perhaps add the word "remember" written on some paper.

Gospel

Jesus, before leaving his disciples, asked them to remember him, to remember all the good times they had had together and to remember everything that they had said to each other. Jesus did not want them to forget him when he is in heaven.

Prayer

Jesus, today we would like to remember all those people who are living in heaven. We want to pray for them.
At this point, the children are asked to name out loud or to think silently of people who are in heaven and whom they would like to pray for.
We promise always to remember those who are now living with you and to be glad that we know them.

Share

The work from the activities.

Sing

"Jesus, remember me, when you come into your kingdom"

4th Sunday of Easter

1. Introduction to the theme of the day

“I am the good shepherd”

Aim: To look at the way Jesus used everyday things around him in order to explain about God, and to try to understand the meaning behind these comparisons.

Leader’s Reflection: Jesus’ ministry and preaching are full of everyday images that were common to the people of his time. Jesus often drew comparisons between God and his kingdom and the natural world, speaking of animals like sheep and goats; plants like thorn bushes, fig trees, grape vines and mustard seeds; food like bread, eggs and fish; and events like harvest time, weddings and journeys. How can we, therefore, understand Jesus’ words about the kingdom of God if we have never seen or experienced such things? How can we truly understand his parable today if we have never seen sheep or a shepherd? How can we therefore change the setting of the stories to something we experience in our everyday lives without changing the original meanings? This challenge of setting Jesus’ message into the cultural environment of today is referred to as “inculturation of the Gospel”.

2. We arrive

We sit in a circle ready to listen to the Gospel.
Has anyone anything to share from last week’s Family Sheet?

Focus

A lighted candle on white fabric for Easter time. You may wish to place a picture of Jesus as a shepherd with some sheep in order to help understand the Gospel better.

Gospel: John 10:11-18

Read from the Lectionary or the Children’s Lectionary.

3. We respond

What is the Gospel asking of us?

If appropriate, work in age groups but join together as one community at the end of the session.

Young ones

Jesus is using a story or a "parable" in order to explain about God. God is like a shepherd and we are like sheep. God looks after us, keeping us from danger and protecting us, like a shepherd watches over his sheep. There are many ways of illustrating how God cares for us: for example, God cares for us like a mother cares for her new baby or God cares for us like a gardener looks after his prize roses.

Story

For his birthday, Gerald's parents gave him a puppy dog. Gerald was so happy because he had always wanted a puppy to play with and to do tricks. His parents, though, had always said that he had to wait until he was older. Now that it was his birthday, Gerald's mum and dad had decided that Gerald could now be responsible enough to look after a dog.

Gerald first gave the dog a name. He had a big brown patch on his back, and so he called the dog "Patch". Every day, Gerald would feed him dog food and give him water because he knew that Patch needed to eat and grow strong. Gerald would take Patch for walks so that Patch could be fit and healthy. He would stroke Patch and scratch his ear because he knew that Patch needed love and attention.

One day, Patch was playing in the garden when some bad boys were passing Gerald's house. When they saw the dog they started to throw stones at Patch and started to call Patch bad names. Gerald was very scared of these boys because they were much bigger than him, but he hated seeing Patch being bullied like this. Gerald, forgetting his fear because of his love for Patch, ran into the garden and screamed for the boys to go away. They were so surprised that they dropped their stones and went away.

Gerald's parents were very happy that Gerald was so brave for defending Patch and for always looking after Patch so well. They gave Gerald a big hug and told him, "You are such a good boy. Patch is a very lucky dog to have you to look after him!"

Juniors

Discuss what makes a good shepherd. He cares for the needs of his sheep: food, shelter and protection. How would the children describe a sheep? Was Jesus only talking about sheep? What did he mean when he said he would give up his life for his sheep?

Story

In Kenya, many parents cannot afford to send their children to school. Instead, they send them into the fields where the children look after sheep and goats. If the parents are so poor that they have no animals of their own, then the children are paid to look after the animals of a rich person in the village. The children take greater care, however, if the sheep are their own as they know that without the animals their family would have no milk or meat or money.

In Tanzania, however, many children are from the Masai tribe. The Masai tribe do not look after sheep but instead they keep cows. The children bring the cows out of the "boma" (a place where the Masai family and their animals sleep at night) early in the morning and lead them to grass and water. If there are any wild animals like lions that come to attack the cows, the children carry spears, knives and clubs in order to protect the cows. It is a great loss if even one cow is lost from the herd.

In some Pacific islands there are no cows or sheep or goats. Instead, people keep pigs for money and meat. However, they too look after the animals in the same way as the African children, making sure that they have enough to eat and drink, and that the animals are safe from thieves and predators.

In the UK, children do not look after sheep, cows, pigs or goats. But children often have a pet animal like a cat or a dog, a rabbit or a fish. These children too look after the animals, by feeding them and washing them, and making sure that they have medicine when they are sick and that they do not run out into the road where they can get killed.

If Jesus had been born in Africa, today's Gospel may have been about herding cows. And if Jesus had been born on the Pacific islands, he would have talked about caring for pigs. If Jesus had been born today in the UK, today's Gospel story may have been very different but the meaning would have been the same... that God looks after us in the same way as humans care for their own pets and animals.

4. Activity

Young ones

Draw a picture of something or someone you care for. Then write below the picture "I care for _________ like God cares for me".

Juniors

Rewrite today's Gospel story as if Jesus had been born in the UK today. Use the template of the frame. What would he be looking after? What would he have called himself? What dangers would he have fought against?

Tips for learning difficulties

Have pictures of people helping each other or people caring for animals. Explain that God loves us like these people are showing love to others in the pictures.

5. We come together

Parents can be invited to join in at this stage.

Focus

Gather together all the children's work and place it in the centre of the circle. Light a candle and put it at the centre of the display with the shepherd and sheep.

Gospel

"I am the good shepherd.
I know my sheep, and they know me.
Just as the Father knows me, I know the Father, and I give up my life for my sheep."

Jesus uses many examples to explain how God is, examples that were easy for the people at the time to understand. However, the central message behind the examples is the same for everyone everywhere, for ever.

Prayer

Jesus, you want so much for us to understand who you are that you tell us very difficult things in very simple ways. Thank you for being such a good teacher and for helping us to come to know you through everyday things that we see and touch.
Amen.

Share

The work from the activities.

Sing

"The Lord's my shepherd, I'll not want"

I CARE FOR ____________ LIKE GOD CARES FOR ME

5th Sunday of Easter

1. Introduction to the theme of the day

Aim: To reflect on our own dependence, how we need so many things in order for us to live.

Leader's Reflection: It is only when we are lacking something that we realise how dependent we are. Not only do we need water, food, clothes, money and shelter, but we also need security, family and friendship. Indeed, without these things, we cannot live. But often we can be so preoccupied with fulfilling these needs, that we forget also that we need God in our lives: that we are in fact utterly dependent on God for all our needs. Once we come to understand this, we begin to see that alone we can do nothing. Our dependence can then become a great source of humility in our humanity and of trust in our creator.

2. We arrive

We sit in a circle ready to listen to the Gospel.
Has anyone anything they would like to share from last week's Family Sheet?

Focus

A lighted candle on white cloth for the Easter season. You may like to add some grapes and some flowers/plants to help understand the Gospel.

Gospel: John 15:1-8

Read from the Lectionary or the Children's Lectionary.

3. We respond

What is the Gospel asking of us?

If appropriate, work in age groups but bring everyone together as a community at the end of the session.

Young ones

Jesus is reminding us how dependent we humans are. We sometimes forget how many things we need in order to live. We need air to breathe, water to drink, food to eat, friends to love. But most importantly, we need God so that our lives can be truly complete.

Story

John was so excited about going to school for the first time. He could not wait to go and see his new teacher and to meet new friends and to play new games. He was thinking so much about these things that, when his mummy left him at the school gate, he forgot to take his schoolbag with him and instead left it in the car. Then he ran inside the school playground and began to play with the other children.

The school bell rang, and all the children and John went in to begin their lessons.

"Today, we are going to draw pictures," said the teacher. John was really happy because he loved drawing. But when he went to take out his crayons and paper from his bag, he saw that he had forgotten them.

"Oh no," he thought. "Now I cannot draw because I have no crayons or paper." Just then, the bell rang for lunchtime. All the children took out their sandwiches and crisps and drinks and began to eat.

"Oh no," said John. "My lunch was in my bag and now I feel so hungry and thirsty." Everyone was so busy eating that they did not see that John needed some food too.

Just then there was a knock on the classroom door. It was John's mum. And she was holding his schoolbag for him.

"You were so excited this morning that you forgot your bag. Here, I have brought it for you."

"Thank you, thank you, Mummy," John shouted. "Look inside my bag. Here are the crayons and paper I needed to draw with, and here is my lunch which I want to eat. And here is my mummy who I need to look after me and help me to remember to bring my bag to school!"

Juniors

Discuss the word "pruning": cutting away dead or damaged stems to make room for new growth. Who was the vine and who was the gardener?
Jesus explains that we are all part of him.
What fruits does he want us to bear?

Story

In Africa, people depend on water very much. In Eastern Africa, it rains twice a year: the long rains come from March until May, and then the short rains come in October and November. During these rains, people plant seeds on their land and then wait for the seeds to grow into food such as maize, beans, sorghum, sugar, cabbages and tomatoes.

If the rains do not fall, the seeds will not grow because there is no water available for them to live. And if the seeds do not grow, then the people have no food to eat. They do not have money to go and buy food either, and sometimes people die because there is no rain and no food. Also, when it does not rain and water is hard to find, people suffer from many diseases such as cholera and typhoid because they begin to drink dirty water that is bad for them. Many animals like cows and goats die because without water there is no grass for them to eat.

Every year, before the rains come, people go to church and pray that the rains will fall. They realise how much they need water in order to live because with water they can drink and eat and be healthy. When it does begin to rain, people say that it is a blessing from God. They know that without God there would be no rain, no water, no food and no life. African people are very aware of how dependent they are on God and his blessings.

4. Activity

Try to explain to the children Jesus' parable from today's Gospel. Take a plant and break a leaf off it. What will the leaf look like after one week? Can the leaf live if it is not attached to the plant? What does it get from the plant that allows it to live?

Young ones

Using the template colour in and name pictures of things we need to live (water, food, friends, air, shelter, trees).

Juniors

Jesus tells us that we are like leaves and he is the plant. Have a plant to focus the discussion.
• How do we stay close to Jesus like a leaf stays close to a plant? (prayer, going to church, doing good etc.)

Jesus tells us that we need him like leaves need a plant in order to grow. And when leaves grow, fruit is produced.
• What type of fruits do you think Jesus is talking of? (patience, kindness, humility, holiness etc.)
• Can a leaf grow fruit if it is not part of the plant? Can we do good if we are not close to God?

Jesus says that God prunes the branches so they bear more fruit.
• What is pruning? (cutting away of dead branches)
• How do we cut away the dead branches in our lives? (through confession, saying sorry, changing our behaviour etc.)

Write all the answers of the children on large sheets so that everyone sees the variety of answers.

Tips for learning difficulties

Have many pictures of things and ask the children to show which ones we need. Show them how we really need many things in order to live.

5. We come together

Parents can be invited to join in at this stage.

Focus

The lighted candle on white cloth for the Easter season and the plant used during the activity.

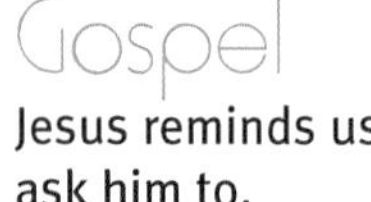

Gospel

Jesus reminds us of how we humans have many needs but that God can fulfil them all if we ask him to.

Prayer

Jesus, thank you for reminding us how much we need you and depend on your blessings every day. We promise to thank you every day for giving us all that we need so that we can live and love you. Amen.

Share

The work from the activities.

Sing

"Take our bread, we ask you,
take our hearts, we love you,
take our lives, O Father we are yours, we are yours"

Air

6th Sunday of Easter

1. Introduction to the theme of the day

Aim: To explore what it means to love, how Jesus loves us and how we can love others.

Leader's Reflection: Often in our world, love is understood primarily as the Greek word "eros", this being the term for erotic love. However, eros is not referred to in the Bible. Rather it is "agape", the seeking of a neighbour's welfare, and "philia", the love between friends and relatives, that are talked of. However, it is these elements of love that are the hardest to live out, but are in most need of practice today.

Love, though, is a difficult and complex emotion to understand. Fortunately, Jesus led us by example and through seeing his actions we are able to follow more closely his command to love others as he himself did.

2. We arrive

We sit in a circle, ready to listen to the Gospel.

Does anyone want to share something from last week's Family Sheet?

Focus

In the centre of the circle is placed a lighted candle on white cloth for Easter time. You may wish to place some pictures of couples, families, friends who are helping and loving each other.

Gospel: John 15:9-17

Read from the Lectionary or the Children's Lectionary.

3. We respond

What is the Gospel asking of us?

If appropriate, work in age groups but join together as one community at the end of the session.

Young ones

Jesus tells us that we should love one another. How do we show love for others? How did Jesus show love to others? Should we do the same as Jesus?

Story

Peter was the second child of three in his family. He had an older brother, Jack, and a younger brother, Alex. Jack was a very good brother. He would spend long hours with Peter, reading him stories, watching TV with him and laughing together with him. Jack even lent Peter his new bike so that Peter could learn how to ride it! Peter liked his older brother a lot because he was always so good to him.

Peter did not, however, like Alex, his younger four-year-old brother. When Alex wanted to play with Peter's toys, Peter would get very angry and shout and scream at him. When Alex wanted some of Peter's crisps, Peter would run away with the packet. When Alex was watching TV, Peter would come in and change channels without asking him.

Jack, Peter's older brother, began to see how Peter was treating Alex and did not like it. So, one day, Jack went on a long walk with Peter. They began to talk.

"Remember how I gave you my sweets when you asked me for them?"

"Yes," said Peter. "I was so happy that you shared them with me."

"And do you remember when I gave you my toy car, the one I always played with?"

"Yes, I do remember," said Peter. "That is my favourite toy now because you gave it to me."

"Well then," said Jack. "If I share my things with you and spend time with you, why do you not do the same with Alex, your younger brother?" Peter was quiet for a while and thought to himself, "Jack is right. If Jack treats me so well, then I too should be good to Alex."

And from that day on, Peter loved his brother Alex. He played with him and shared his sweets and toys with him. Jack was very happy that Peter had finally learnt how to be a good big brother!

Juniors

What did Jesus ask his disciples to do? What did Jesus do for us? How can we share Jesus' love with each other?

Story

St Paul talks of what love is (1 Cor 13). When we show love, we are patient and kind. Loving people are not jealous of others, neither are they boastful or arrogant. To be rude to others is not love. Loving people help others and do not get angry quickly. They forgive quickly. They do not like it when people are bad but are happy when others are honest and speak the truth.

St Paul also tells us that we can be the best musician or sportsperson or top of the class. But if we play music or sport or do schoolwork without love in order to be praised or to beat others, then what we do is worthless. He tells us that we can believe in God so much that we can say wise things and pray for many hours and even move mountains, but if we do it in a way that is proud and boastful, then it is pointless. We may even share all our things with our friends and family and give away our best toys and books, but if we then are people who easily get impatient or angry, or we criticise others, then our generosity has no meaning. No, we must do all things first with love in our hearts, and then our actions will have meaning.

4. Activity

Young ones

A picture of a heart is a symbol of love because people say that love comes from the heart. When you love someone, how do you feel inside? On the template, ask the children to write in two names of people they love, inside two hearts, and two names of people they will try harder to love, in the other two. Allow them to colour the hearts in.

Juniors

Write out, in large letters, words that show love and words that show hate. Get the children to divide the words into two sections and then paste them onto posters saying "How to love" and "How not to love". Examples of words include patience, honesty, kindness, boastfulness, arrogance, listening, hopefulness, keeping secrets, correcting others, competing (include some words that can depend on how the action is done so that the children can discuss the meaning between themselves).

Tips for learning difficulties

Have a variety of pictures and allow the children to pick the ones that show love, e.g. pictures of family, war, people shouting, children playing etc. Help them understand what it is to love others. Stick them onto a poster.

5. We come together

Parents can be invited to join in at this stage.

Focus

Gather together the two posters and the pictures of the hearts and pictures of love and place them around the candle.

Gospel

Before leaving them, Jesus asks his disciples to think back and to remember how he showed love to others. And then he asks them to copy his actions so that they too can be his friends.

Prayer

Dear Jesus, we remember today how you showed love to others:

you listened to people who were worried; you hugged the sick and dying; you helped the old; you shared your food with hungry people and you even died so that we could live. Teach us also to love like you did, so that we can always be like you in all ways. Amen.

Share

The work from the activities.

Sing

"Love is his word, love is his way"

The Ascension of the Lord

1. Introduction to the theme of the day

"Jesus disappeared from their sight"

Aim: To think about the events of the Ascension as Jesus says goodbye to his friends.

Leader's Reflection: At the Ascension we are usually left standing with the apostles as Jesus disappears from sight. This is so often our perspective and we get very used to standing with our faces pointing upwards, looking quizzically at the clouds. Among the many different forms of prayer which are available to us, there is one in which we take on the role of some person in a biblical story and re-enact the story in our mind. Taking on the role of Jesus in this way can lead to some lovely insights into his humanity.

2. We arrive

We sit in a circle ready to listen to the Gospel.
Has anyone anything to tell us about last week's Family Sheet?

Focus

A lighted candle, white fabric for Eastertide, a depiction of the Ascension – from a book, or try http://biblia.com/jesusm/passion.htm#Ascension

Gospel: Mark 16:15-20 (Catholic)
Luke 24:44-53 (Anglican)

Read from the Lectionary or Children's Lectionary.

3. We respond

What is the Gospel asking of us?

Work in age groups if appropriate.
Today Jesus went back to heaven. We think about how that might have felt for him.

Young ones

Story

Aelred was looking for Jesus – he was Jesus' guardian angel. Ever since the Resurrection when Jesus rose from the dead, Aelred had found it difficult to keep his eye on exactly where Jesus was. He kept popping up all over the place: at the table when his friends were eating; on the beach when they were fishing; walking with them along the road. Aelred was kept really busy flying around on his angel's wings trying to keep up with him.

At last he found him. This time he was on his own, sitting in a field under a tree. He looked a bit strange, sort of happy and unhappy at the same time. Aelred sat down next to him.

"What are you thinking about?" he asked.

Jesus smiled at him gently, "Sorry," he said, "I should have told you. Today is our last day on earth."

"What do you mean?" asked Aelred. "I thought now you had risen from the dead, you were going to live here for ever."

"Well, I will live for ever," said Jesus, "but not here, or at least, not in the same way. I have to go back to heaven, so that my friends can get on with telling people about me. I can help them much better from heaven, than if I stay here."

Aelred went very quiet. "But what about me?" he whispered, trying not to cry. "What will I do? I can't be your guardian angel in heaven. You won't need me any more!"

Jesus laughed, "Don't you worry about that!" he said. "I will have plenty of work for you in heaven. Even when I am up there, I will still be keeping an eye on things down here. Who else do you think I can trust to run my messages for me and to help me look after everything on earth? Besides, it won't be too long before some of my friends come to heaven to live with me for ever, and there will be lots of cleaning and cooking to be done before they arrive. Don't you worry about what you are going to be doing. You will be kept very busy!"

Juniors

At the Anglican shrine in Walsingham in Norfolk, there is a small side chapel dedicated to the Ascension of the Lord. At first it appears to be completely empty, until you are directed by a friend or some helpful passer-by to look upwards. There, disappearing into a cloud painted in the middle of the ceiling, are stuck a pair of plaster-cast feet. It is left to your imagination to picture the rest of Jesus' human form hovering in suspension above you.

Because we can only imagine the events of the Ascension from ground level, it can be difficult to represent them without them appearing slightly ridiculous – a sort of disappearing act, or a balancing act on a cloud, or maybe even zooming off like a rocket into the sky.

Again from ground level, we often think about how the apostles felt when Jesus disappeared from their sight – shocked, upset and frightened probably – but I wonder how did Jesus feel? It was the end of his time as a man living on the earth: he would still be with his friends, but it would be in a different way – no Peter to give him a hug when he was feeling fed up, no more sorting out the squabbles between Philip and Andrew, no more home-cooked meals with Martha, Mary and Lazarus, no more intimate nights around the campfire with his friends, no more walking through the fields with the sun on his face, no more crowds, and no more quiet times.

Jesus had to leave his friends so that they could receive his Spirit for themselves, and begin to do the work he had prepared them for, but maybe the parting was just as difficult for him as it was for them.

4. Activity

Young ones

Aelred wants to tell his friends all about his trip back to heaven with Jesus.

Using the template picture of the postcard, cut around the solid outside line and fold along the dotted line. You now have a front and a back to your postcard. Stick or tape together.

On the front, draw a picture of heaven.

On the back, write a few words for Aelred, describing his trip to heaven.

Juniors

Imagine you found out that you were going to ascend to heaven tomorrow. You would be very excited, but probably a bit sad as well because you would be leaving so much behind. Which places would you want to visit again, and which people would you want to talk to? Imagine how you would spend that last evening. Find a space to be quiet by yourself and just think about it. Your leader might play some quiet music to help you think.

Tips for learning difficulties

Some children might find it easier to focus if they are shown photographs of people and places that are special to them.

5. We come together

Parents can be invited to join in at this stage.

Focus

Gather around the candle and the pictures.

Gospel

Jesus said to his apostles, "Go out to the whole world and tell them the Good News. Baptise people in my name, and teach them everything I have taught you." And after he had spoken to them a cloud covered him and he was taken up into heaven and they could not see him any more.

Prayer

Jesus, today you went back to heaven. The apostles missed you and would have liked you to come back. Sometimes we think it would be nice for you to come back and visit us as well. Help us to remember that you are always with us. Amen.

Share

The young ones can give their pictures to somebody that Jesus loves. If there is time, juniors might wish to share their experiences, however, as these are essentially private, there should be no pressure.

Sing

"Be still and know that I am God" – you could substitute these lines for verses 2 and3:

"Today I go to be in heaven"

"But I am with you for all time"

back

Dear ....

To all my angel friends

With love from,

Aelred

Heaven

front

7th Sunday of Easter

1. Introduction to the theme of the day

"Waiting for the Spirit"

Aim: After Jesus' ascension, the apostles had to wait a short time until the Holy Spirit came to them. We wait with them.

Leader's Reflection: These few days between the Ascension and Pentecost are a time of waiting. In many respects, waiting has become unacceptable to us. We live in a world of instant make-overs; banks, supermarkets, petrol stations, all are designed to minimise our waiting times. We regard waiting as a waste of time, an imposition on our important, busy lives. In God, we must learn to wait patiently, joyfully even. Waiting is part of the process. He comes to us, as and when we are ready for him.

2. We arrive

We sit in a circle ready to listen to the Gospel. Invite some comments regarding the Family Sheet used during the week.

Focus

A lighted candle, a ticking clock, preferably one with a second hand. White fabric for Easter.

Gospel: John 17:11-19

Read from the Lectionary or Children's Lectionary.

3. We respond

What is the Gospel asking of us?

For one minute, just sit and listen to, and watch the clock. Does time seem to pass slowly or quickly? Talk about the things we expect immediately, and the things we are prepared to wait for. What are the things we don't like about waiting? What makes it worthwhile? What can happen if we try to rush things we need to wait for?

If appropriate, split the children into age groups for the stories and activities.

Young ones

Story

Henry, the honey bee, was painting the inside of his hive. He had chosen the colours himself – blue and yellow – and imagined how bright and cheerful it would all look when he had finished. He was very careful. He took all the pictures off the walls, and put the chairs outside; he rolled up the carpet and took down the lampshades, then he covered the table with a large cloth and started work.

First of all he got on his step ladder and painted the ceiling bright yellow, and then he painted the door and the skirting board yellow as well. Finally he got out the big pot of blue paint, and painted all the walls a deep, beautiful blue. It did look lovely when he had finished. Although the paint was still wet, he wanted to finish his work quickly, and get all the furniture back in, so very carefully he took the cloth off the table, then he unrolled the carpets, and then he climbed onto his step ladder to put the lampshades and pictures back. Henry was right at the top of the ladder, when, disaster!

The ladder wobbled a bit this way, and then wobbled a bit more the other way, and then wobbled and wobbled until finally, it toppled right over. Henry was at the top of the ladder. As it wobbled he put both his hands on the ceiling to stop himself falling. As it wobbled some more, he put both his hands on the wall to stop himself falling, and as it toppled over, he put both hands in the air as he hit the carpet with a thud.

Ouch! Henry needed to sit down, so he went outside to bring in one of the chairs, and sat on it to look at the mess. Oh dear! The yellow paint on the ceiling was all smudged and messy where he had put his hands; the beautiful blue wall had bright yellow handprints on it where he had put his hands; and the beautiful yellow door had deep blue handprints on it where he had put his hands.

Henry was very upset! Now he would have to do all his work again. But this time he would wait until the paint was quite dry before getting on the step ladder again.

Juniors

Story

St Romuald was a hermit. Hermits are people who spend their lives on their own, waiting for God. Romuald was born at a place called Ravenna in the tenth century, and should have grown up to be a duke.

As a boy, he enjoyed wild parties and behaved appallingly, until one day he saw his father kill another man who owed him money. Romuald was so shocked and upset that he ran away from home and became a monk. He was a very good monk, and was soon put in charge, but Romuald felt that life in the monastery was too easy. He tried to make it harder but the other monks did not like this at all, so Romuald left the monastery and joined an old man called Marinus who was a hermit.

Marinus also liked to live life the hard way. He would take Romuald into the forest and make him recite all 150 psalms in the Bible by heart. If Romuald made a mistake, he would hit him on his left ear. After a while, this ear became so swollen that Romuald couldn't hear with it, so he asked Marinus to hit him on the other ear instead!

Romuald spent many years as a wandering hermit, living alone, or visiting different monasteries until in 1012 he came to a place called Camaldoli. There he had a dream, telling him to build a monastery just for hermits. Romuald built his monastery, and wrote a set of rules for the hermits. Romuald taught his monks to be joyful and happy as they waited for God. He wrote,

"Wait in your room as in Paradise, content with God's gift, like a little chick, tasting and eating nothing but what its mother brings. Sing in your heart. If you get frustrated and impatient with yourself, don't give up, but realise that you are in God's presence: wait there and hold your heart in wonder."

4. Activity

Young ones

You will need two sheets of paper, some blue paint and some yellow paint. Paint one sheet blue all over, and paint the other one yellow. Whilst they are still wet, put your hand on one, and then the other. You will get some lovely hand prints, just like Henry!

Juniors

In a newspaper or magazine, find all the articles or advertisements that use words or phrases like "instantaneous", "immediate", "at the push of a button", "at your fingertips" etc. Make a collage of them using the template.

Think of an advertising slogan for God which emphasises the need to be patient, e.g. Life happens at once ... Eternity takes a little longer.

Tips for learning difficulties

Have some samples of wet paint and dry paint. Work through some activity to show the passing of time, before you can fold the dried sheet and use it.

5. We come together

Parents can be invited to join in at this stage.

Focus

Gather around the clock and candle.

Gospel

Before Jesus ascended to heaven on Ascension Thursday, he prayed for all his friends.

"Father, I am coming to heaven soon, but my friends cannot come with me yet. I have taught them all about you. Help them still to believe in you, even when I am not here to remind them. Look after them while they are waiting for our Holy Spirit, then they will know how to teach other people about you as well."

Prayer

Dear Father, after the angel visited Mary, she *waited* nine months until Jesus was born. Jesus *waited* thirty years before he started to preach to the people.
After he died on the cross the apostles *waited* three days until the Resurrection.
After he ascended to heaven the apostles *waited* ten days for the Holy Spirit to come to them. Some things are worth waiting for.
Help us to wait for you patiently and to enjoy our waiting. Amen.

Share

Discuss the activities from each group.

"Be still and know that I am God"

INSTANT
MAKE-OVER!
EXPRESS CHECKOUT
ZERO WAITING TIMES!

Pentecost Sunday

1. Introduction to the theme of the day

"The gifts of the Spirit"

Aim: Today the Holy Spirit comes to us to help us live in God's way.

Leader's Reflection: Fire always leaves an indelible mark on things, even changing the nature of some things completely. When the Holy Spirit arrived at Pentecost in tongues of flame, it was an indication that we should be prepared for God's life in us to change us completely.

2. We arrive

We sit in a circle ready to listen to the reading.
Has anyone anything they would like to tell us about last week's Family Sheet?

Focus

If possible, a bonfire; if not then a paraffin lamp or a lighted candle; red cloth for Pentecost.

Reading: Acts 2:1-11

Read from the Lectionary or Children's Lectionary.

3. We respond

What is the reading asking of us?

Work in age groups if appropriate.
Alternatively, choose the discussion ideas, story and activity most suitable for your group.

Young ones

Story

The animals were having a bonfire. Monica had been cleaning her mouse hole, and had made a huge pile of all the leaves, and bits of paper and broken furniture which had gathered there over the winter. Henry the honey bee had added to the pile all the rubbish that he had found when he was decorating the hive. Everybody had found a stick or two to put on the pile. Now the day had come, and they all gathered round to watch Owen the owl (who was the eldest and most sensible of them all) light the match and set the fire alight.

They all stood around warming their hands as the flames blazed high in the sky, until Daphne came quacking along with a sack of potatoes that she poked one by one into the bottom of the fire, so they would cook.

Michael the mole had brought along a plate of worms marinated in barbeque sauce. Everybody stuck them onto the end of sticks and held them over the flames until they sizzled: they were quite delicious. By then the potatoes were ready. They were black and burnt on the outside, but inside they were all white and fluffy. With a little bit of butter on top, they went down a treat.

By now it was evening, and the animals could only see each other if they stood close to the light of the bonfire. "How wonderful a bonfire is," sighed Monica. "It has burnt up all my rubbish, and it has kept us all warm, and it has cooked our food for us, and now it still gives enough light to see each other." And everyone else had to agree.

Spend some time talking about the changes the Holy Spirit makes in our lives.

Juniors

Story

St Barnabas was a friend of St Paul. Barnabas was not with the apostles when the Holy Spirit arrived at Pentecost in the form of fire. Nor was he with St Paul when the Holy Spirit came to him as a great bright white light, but still the apostles often said, "Barnabas is a man filled with the Holy Spirit", because he was very good at encouraging people and cheering them up.

Barnabas was a friend of the apostles and quickly became a Christian. This was at about the same time as St Paul had his vision on the road to Damascus. Paul wanted to join the other Christians in Jerusalem, but they were all very scared of him, because he used to be one of their persecutors. Only Barnabas was brave enough to go to Tarsus and meet him. Barnabas got on very well with Paul, and talked to him about Jesus, and about the other Christians. Eventually he convinced them that Paul was to be trusted, and Paul joined their community.

Paul and Barnabas travelled a lot together, spreading the news of Christianity. Once they went to a place called Paphos and met a man called Sergius Paulus who was extremely intelligent. He asked Paul and Barnabas to tell him about Christianity. Sergius had a magician working for him called Elymas. Every time Barnabas started speaking, Elymas kept interrupting and trying to stop him. Paul looked at the man intently and said, "You utter fraud, you impostor, you son of the devil; to stop you interrupting and twisting our words, you will go blind for a while and will not even see the sun!"

That instant, everything went misty and dark for the magician, and he started to grope around to find his way. Sergius became a Christian straight away.

Another time, Paul and Barnabas cured a man who was a cripple. The people around were so impressed by this that they started to call Barnabas "Zeus", and Paul "Hermes" (these are the names of Greek gods). They were about to sacrifice a bull for them, but Paul and Barnabas were so upset that they started to tear all their clothes off to prove that they were human beings like everyone else. Now the people were not impressed, and started to throw stones at them instead. They left that town very quickly!

Spend some time in discussion.

We are very like Barnabas. Like St Barnabas, when the Holy Spirit comes to us, it will not be in the form of fire or bright lights, but people will know we are filled with the Spirit because of the way we live.

We can ask St Barnabas to pray for us and to help us.

4. Activity

If possible build a bonfire. If not, use a paraffin lamp or a candle.

Think of all the things which fire can do – heat, light, destroy, cook food, melt things, cause chemical reactions (fireworks etc.), provide power.

Fire always changes things. So when the Holy Spirit comes in the form of fire, we can expect that he will change us as well.

Young ones

Make a model of a bonfire on a sheet of paper using orange and yellow tissue paper, twigs and leaves. Write the word "God" on it to show that God is like fire.

Juniors

In the frame from the template page, draw a picture of yourself. Stick on yellow and orange tissue paper flames around yourself so that you are in the middle of the fire. Write a prayer at the top, beginning "Holy Spirit, come to me and change me ..." (and continue with words describing how you want to be changed).

Tips for learning difficulties

Around the bonfire model, talk about God being warm and powerful. He can make things happen and make things light so we can see where we are going.

5. We come together

Parents can be invited to join in at this stage.

Focus

Gather around the fire/candle/lamp.

Today's Readings

After the resurrection, the apostles were all praying together. Jesus appeared in the room with them. He said to them, "Receive the Holy Spirit", but they did not really know what he meant.

A few days later, after Jesus had ascended to heaven, the apostles were praying together again. A great wind shook the house they were in, and flames of fire appeared in the room with them. Jesus had kept his promise, and sent his Holy Spirit to be with them. They were filled with joy and started shouting and praising God.

Prayer

Holy Spirit, come to us, not as fire or as bright lights but in a way which will help us to grow and to change so that we can live the way Jesus wants us to live. Amen.

Share

The work from the activities.

Sing

"Abba, Father, send your Spirit"

Young ones

Story

The animals were having a bonfire. Monica had been cleaning her mouse hole, and had made a huge pile of all the leaves, and bits of paper and broken furniture which had gathered there over the winter. Henry the honey bee had added to the pile all the rubbish that he had found when he was decorating the hive. Everybody had found a stick or two to put on the pile. Now the day had come, and they all gathered round to watch Owen the owl (who was the eldest and most sensible of them all) light the match and set the fire alight.

They all stood around warming their hands as the flames blazed high in the sky, until Daphne came quacking along with a sack of potatoes that she poked one by one into the bottom of the fire, so they would cook.

Michael the mole had brought along a plate of worms marinated in barbeque sauce. Everybody stuck them onto the end of sticks and held them over the flames until they sizzled: they were quite delicious. By then the potatoes were ready. They were black and burnt on the outside, but inside they were all white and fluffy. With a little bit of butter on top, they went down a treat.

By now it was evening, and the animals could only see each other if they stood close to the light of the bonfire. "How wonderful a bonfire is," sighed Monica. "It has burnt up all my rubbish, and it has kept us all warm, and it has cooked our food for us, and now it still gives enough light to see each other." And everyone else had to agree.

Spend some time talking about the changes the Holy Spirit makes in our lives.

Juniors

Story

St Barnabas was a friend of St Paul. Barnabas was not with the apostles when the Holy Spirit arrived at Pentecost in the form of fire. Nor was he with St Paul when the Holy Spirit came to him as a great bright white light, but still the apostles often said, "Barnabas is a man filled with the Holy Spirit", because he was very good at encouraging people and cheering them up.

Barnabas was a friend of the apostles and quickly became a Christian. This was at about the same time as St Paul had his vision on the road to Damascus. Paul wanted to join the other Christians in Jerusalem, but they were all very scared of him, because he used to be one of their persecutors. Only Barnabas was brave enough to go to Tarsus and meet him. Barnabas got on very well with Paul, and talked to him about Jesus, and about the other Christians. Eventually he convinced them that Paul was to be trusted, and Paul joined their community.

Paul and Barnabas travelled a lot together, spreading the news of Christianity. Once they went to a place called Paphos and met a man called Sergius Paulus who was extremely intelligent. He asked Paul and Barnabas to tell him about Christianity. Sergius had a magician working for him called Elymas. Every time Barnabas started speaking, Elymas kept interrupting and trying to stop him. Paul looked at the man intently and said, "You utter fraud, you impostor, you son of the devil; to stop you interrupting and twisting our words, you will go blind for a while and will not even see the sun!"

That instant, everything went misty and dark for the magician, and he started to grope around to find his way. Sergius became a Christian straight away.

Another time, Paul and Barnabas cured a man who was a cripple. The people around were so impressed by this that they started to call Barnabas "Zeus", and Paul "Hermes" (these are the names of Greek gods). They were about to sacrifice a bull for them, but Paul and Barnabas were so upset that they started to tear all their clothes off to prove that they were human beings like everyone else. Now the people were not impressed, and started to throw stones at them instead. They left that town very quickly!

Spend some time in discussion.

We are very like Barnabas. Like St Barnabas, when the Holy Spirit comes to us, it will not be in the form of fire or bright lights, but people will know we are filled with the Spirit because of the way we live.

We can ask St Barnabas to pray for us and to help us.

4. Activity

If possible build a bonfire. If not, use a paraffin lamp or a candle.

Think of all the things which fire can do – heat, light, destroy, cook food, melt things, cause chemical reactions (fireworks etc.), provide power.

Fire always changes things. So when the Holy Spirit comes in the form of fire, we can expect that he will change us as well.

Young ones

Make a model of a bonfire on a sheet of paper using orange and yellow tissue paper, twigs and leaves. Write the word "God" on it to show that God is like fire.

Juniors

In the frame from the template page, draw a picture of yourself. Stick on yellow and orange tissue paper flames around yourself so that you are in the middle of the fire. Write a prayer at the top, beginning "Holy Spirit, come to me and change me ..." (and continue with words describing how you want to be changed).

Tips for learning difficulties

Around the bonfire model, talk about God being warm and powerful. He can make things happen and make things light so we can see where we are going.

5. We come together

Parents can be invited to join in at this stage.

Focus

Gather around the fire/candle/lamp.

Today's Readings

After the resurrection, the apostles were all praying together. Jesus appeared in the room with them. He said to them, "Receive the Holy Spirit", but they did not really know what he meant.

A few days later, after Jesus had ascended to heaven, the apostles were praying together again. A great wind shook the house they were in, and flames of fire appeared in the room with them. Jesus had kept his promise, and sent his Holy Spirit to be with them. They were filled with joy and started shouting and praising God.

Prayer

Holy Spirit, come to us, not as fire or as bright lights but in a way which will help us to grow and to change so that we can live the way Jesus wants us to live. Amen.

Share

The work from the activities.

Sing

"Abba, Father, send your Spirit"

This is how I want the Holy Spirit to change me.

2nd Sunday in Ordinary Time

The 2nd Sunday of Epiphany

1. Introduction to the theme of the day

"Come and see where I live"

Aim: To see in the call of Jesus an invitation to get to know him personally.

Leader's Reflection: We often hear people speak of their "calling" or "vocation" and recognise it as something they feel almost compelled to respond to. We tend to interpret our sense of being called as something we have to do – and that can often be the case. However, the call to be a Christian has another element: the call to get to know Jesus and to develop a living relationship with him. Unlike Andrew and the other disciples, we do not have the opportunity to go to Jesus' home and spend hours in discussion and prayer. There are other ways in which we can allow our relationship with him to grow. Prayer is an obvious one. Another is to read the Gospels as if we were actually present – or to read the words of Jesus as though directed personally at ourselves. At times, this can be challenging; at times, it can be comforting. It can, at times, be boring. That is the way of many close relationships. Time spent getting to know and love Jesus more deeply will inevitably enrich us and make the active side of our calling vastly more fruitful.

2. We arrive

We sit in a circle ready to listen to the Gospel.
Has anyone anything they would like to tell us about last week's Family Sheet?

Focus

Green cloth.
Candle.
Bible or Lectionary open at the Gospel.

Gospel: John 1:35-42

Read from the Lectionary or Children's Lectionary.

3. We respond

What is the Gospel asking of us?

Work in age groups if appropriate. Alternatively, choose the discussion ideas, story and activity most suitable for your group.

Young ones

Invite the children to think about the Gospel. Imagine you are one of the two disciples who followed Jesus. Jesus looks around and questions you. What do you feel like? He invites you to come to his house. Now, what do you feel like?

Story

Judith liked living next door to Mrs Marshall who had recently moved in. After her first visit with her mother she went round to see her at least twice a week and they would enjoy tea – or lemonade in Judith's case – and some of Mrs Marshall's home-made cake.

Mrs Marshall told Judith all about when she was a little girl and how different everything had been. "No computers in those days," she would say.

She taught Judith some of the games that she had played as a child and said that when she was young, she and her friends would go off for whole days with a packet of sandwiches and a jam-jar with string on to catch tadpoles and sticklebacks. Judith thought she must have been very adventurous.

When Judith went to school, she told her friends about Mrs Marshall and when she went to Mrs Marshall's she told her about her friends at school.

One day, Mrs Marshall said, "Now I've heard about Michelle, Kate, Josh and Gaurav – but I have never met them. Do you think their parents would let them come to tea with us one day?" Judith thought they might and the next time she went to visit, Mrs Marshall gave her five envelopes – one with her name on and the others for her friends.

Everyone's parents agreed and so, one sunny afternoon, they all trooped to Mrs Marshall's front door. She opened it and led them into her sitting room where the children saw all sorts of interesting things.

"Does your budgie talk?" asked Gaurav.

"Not much," said Mrs Marshall, "but we had a parrot once who could sing Happy Birthday."

The children had a wonderful afternoon with Mrs Marshall. She told them stories and taught them games and the end of the day came far too soon.

"Next time you come," she said, "I'll show you how to make peppermint creams."

As they went back to Judith's house, Kate said, "Mrs Marshall is so cool. I wish I lived next door to her."

Judith was glowing with pride. She did live next door and now her friends had met the best next-door neighbour ever.

Invite the children to respond to the story. Do they know who their neighbours are? What are their neighbours like? What might living next to Jesus have been like?

Juniors

Invite the children to think about the characters in the Gospel story and how they might have felt as events unfolded. How did John the Baptist feel when he recognised Jesus again? What about Andrew when he heard John identify Jesus – and when Jesus turned and invited him to his home? And Simon – hearing Jesus change his name to Cephas (or the name we would more readily recognise, Peter)?

Ask the children to close their eyes and relax. Use the following words to lead the children in a guided meditation on this week's Gospel. Read or speak slowly – giving the children time to build up the picture and allowing the story to unfold.

Story

Imagine the scene in the Gospel... the River Jordan in the background, palm trees, blue sky. Try to hear the water flowing... the sound of people talking; perhaps dogs barking.

Now bring John the Baptist into the scene with his camel-hair clothes; watch him baptise people and then, seeing Jesus and watching him go past, he says, "Look, there is the lamb of God."

Imagine yourself turning round to see Jesus... what does he look like?

Watch Andrew and his friend follow Jesus... and see Jesus turn around... hear him ask, "What do you want?" In your imagination tell him something that you would really like... Let him invite you to go to his home... What does it look like?... What does Jesus do?... What does Jesus say?

When you feel ready, say "goodbye" to Jesus in your head... and open your eyes.

Invite the children to share the fruits of their reflections with you and the group ... Respect the fact that they may not want to share certain details but encourage them to savour the time they have spent with Jesus. Explain that this is a way of praying that helps us to get to know Jesus better.

4. Activity

Young ones

Cut out enough footprints for your group using the template provided. Write each child's name on their footprint in large writing and encourage them to decorate it. On the reverse side, the children can draw a picture of themselves and Jesus walking together.

Juniors

The children cut out the footprint and write their name in "bubble-writing" which they colour in and decorate the rest of the print. On the reverse side, they can write or draw something from their reflection. Assure them that no one in the group is going to see what they have drawn or written.

Tips for learning difficulties

Have the footprints ready cut out and the children's names written on them. Where necessary, ask the children what they would like to be doing with Jesus and draw an outline of Jesus and the child on the reverse for the child to colour.

5. We come together

Parents can be invited to join in at this stage.

Focus

Use the focus prepared for the beginning of this session. Light the candle. Invite those gathered to become still.

Gospel

John has baptised Jesus. Some time later, he sees Jesus and, when he realises that it is him, tells his own disciples that this is the one whom he had spoken about.

Andrew and one of his friends follow Jesus and he invites them to his home. Andrew is so impressed that when he next meets his brother Simon, he immediately tells him about the Messiah.

When Jesus and Simon meet, Jesus looks hard at him and renames him "Cephas" which means Rock.

Prayer

Jesus, you want us to get to know you.
Help us to grow in love
and to listen to your word
so that we can be like Andrew and Peter
and become your friend.
Amen.

Share

Talk about what happened in the session – what the children have learnt. Invite the children to place their footprints (name side up) on a path made of fabric or card. Explain that this is a sign of walking with Jesus.

Sing

"Follow me, follow me"
"One more step along the road I go"
"My God said to me 'Follow'"

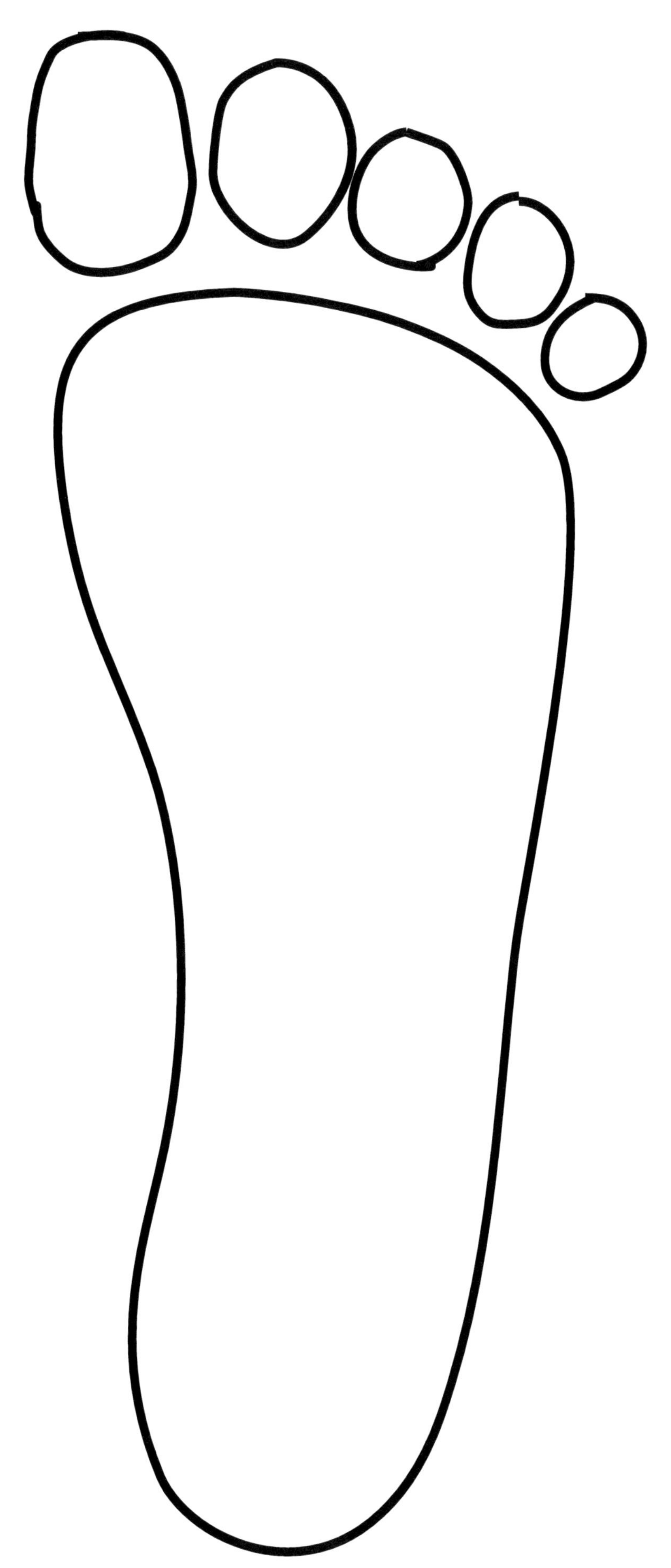

3rd Sunday in Ordinary Time

The 3rd Sunday of Epiphany

1. Introduction to the theme of the day

Aim: To explore the diversity of the "fish" in the fisherman's net.

Leader's Reflection: This week, we have a second encounter between Jesus, Andrew and Peter, but this time it is much more decisive. John the Baptist has been arrested and the mission of proclaiming the kingdom now passes into new hands.

Jesus knows that the mission is now his, but that it is not one he can do alone. It is likely that he knew Andrew, Peter, James and John beforehand as they had been disciples of John the Baptist. However, under Jesus' leadership, the group finds a new mission and level of commitment. Where John seemed content that they continue with their daily work, Jesus brings a new sense of urgency. The kingdom is close at hand. He needs them to follow him at once.

Our calling does not usually require us to leave everything – but a sense of urgency remains. The world is as much in need of Good News as it was two thousand years ago. One of our roles is to fire up those around us so that they encounter the risen Lord in his word and grow in love and commitment to him. How each will receive the Word will be different, and part of our work is to create a variety of activities, situations and settings in which others can most readily open themselves to the love of God.

2. We arrive

We sit in a circle ready to listen to the Gospel.

Has anyone anything they would like to tell us about last week's Family Sheet?

Focus

Green cloth. Candle.

Bible or Lectionary open at the Gospel reading.

Gospel: Mark 1:14-20

Read from the Lectionary or Children's Lectionary.

3. We respond

What is the Gospel asking of us?

This week there is one story for all, but work in age groups, if appropriate, for the activities.

Young ones and Juniors

We think of fishermen catching fish mainly for food. But some people catch or breed fish for others to keep in an aquarium. Does anyone have fish at home? Where do they keep them? Are they all the same? Some fish, like goldfish, are fairly easy to look after, but some are more complicated... like the ones Uncle William keeps...

Story

Duncan's Uncle William kept fish. They were not ordinary goldfish like Duncan's, but tropical fish. He had lots of different tanks because, as Uncle William said, different fish needed different conditions.

Some of the fish were in cool water and some were in warm water, heated with a special heater that kept the water at just the right temperature. Some had gravel and some had pretend coral.

Duncan's favourite was the marine tank. This had salt water in it and the coral made hiding places for the fish. Uncle William had prawns in it and anemones and the fish in there were the most beautiful – their colours sparkled in the water. He even had sea horses!

Uncle William had invited Duncan to go to his house this weekend to show him how to look after the fish. It was more complicated than looking after Duncan's goldfish. Uncle William had a special testing kit. They had to test the water to make sure it was just salty enough. "If it is too salty," said Uncle William, "we will have to take some water out and add some cooled boiled water. If it isn't salty enough, we will have to add some more salt."

They had to check the temperature too. "I have to do this every day," said Uncle William, "to make sure that they don't catch cold – or get cooked!"

"What if the power goes off?" asked Duncan.

"Well, I have to wrap the tank in sleeping bags and blankets and, if the fish get cool, I have to warm them up very slowly so that the shock does not kill them."

Duncan thought it would be fun to see the tanks wrapped up in cosy blankets but he knew that it would not be very nice for the fish.

"If the power goes off, we could have problems with the light too," continued Uncle William. "The fish like twelve hours of light every day."

"Fussy fish!" thought Duncan.

"You'll like this bit," said Uncle William.

He gave Duncan a pot of fish food. "Just a pinch now – otherwise it makes the water go stale." Duncan gave the fish a pinch of food but was amazed when Uncle William said that he would have to put his hand in the water to feed some of the creatures in the tank.

"The fish eat most of the food, so we have to feed the anemones and sea horses by hand, otherwise they won't get their fair share."

"Will they bite me?" asked Duncan.

"No," said Uncle William, "they're not interested in humans, they just want their food."

Duncan loved feeding the sea anemones and sea horses by hand.

"I think I'll have a marine tank when I grow up," said Duncan.

"Great," said Uncle William. "But remember that you'll have to work hard to care for your fish every day – but they're well worth the effort."

Duncan agreed. "Can I come back next week, to get some practice?"

"You surely can," said Uncle William. "Most people think I'm mad spending so much time with the fish, it will be nice to have somebody on my side for a change!"

Invite the children to respond to the story. Explore the ideas brought up in the story: fish needing to be cared for; their different needs; some needing individual attention and so on. Ask them to think about how this is like people in the Church: people need to be cared for – who does it? What are the different needs/ settings in which people need to be looked after? Talk about the specific vocations of priests and religious who dedicate their lives to caring for others.

Alternatively, read *The Rainbow Fish* by Marcus Pfister, a beautiful storybook which younger – and older – children will enjoy.

4. Activity

Young ones

Cut the fish out of card using the template provided. Provide shiny paper and sequins that the children can use to decorate their fish. Attach a paper-clip to the fish ready for the closing prayer session.

Juniors

As with the younger children, decorate the fish using shiny paper and sequins but allow the children to decide on the shape of fish they would like to create.

Tips for learning difficulties

Have the fish and shiny scales ready cut out and help the children use the resources to decorate their fish.

5. We come together

Parents can be invited to join in at this stage.

Focus

Use the focus from the beginning of this session. Light the candle. Have a net resembling a sea-fisherman's net ready. Invite those gathered to become still.

Gospel

Jesus calls Andrew, Simon, James and John to follow him. They are to move away from their work as fishermen and become "fishers of men", gathering people into the kingdom of God.

They could not have imagined just how far the new spiritual nets that Jesus was giving them would spread... even as far as *N*... (name of the place where you are meeting).

Prayer

Jesus, you ask us to be your friends and to follow you. Help us to be true disciples and help others to come to know you through the things we say and do.

Amen.

Share

Talk about what happened in the session – what the children have learnt. Talk about the fact that we are gathered because the apostles did as Jesus asked; we are the fish that Jesus said that they would catch. Explain that the net represents Peter's net and invite the children to come and clip their fish onto it.

Sing

"Follow me, follow me"

"I want to build my life"

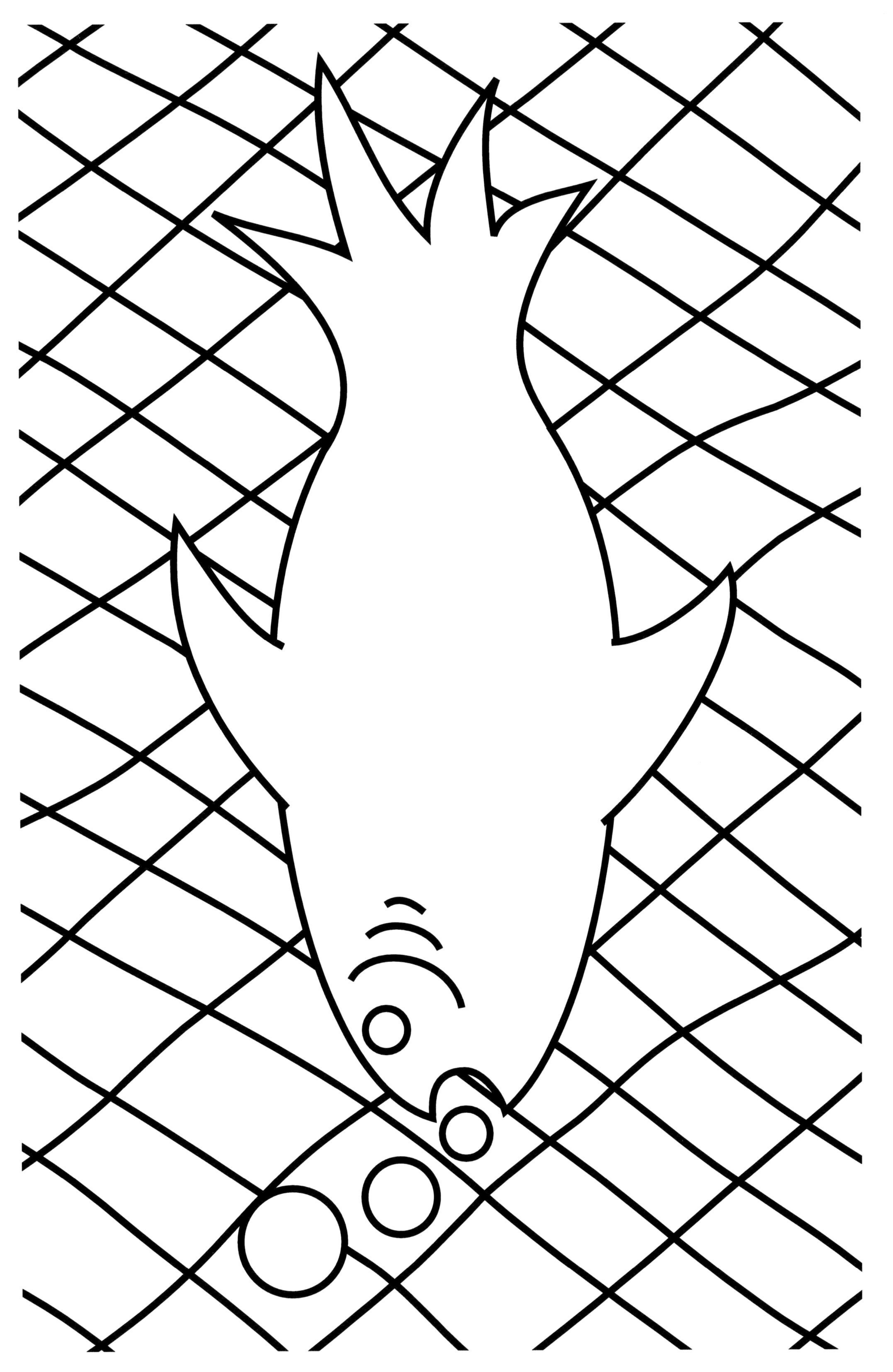

4th Sunday in Ordinary Time

The 4th Sunday of Epiphany

1. Introduction to the theme of the day

Aim: To help the children understand that Jesus speaks with the power of God. It is imperative that we listen to him.

Leader's Reflection: The things that Jesus said were important, but most of them were not new. The people who heard him listened because of the authority with which he spoke. Those who believed him did so because of the person he was, the power evident in him. Getting that authority across to our children, that we must listen and act, is a difficult aim to achieve.

2. We arrive

Invite the children to gather around today's focus to listen to the Gospel.
Has anyone anything they would like to tell us about last week's Family Sheet?

Focus

The open book of the Gospels on a green background.

Gospel: Mark 1:21-28

Read from the Lectionary or Children's Lectionary.

3. We respond

What is the Gospel asking of us?

Work in age groups if appropriate, but join together at the end of the session as one community.

Young ones

Story

Grace's mum had come home from work with a surprise. She had a big cardboard box in her arms when she got out of the car. She carried it very carefully into the house.

"Whatever have you got in the box?" shouted Grace.

"Hold on, Grace," said her Auntie Jo. "Give your mum a chance to get in."

Mum managed to put the box down.

"Go on, open it," she said to Grace.

Grace lifted the lid and inside the box, but only for a moment, was a small, black puppy. He jumped out very quickly, and in a second had rolled over at Grace's feet.

"I promised you that we'd have a dog, when we had settled into our new house. Now, what do you think we should call him?"

Grace was very excited, she thought of lots of names while the puppy rolled about, then sniffed about and finally made a big wet patch on the carpet.

"Blackie, Darkness, Beauty, Bill, Bob, Sam, Jack..."

"It's important to choose a name quickly, so he can get used to it."

"I think he should be called Drippy, after that," said Auntie Jo, pointing at the wet patch that she had been mopping up.

"No," said Grace, "you don't call friends names like that."

"I know," said mum. "What's the word for friend in French?" (Grace was learning French at school.)

"Ami," said Grace.

"Well, he belongs to you so how about mon ami: my friend. Make it all one word: 'Monami'."

So that was how the puppy got his name.

"Now, we can start to train him. He has to know his name, come when we call him, learn to go outside when he needs to ... he has to know who's in charge. If he doesn't believe you mean the things you tell him to do, and he doesn't listen when you call he'll be a nuisance and a danger to himself and other people."

"You mean things like running across roads and jumping up and knocking people over?"

"Yes," said Auntie Jo. "Everyone has to learn who's in charge and it's very important for dogs... look, get him into the garden quickly, he'd better start learning straight away who's boss, before the next accident!"

How do you get a puppy to learn to behave properly?

How do you learn what are good things to do?

Jesus showed everyone that he was in charge when he healed the man in the synagogue. He taught everyone in a way they never forgot. He spoke with power and authority.

Juniors

Story

Lead a discussion around the Gospel: make sure all the children can join in and that they listen to each other. There are no right and wrong answers.

See if the children can suggest all the people they know who have power, "authority" over other people.

Parents, police officers, judges, teachers, nurses and doctors, firefighters, soldiers, older siblings, bullies, priests, sports coaches...

Why do we do what these people say? Why do we listen to them?

Can they suggest where the "authority/power" comes from?

Now look at today's Gospel. Why did the people listen to Jesus and why did what he say make such an impression on them?

Why do the people believe Jesus speaks with authority?

Where does his authority come from?

What has Jesus said that made an impression on you? Be honest. Why are you a follower of Jesus?

Remember Jesus is in control, in power.

4. Activity

Young ones and Juniors

Make an "authority triangle" using the template provided.
In the bottom centre box ask the children to draw a picture of themselves.
In the boxes on the second line ask the children to draw and name all the people who have real authority over them (people they really listen to).
Now can they draw in the next line some of those people who have authority over the second line people.
Now colour in the border words: "All authority and power comes from our God who holds all things safe in his hands".

Tips for learning difficulties

Concentrate on the first two lines of drawing, the child and his/her carers only.

5. We come together

Parents can be invited to join in at this stage.

Focus

Gospels open on green background.
Gather the children around the focus and add to it the authority triangles.

Gospel

Ask one of the children to read out this summary:

"Jesus went into the synagogue. His teaching was not like the scribes because he taught with authority."

Prayer

Father God, you are in charge. Thank you for creating our world and for keeping all things safe in your hands. Help us to listen to you.
"For the kingdom, the power and the glory are yours, now and for ever."
Amen.

Share

Some of the work on the authority triangles.

Sing

"He's got the whole world in his hands"
"How great is our God"
"Be still and know that I am God"

ALL AUTHORITY AND POWER
COMES FROM OUR

GOD WHO HOLDS
ALL THINGS SAFE IN HIS HANDS

5th Sunday in Ordinary Time

Proper 1

1. Introduction to the theme of the day

"Jesus touched her and she served him"

Aim: God touches us and changes us for the better. Today, our hands and feet are his, and we are sent out to carry his love everywhere.

Leader's Reflection: Jesus touches Peter's mother-in-law: no fear of infection or of becoming ritually unclean. He wishes to avoid publicity but agrees to cure many people. He makes time to pray.
Peter's mother-in-law is one of those intriguing walk-on characters in the Gospel. Not just a passive recipient of grace, she gets up and serves Jesus as soon as she is cured. An example of doing everyday jobs well – all for the glory of God. We can be sure Jesus was ready for a meal after a busy morning at the synagogue.

2. We arrive

We sit in a circle. Look at each other. Is God's light shining in our hearts? Are we ready to listen to the Gospel?

Focus

Green cloth reminds us that we are growing in understanding of Jesus. A Red Cross or Maltese Cross (St John's) can remind us that healing is Jesus' work and our work today.

Gospel: Mark 1:29-39

Read from the Lectionary or the Children's Lectionary.

3. We respond

What is the Gospel asking of us?

If appropriate, work in age groups, but join together as one community at the end of the session.

Young ones

We receive God's healing power through each other – healing for our hearts as well as each other. We must be ready to give and to receive.

Story

Have you ever felt really sad? Mary did once. She went to feed her rabbits and found the hutch on its side, the door open, and blood and fur splashed around. The fox had been!

Mum and Dad had to go to work, and Mary had to go to school. She had no time to think about the disaster until everyone was working quietly.

Mary could not work. Her mind was full of the awful thing that had happened. Tears began to roll down her face, though she did not know she was crying.

"What's the matter?" said Zoe, as she put her arm round her.

Mary ran out, followed by Zoe. Mrs Davies found them on the cloakroom benches, and heard all about it. She helped Mary wipe her face. Zoe and Mrs Davies did not take the sadness away, but they helped Mary through the day.

At three o'clock Mum was waiting. They both needed a big hug, then went home holding hands. It was difficult to go out and tidy up, but they did it, and when Dad came home they had tea waiting for him.

Sometimes when our friends are ill or sad we can be like Zoe and Mrs Davies, ready to help, just by being friends.

Juniors

Jesus can touch us in many ways but, if we accept his help when we are feeling sad, we will feel better, and be prepared to help others when they feel sad.

Story

You never know what's going to happen when you go collecting sticks. This is what happened to Bernadette, the eldest child of a miller, when she was searching for firewood. She tells the story herself: "I had gone with the two girls to collect wood by the bank of the river Gave. I heard a sound. I turned toward the meadow and the trees were not moving at all. I looked up and saw a grotto. And there was a 'Lady' wearing a white dress with a blue sash. On each foot she had a yellow rose; her rosary was the same colour. When I saw her, I rubbed my eyes. I thought I must be mistaken..."

The beautiful "Lady" urged Bernadette to pray and do penance and to encourage others to do the same. Guided by the "Lady", Bernadette uncovered a small spring of fresh water from which to drink. At first the girl wasn't believed. The authorities were suspicious. For some years Bernadette suffered greatly from the disbelief of some and from the silly enthusiasm of others. However, she bore all this, along with much ill health, with impressive dignity and patience. Bernadette was canonised as a saint, not because of the visions she had, but because of the way she responded to them, in humility, prayer and penance.

Thus began the story of Lourdes: the shrine of Our Lady in the South of France that has become one of the greatest pilgrim shrines in the history of Christianity.

Thousands go to Lourdes every year in prayer and penance, and thousands find new strength, spiritual and physical, to do God's will and help build up the kingdom of God.

Bernadette was just doing an ordinary job, collecting firewood, when she had this extraordinary experience. God was able to communicate a message through her because she was willing to receive it. Who knows what God is asking of any of us, except to know his will and get on with it.

4. Activity

Young ones and Juniors

Act out a mime with the children.

Split the children into groups with a helper or parent on hand, but let the children lead. Give each group a scenario to enact, and delegate one person to explain the scene to everyone else. Ideas could include:

- A playground accident
- A new child in the class
- A very tired parent
- A pet has died
- Someone is told off unfairly

Tips for learning difficulties

Let each person join in as they are willing and able to. Children could colour in the hand from the template.

5. We come together

Refer to the mimes and talk about how the plays bring out our duty to heal each other. All the parents can be invited to join in at this stage.

Focus

The Red Cross or Maltese Cross reminds us that we are called to heal each other, as we did in the mimes. The green fabric reminds us that we are growing in God's love.

Gospel

Peter's mother-in-law was sick in bed.
Jesus touched her and her fever went away.
She got up and served them a meal.

Prayer

Let us pray that Jesus will live in us this week.

Ask the children to repeat each line after the leader:

God be in my head and in my understanding,
God be in my eyes and in my looking,
God be in my mouth and in my speaking,
God be in my heart and in all my doing,
God be at my end and at my departing. Amen.

Sing

"He's got the whole world in his hands" with appropriate verses:

"everybody here"
"all the sick people"
"doctors and nurses"
"We're all safe together in his hands"
"He loves and heals us with his hands"

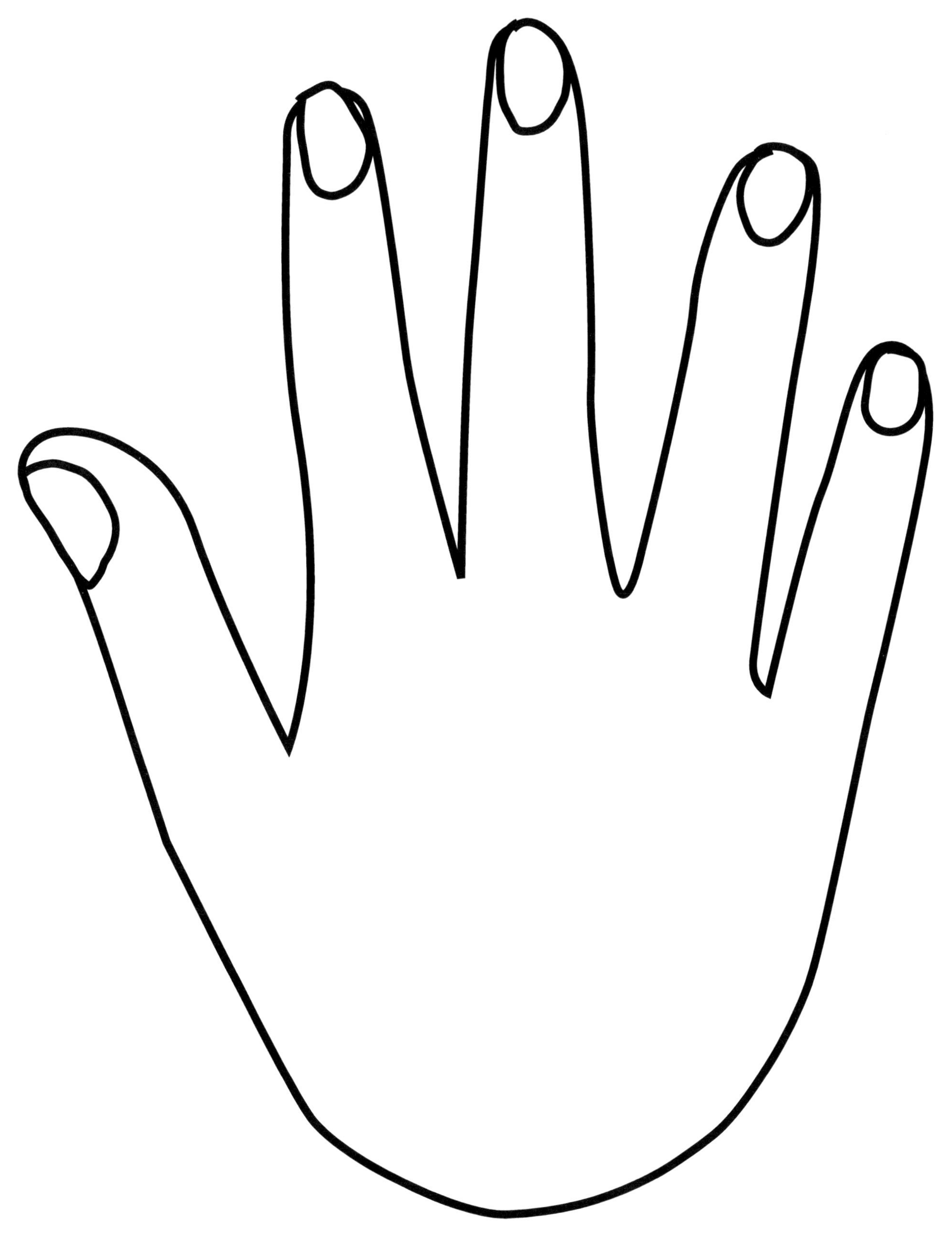

6th Sunday in Ordinary Time

Proper 2

1. Introduction to the theme of the day

"Jesus renews our hearts and our bodies"

Aim: Hope; Jesus has time for everyone; he wants everyone to belong to his family and is ready to heal each one of us.

Leader's Reflection: Leprosy was, until very recent times, a nasty physical and social affliction. The fear of contagion led to lepers being excluded from society. But Jesus had time for the members of this underclass. Not that he wanted them to stay that way, for he told the leper to do what was required for his cure to be accepted by the authorities and allow him to return to his family. But first the leper asked for help – and Jesus touched him. We ask for God's healing touch in our own lives, and we pray that our hands may be his, helping and healing others.

2. We arrive

We all sit in a circle, ready to listen to the Gospel. Does anyone have anything to say about last week's Family Sheet?

Focus

Green fabric for our time of growth in Jesus. Perhaps a picture of Fr Damien, the priest of the lepers of Molokai. Some early new leaves or evergreens.

Gospel: Mark 1:40-45

Read from the Lectionary or the Children's Lectionary.

3. We respond

What is the Gospel asking of us?

If appropriate, work in age groups, but bring everyone together as a community at the end of the session.

Young ones

Whatever mess we may be in, God loves us. He does not worry if it's our fault or not, he just loves us. That's why he sent Jesus to call us back to his family. Listen to this story about Horace the park-keeper. He taught people a lot about gardening, and about caring for people and animals too.

Story

There was a gang of dogs that hung around the park. Most of them would disappear home at tea-time or when Horace, the park-keeper, came to round them up. Horace wanted a clean, safe park.

There was one little dog that Horace could never catch. It was a Yorkshire terrier. Its long hair was matted and filthy. No one seemed to own it. It scurried away through the fence if Horace came in sight.

Yorkshire terriers are not made to be wild dogs. As his fur got heavier with caked mud, the little lost dog could no longer catch the rats and rabbits he was living on. Horace hated to see him like that.

One closing time Horace was checking the benches and gates with his spaniel, Suzie. He heard Suzie whining beside a holly bush, and pointing with her nose. Horace used his big stick to part the branches, and saw the little terrier caught by his fur. He must have been there for hours.

He lay quite still while they freed him. Back home, while Horace fed him a little bread and milk, he had a good look at his fur. Most of it had to be cut off, very gently, which left the little dog feeling strange. But that night he shared Suzie's basket, and he stayed with Suzie and Horace for the rest of his life.

Juniors

Leprosy is a nasty disease. For hundreds of years the law kept lepers away from healthy people. They often roamed the land, begging. The Gospel tells how Jesus changed one man's life, and this story is also about changing people's lives. Leprosy really caught hold in Hawaii, even the royal family was afflicted. One man's work there eventually led to the cure that is available today. Can you think of someone who needs the touch of Jesus?

Story

Jef was a farmer's boy in Belgium, but he knew God wanted him to become a priest. He took the name Damien, after a Roman doctor who became a saint.

He was sent to Hawaii, where he found in his parish a village of lepers called Molokai. They were sent there to stop other people from catching the disease.

The first time Damien visited to say Mass he was nearly sick, because of the smell of all the sick people. They had open sores with maggots in them. Damien stayed to work with these abandoned people. Although he knew the risk he was taking, he would clean their wounds and give them Holy Communion and eat with them.

He organised the lepers to care for themselves and each other. He persuaded the government to provide decent buildings and medical care. Although a cure had not yet been discovered, Damien found ways to make life easier for the people of Molokai. Clean homes and a modern hospital, good food and medicine for the sores all helped. Most important was Damien's love, which gave the lepers hope to live and care for each other. Damien caught the disease, and died aged forty-nine, among his lepers.

Because of his work, scientists and doctors understand leprosy better and have found a cure. Mother Teresa honoured him for taking fear away from those who care for lepers, and from lepers' own hearts, so that they can come forward and ask for help – and receive it.

4. Activity

Young ones and Juniors

Older children can help younger ones or those with learning difficulties.
Sing the following song, with gestures made up by yourself, or taken from Makaton or British Sign language.

(tune of "Twinkle, twinkle")
Listen to me when I say
Jesus touched my heart today.
I will share his love with you
Just as Jesus told me to.
He will help me every day
Love my friends at work and play.

Using the template of a large hand reaching out to a smaller hand, colour the picture and write a name on each hand.

5. We come together

Parents can be invited to join in at this stage.

Focus

All hold hands. We are growing, like the green leaves on the trees. And like leaves on the tree, we grow together, helping each other.

Gospel

A leper asked Jesus to cure him. He trusted him. Jesus touched the man, and he was cured. Jesus sent him to thank God and go back to his family.

Prayer

Lord, you broke the law to touch the leper and heal him.
Help us to trust you as he did.
Help us to love each other
and heal each other as you did. Amen.

Share

Talk about what the children have learned in the session.

Sing

Reprise the action song from the activities.
You could also sing:
"Jesus' hands are kind hands"

7th Sunday in Ordinary Time

Proper 3

1. Introduction to the theme of the day

"Friends can bring each other to God"

Aim: To remember that Jesus wants friends to bring each other to him. Together we can be forgiven and cured.

Leader's Reflection: Mark crams so much into one story! Let us set the friends centre-stage, rather than the Pharisees. Their faith has brought them to the house where Jesus is, and it is not confounded by the obstacle of the crowd. No, it leads them, and their charge, home: home to Jesus, in the first place, but then home to a fuller life in Capernaum, and in the comfort of being reconciled to God. Finally, we trust, their faith led them home to heaven.

2. We arrive

We sit in a circle, ready to listen to the Gospel. Does anyone want to share something from last week's Family Sheet?

Focus

Green cloth, flowers growing amid green leaves – crocus or other spring bulb, crucifix.

Gospel: Mark 2:1-12

Read from the Lectionary or the Children's Lectionary.

3. We respond

What is the Gospel asking of us?

Work in age groups if appropriate, but join together as one community at the end of the session.

Young ones

The man in the Gospel had good friends, didn't he? Do you think you could be helpful like that? Jesus is very happy to help us. He is especially happy when we take care of each other, like the good friends in the Gospel. We can trust him to take care of us and our friends and family.

Anthony was only three and a half, but very brave and very sensible. He had a mother who was diabetic. Most of the time if she ate certain foods and had special injections, she could live a normal life. But one day she sat down on the sofa, and seemed to go to sleep. Anthony thought she might like a cuddle with him, but her arms did not go round him.

Sensible Anthony knew what to do. Tiptoe to the telephone, and ring 999! He told the lady, "Mummy's gone to sleep and she won't wake up," and gave her his name and address.

The ambulance soon came, and the men knew just what to do. They gave the right injection and took Mummy to hospital for a check-up. Soon everything was all right. Thanks to brave, sensible Anthony!

Anthony knew the ambulance people could help his mother when he could not. What would you do if your friend hurt her knee in the playground? Or if you lost your dad in town? God gives us special helpers and everyday helpers, but our most special helper, Jesus, is with us every day, every moment. He promised: "I am with you always; yes, to the end of time."

Juniors

Jesus wants to heal us: body, mind and soul. This happens through ordinary people like us, even when we do not realise it. Did you know that the polio vaccination you received also helps keep a child in Ghana free from the disease? If the germ cannot live here, no one can take it to Ghana. In a similar way, forgiveness repairs friendships and lets happiness grow in all directions.

Bill and Mike became friends in hospital. Mike was suffering from polio. One of his legs was paralysed, like the man in the Gospel.

Their mums became friends too, as they travelled to the hospital to visit the boys. They chatted together on the train. Bill's mum was putting her worries in the care of God and praying for a good recovery. Mike's mum was in despair, thinking Mike would die. She felt there was no God.

Very gradually, as the two mums chatted over their worries day by day, Mike's illness became a chance for his family to know God, just as illness led the man in the Gospel to Jesus.

Mike, his mum and their family became Christians. Mike got better, though he always walked with a limp. When they were baptised the priest told them, "Your sins are forgiven."

This promise is made to us, too. God has given us many clever doctors and nurses who can help cure our bodies, but he wants to cure our hearts as well, to forgive our sins. We only have to ask.

Thank God that a modern miracle – men and women working together, all over the world – has nearly wiped out polio. The germ has gradually been killed off. You helped too. The special polio medicine you were given stopped you getting the disease and also passing it on to other people.

4. Activity

Young ones

Act out today's Gospel story. You won't need a stretcher: the patient can be supported with arms around the shoulders of two others. A space between two chairs can serve as a hole in the roof, if it is directly next to "Jesus". All other access to be taken up by listeners. Talk about it afterwards; how did different people in the story feel?

Alternatively, the children could colour in the flowers on the template page.

Juniors

Talk about prayer. Who do we bring to Jesus in prayer? Ourselves and ... ?

Give each child an envelope and a sheet of paper. Invite them to write a letter beginning "Dear Jesus, I bring to you ..." Ask the children to add an intention such as "...my brother because he is worried about his exams."

Envelopes can be addressed to Jesus and decorated. Intentions can be shared or not, as the children wish; the sealed envelopes to be put in a basket.

Tips for learning difficulties

Some children may prefer to be with a friend on the edge of the crowd, others may be the most enthusiastic participants. Allow the children to participate as far as they are willing and able to do so.

5. We come together

Parents can be invited to join in at this stage.

Focus

Basket of envelope intentions. Green cloth, flowers. Notice how the leaves raise the crocus flower up to God.

Gospel

Some friends brought a paralysed man to Jesus.

Jesus said, "Your sins are forgiven."

Then he told the man to pick up his bed and walk home.

The man did. He was cured.

Prayer

Dear Jesus,

we bring before you all the people who need your help. We ask you to bless and care for the people we wrote about in our letters to Jesus. We trust that you are always here to help us. Thank you, dear Jesus, for your love. Amen.

Share

Share the drama and talk about the letters to Jesus.

"Trust is in the eyes of a tiny babe"

"Trust and obey"

8th Sunday in Ordinary Time

1. Introduction to the theme of the day

"New wine, fresh skins!"

Aim: Jesus comes to tell us that there is a new way to God; not by our own efforts, but through his saving help – if we will listen to him.

Leader's Reflection: The story of the Jewish people in the Old Testament is one of increasing complexity. From the initial encounters of Genesis, and the deliverance of Exodus, and despite the warnings and encouragement of the prophets, the people evolve ever more complex ways of approaching God, through adherence to the law, the sacrificial liturgy and demonstrations of penance. Not surprisingly they are easily discouraged.
Today's readings remind us that God takes the first step and every step in our relationship with him. The way to God is not through esoteric practice, but through listening to his Word and allowing it to ferment gently in our daily living.

2. We arrive

We sit in a circle ready to listen to the Gospel.
Does anyone want to share how they brought God's love to someone last week?

Focus

A lighted candle, green fabric for ordinary time.
A picture of Jesus' face (an icon, work of art, or a picture from a children's book would all be suitable).

Gospel: Mark 2:18-22

Read from the Lectionary or Children's Lectionary.

3. We respond

What is the Gospel asking of us?

Work in age groups if appropriate, then come together as a community to end the session.

Young ones

We can tell by the way somebody is behaving, how they are thinking or feeling. Jesus cares about the way we feel as well as the way we behave. You can illustrate the story by acting out happy, sad, bad-tempered etc. The children could join in.

Story

Camilla the cow had found a bright red ball in the field. She was kicking it around and having a great time.

Then, plop! The ball had landed in the river. The water was too deep for Camilla, and she stood on the bank looking at the ball. How could she ever get it back?

Just then along came Daphne the duck with her family of ducklings. Daphne was feeling grumpy. She had overslept that morning, and her ducklings had been fighting and quarrelling ever since she had got them up. Now they were all very late and there would be no food for supper.

"Good morning," mooed Camilla. She had an idea. "I wonder if you can help me?"

"Morning," muttered Daphne. She did not feel like being helpful.

"My ball has landed in the river," mooed Camilla, "could you fetch it for me?"

"Oh, for goodness' sake," exploded Daphne, "I am late enough already without having to go chasing after balls for silly cows. This will make me even later. Where is it anyway?"

Camilla looked very hurt. "I'm sorry," she whispered. "It doesn't really matter, it was just that I was having such a good time, and I can't swim to fetch it, and you can. But I don't want to make you cross, so it doesn't matter at all."

Daphne saw she had upset Camilla and was very sorry. Being bad-tempered was not helping anybody. The food could easily wait five minutes. "I'm sorry, Camilla," she quacked gently. "It is me that is being silly. Of course I can fetch your ball," and off she swam.

When she got back, Camilla was entertaining the ducklings showing them grass-eating tricks. Everybody was much calmer. "Why don't I look after them whilst you fetch the food?" Camilla suggested. What a good idea! Daphne felt much happier already.

Juniors

Sometimes we think that we have to behave in very special ways if we want to get to know God. Jesus tells us that it is the way we do ordinary things that is most important.

In the early days of Christianity, holy men sometimes went off to live in the desert. They spent hours in prayer, and made life difficult for themselves by wearing hair shirts and fasting for days on end. This is one of the stories told about them.

Story

A monk was in his cell busily at work. The monk was wearing a hair shirt that was very itchy. When the abbot saw the hair shirt he said, "Why are you wearing that? Take it off; it won't do you a bit of good."

The monk said, "I am wearing it because I am worried about three things. The shirt is so itchy that I spend all my time scratching and so I don't have time to think about my worries." So the abbot asked him what was worrying him.

The monk answered, "I want to please God, and I dreamt that I have to do three things to please him, but I don't want to do any of them. The first is to go into the wilderness where the wild beasts might attack me and I might die of thirst. The second is to go to a foreign land where no one knows me and no one will talk to me. The third is to shut myself in my cell and eat only one meal every other day."

The abbot said to him, "God does not want you to do any of these things. Instead you should just carry on working and eating and sleeping as normal. Think kind thoughts about your brothers and listen to the words of Jesus in the Gospel. In this way you will please God most."

Encourage comments relating the story to the Gospel.

4. Activity

Young ones

On a large sheet of paper, draw the outline of a happy face. Ask the children how the person is feeling. Do the same with a cross face. Ask for more suggestions of feelings, and draw each on a separate piece of paper. Label each one. The children can each choose one face, add hair, eye colour, lip colour etc.

Juniors

Work in pairs. In one of the heads you are given, draw or write as many different helpful attitudes (an attitude is a way of thinking). Fill the circles round the edge with the sort of things somebody with these attitudes is likely to do. In the other head, do the same, but think about unhelpful attitudes.

Think of one helpful attitude which you have yourself and write a short prayer thanking Jesus for giving it to you.

Tips for learning difficulties

Enlarge two heads using the template. Have ready a selection of photographs which show people with different facial expressions. The child can sort them into helpful or unhelpful attitudes and stick them onto the heads.

5. We come together

Parents can be invited to join in at this stage.

Focus

Gather around the face of Jesus. Light the candle.

Gospel

John the Baptist taught the people he baptised that fasting (that is, not eating for a long time) was one way of showing they were sorry for their sins. The Pharisees noticed that Jesus' disciples did not fast. So they asked him, "Why don't your disciples fast?" Jesus answered, "Nobody puts new wine into old wine skins. If he did the wine skins would burst." He was telling them that he had come to show them a new way of knowing God. It was more important that the people listened to what he had to say, than that they went about fasting all the time.

Prayer

Jesus, I want to be like you, and do things in the way that you would do them. But that is difficult until I learn to think like you. Help me to think in your way, and to want the same things that you want. Thank you for helping me. Amen.

Share

Children can read out the prayers thanking God for their helpful attitudes, and show their "feeling faces".

Sing

"Give me joy in my heart"

9th Sunday in Ordinary Time

Proper 4

1. Introduction to the theme of the day

"Jesus is Lord ... every day"

Aim: To encourage the children to see Sunday (our Sabbath) as a special day, but to recognise Jesus' Lordship over not only Sunday but all days.

Leader's Reflection: For us Sunday is the day we remember God formally. We come to church, celebrate the Eucharist and pray together. Jesus, as a Jew, kept Saturday as the Sabbath. Like us, it was his custom to read scripture and pray with his friends formally, in the synagogue. But Jesus is Lord: the laws relating to Sabbath observance do not bind him or prevent his doing good on that day, just as he does on the other weekdays. For us, worship needs to spread out beyond the "special" day to the "ordinary" days of our lives.

2. We arrive

We sit in a circle ready to listen to the Gospel.
Welcome the children and their parents by name.
Has anyone anything they would like to tell us about last week's Family Sheet?

Focus

Open book of the Gospels on a green background.

Gospel: Mark 2:23 – 3:6

Read from the Lectionary or Children's Lectionary.

3. We respond

What is the Gospel asking of us?

This week, there is one story for all the children – it can be used as a common experience, but how you make use of it will differ according to the age of the children.

Story

It was the start of the new school year. For Year 2 this was their first day in their new class. They had come back from assembly, ready for work, and now they were all sitting together on the carpet in the quiet area of the classroom. Mr Gavin waited until everyone was still.

"Now," he said, "the first piece of work is for us to agree the rules for the classroom for this year. I don't make the rules, you do, and you all have a chance to say what you think today. Once we have agreed the rules everyone must keep them."

"Why do we have to think them up?" asked Jack.

"Well... why do you think?" said Mr Gavin.

"I think it's because that way we can't argue that it isn't fair," answered Bet.

"People always do better with rules they can see some sense to, ones that they have suggested," Mr Gavin said, "so let's make a start."

Everyone joined in the discussion and eventually a long list of rules emerged. They were things like:

Don't borrow someone else's things without asking.
Don't hurt anyone.
Don't fight.
Tidy things away carefully.
Listen to what the teacher says and listen to what other children say in a discussion.
Work hard.
Don't say rude things about someone else.

The list went on and on.

"There are an awful lot of rules here," said Mr Gavin. "They are all very sensible, but there is such a lot to remember. Can you think of a way we could make things simpler?"

Everyone thought long and hard, then Siobhan put up her hand ... (because that was one of the suggested rules).

"At my special class at church our teacher said every religion has a golden rule. It's usually something like this:

"Treat other people the way you would like them to treat you."

"That's clever," Salvatore said, forgetting about putting his hand up. "That covers all the things we thought of. Everyone wants to find things in the right place, no one wants people fighting them or being rude about them or not listening to them."

"Yes," Mr Gavin agreed, "and no teacher likes working in a noisy, untidy room with children who don't work hard, and teachers are people too."

Everyone laughed, but everyone understood.

"Shall we make that our rule, to cover all rules then?" asked Mr Gavin. "When we think someone has broken our class rule, we'll talk it over and see if we can see where the problem is."

Young ones

Do you have rules in your school? What are they like? Who makes you keep them?

Jesus and his friends had rules they kept. Today's Gospel is about one of these.

The rule was that no one should do any work on the Sabbath day – it was a special day. The trouble was that there were arguments about the rule: what was work?

What could you do on this special day?

Over the years the Jews discussed the rule and added little ones to it: you couldn't cut corn if you were a farmer; that was work. But even boys and girls like you couldn't pick a few ears of corn because that was doing the same job as a farmer.

When Jesus cured the man in the synagogue, he was doing the work of a doctor, so they said he was breaking the rule.

How did Jesus explain in today's Gospel that it was more important to break the rules on that Sabbath day?

Do we have rules about a special day? Which day is it? What are the rules?

Juniors

Recap the Gospel story – explain anything the children don't understand – take the story further...

Jesus gave a golden rule to his friends. Do you know what it was?

It has the word "love" in it.

"You shall love God with all your heart, your soul, your strength and your mind and your neighbour as yourself."

Jesus wants us to put some effort into treating other people as well as we do ourselves and he wants us to put effort into loving God.

That might mean that we have to put effort into what we do on Sunday, our special day. What could that mean we have to do?

Does having a "special" day mean we don't have to put effort into loving God on other days?

What about the people we meet, our friends and family... what does Jesus want us to do to them to keep his golden rule?

4. Activity

Colour the pictures from the template page and add words on the lines to say why Sunday is special.
In the bottom space draw a picture yourself of something which makes another day important and say why.

Tips for learning difficulties

Talk about the differences between Sunday and other days. Help the child to record (in words or pictures) one thing that makes Sunday special.

5. We come together

Parents can be invited to join in at this stage.

Focus

The open book of Gospels and samples of the children's work on a green background.

Gospel

Jesus said,
"I am the master, even of the Sabbath day.
It is important to do good things on the Sabbath,
just as it is on other days."

Prayer

Be still for a while and remember how much God loves you.
Help us to share your love with everyone around us. Amen.

Share

Some of the work from the activity sheets.

Sing

"His banner over me is love"
"The love of God is truly wonderful"
"Love is his word, love is his way"

Sunday is special because

But all the other days are important too

10th Sunday in Ordinary Time

Proper 5

1. Introduction to the theme of the day

> "Anyone who does the will of God is my brother and sister and mother"

Aim: To concentrate the children's minds on the verb "to do" in the context of being a Christian.

Leader's Reflection: Those of us caught up in the work of encouraging children in the faith must ask ourselves if we "do" what we encourage the children to do. It isn't through thinking about the faith, talking about it or teaching it (though these are very important), but in "doing" God's will that we become part of his family.

2. We arrive

Greet the children and their parents by name. Has anyone anything they would like to share from last week's Family Sheet? Sit in a circle ready to listen to the Gospel.

Focus

A lighted candle on a green background.

Gospel: Mark 3:20-35

Read from the Lectionary or the Children's Lectionary.

3. We respond

What is the Gospel asking of us?

Work in age groups if appropriate.

Young ones

Story

Sean had listened to the Gospel, and this time he had heard something really interesting. It was to do with family.

When Sean thought about his family he struggled to remember all the people who were part of it. In his house were his mum and his sisters Kate and Alice. His dad lived in a flat not far away and Sean always went to see him on Saturdays. His gran and granddad lived just along the street but mum said he had another granny and granddad who lived in Ireland. He couldn't work out how many uncles and aunts he had, but he liked playing with Tom, who was Uncle Nick's son and went to Sean's school.

Sean's family were very important to him. Those in his house, and his dad, looked after him, loved him, nagged him and worried about him when he had a problem. It would be terrible to have no family, no one who thought you were really special.

"Mum," he said after they had been to church, "when Jesus said, 'Who are my mother and my brothers?' what did he mean? He knew Mary was his mother and she loved him and looked after him."

"Yes," said mum, "I'm sure he didn't mean that she wasn't important, his family must have been special to him."

"Well then..." said Sean.

"But Jesus has a huge family who are special; all of us who try to do what God wants. He's telling everyone that when we are doing the best we can then we are his relatives: he looks after us like we look after each other in our family. Anyway Jesus knew that Mary did what God wanted."

Who is in your family? They may live in your house or somewhere else. What makes these people "family", how are they different from your friends?

Are you a member of Jesus' family?

What do you do that shows you are in this special family?

Juniors

Story

We had had a busy day. Jesus had been teaching the crowds about God's kingdom. Then when he had finished many people with problems of their own wanted to speak to him. Some of them were sick. Jesus always took time to talk to people who were ill and often to heal them. It all took a great deal out of him – he was tired.

When nearly everyone had gone, Andrew turned to Jesus:

"Come home now, you need a rest, something to eat."

Jesus went with him. His other friends followed on behind talking about the events of the day in quiet voices.

Word went around quickly and soon a new crowd built up following Jesus.

"Tell them to go away," said James, "you need time for yourself."

"No," said Jesus. "Let them come, they need what I can give."

"You can't go on giving without a rest and a meal, everyone needs that."

It seemed that the crowds would never go away. Then members of Jesus' own family came, they were sure he could not be sane.

"He's not in his right mind, going about like this, the stress has got to him."

"You're right there," said one of the scribes who had come from Jerusalem. "In fact he's probably possessed by the devil."

Jesus was angry:

"You're not being sensible, the devil would not want good things to happen. Don't make the mistake of calling the good things, healing, learning, people turning to God, bad. My family are calling for me, but what I'm telling you is that my family are the people who do what God wants."

What sort of things does Jesus like us to do as members of his family?

What do we really do each day, or is it only on Sundays when we think about God? What could you find to do this week that is something God would really like?

It might be being grateful for the world we live in – caring for it. It might be doing what your parents tell you. It might be asking someone who often gets left out to join in your game...

4. Activity

Young ones and Juniors

Using the template, find the words that describe the sorts of things members of God's family should do, or be like. There are 20 to find – you could use different colours to make them show up.

When you have finished draw a picture inside the frame that illustrates the meaning of one of the words.

Tips for learning difficulties

Concentrate on the picture. Talk about what makes the child happy. Draw a picture of that and the joy shared by the family when the child is happy. How do you feel if you see them again? (Happy/sad)

5. We come together

Parents can be invited to join in at this stage.

Focus

A lighted candle on a green background. Display some of the children's work.

Gospel

Jesus said:
"Anyone who does what God wants is my brother, sister and mother. They are in my family."

Prayer

Start by keeping quiet and still for a moment, remembering that Jesus is always with us.

Dear Lord, help us to live in the way you expect from members of your family. Help us to be kind to the people we meet. Amen.

Share

Some of the work from the activity sheets.

"Let there be peace on earth"
"I belong to a family, the biggest on earth"

word search

w	x	c	p	r	a	i	s	e	l	r	d
o	t	m	o	s	s	e	n	d	n	i	k
r	r	u	n	d	e	r	s	t	a	n	d
k	o	h	g	o	o	d	h	j	k	k	u
n	p	s	o	w	p	e	a	c	e	j	e
a	p	m	o	p	c	a	r	e	u	o	h
h	u	i	p	m	e	g	e	v	o	l	t
t	s	l	q	r	n	c	v	i	r	y	i
k	e	e	a	z	a	a	u	g	d	h	a
h	s	e	n	j	o	y	p	p	a	h	f

work, kindness, understand, share, help, pray, smile, love, care, enjoy, thank, praise, give, support, hope, faith, peace, aid, happy, good.

11th Sunday in Ordinary Time

Proper 6

1. Introduction to the theme of the day

"The kingdom of God is like a mustard seed"

Aim: To think about what Jesus was trying to tell us about God's kingdom.

Leader's Reflection: The parables can become so familiar to us that we think we know immediately what they are trying to teach us. Today we spend some time looking more closely at the parable of the mustard seed, to see what we might have missed.

2. We arrive

We sit in a circle ready to listen to the Gospel.
Has anyone anything they would like to tell us about last week's Family Sheet?

Focus

A lighted candle, green fabric for ordinary time, mustard seeds, large shrub or branch held upright in a pot.

Gospel: Mark 4:26-34

Read from the Lectionary or Children's Lectionary.

3. We respond

What is the Gospel asking of us?

Jesus often spoke in parables; he used the things which were around him to try and explain what God was like. But Jesus lived in the first century, and we live in the twenty-first century, so sometimes we need to work a little bit harder to try and find out what he was really trying to say.

Work in age groups if appropriate, but join together as a community at the end of the session.

Young ones

Story

The mustard tree gave a great sigh. She was lonely. It hadn't been like this when she was little; then she had been surrounded by all the other plants her own size. They had a great time together, swaying in the wind, and splashing raindrops at each other. But now she had grown up ... and up ... and up. She was far taller than any of the other plants in the garden. She could hear them still chittering and chattering down in the shade below, but she was too high up now to join in.

It wasn't all bad. Now that she was tall and so very strong, the birds loved to come and sit in her branches and groom her leaves with their beaks. She couldn't understand what they were saying, but they tickled her and made her giggle. And she did get the views. She could see sights that the plants below her never even dreamed of. Even so, it wasn't much fun being on her own. She sighed.

Just then a man came over the hill with his friends: they were talking together.

"Tell us about the kingdom of God," one of them said. The mustard tree listened carefully – the kingdom of God – now she had heard of that, and often wondered about it. It was supposed to be a wonderful place, where everybody was kind and there was room for everybody, and nobody was ever lonely.

"Well," said the man, looking round him, "the kingdom of God is like ... is like ... a mustard tree!" The tree could hardly believe her ears. How could she be like the kingdom of God, stuck up here with no one to talk to?

"The kingdom of God is like a mustard tree," explained the man, waving in her direction, "because it grows so quickly that it is bigger and taller than all the other plants, and it can be seen from a long way off, and it gives shade to the plants that grow underneath, and there is room in it for all the birds to come and make their nests." And then the man and his friends moved on.

The mustard tree was stunned. The kingdom of God! She was like the kingdom of God! It was true all the things that the man had said. She did grow quickly, and she was the biggest and tallest, and she could see a long way, and the plants did grow in her shade, and the birds did nest in her branches. The kingdom of God! Fancy that! She rustled her leaves and stood up a little bit taller. The kingdom of God! Now that was really something.

Talk with the children about the meaning behind the imagery used in this story.

Juniors

Perhaps have some mustard seeds ready to show the children.

Some facts about the mustard seed:

The horticultural name is *sinapis* and they are part of the brassica family (the same as cabbages, sprouts and broccoli). In the Holy Land three different varieties of mustard are found – *sinapis arvensis* (field mustard), *sinapis alba* (white mustard) and *sinapis nigra* (cultivated mustard). The first two of these are very common weeds, and all three have very tiny seeds. Mustard plants are annuals – they need to be sown each year. Once sown, they grow very easily, even in the most inhospitable places, in nooks and crannies, and even on stony ground, wherever there is a bit of moisture and something for their roots to hold on to. They grow extraordinarily quickly. They soon outstrip all the other common herbs, and cultivated mustard can grow to be as tall as 3–4 metres, a tall shrub rather than a tree by British standards, but much taller than some Mediterranean trees. Their stalks ripen into "branches" which make great perches for the birds that are attracted by the mustard seeds. Once the tree has flowered, they are often covered by small flocks, pecking away at the pods.

Once they are harvested and dried, mustard seeds are full of flavour, and are used in lots of Middle Eastern recipes.

Allow the children to have a taste from a little pot of mustard.

4. Activity

Young ones

Draw a mustard tree on a large sheet of paper, or bring in a large shrub or branch held upright in a pot. Children can stick or hang photos or pictures of themselves in its branches. Talk to them about the significance of doing this.

Juniors

Have a look again at the Gospel story. Jesus says that the kingdom of God is like a mustard seed. Read the description of the mustard seed carefully. Try and work out in how many different ways it is like the kingdom of God (use the chart from the template page). Why did Jesus use the mustard seed for his parable?

Tips for learning difficulties

Use the tree made by the young ones. Label the ways in which it is like the kingdom of God.

5. We come together

Parents can be invited to join in at this stage.

Focus

Gather around the candle and the "mustard tree".

Gospel

Jesus said, "The kingdom of God is like a mustard seed. It is the smallest of all the seeds, but once it is sown, it grows into the biggest shrub of them all, and the birds come and rest in its branches."

Prayer

Jesus, you used the things around you to try and teach us about God. Thank you for making things easier to understand. When we look at the things around us, help us to see what they can tell us about God. Amen.

Share

The children can show the work they have been doing.

Sing

"He gave me eyes so I could see"
"All things bright and beautiful"

How is a mustard seed like the Kingdom of God?

MUSTARD SEED	KINGDOM OF GOD

12th Sunday in Ordinary Time

Proper 7

1. Introduction to the theme of the day

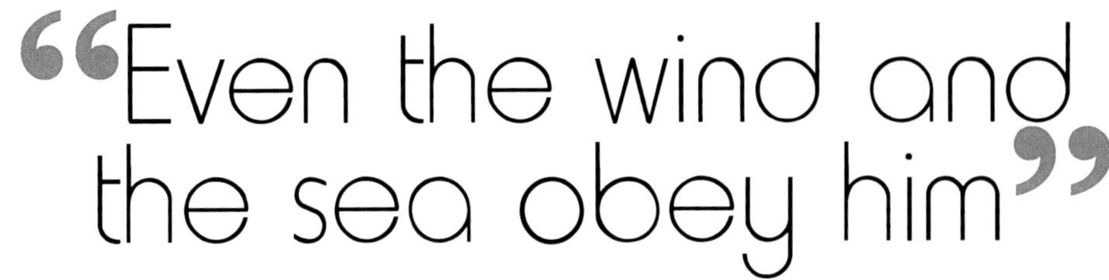

Aim: To think a little more of the historical Jesus, to locate him in a physical environment.

Leader's Reflection: There are very few references in the Bible to the weather, and when it is mentioned it is usually as a vehicle for some forthcoming event – "it was hot, and Jesus was thirsty" or as a manifestation of God's presence: the storm of Jonah, the quiet breeze of Elijah. If it were all located in the British Isles, it might be a very different story!

2. We arrive

We sit in a circle ready to listen to the Gospel.
Has anyone anything they would like to tell us about last week's Family Sheet?

Focus

A lighted candle, green fabric for ordinary time, protective weather gear: waterproofs, wellies, hat etc.

Gospel: Mark 4:35-41

Read from the Lectionary or Children's Lectionary.

3. We respond

What is the Gospel asking of us?

This is a version of the Gospel story set somewhere in the British Isles, for both young ones and juniors.
Work in age groups, if appropriate, for the activities but join together as a community at the end of the session.

Young ones and Juniors

Story

Peter stared gloomily out of the window of the fisherman's hut where they had all spent the night, cooped up in the muggy darkness. Raining again. None of them had slept very well in these cramped conditions, and now Jesus was insisting they get out the boats and cross to the other side of the lake. A storm was brewing, he could see that – he hadn't spent twenty years on the lake in all weathers without learning to recognise the signs – but the Master was the Master, seemed to think he knew what he was talking about.

The oilskins were hanging behind the door. Peter shivered, still damp from yesterday's excursion. Really, you had to hand it to the man, all those people standing on the hillside in the pouring rain just to hear what he had to say. Even under all his gear Peter had felt cold and miserable and he had been glad when Jesus had finally decided he had had enough. The whole village would be down with the flu at this rate!

He called to James and Andrew to give him a hand. They were feeling stiff and grumpy too, but barely raised an eyebrow when Peter explained what Jesus wanted. Reckoned they could handle themselves in any weather, that pair!

Oh well, best get on.

Two hours later Peter was feeling a bit more cheerful, the weak sunshine had warmed him up a bit, and it was always good to be out on the waters and moving. Jesus, bless him, after getting them all going, had promptly fallen asleep at the back of the boat. He was a useless sailor anyway, so he was probably best off out of the way back there; their very own holy mascot!

Oops, what was that? The waves were slapping a bit harder at the stern now. Peter grinned to himself: that might wake the man up! But no, Jesus slept right on – quite oblivious. Peter, on the other hand, was suddenly very alert. He had been right to rig the boat up ready for a gale and now it was going to need his full attention. He shouted orders to the others who were already busy trimming the sails and laying out the sea anchors. This looked like it could be a big one.

The storm, when it arrived, was like nothing they had experienced, and they were very experienced. At first they tried to make a bit of headway, but that quickly became dangerous; the wind screamed around them and threatened to rip the sails, so they yanked them down, threw over the anchors and tried to ride it out instead. The boat was tossed about by each wave smashing against them; water poured in, and they were blinded and deafened by the torrential rain. Soon each man was clinging to the boat for dear life, praying for the strength to hold on when the capsize, which seemed inevitable, finally happened. Only Peter, yelling out curses to the wind, the rain, and whoever else happened to be listening, tried to keep some sort of control. But in the end even he gave up. They were all going to drown.

"Jesus!" Peter suddenly remembered. He was probably already thrown overboard. Wind roaring in his ears, and rain scouring his face, Peter dragged himself hand over hand down to the back of the boat. "Jesus!" Thank God, he was still there. "Jesus!" Peter screamed into the wind. Nothing seemed to stir him. Groaning with the effort, Peter dragged himself that extra yard. He shook the man roughly. Jesus woke instantly. "What is it?"

"What is it?" Peter was beside himself with anger and worry. "What is it?" Couldn't he see what it was?

"Quiet now," Jesus said, "be calm."

Peter could never quite explain what happened next. By the time they reached the shore, the sun was shining again and everything was calm. James and Andrew were congratulating themselves on their ship-handling skills whilst Jesus was calmly talking about his plans to visit Nazareth next week. Only Peter sat in the stern of the boat, his mouth still dropped open with astonishment. It had happened. He looked at his little boat, battered and torn from the storm. It had happened. Even the wind and the sea had obeyed him.

4. Activity

Young ones

Re-enact the story. An upturned table makes a great boat, with a broom and curtain for a sail. Don't forget a cushion for Jesus to sleep on in the stern.

Juniors

You are going to present the weather forecast and news report for Lake Galilee on the day of the storm. You will need a large map of Lake Galilee copied from an atlas. The lake is roughly egg-shaped with the blunt end in the north. Capernaum is on the northern shore where it is likely that Jesus embarked. Nazareth is to the west of the lake, a bit further inland. Use the weather symbols on the template sheet to help your presentation. Refer to the story and report in your own words.

Tips for learning difficulties

One child could be assistant to the "weather presenter" and stick the symbols onto the chart. Colour code these with corresponding dots on the back and the place on the chart.

5. We come together

Parents can be invited to join in at this stage.

Focus

Gather around the candle, and protective clothing.

Gospel

Jesus was in a boat with his friends. He was very tired, and had just settled down for a nap at the back of the boat when a great storm blew up. Jesus' friends were very frightened and thought they were going to be shipwrecked, so they woke him up, but Jesus just looked at the wind and the sea. "Quieten down!" he said. And the wind settled and the sea became calm again.

Prayer

Jesus, we thank you for being our friend. You have done great things for us. Help us, Jesus, to recognise you in the world around us. Amen.

Share

Juniors can present their "broadcasts" to everybody.

Sing

"A word from Jesus calms the sea"

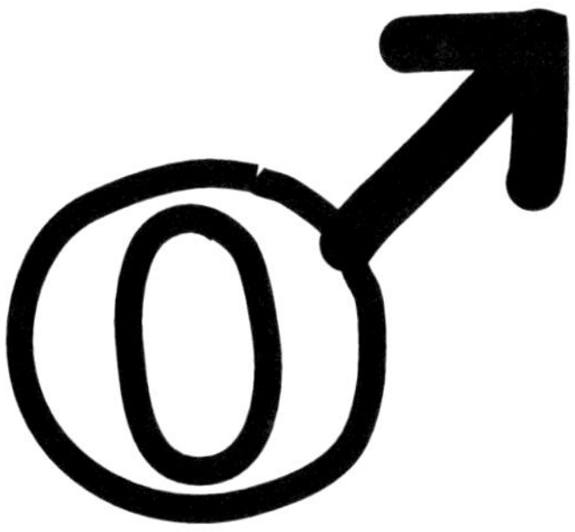

0 = calm (water like a mirror)

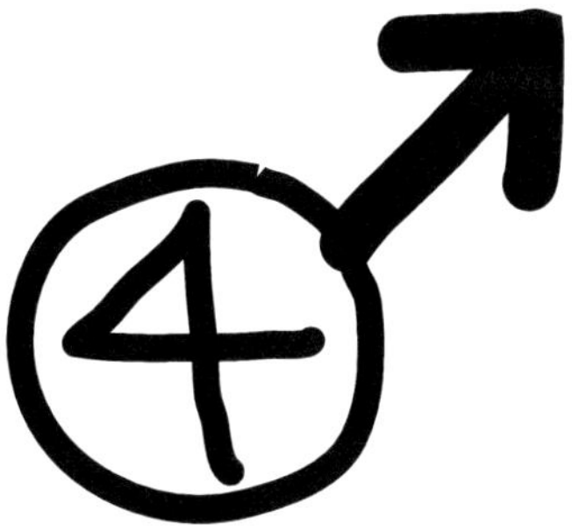

4 = breeze (small waves)

8 = gale (waves 2-3 metres)

11 = violent storm (waves 9-10 metres)

13th Sunday in Ordinary Time

Proper 8

1. Introduction to the theme of the day

"If I can only touch his cloak"

Aim: We recognise that when we really need something, nothing can come between us and God.

Leader's Reflection: In today's Gospel, two very different people overcome very different obstacles in order to approach Jesus. The first is a man of high standing; a synagogue official. He must give up his rank and self-importance in order to approach Jesus for help. The second is a woman suffering a shameful disease who must give up her secrecy in order to approach him. They are similar in that both must give up a mask of respectability and approach Jesus simply as a person in need.

2. We arrive

We sit in a circle ready to listen to the Gospel.
Has anyone anything they would like to tell us about last week's Family Sheet?

Focus

A lighted candle, green fabric for ordinary time, a cloak.

Gospel: Mark 5:21-43

Read from the Lectionary or Children's Lectionary.

3. We respond

What is the Gospel asking of us?

Jesus needs us to need him.
Today's story is for everyone. We think about the difficulties which can be overcome when we really want to speak to Jesus.

Young ones and Juniors

Story

Rose had woken up with a headache. It was worse than her usual headaches, because she was so anxious and nervous about today. Today Jesus was coming to town. Today she had to do something terrible. Today everyone would find out.

Jairus hadn't slept at all. His eyes were sore and red-rimmed. He had been pacing up and down in his little girl's room all night. He must make a decision. He was Jairus, the custodian of the synagogue, an important and respected man. Could he really stoop to begging a peasant carpenter for help. What would all the people think? He looked at his daughter on the bed – she was dying. There was no more time. He had to decide now.

Rose pulled on a long dark coat, and wrapped a scarf around her head so nobody could see her. Maybe if she could just get close to Jesus; maybe if she could brush against him in the crowd; maybe that was all it would take to cure her of this terrible disease. She thought of them all, of her neighbours, of Jairus and the men from the synagogue, and all his friends. How could she explain to Jesus in front of all of them? She shuddered with embarrassment. There had to be a way, without anyone knowing.

Jairus stared out of the window. Maybe he could invite Jesus for dinner, maybe that was the way; maybe he could talk to Jesus privately, explain that he didn't want any publicity, that he was a respectable man. Jesus would understand, surely. A great cheering suddenly arose in the street below: Jesus was on his way. One last look at his dying daughter, and Jairus left the room.

Down in the street it was bedlam. Jesus was fast approaching. Jairus saw immediately that there could be no whispering in Jesus' ear, no discreet invitations, even shouting wouldn't be enough. His daughter was dying and there was only one thing to do. He pushed his way through the crowd and hurled himself onto the ground in front of Jesus.

Jesus had stopped suddenly, almost stumbled over something it seemed. Rose wondered why, but was very relieved. She tried to catch her breath. It was a long time since she had been out in a crowd like this and she was terrified, she had never imagined so many people. Jesus had seemed to be getting further and further away – but now that he had stopped, she had to take her chance. She squeezed through the crowds, not wanting to push against people. If they knew ... she trembled at the thought. Then, there was Jesus, just inches away from her. She crouched down and reached forward – just his cloak, if she could just touch ...

Jesus looked up from the man on the ground in front of him. "Who touched me?"

Rose kept her eyes down, staring at the ground, maybe he wouldn't see her ... but she could feel him turning around, searching her out. Dear God, he wasn't going to let her escape. Then Rose slowly became aware of another face staring at her; the face of a man on the ground like she was, the face of a man called Jairus. It was Jairus, the man from the synagogue, the man who had sent her away in disgust because of her disease. Rose felt faint with fear of what was to come. Slowly she lifted her eyes to meet Jairus' gaze, to plead with him. It was only then that she saw he had been crying. Why on earth should a man like Jairus be crying out here in this public place? What was he doing on the floor anyway in front of Jesus? Rose was confused. What was even more confusing, Jesus seemed to be smiling at her, as if he understood, almost as if he admired her. He wanted her to say something. She looked up at Jesus. "It was me who touched your cloak," she said.

The worst of it was over then. Jesus didn't seem disgusted when she told him about her disease; she knew he had cured her; he didn't need to tell her. And all the time there was Jairus behind him, anxious about something, but patient, encouraging her with little smiles and nods. Even when the messenger arrived to tell him his daughter was dead, he still stood there, with tears rolling down his cheeks, supporting Rose, trying to be happy for her, even though it seemed as if Jesus had forgotten him.

When finally Jesus let her go and turned around to talk to him again, Jairus just shook his head sadly. It was too late. "Take me to her," said Jesus, and Jairus looked up at him, wondering, not quite daring to hope. Even now, even when the girl was dead, could he ...? Rose smiled. Maybe, maybe it could happen, maybe even that was possible for this man.

4. Activity

Young ones and Juniors

The children can act out the story, then they can try to imagine what happened next. How do Rose's neighbours react to her cure?

How does Jairus celebrate his daughter's recovery? Do they become friends?

The picture from the template page can be coloured at home or used as an alternative activity in the session.

Tips for learning difficulties

Everyone can be given a part within the drama, if necessary supported or prompted by another child.

5. We come together

Parents can be invited to join in at this stage.

Focus

Gather around the candle and the cloak.

Gospel

Rose was very poorly; Jairus' daughter was dying. Both of them wanted Jesus' help but they didn't know how to get it, and they didn't want other people to know. In the end they wanted his help so much that they asked him, and so he helped them.

Prayer

Jesus, sometimes we really need help, but we don't know how to get it, or we don't want other people to know, or maybe we just can't be bothered. Help us to remember to ask you for help, and help us not to be afraid to ask other people as well. Amen.

Share

The children can act out the second part of their play – what happened next.

Sing

"Reach out and touch the Lord"

"Oh my Lord"

Jairus jumping with joy
Jesus
Rose, thanking Jesus

14th Sunday in Ordinary Time

Proper 9

1. Introduction to the theme of the day

"Who'd be a prophet?"

Aim: To recognise that the role of prophet or person of faith is not always comfortable or welcome.

Leader's Reflection: Everyone likes to be popular – especially when, like Jesus, you are seeking to do the very best for people. His reputation in the surrounding countryside was already high and on the increase. It was natural for him to want to take his gifts of healing and preaching back to his home town – of all people surely they should be among the first to benefit.

The problem lies in the fact that the people knew him too well. They had grown up with him – how could he now be a preacher and healer? And even Jesus was unable to overcome their preconceptions.

People change, especially when their lives are touched by the power of the Good News. Perhaps you have undergone such a change, how did people around you react? Perhaps you have witnessed dramatic changes in others, how did you react? How can you help the children to be open to change and growth, remembering words of Cardinal Newman: "To live is to change – to change often is to become perfect"?

2. We arrive

We sit in a circle ready to listen to the Gospel.

Has anyone anything they would like to tell us about last week's Family Sheet? Did the children help anyone in need last week?

Focus

A green cloth, candle and open Bible.

Gospel: Mark 6:1-6

Read from the Lectionary or Children's Lectionary.

3. We respond

What is the Gospel asking of us?

Work in age groups if appropriate. Alternatively, choose the discussion ideas, story and activity most suitable for your group.

Young ones

A story to finish

Dominic had lots of friends. They played together at playtimes, went swimming together and had had a great time last weekend at Dom's (as his friends called him) when they had all watched (name of currently popular film).

The trouble was that there was now a big argument. Martin's older brother had told them that he had made a den in the woods and wanted to take them with him. He said he had matches and would cook something for a picnic.

Dom didn't like the sound of it. His mum had warned him not to go into the woods without an adult and though Martin's brother was twelve, Dom was sure that wasn't grown up enough. He also wasn't sure about lighting fires in the wood.

When he said this to his friends they said he was being a baby. He said he wasn't, and tried to explain why. They wouldn't listen – what Martin's brother said was much more exciting.

He knew they weren't going to listen when they started saying "Dominic is a softie," "Dominic's a scaredy cat," "Dominic's no fun."

Dom was upset – but even more worried for his friends when he saw them going to the woods.

What should he do? He didn't really want to tell tales – but what if something happened?

Invite the children to think about Dom's dilemma – what might happen in the woods? What should he do? What will they think if he tells his mum – and they arrive just in time to stop a nasty accident – or help someone who has been hurt? How would Dom feel if something awful happened and he hadn't said anything?

Have the children ever been in a similar situation? How did they deal with it?

Juniors

Story

It may be useful to have a photograph of Nelson Mandela available to show the children

Nelson Mandela was a prophet in his own country, South Africa, and like Jesus saw his message rejected.

For many years, South Africa had lived under an unfair system called apartheid. It kept black and white people apart, with almost all of the power in the hands of a few white people.

Nelson became a lawyer and saw so many cases of black people being treated unjustly that he decided he had to speak out against it. Although he tried to use non-violent means, others chose violence and he ended up being imprisoned on Robben Island. As he started a sentence that was to last nearly thirty years he said, "During my lifetime I have dedicated myself to the struggle of the African people. I have fought against white domination, and I have fought against black domination. I have cherished the ideal of a democratic and free society in which all persons live together in harmony and with equal opportunities. It is an ideal that I hope to live for and to achieve. But if needs be, it is an ideal for which I am prepared to die."

These words encouraged others and, though there was much bloodshed, eventually the Government of South Africa realised that they had to listen to the prophet they had imprisoned.

In 1990, Nelson Mandela took the last steps in what he called his "long walk to freedom". Later he was elected as the first black president of South Africa. He is recognised as a great person who dared to speak for the truth even at the risk of his own life.

Have the children heard of Nelson Mandela? You might like to talk a little more about the apartheid system – black people having to carry passes and only being able to live in certain areas. Were these laws fair? Why did the South African Government want to stop people like Nelson Mandela speaking out? Can the children identify similar situations in the world today?

4. Activity

Young ones

Complete the drawing of Dom and draw in two thought-bubbles. In one, the children can draw how Dom thinks his friends will react if he tells his mum. In the other, they can draw how his friends react when Dom and his mum come to the rescue.

Juniors

Invite the children to think about things they have heard on the news and to think of something that they think is wrong. What would they like to say to those with power to change things? The children can write this on a speech bubble in readiness for coming together.

Tips for learning difficulties

Use the story and picture of Dom. The children may be able to illustrate the story as for the younger children. Alternatively, they could draw Dom: happy because he has saved his friends in one bubble – and sad because he did not say anything and something happened.

5. We come together

Parents can be invited to join in at this stage.

Focus

Light the candle. Invite those gathered to become still, ready to listen to the Word of God.

Gospel

In the Gospel, we hear that Jesus went back to his home town to heal people there and to tell his family and friends about the Good News.

They refused to listen. They could not believe that someone they had grown up with could possibly be a great prophet and miracle-worker.

Jesus was very sad, amazed that they did not believe in him.

Prayer

Jesus, you ask us to be like you;
to stand up for what is right even when it makes us unpopular.
Help us to grow more like you on the inside,
so that we are strong and brave like you.
Amen.

Share

Talk about what happened in the session – what the children have learnt. Explain Dom's dilemma and share some of the thoughts the children had. Juniors might like to have a soapbox from which to read their declaration on how things should change (explain the hallowed tradition of the soapbox and its role in people telling their truth). Dom and the declarations could then be pinned to a display board headed "Speaking up for Truth".

Sing

Use the tune of "Give me joy in my heart" with the verses:

1. Give me truth in my heart, keep me speaking
2. Give me strength in my heart, keep me serving
3. Give me hope in my heart, keep me loving

15th Sunday in Ordinary Time

Proper 9

1. Introduction to the theme of the day

"On the road"

Aim: To explore the missionary dimension of the Church's life.

Leader's Reflection: Most of the work we do with children is done in familiar places – churches or parish rooms. For many Christians, it may be far less secure – and certainly throughout the course of history, many of those charged with the mission of spreading the Good News have fallen foul of governments, rulers or even simply local factions. However, had people not had the courage to take to the road and proclaim the Gospel we would not be here now. Though we are unlikely to be asked to be missionaries in the traditional sense of going abroad, we are still called to be missionary. People do not know the joy of the Gospel, or are confused by the message. We may find that some of the things we say are unwelcome in wider society, but we are called to take the risk so that a new generation of children come to know the call of Jesus for them to follow him.

2. We arrive

We sit in a circle ready to listen to the Gospel.
Has anyone anything they would like to tell us about last week's Family Sheet?

Focus

Green cloth, candle, open Bible, one or more handkerchiefs or checked tea towels, tied to a pole (as travellers' packs).

Gospel: Mark 6:7-13

Read from the Lectionary or Children's Lectionary.

3. We respond

What is the Gospel asking of us?

Work in age groups if appropriate. Alternatively, choose the discussion ideas, story and activity most suitable for your group.

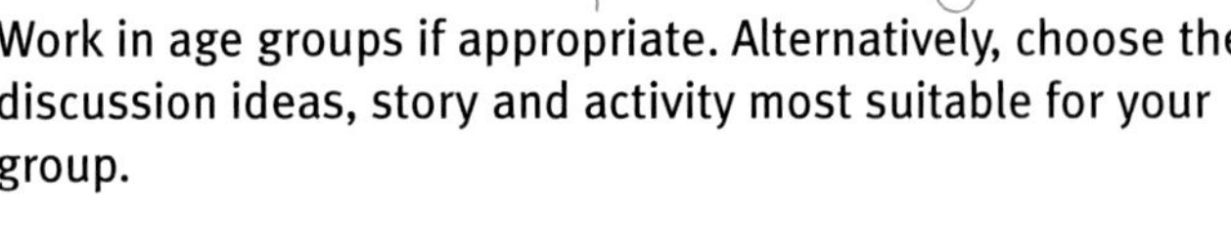

Young ones

Story (read with help from the children)

Jack and Jessica were going on holiday.

"We're going camping," said Dad. "We have to take the tent, camping stove and beds, so we are short of space. You can only take as many books and toys as you can fit in these bags."

The children were very excited and took the bags up to their rooms.

It wasn't as easy as they thought, though.

Jessica collected all her colouring pencils and drawing books, her Barbies, Barbie's caravan, her six favourite bedtime books, and ...

(invite the children to make suggestions as to what else she might have wanted to bring)

Jack got his books, his colouring pencils, his box of Lego, and ...

(again, invite the children to make other suggestions)

But there was a problem – what was the problem?

(Let the children tell you)

Jessica went into Jack's room.

"Can you fit everything in?" she asked.

"No," said Jack, looking at a pile of things he wanted to put in the already full-to-bursting bag. "I think we need to see if we can get more space."

Jack and Jessica went downstairs. Mum was packing four plastic plates in with four mugs and cereal bowls.

"Can we have another bag each, please?" they said.

Mum picked up the knives and forks.

"Well," she said, "only if you're happy for me to leave some of these behind."

Jack and Jessica decided that they did want to eat while they were away.

"Tell you what," said Jessica, "let's do it together. I'll help you to choose, and you help me."

"Yes," said Jack, "then we can bring things to share – no point taking two of everything!"

So they ran up the stairs, took everything out of the bags and started again.

What do you think they took?

Invite the children to suggest what Jack and Jessica took, and then to tell you what they would want to take if they could only take a few things.

Juniors

Invite the children to think about Jesus' instructions to the disciples in today's Gospel.

Can they think of people who would also have had to make decisions about what to take and, more importantly, what not to take? Think about explorers, missionaries... try to create a sense of excitement and admiration for people who are prepared to leave everything behind in search of something bigger, especially those who go out to take the Good News.

Take in photos of contemporary missionaries: many missionary societies have material available for educational purposes either by post or on the Internet. What do the children think motivates the missionaries? Look particularly for pictures of catechists/Sunday school teachers in Africa/India/South America. Perhaps look at the places where they are working on a globe or world map.

Talk about the fact that they are doing the same job as you, helping people to come to know and love God.

You may also like to extend the discussion to help the children to see that, having made such sacrifices, catechists and missionaries need our support. How can we give it?

4. Activity

Young ones

Have a selection of items ready – obvious necessities like soap, toothbrushes, along with luxuries like computer games, large toys. (Ensure that there are far more things than can be fitted into the tea towel.) Open the tea towel, and invite the children to select the things that they think someone would need to take on a mission journey. Encourage them to explain why things should be included, or not.

When the tea towel is full, tie it back onto the pole.

Or, using the template drawing of a small ruck sack, write a list of what essentials to pack. The children will have to decide which luxury items to leave behind!

Juniors

As with the younger children, but include things like family photographs, certificates, keys (e.g. to home) and other things that are harder to choose from. Use the exercise to emphasise the radical nature of what Jesus asked of his first disciples, and his missionaries today.

Again tie this tea towel back onto its pole.

Tips for learning difficulties

Have a selection of things that someone travelling light would need, with one or two very obvious "mistakes" – something far too large, for example.

Help the children to pack their tea towel and take turns to carry it to the focus.

5. We come together

Parents can be invited to join in at this stage.

Focus

Light the candle. Invite those gathered to become still, to look at the tea towels and think about what might be in them.

Gospel

Jesus sends his first disciples out as missionaries to spread the Good News. He tells them to travel light, not to carry more than they need.

He also tells them how to deal with people who don't make them welcome. If someone offers hospitality, they are to take it, but if they are not treated well, they are to walk away and not even take the dust from the place away with them.

Prayer

Jesus, you send special people to tell the world about you.
Help us to be proud of them, and to pray for them.
Keep us open to the possibility that you have called us,
and help us to be willing to leave things behind and follow you.
Amen.

Share

Explain to the parents that the children have been preparing for the holidays: learning how to pack.

Go on to say that the children have been exploring what it means to be a missionary, and how hard it is to choose what to take and what to leave behind.

Encourage the children to say what is in the tea towels, and what they left out and why.

Sing

"God's Spirit is in my heart"
"One more step along the road I go"

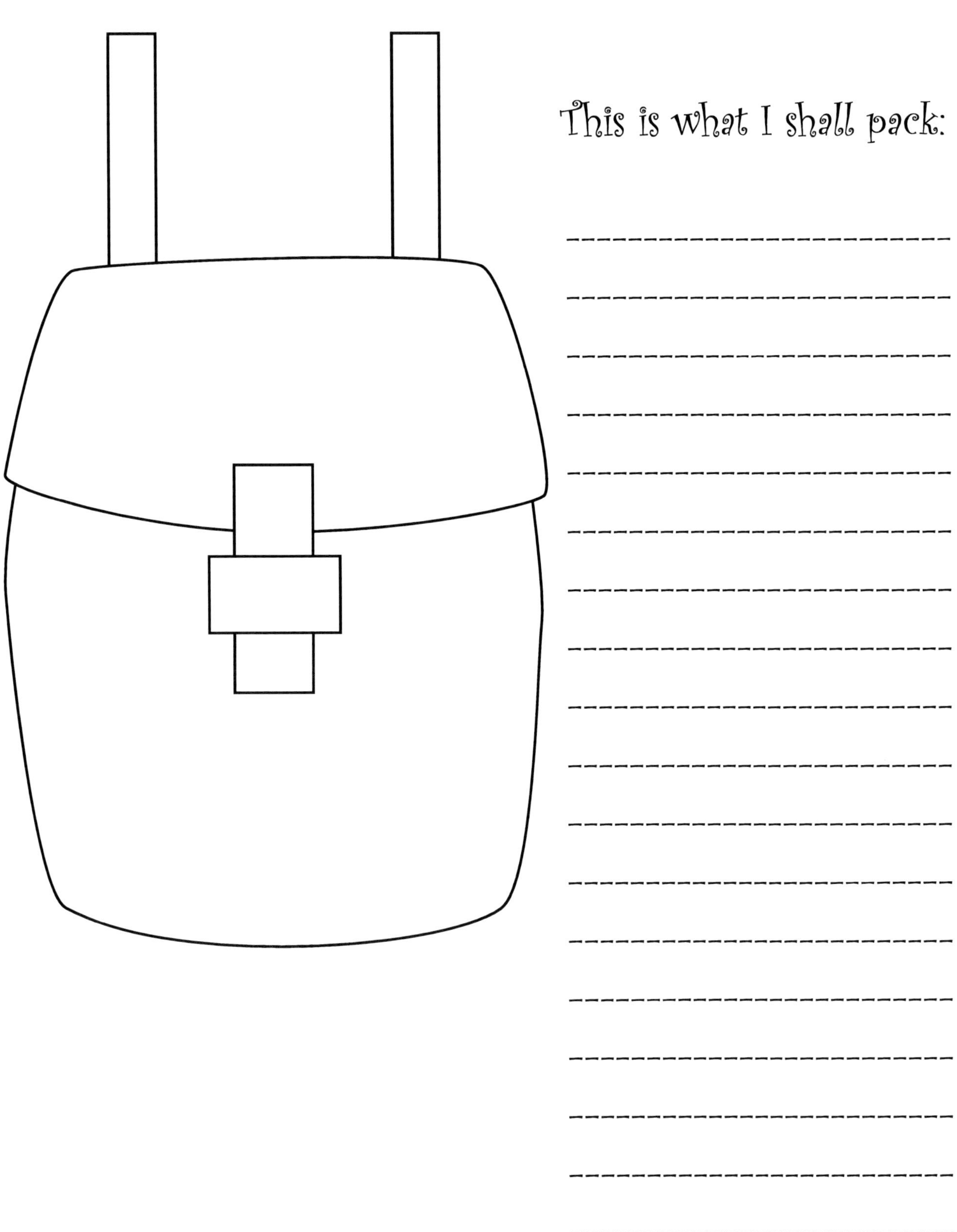
This is what I shall pack:

16th Sunday in Ordinary Time

Proper 11

1. Introduction to the theme of the day

"Rest for a while"

Aim: To reflect on the importance of taking time to rest and recreate.

Leader's Reflection: The disciples had gone at the Lord's bidding and done great things, beyond anything they could have asked or imagined. They probably thought they could go on and do more, but Jesus is a wise and loving Master. He knows from his own experience that there comes a time when one needs to withdraw, to rest, and to recharge the batteries.

It is a strong factor in the life of many committed Christians, the desire to serve, to give unstintingly through our love of God and of those placed in our care.

Jesus honours that desire but knows that we need rest... and, when we are tired and taking our rest, he comes to the people and cares for them himself.

We are not indispensable, nor do we work alone. We serve a Master who gave himself for his sheep. We work, in fact, in partnership with him, not as slaves who must work themselves to death to prove their love for him.

2. We arrive

We sit in a circle ready to listen to the Gospel.

Has anyone anything they would like to tell us about last week's Family Sheet?

Focus

Green cloth, candle, open Bible – and a symbol of rest or holidays... e.g. a pillow, sun cream, a set of balance scales.

Gospel: Mark 6:30-34

Read from the Lectionary or Children's Lectionary.

3. We respond

What is the Gospel asking of us?

Work in age groups if appropriate. Alternatively, choose the discussion ideas, story and activity most suitable for your group.

Young ones

Story

Maisie had been in school a whole year. She had been in the Christmas play as an angel. She had learnt to write her name, the names of her friends and the days of the week. She could add numbers up to ten and do some take-aways. She knew where Mrs Willis's office was, and she had taken the register to the office five times. She had done three assemblies in front of the whole school and could do up her own shoes.

"What a lot you have learnt this year!" said Gran. "Your brain must be absolutely full!"

Maisie thought about it.

"Not really, there's lots more to learn. I took my work to show Miss Jones in Year 6 and they do really hard stuff."

"But they are nearly all eleven and will be going to secondary school soon," said Gran.

"I know that, but to be as good as that, Mrs Kent says I have to work very hard," said Maisie.

Gran smiled. "Yes, but do you know something? Mrs Kent knows that you have to do other things too."

Maisie looked at Gran. How did she know what Mrs Kent knew?

Gran said, "When Mrs Kent and I were little we had a saying: All work and no play makes Jack a dull boy."

"But I'm a girl, Gran!" exclaimed Maisie.

"All right – All work and no play makes Maisie a dull girl. What it means is that if you work hard you need time to play too."

"Oh," said Maisie thoughtfully, "is that why Mrs Kent is asking us to tell her if we're going on holiday, or going on a playscheme? She says, 'You need to have time to play and enjoy yourselves.' Is that what she means?"

"Hmm, not just children," said Gran, "we all need time to play and to relax!"

"Grans don't play!" giggled Maisie.

"I'll race you to the swings," shouted Gran.

"That's not fair," laughed Maisie, "you had a head start!"

What do the children enjoy doing in the summer holidays? Encourage them to enjoy the break and to use it well!

Juniors

Use the story below to remind the children of the Song of Creation (Genesis 1) which shows how God created something new each day – encourage them to join in the "chorus".

Story

In the beginning the earth was a formless void – and then the Spirit of God swept over the waters.

God said, "Let there be light!"

And there was light – separating night from day.

Chorus: **And evening came and morning came – the first day.**

On the second day, God said, "Let there be a dome in the heavens." And God called the dome "Sky".

Chorus: **And evening came and morning came – the second day.**

On the third day, God said, "Let dry land appear." He called the dry land Earth and the waters the Seas.

Chorus: **And evening came and morning came – the third day.**

On the fourth day, God said, "Let there be lights in the sky." And he made two great lights: the sun and the moon – and the stars.

Chorus: **And evening came and morning came – the fourth day.**

On the fifth day, God said, "Let the waters and the skies be filled with living creatures!" And fish swam in the waters and birds flew in the sky.

Chorus: **And evening came and morning came – the fifth day.**

On the sixth day, God said, "Let the earth be filled with animals of every kind!" And God made every species of animal that has been known, lives now, and has yet to be born.

And God said, "Let us make human beings now, in our own image and likeness."

And God made human beings, men and women in God's own likeness to be stewards of his Creation.

Chorus: **And evening came and morning came, the sixth day.**

And, after God's mighty work of Creation, on the seventh day ...

Chorus: **God rested!**

4. Activity

Young ones

What sort of things are the children going to be doing over the summer? Invite them to draw them in the "My Summer Holiday" frame.

Juniors

Talk about the need for balance in everyone's life: Jesus went to pray and encouraged his disciples to do the same. God created a whole universe and then rested (note: it may be appropriate to say that this is a "Song" – and God's days are not necessarily 24 hours long).

What work have the children done over the last academic year? Invite them to write this down on a piece of paper and put them on one side of a balance – either a picture or, if possible, a real set of scales. Now invite them to write down what they are going to do to balance their work with rest, and put these on the other side of the balance. (Perhaps making the point that God worked for quite some time before taking rest! One day's rest for God made up for six days' work.)

Tips for learning difficulties

What are the children going to do on holiday? Invite them to draw it on the "My Summer Holiday" frame.

5. We come together

Parents can be invited to join in at this stage.

Focus

Light the candle. Invite those gathered to become still, to be aware that we are on the threshold of the summer holidays for the children.

Gospel

Jesus welcomes his disciples back and shares their joy at the great things they have done. But he knows, from his own experience, that great things come at cost. The disciples need to rest but the crowds think they need the disciples and have followed them.

Jesus takes that work to himself – while the disciples rest, Jesus speaks to the crowds.

Prayer

Jesus, you love our work and all we try to do for you.
But you know that we need rest, that we need re-creation.
Give us happy holidays, whether at home or away,
so that we remember that you are the Lord of Rest,
as well as the Lord who calls us to serve.
Amen.

Share

The children have been thinking about balance in people's lives. Many of us work very hard, some of us too hard! This isn't actually God's will for us. What can we do to redress the balance in our own lives so that our rest gives as much glory to God as our hard work?

Sing

"Take the word of God with you as you go"
"You shall go out with joy"

My Summer Holiday

17th Sunday in Ordinary Time

Proper 12

1. Introduction to the theme of the day

"A little goes a long way"

Aim: To explore how God takes our apparently small offerings and does great things with them.

Leader's Reflection: We leave Mark's Gospel for a few weeks and spend time with John, focusing on chapter 6 in which he reflects on the eucharistic significance of Jesus feeding the five thousand. The simple gift from a small boy, placed into the hands of Jesus, opens up the mystery of the gift of Christ's own body as the bread of life.

We might speculate what the reaction of the disciples was when the child offered five loaves and two fish to feed a crowd which, as Philip suggested, needed at least two hundred denarii. Did they try to send him away? Did they smile condescendingly? And what of Jesus?

When we think that what we offer is small and inadequate, we might reflect on how Jesus might have looked at the child, and see that look in his gaze upon us. Then, perhaps, we will have the confidence to hand to him the little we have and trust that he will transform it.

2. We arrive

We sit in a circle ready to listen to the Gospel.

Has anyone anything they would like to tell us about last week's Family Sheet?

Focus

Green cloth, candle, open Bible and a basket.

Gospel: John 6:1-15

Read from the Lectionary or Children's Lectionary.

3. We respond

What is the Gospel asking of us?

As the holiday season is upon us and children's numbers are likely to be reduced one long story is offered this week with different discussion ideas and activities for different age groups. Use those most appropriate for your group.

Young ones and Juniors

Story

Samson had been called Samson after the great Hebrew warrior. He guessed his parents had thought that giving him that name would make him grow up big and strong – but it had not worked. Samson was very small for his age and, after a bad fall when he was a toddler, walked with a limp.

His parents had decided to take him to see someone called Jesus. He had cured lots of people and they hoped he might cure Samson. Mum had packed a picnic and they had set off. It was a long way and Dad had given him a piggy back when he got tired.

When they arrived, Samson saw thousands of other people but could not see a great man who looked like Jesus. Samson thought he would be like – well, big and strong and standing out from the crowd... but there was no one like that.

Suddenly, he saw his Uncle Andrew. He knew that Uncle Andrew was a follower of Jesus so asked his mum if he could go and see him.

Mum said yes and told him to take some of the picnic with him to give to Uncle Andrew. "I don't suppose he thought to bring anything!" she said.

As Samson got close to Uncle Andrew, he saw a lot of worried faces, and one very kind one smiling quietly to himself as everyone else was fretting about how they were supposed to feed all these people. The kind man caught sight of Samson and gave him a wink. Samson guessed that this was Jesus and winked back.

At last, Uncle Andrew noticed Samson and beamed at him, "Samson! Well, here's a start with some food. Can we have this?"

Samson was feeling a bit hungry himself, but saw how worried everyone was, so said yes.

Jesus beckoned him over and Samson gave him the bread and fish.

Jesus gave thanks for the bread and the fish and then asked the disciples and Samson to hand them out. Every time Samson had given one lot out he came back for more, and there always was a lot more waiting. He could not understand it, though he noticed Jesus was smiling broadly every time he looked at him.

When everyone had had enough to eat, Samson went over to Jesus.

"How did you do that?" he asked.

"Ah," said Jesus, "that's between me and my Father. Maybe it's time for you to run back to your mum and dad."

Samson was about to say that he could not run, until he realised that all the time he had been giving out the food he had been running – running backwards and forwards to share the food as quickly as he could.

Jesus winked at him again. Samson winked back and then gave Jesus a huge hug.

Young ones

Invite the children to respond to the story. Have they ever felt like Samson – very small and not very strong? What do they think Jesus is like? How did people feel when they received the food?

Juniors

Invite the children to respond. Why were all the people following Jesus? How do they think Jesus felt when he saw them all coming? Did Jesus know in advance what he was going to do? How did the small child feel in front of all those people – and when he saw what Jesus did with his small offering? Have the children ever done something small that turned out to be special?

4. Activity

Young ones

Allow the children to choose either a loaf or fish outline from the template. Help them to think of one small thing they could do or share with someone else. They can draw themselves doing it in either the loaf or the fish – and colour in the rest.

Juniors

Think about the child's offering and introduce the idea that Jesus was not just feeding the people but was setting the scene for explaining that he was the bread come down from heaven... the people needing something practical to start them off.

Talk about our own Presentation of Gifts at the Eucharist. What do we offer? What does God do with them? Draw out that our simple gifts of bread and wine become the Body and Blood of Jesus. We do not know how, any more than the disciples knew how Jesus had fed five thousand people, but we know it happens.

We can also offer the things we do and say. Encourage the children to think of one thing they would like to offer at the Presentation of Gifts next time. They can write it on one of the loaf outlines.

Tips for learning difficulties

Have the outlines ready cut out. Help the child to think about something good about themselves and to draw this onto their loaf or fish.

5. We come together

Parents can be invited to join in at this stage.

Focus

Light the candle. Invite those gathered to become still.

Gospel

We are leaving Mark's Gospel for a while and over the summer will be reading John's account of the sign or miracle story of Jesus feeding the five thousand. His reflections help us to understand that Jesus is the living bread come down from heaven. Today, we hear about the people following Jesus into the desert and having no food. A small child comes forward with a very small offering which Jesus takes and uses to feed all the people, with twelve baskets of food left over.

Prayer

Jesus, you invite us to offer the things we do so that you can transform them into something great.

Some things that you do we will know about and some things you keep as secrets for us in heaven.

Help us to trust you in all we do.

Amen.

Share

In our session, we heard the story about the small boy who we called Samson. He offered Jesus his lunch and Jesus fed five thousand people. We have been thinking about the things we could offer Jesus. (Invite the children to talk about what they drew or wrote if appropriate.)

During our song, we will put our own coloured-in loaf or fish into the basket as a sign of offering it to Jesus.

Sing

"All that I am"
"Take my hands"
"Take oh take me as I am"

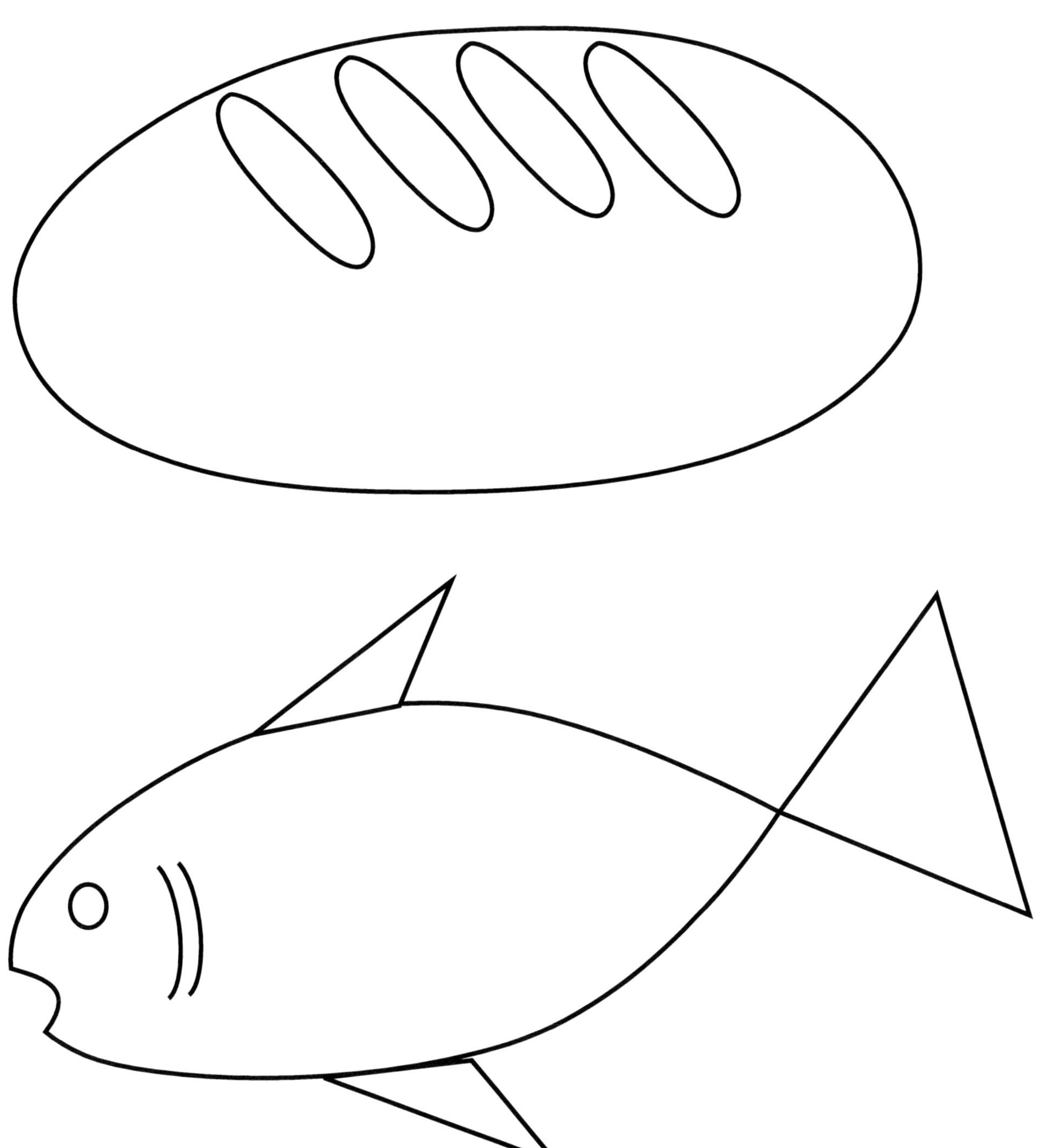

18th Sunday in Ordinary Time

Proper 13

1. Introduction to the theme of the day

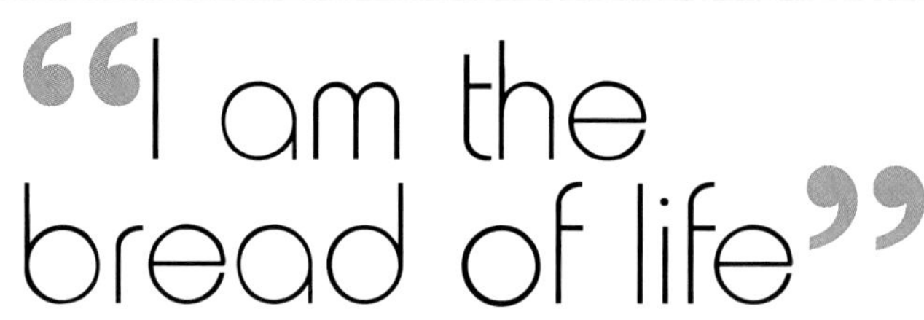

Aim: To help the children develop a deep awareness of meeting Jesus in the Eucharist.

Leader's Reflection: Attracted by the miraculous feeding of five thousand people, crowds continue to follow Jesus. He is aware, though, that they are looking for more miracles, perhaps more free lunches, and are not yet ready to look behind the miracle to find its meaning.

This is the great danger with miracles; we can be tempted to stay at the level of marvelling, of wanting more of the same, particularly if it looks as if it will spare us work. Signs and wonders are wonderful things, but they can lead us to focus on them, waiting for the next one, hoping it will be bigger and better and even more convincing. They can be an excuse for not actually getting on and doing something.

Perhaps this is one reason why Jesus avoided the dramatic and complicated as a way of being with us always, giving us the greatest sign of all hidden in a basic staple of life: the living presence of Jesus in a simple wafer.

2. We arrive

We sit in a circle ready to listen to the Gospel.
Has anyone anything they would like to tell us about last week's Family Sheet?
Did anyone have a go at baking bread?

Green cloth, candle, Bible or Book of the Gospels open at today's reading, a loaf.

Gospel John 6:24-35

Read from the Lectionary or the Children's Lectionary.

3. We respond

What is the Gospel asking of us?

As this is the holiday season and children are likely to be away, use the story for all the children and then choose the activity most suitable for the group you have this week.

Young ones and Juniors

Story

John was not a very clever boy. In spite of everything his teacher tried, he just could not get the hang of even simple maths. The biggest problem he had was with a language called Latin. Even when his friend gave him extra help, John thought his brain just was not big enough for the words to go in.

And why did it matter if John could not learn to understand and speak Latin? Well, John really wanted to be a Catholic priest and in those days the Mass and lots of the prayers were said in Latin.

This is what "The Lord be with you" sounded like: "Dominus vobiscum"; and the congregation would say: "Et cum spiritu tuo."

Shall we try to say that together?

Most people learned just enough Latin to join in with some of the Mass, but priests needed to know much more.

John tried very hard and everyone realised that he was meant to be a priest. Unfortunately, he was called up into the army. John being John, he spent the morning he was due to go into the army in church praying. He lost all track of time and when he came out, everyone else had left without him!

Eventually, though, John was ordained a priest, one of the happiest moments of his life.

Because he was not very clever or ambitious, he was sent to be parish priest of a sleepy little village deep in the countryside. But something very strange began to happen. People started coming from all over France to talk to him. They would talk about the things they had done wrong, and John would absolve them from their sins. This is known as "confession". People who were wondering whether God was calling them to be a priest or nun would go to John to hear his advice. So many people came that sometimes John would be hearing confessions for sixteen hours a day. In one year twenty thousand visitors came to the tiny village just to see John.

His favourite time, though, was when everyone had gone and he could be in the church on his own or with a few of his parishioners. One day, he met one of the poor farmers. He was too old to do heavy work and spent a lot of time in the church too. John asked him what prayers he used and the farmer looked puzzled for a moment. Then he smiled broadly and said, "Well, Jesus is there, isn't he?" pointing to the tabernacle. "I just sit and look at him – and he sits and looks at me!"

John smiled back, "Yes," he said, "that is the best kind of prayer, isn't it?"

John lived to be 73 years old and was much loved. People began to realise that miracles were happening when they prayed to John for help and, eventually, John was made a saint. His full name is St John Vianney and his feast day is 4 August.

Spend some time talking about prayer: when you pray, how you pray and ways in which we can help each other to pray.

4. Activity

Young ones

Do the children have things that they find hard? How does hearing about someone like John Vianney help?

Have the children had times when they have enjoyed peace and quiet in church or another building or open space? Have they ever felt Jesus close to them?

If possible take the children into church to see the tabernacle and show them the consecrated hosts safely inside.

Use the template of the tabernacle. The children can decorate the "outside" and then colour in the ciborium (a chalice in which the consecrated elements are held) inside – folding the tabernacle closed when they have finished. You may like to have a ciborium shape ready cut out in kitchen foil or shiny paper for the children to stick in place

Juniors

If possible, take the children into the church. Show them the tabernacle and the ciborium (a chalice in which the consecrated elements are held). It may also be possible to show the children a monstrance, explaining that the Blessed Sacrament is placed in it and people can spend time in quiet prayer during a period of Exposition, with Benediction.

Use the tabernacle template. The children can decorate the inside and outside – adding notes: e.g. the tabernacle is where the Blessed Sacrament is kept. The ciborium holds the consecrated hosts and is made of precious metal. A monstrance is used for Exposition and Benediction.

Tip for learning difficulties

Have the tabernacle templates ready cut out with ciborium-shaped pieces of foil or shiny paper. As the children work, talk about how this is a precious, special place where Jesus lives. The children can then decorate the outside.

5. We come together

Parents can be invited to join in at this stage.

It may be appropriate to go into the church for a short time of Exposition. Help the children to be still and at ease with the quiet. Invite restless children to sit with you, sharing your stillness with them. If this is not possible, gather around the focus material used at the beginning of the session.

People are asking Jesus for another miracle, another sign so that they will believe in him. They talk about Moses giving their ancestors bread in the desert, but Jesus reminds them that it was actually God who gave them bread.

It is also God who is giving them this new bread – the bread of life. This bread is Jesus.

Prayer

Lord Jesus,
you come to us looking and tasting like simple bread.
Our hearts tell us that it really is you.
Thank you for this great gift.
Help us always to be grateful,
and wanting to spend time just being with you.
Amen.

Share

Talk about what happened in the session – what the children have learnt about the tabernacle, ciborium, monstrance, etc.

"Eat this bread" (Taizé)
"Jesus the Lord said 'I am the bread'"

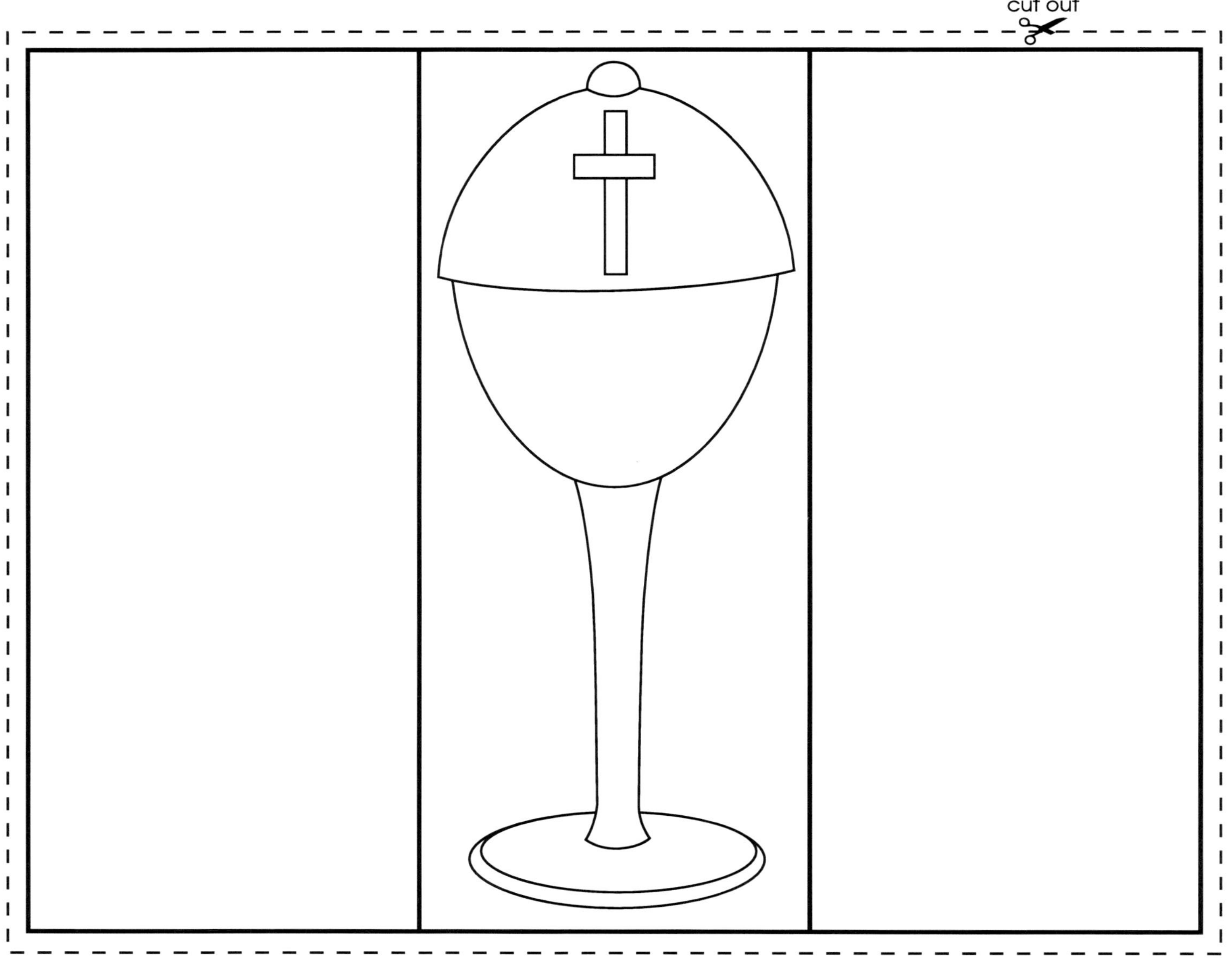
cut out

19th Sunday in Ordinary Time

Proper 14

1. Introduction to the theme of the day

Aim: To think about how we see other people and Jesus.

Leader's Reflection: Jesus is continuing to try to open the minds of his listeners, to enable them to see beyond the literal and take the leap of imaginative faith that will reveal the truth of what he is saying to them. Some, understandably, cannot get beyond the fact that they know his family. Putting ourselves in their shoes, we might be humble enough to see their point. Often, though, our mindset is similar: things have "always" been like this, people have "always" behaved in this way. We find it hard to believe that things can change or that there is another way of looking at them.

Faith is not about closing our minds and ceasing to think. It is about opening minds and hearts to God and letting him reveal more and more of his truth to us. Part of the work we do with children is to open their minds so that they learn to love exploring the mystery of God and are not afraid to allow imagination and insight to take them beyond the literal and rational.

2. We arrive

We sit in a circle ready to listen to the Gospel.

Has anyone anything they would like to tell us about last week's Family Sheet? Did anyone find some unusual breads?

Focus

Green cloth, candle, Bible or Book of the Gospels open at today's reading, a loaf (perhaps a different shape from last week).

Gospel: John 6:41-51

Read from the Lectionary or the Children's Lectionary.

3. We respond

What is the Gospel asking of us?

One long story is offered this week for both young ones and juniors. Work in age groups, if appropriate, for the activities.

Young ones and Juniors

Story

Harry and Charlie were twins. “Not that you’d think it,” their mum often said, “like chalk and cheese you two are.”

In fact, Harry and Charlie were not identical in any way. For a start, Harry was a boy and Charlie was a girl (Charlie was short for Charlotte). Harry was quiet and loved reading and drawing. Charlie was noisy and loved anything that meant getting dirty.

Harry had fair hair and blue eyes. Charlie had brown hair and brown eyes.

Even though they were different they usually got on well together. “Which is at least one blessing,” sighed their mum.

The family had promised themselves a holiday this year, their first for five years. They had booked a caravan near the sea and everyone was getting more and more excited. Charlie was noisier than ever, running up and down stairs every five minutes to get something else she had forgotten. Harry made lots of lists and stuck them to the fridge, ticking things off as he put them out to be packed. He made sure he had his paper, paints and crayons with him. Charlie made sure she had her Frisbee, her kite and football.

“Like chalk and cheese,” said their mum, yet again.

The caravan was in a field with hundreds of others that all looked the same. The children could see people of all ages, some running and playing, others sitting in the sunshine.

Mum insisted that everyone help get things into the caravan. “This is my holiday too,” she reminded them.

Once the car was unloaded and homes found for Harry’s books and paints and Charlie’s Frisbee, kite and football, Mum said that the children could go and explore the caravan park but must stay together and must not forget where their caravan was.

They found a playground where Charlie quickly made friends and introduced Harry to them.

Harry had a few turns on the swings and the slide but was more interested in watching the others. He often did this and Charlie was quite used to it, though some of the other children thought it was a bit strange.

“Doesn’t he like playing?” they asked.

“Yes,” said Charlie, “but he likes looking at things more.”

After tea, which Mum had cooked on a tiny stove, the children went out to play again. This time Harry took his drawing pad and pencils. While Charlie and the other children ran around like mad things, Harry sat and drew. Eventually, Charlie came over to get her breath back.

“Let’s see,” she said.

Harry smiled and handed her the picture. It was of Charlie, but not the Charlie wearing a T-shirt and shorts with mud on her knees and her nose. The Charlie in the picture was wearing a long cloak which billowed out after her as she ran. She carried a banner decorated with stars and was running towards something. As she looked closer, she realised, “That’s our caravan!” but this caravan had flags flying from the television aerial and was decorated with wonderful animals, plants and swirly designs.

In front of the caravan was a luxurious-looking hammock on which a beautiful lady relaxed. There was a long, cool drink with a little umbrella in it next to her.

“Mum?” queried Charlie.

“Yes,” said Harry, “as she said – it’s her holiday too.”

4. Activity

Young ones

What do the children think Harry drew Charlie as? What about their mum? How would they draw their parents, or brothers and sisters? How would they like to be drawn?

Show the children a selection of pictures of Jesus. Which is their favourite? Which one is the most like the Jesus they imagine?

Using the template invite the children to draw a picture of Jesus in the portrait frame.

Juniors

What does Harry's picture tell us about how he sees his sister and his mum? How would they draw members of their family? What does this tell them about how they feel about their families? Does that change sometimes?

How do the people in the Gospel see Jesus?

How do the children see Jesus?

Invite the children to look at a selection of pictures of Jesus. Talk about which is their favourite, which most like the Jesus they imagine. What do the pictures tell us about Jesus? Help the children to identify the characteristics they imagine Jesus to have.

Invite the children to draw a picture of Jesus as they see him, a great king or shepherd perhaps. Encourage them to think about the details that will help to show what they think of Jesus.

Tips for learning difficulties

Look through pictures of Jesus and invite the children to show you their favourite. What do they think Jesus is like? Invite them to draw Jesus, offering help if the child expresses the need for it.

5. We come together

Parents can be invited to join in at this stage.

Focus

Light the candle. Invite those gathered to become still.

Gospel

Jesus is continuing to talk to the crowds about being the bread of life. They could not understand, they just saw the Jesus they had always known. Jesus promises that anyone who can see him as he is and believe in him will live for ever.

Prayer

Jesus, we see you in so many ways:
you are strong, and kind,
you are loving, and want everyone to be happy
and live with you for ever.
Help us to learn more about you
so that we become more like you.
Amen.

Share

Talk about what happened in the session. Explain that you have been looking at different ways of seeing Jesus and using imagination to think about what he is like.

Perhaps show the parents the pictures of Jesus that the children were looking at during the session. Which do they like?

Sing

"This is my body, broken for you"

20th Sunday in Ordinary Time

Proper 15

1. Introduction to the theme of the day

"Jesus lives in me"

Aim: To reflect on the promise that believing in Jesus and sharing in the Eucharist brings the promise of eternal life.

Leader's Reflection: The fear of death is part of the human condition. Part of it is the fear of the unknown – what awaits us? There is also the fear of oblivion, of ceasing to exist. Most cultures in the world have rituals surrounding death, many showing a belief in an afterlife. What is, perhaps, different about our view of life after death is that we do not see it as more of the same, but that we will become more like Christ. As St Paul says, what is mortal and perishable will be no more, our risen bodies will be imperishable and glorious.

It is often hard to hold on to that truth, especially when we are directly affected. The Gospel today offers us reassurance that God's promise is not empty.

2. We arrive

We sit in a circle ready to listen to the Gospel.

Has anyone anything they would like to tell us about last week's Family Sheet?

Focus

Green cloth, Bible or Book of the Gospels open at today's reading, a loaf and, perhaps, a picture of Mary.

Gospel: John 6:51-58

Read from the Lectionary or Children's Lectionary.

3. We respond

What is the Gospel asking of us?

One long story is offered this week for both young ones and juniors. Work in age groups, if appropriate, for the discussion ideas and activities.

Young ones and Juniors

Story

Jack had been ill for a long time. He had an illness called leukaemia and had had all sorts of treatment. He had had something called chemotherapy which had made him sick and his hair had fallen out and he had missed loads of school.

The hospital was brilliant. There was a special family house where Mum could stay when Jack was in the hospital and at weekends, Dad, Jack's older brother Dave and big sister Laura could come and stay too.

Jack did really well but after four years of feeling absolutely great, Jack knew his illness had come back and that this time there was not much the doctors could do. His mum and dad were really upset and Dave and Laura were very unhappy. Jack wasn't sure how he felt. Sometimes, he felt afraid – sometimes he felt sad. But quite often, he just felt sick and tired of feeling sick and tired.

Eventually, Jack went into a children's hospice. If the hospital was brilliant, the hospice was amazing. Everything he and his family could ever want was there and being with other families in the same situation was really good.

There was a hospice chaplain but Jack's parish priest, Fr John, came to see him too. Fr John brought him Communion and sometimes anointed him with Oil of the Sick.

One day, Jack turned to Fr John and asked him a question that had puzzled him for some time.

"Fr John, how do I do it? What do I have to do when I die?"

Fr John thought for a moment, "Well, can you remember being born?" Jack shook his head. "Did someone tell you how to be born?" Jack smiled and shook his head again. "I think it is a bit like that. When the time comes, people just know what to do. I have been with quite a few people when they have died and most of them become very quiet and peaceful and seem to know they are going somewhere wonderful. I think you'll find that too."

Jack gradually got weaker and, one day, he slipped into a coma. Although he could still hear what was going on around him, he did not feel much like joining in. He could hear Mum crying quietly and could vaguely feel her and Dad holding his hands – and then Fr John anointing his head with oil and saying, "Go forth, Christian soul..."

... and Jack did. The next thing he knew, he had rushed down a dark tunnel and burst into a world of light.

He looked around and there was Gran!

"Eeh pet – you've come here a lot sooner than we'd have liked – but, here, come and give me a hug!"

Jack could still just hear Mum's distant crying and wanted to rush back and say, "Mum, Mum it's OK! I'm with Gran!" But he knew he couldn't.

Then he looked up and saw a beautiful motherly looking woman coming towards him. She crouched down in front of him and smiled, "Welcome to heaven, Jack."

"Are you ... Mary?" asked Jack.

"Yes," said Mary.

"Can you look after my mum? She's really sad and doesn't know I'm going to be OK here."

"I can do that," said Mary, "remember I had a son who died too." And she turned and pointed to a man who was coming towards them smiling broadly.

"Is that...?"

Mary smiled and nodded.

"Wow," gasped Jack as the man came to him, gave him a huge hug and said, "Welcome home, Jack!"

Young ones

Who was the man who came to meet Jack? Is Jack going to be happy in heaven? What do they think heaven will be like?

Juniors

Some children may have experienced the death of someone. Sensitively help them to tell you about it. How do Jack's story and our faith offer us hope for them – and for ourselves? What might it be like to meet Mary and Jesus?

4. Activity

Young ones

If possible, take the children into a church and show them the Lady Chapel – or bring in a statue or favourite picture. Invite them to light a candle and say a prayer; perhaps the Lord's Prayer or the Hail Mary. Explain that this is something we can do when we are sad or want to pray for someone. Colour in the picture of Gran, Mary and Jesus greeting Jack in heaven.

Juniors

As with the little ones, take the children into church. Talk about the tradition of lighting candles as a way of praying and, if appropriate, encourage them to light one and pray quietly. Colour in and add details to the picture of Jack's arrival in heaven, and add a big welcoming smile to Jesus' face.

Tips for learning difficulties

Help the children to light their candle and talk about the light and warmth.
As they colour in the picture, talk about how happy Jack is – even though he is sad that his family do not know that yet.

5. We come together

Parents can be invited to join in at this stage.

Focus

Light the candle. Invite those gathered to become still.

Gospel

Jesus reminds us that he is the bread of life and promises us that anyone who eats this bread will live for ever.

Prayer

Jesus, you give us the promise of life for ever with you.
Help us to meet you in Communion as often as we can.
Bless those people who cannot receive you in Communion as often as they would like.
Bring us all one day to be with you in heaven.
Amen.

Share

We have been thinking about Jesus' promise that those who believe in him will live for ever.

Sing

"I am the bread of life"

21st Sunday in Ordinary Time

Proper 16

1. Introduction to the theme of the day

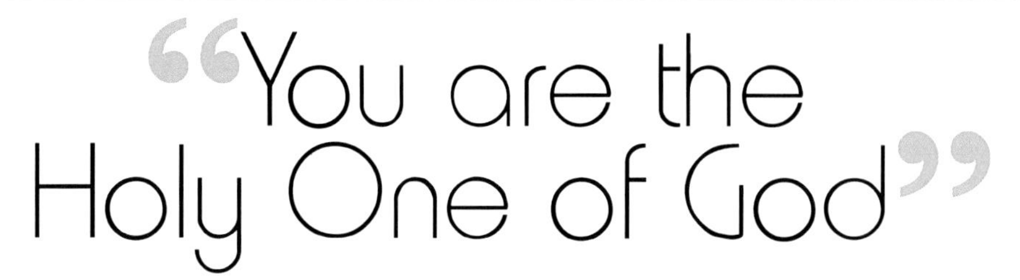

Aim: To help the children to share Peter's conviction that Jesus is the Holy One of God.

Leader's Reflection: After leading the people through from a miraculous feeding of five thousand to the point of saying that it was necessary to eat his flesh to gain eternal life, Jesus has reached a point beyond which many cannot go. His words are intolerable; how, people ask, can anyone accept this? At one level, their position is understandable but Jesus tries to push them towards an understanding that his words are spirit and they are life. Some parts of the Christian message are unwelcome in the secular world. Many are unable or unwilling to take the risk of faith. Our task is to encourage those with whom we work to dare to believe, sharing our own conviction that ultimately there is nowhere and no one who can offer what Jesus does, the words of eternal life.

2. We arrive

We sit in a circle ready to listen to the Gospel.
Has anyone anything they would like to tell us about last week's Family Sheet?

Focus

Green cloth, Bible or Book of the Gospels open at today's reading, candle.

Gospel: John 6:60-69

Read from the Lectionary or the Children's Lectionary.

3. We respond

What is the Gospel asking of us?

One long story is offered this week for both young ones and juniors.
You may like to remind the children briefly about Samson who appeared as the boy who shared his lunch (17th Sunday in Ordinary Time/Proper 12) and introduce him for those who were not there.

Young ones and Juniors

Story

Samson had not understood very much about what Jesus was talking about. In fact, he had not done much listening at all. The novelty of being able to run was still too great and, apart from the time in the boat crossing to their home in Capernaum, he had spent the last few days practising.

A few people had left the town. Samson guessed it was because Jesus was not feeding them and that was all they had been interested in. As his mum said, "We're near enough to the town to buy food for ourselves now!"

The people who were left seemed to spend a lot of time discussing things with Jesus and with each other. Samson asked his mum and dad what it was about and they just said Samson was too young to understand. He was not impressed.

Late one afternoon, Samson's mum told him to go and ask Uncle Andrew if he wanted to bring Jesus for a meal. She had seen how busy he was and guessed he probably was not eating properly; Mum was good at spotting things like that.

As Samson got closer, he heard angry voices. He saw Jesus in the middle of a group of people and it was clear that no matter what Jesus said, they were not going to be convinced. Then, they turned away and stalked off, shaking their heads and muttering, "He's mad!" "He's got evil in him, saying things like that." Samson hid behind a tree until they had gone past.

When they had gone, Samson came out from behind the tree and ran over to Uncle Andrew just in time to hear Jesus say, "What about you, do you want to go away too?"

Uncle Andrew and all the other disciples were looking embarrassed and no one knew what to say.

Samson tugged Uncle Andrew's sleeve, but Uncle Andrew took no notice. Samson tried again. "What is it Samson?" he said, and it was so quiet that even though he was nearly whispering, it sounded really loud and everyone looked at them. Samson looked down at the ground, but no hole appeared to swallow him up. So, he took a deep breath and blurted out, "Mum sent me to see if you would come and join us for tea, all of you."

He knew it wasn't quite what Mum had said but was sure he could explain. He did not want Uncle Andrew and Uncle Peter to leave Jesus. Jesus needed all the friends he could get, and he was not evil, nor mad. He was the best and kindest person Samson knew.

"Well," said Jesus, "do you want to leave me? Or shall we join Samson for tea?"

No one said anything but Samson noticed Uncle Peter looking at him and thinking hard. Samson wondered if he was remembering how Jesus had managed to share his lunch with all those people, and he was definitely looking at Samson's new strong leg.

It was Uncle Peter's turn to take a deep breath.

"Who else could we go to? You are the Holy One of God."

Samson heard Jesus sigh with relief. He walked over to Uncle Peter and gave him a hug.

"Thank you, Peter." Then he turned to Samson and bent down so only Samson could hear. "Are you sure you got that message right?"

Samson looked into Jesus' eyes and knew he did not need to say anything. Jesus knew he had not!

"Well, you'd best just run on ahead and tell your mum we're coming," said Jesus, "but tell her not to worry too much, we know what we can do with a little bread, don't we?"

Samson laughed and set off running as fast as the wind to tell his family that they were in for a party!

4. Activity

School holidays may soon be over. Be like Samson and his family and have an impromptu party. Bring various items for a picnic (even if it is indoors) and allow the children to help you to get it ready: putting cloths down, crisps in bowls, cakes on plates, etc. It need not be lavish but encourage a sense of creating a sense of welcome and hospitality.

Young ones

Children can colour in the picnic scene.

How do the children think Samson felt when he heard the arguing voices?

What about when Peter said that they would stay with Jesus?

Juniors

Spend a few minutes with the children thinking about the story. How did Samson feel at various points? What about the disciples – what might they have been thinking when everyone else left? What made them stay?

Look back over recent weeks and see what the children remember about the tabernacle, ciborium, etc.

Tips for learning difficulties

Talk about Samson and how he felt about Jesus. What made Samson happy? What made him worried? What was the ending of the story like?

5. We come together

Parents can be invited to join in at this stage.

Focus

Light the candle. Welcome the "guests".

Gospel

Jesus has been trying to help people to see him as the bread of life – the way to eternal life. Today, though, most people have had enough and have walked away from him. Jesus is worried that his closest disciples might do the same.

Fortunately, Peter speaks up and asks who else they could go to. Jesus has the message of eternal life. He is the Holy One of God.

Prayer

Jesus,
it is sad that people do not always understand your message.
Help us to believe in you,
and to stay faithful to all the things that you teach us,
even when other people do not understand.
Amen.

Share

Explain to the parents that the children have heard another story about the little boy who shared his lunch with five thousand other people, and how today he has invited Jesus and all the disciples home for tea!

Invite everyone to share the prepared "picnic".

"Seek ye first"
or any song that the children especially like.

22nd Sunday in Ordinary Time

Proper 17

1. Introduction to the theme of the day

"Keep God's law on the inside"

Aim: To show that God's law is for the inside and not just for outer show.

Leader's Reflection: We leave John's eucharistic reflections this week and return to Mark. The children too will be preparing to go back to school; new classes and, for some, new schools. It is a time of new beginnings, some anxieties, and lots of new things to learn.

Mark's Gospel this week looks at rules for living, and how their original meaning has got lost. People adhere to the rules simply because they are rules and have failed to grow in understanding of their purpose. Many primary age children are at a similar stage in their moral development. Others see rules as something to challenge, simply because they are rules. Some go on to make gang rules that are far harsher than anything an adult world might impose.

Part of our role is to help children learn the value of rules for human living: to encourage thinking and reasonable questioning so that our children move from blind adherence, or challenge for the sake of challenge, to a point of seeing that rules are there to ensure human happiness and growth.

2. We arrive

We sit in a circle ready to listen to the Gospel.

Has anyone anything they would like to tell us about last week's Family Sheet?

Catch up on some of the news of people who have been away over the summer.

Focus

Green cloth, Bible or Book of the Gospels open at today's reading, a candle.

Gospel: Mark 7:1-8. 14-15. 21-23

Read from the Lectionary or Children's Lectionary.

3. We respond

What is the Gospel asking of us?

One long story is offered this week for both young ones and juniors. Work in age groups, if appropriate, for the activities.

Young ones and Juniors

A story to finish

When Craig and Darren started Junior school, you could not have had two more different boys. Craig arrived at school in his mother's new car (perhaps use a brand here). His uniform was brand new and everything had his name tapes neatly sewn in. His lunch box was new and had healthy sandwiches in it: a no-sugar drink and fruit for break time. His PE kit was in a new bag with his name clearly written on the outside.

Darren arrived late. Mrs Johnson had taken the register and everyone was writing their names on their new books. Mrs Johnson gave a loud "tut" and told Darren to sit next to Craig. Craig did not look impressed. Darren's uniform was obviously handed down from someone else. His lunchbox was a plastic (name of local supermarket) bag and his PE bag was a (name of another supermarket) bag.

At lunchtime, Darren opened his (supermarket) bag and found the crumpled slices of bread he'd put in there, but where were his crisps?

"Perhaps they fell out when I tripped getting off the bus," Darren thought.

In the afternoon, they had PE and Mrs Johnson checked that everyone had their name tapes sewn in. "Well done, Craig," she said, "tell your mum we're very pleased when everything is labelled."

When she came to Darren's (supermarket) bag, she sniffed. The white T-shirt was grey; the shorts were too big; the trainers were scuffed; and nothing had Darren's name in.

"Sorry, Mrs Johnson, Mum was busy with the new baby."

Things got even worse for Darren when not only did his crisps go missing, but things began to go missing from other people's lunch boxes and trays. Then one day, he opened his tray to find the empty wrapper from a Mars bar and Jenny had told Mrs Johnson that she had lost a Mars bar that day!

"Darren Wilson! How dare you steal things from other people?"

Darren tried to say that he didn't steal, that he had had things stolen from him, but he could not get the words out.

Mrs Johnson told him to go and see the headteacher, Miss Clarke, and "see what she has to say about this!"

He knocked at the door and a voice said, "Come in".

Darren gave Miss Clarke the note from Mrs Johnson.

"Now Darren, I want you to think very carefully before you answer. Did you steal those things?"

Darren did not need to think for long. "No, Miss. I didn't. I wouldn't! I've ..."

Darren was really cross with himself because tears kept coming to his eyes.

Miss Clarke told him to sit down and take his time.

And then he told her how he had had his crisps stolen nearly every day but he hadn't said anything to anyone. He didn't want to get anyone into trouble and he knew Mum would go mad because they did not have a lot of money anyway and she would think he was just being careless.

Miss Clarke did not say anything for a while.

"Darren, whoever is doing this needs to learn that it is wrong. I think you might have to help them by helping me to find out who it is."

Darren wasn't so sure but didn't say anything. Then he said, "I don't know if it's important, Miss, but... well, Craig always seems to have the same crisps as I bring. And I don't think his mum buys (name a cheap brand) like my mum."

Miss Clarke smiled. "I know that wasn't easy, Darren. Don't worry, let me deal with this now."

That afternoon, Miss Clarke visited the class as they got ready for PE. "Just a spot check on name tapes," she said.

Darren gave Miss Clarke his (supermarket) bag. She looked at the, still unnamed, clothes. "Mum still being kept awake by the baby?" she asked. Darren nodded gratefully and beamed, "Yes Miss, three times we were up with her last night!"

"Craig, can I see your things, please?"

"Erm... I forgot them."

"Craig, I can see the bag with your name on, let me see it please."

Inside Craig's bag were his bright white T-shirt and just the right sized shorts and ...

4. Activity

Young ones

What is Miss Clarke going to find in the bag? What could happen next?

Ask the children to think of something good that they would like God to notice them doing. Invite them to draw this on the T-shirt template.

Juniors

What is going to happen next? What do the children think should happen to Craig? What did Miss Clarke mean by helping him to learn that this was wrong? Help the children to see that doing something wrong is not the end, but can lead to repentance and forgiveness.

Invite the children to think of some of the qualities God looks for in people: kindness, sincerity, gentleness, etc and to write some of them on the T-shirt template

Tips for learning difficulties

Talk about how some people seem good on the outside but make us feel uncomfortable inside... and the other way round. Invite the children to draw a person who feels good on the outside and on the inside onto their tee-shirt template.

5. We come together

Parents can be invited to join in at this stage.

Focus

Light the candle – and add a plastic carrier bag from a local supermarket.

Gospel

Much of Jewish Law was very sensible – surgeons still wash up to the elbow as described in the Gospel. The problem was that people had begun to focus on the Law and not what it really meant. They were more concerned with following the letter of the Law and not necessarily thinking about what lay behind it. They allowed human thinking to become more important than what God actually wanted.

Prayer

Jesus, you ask us not just to do what you tell us
but to become people who love,
who forgive, and reconcile people to you.
When we are tempted to believe what we see on the surface –
remind us to look more deeply,
so that we see clearly and truly
what a person is really like. Amen.

Share

In this session we have thought about someone who seemed to be perfect on the outside – but was not so good on the inside. This could apply to any of us. Ask the children to put all the good things they hope God sees in them into the bag and draw out the significance of this.

"God's Spirit is in my heart"

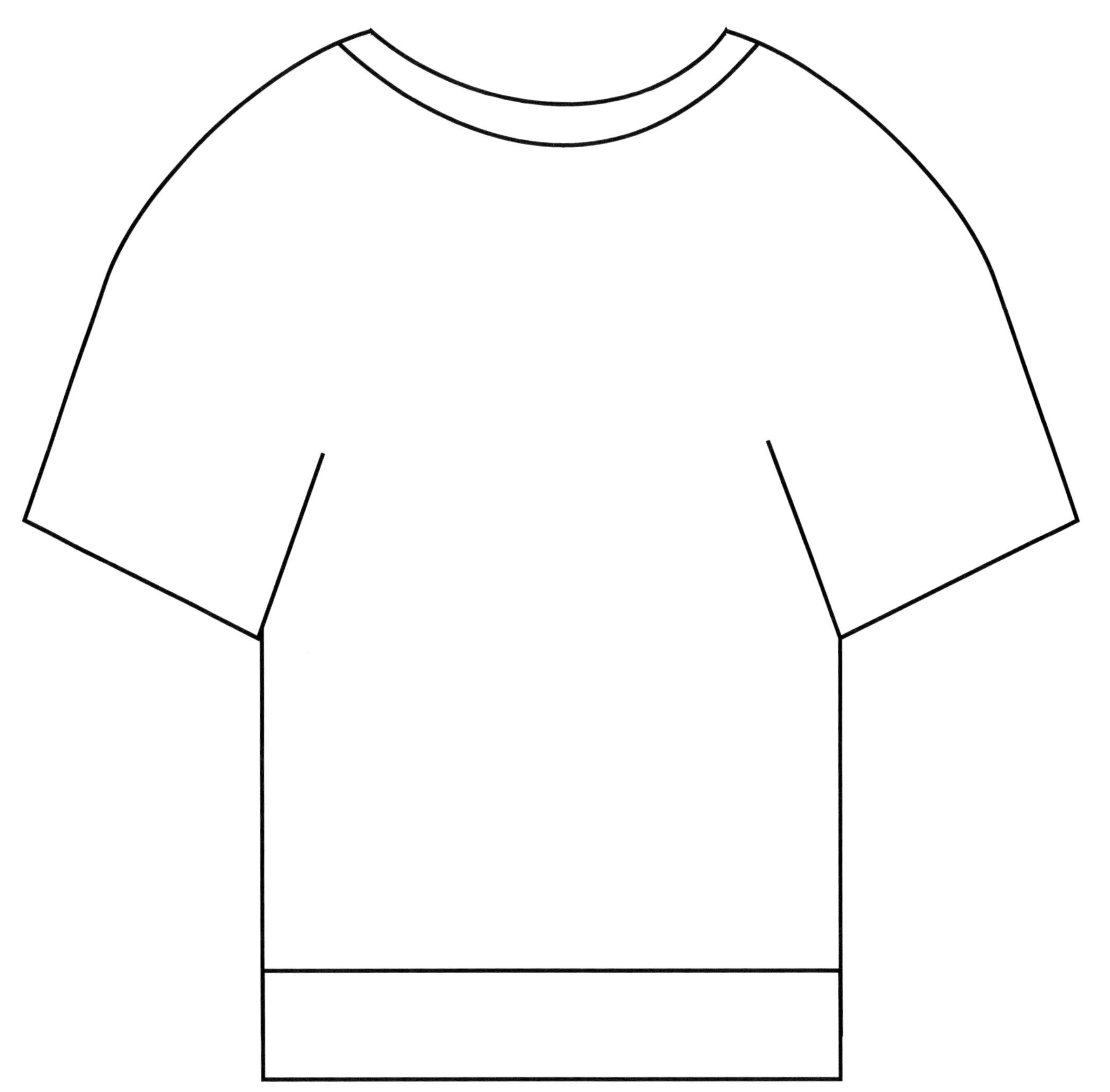

23rd Sunday in Ordinary Time

Proper 18

1. Introduction to the theme of the day

"Our ears will be open"

Aim: Today we focus on hearing God's message. We hear in the readings that God will open our ears, and make us whole. Let us try to understand how best to hear what God is saying to us.

Leader's Reflection: God calls out to us, and God gives us the equipment we need to hear his voice. In the readings for today, we hear how Jesus cured a man of deafness. But God's real gift goes far beyond healing physical deafness, as the reading from Isaiah makes clear. God reaches out and touches us, so that we can hear and understand and celebrate the glory of his love. How can we hear God better?

2. We arrive

We sit in a circle, ready to listen to the Gospel.

Focus

A candle with matches ready to light.

When everyone is ready, ask them whether you can hear a candle burning. Ask them to sit very quietly and listen, as you light the candle. Sit in silence, for a few moments, and listen as hard as you can. Listen as the candle is blown out and lit again.

Gospel: Mark 7:31-37

Read from the Lectionary or the Children's Lectionary.

3. We respond

What is the Gospel asking of us?

Work in age groups if appropriate. Then come together as a community to end the session.

Young ones

Ask: Could you hear the candle burning? What did you hear? Perhaps it was the wick fizzing when the candle was lit, or tiny creaks the wick makes, or the plop of wax falling, or the pop when the flame goes out. You have to listen hard to hear some things. And if you were in a rush, you might not listen hard enough to hear them. God gives us ears to hear his voice, but we have to listen hard.

Story

Will had a problem. He could hear, very well. But he never learned to talk. Some people don't, you know. They never work out what words mean. Will's mother was very sad. "How will he know how much we love him?" she said. But Will was very clever. Of course he knew his mother loved him!

One day, his mother had to go to the hospital. She was very ill, and Will wasn't allowed to visit her, only to talk on the telephone. Well, how could he tell his mother how much he loved her on a telephone, when he couldn't talk? But he knew how! He made the sound of kisses, plopping on her cheek. He made the sound you make when you get a lovely treat: "Mmmmm!" He made excited noises: "Ooooh! Ooooh! Oooooh!" And he made the noise that says "There, there, soon the pain will go."

Will's mum was so happy. At last she understood. He knew how to hear her love in little sounds that most of us hardly notice.

He was a very good listener indeed.

Juniors

Encourage the children to think about what would be missing, if they couldn't hear. Imagine if you couldn't hear the school bell calling you to lessons, or if you couldn't hear the secret that your friend wanted to tell you, or your mother or father telling you that they love you. But sometimes, even people with very good ears don't hear things properly, because they are not really listening. God gives us the tools we need to find him, but we have to pay attention!

Story

Now, think back: how many times have you seen a kettle boil? I'll bet it's hundreds of times. And I'll bet you know just how a kettle sounds when it boils, too: first it sort of rumbles, then it gurgles harder and harder, and steam comes hissing out of the spout. But have you ever really stopped to listen to the water boil? And have you ever really stopped to try to understand what all those sounds mean?

Here's a true story about one boy, who really did listen to a kettle. I forget his name, but that doesn't matter. He lived a long time ago, before there were machines for doing this and that, before there were cars, even before there were trains.

In those days, people didn't have electric kettles. Well, they wouldn't have been much use, as no one had discovered electricity yet. Instead, people had big old metal kettles that sat on the stove or right in the fire (you've guessed, nobody had central heating, so they kept a warm fire burning). You can still see kettles like that in the shops. On the spout there's a little cap, like a hat, that whistles when the steam starts to hiss. You have to lift that little cap off to pour the water out.

This boy I've told you about thought his mother's kettle was very interesting. He'd sit and listen to the noises it made for hours. Why did it do that? It puzzled him. And while he was listening, he noticed something interesting: if you leave the kettle on the fire even after the water has boiled, the steam gets stronger and stronger, and it can even blow that little cap right off the spout – it can blow it right across the kitchen!

Well, of course, everyone knew all about that, which is why they hurried to take the kettle off the fire when it started to boil. You wouldn't want to have that little hot cap flying all over the place like a bullet breaking things, now would you? But this boy worked out something no one else had ever thought of. He realised what the kettle was saying. It was saying: steam is power! Look, it can move things! And that boy went on to invent machines that used steam; machines that people used to make trains and all sorts of things, and he changed the whole world.

I suppose Jesus listened to God just as carefully as that boy listened to his mother's kettle, and Jesus changed the world even more.

4. Activity

Young ones

Use the template of a boy cupping his hand to his ear. What is he listening to? Draw and colour something special we can hear, like Will.

Juniors

Think of all the ways God speaks to us. Make a poster.

Tips for learning difficulties

Ideas like listening or concentrating are difficult for those with learning difficulties to understand. Help the child to notice first the loud sounds in the room, and then the quieter ones, such as the sound of crayons colouring, or someone's breathing. Focus: listening carefully.

5. We come together

Parents can be invited to join in at this stage.

Focus

The lighted candle, the posters and pictures made in the activities.

Gospel

God says: "I want everyone to hear my message of love. I will help you open your ears. Listen and you will hear me."

Prayer

Dear Lord, help us to hear your voice in everything we do today and every day. We thank you, we praise you for all your love for us. Amen.

Share

Share the work from the activities.

Sing

"Give me joy in my heart, keep me praising."

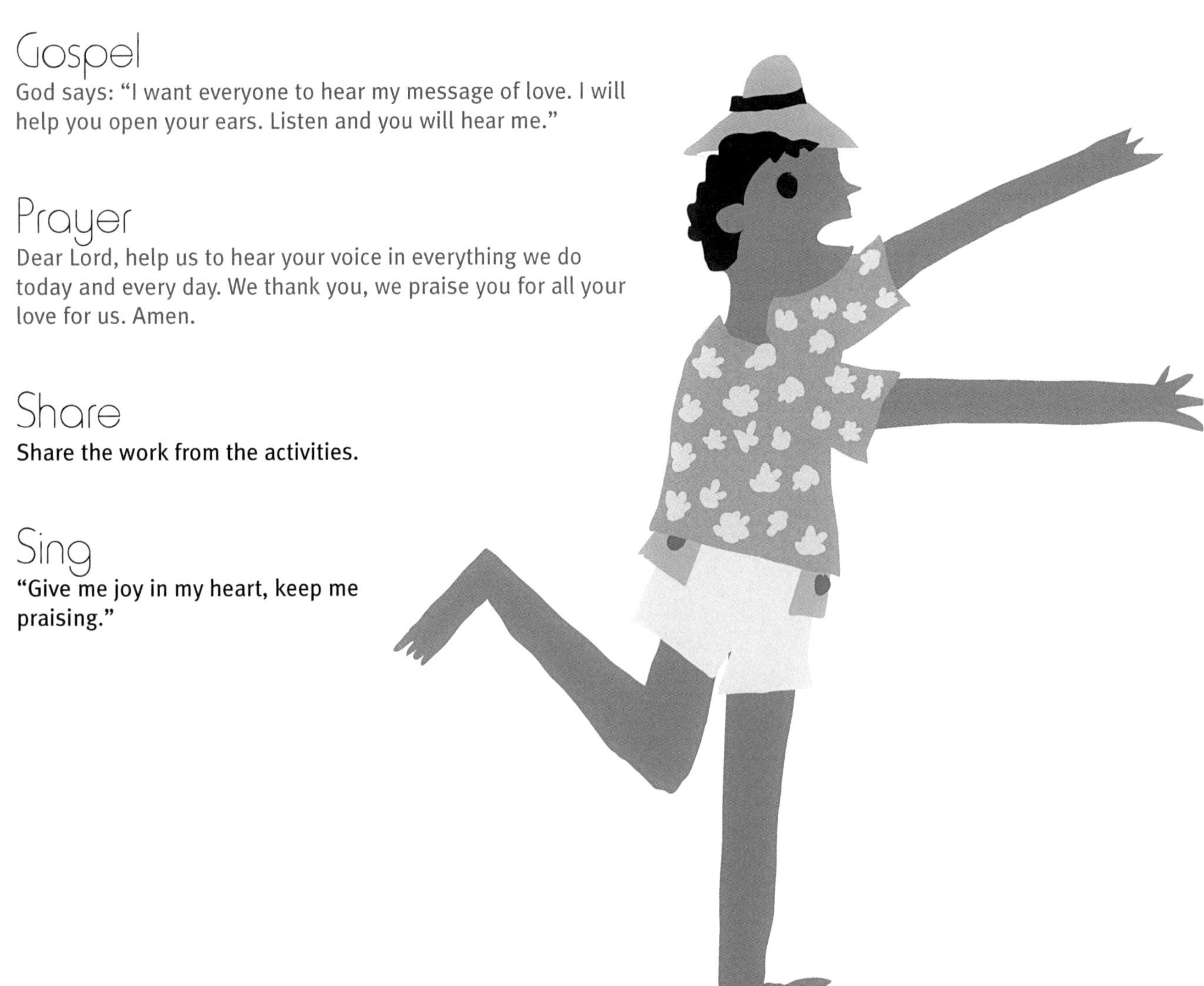

24th Sunday in Ordinary Time

Proper 19

1. Introduction to the theme of the day

"Who do you say I am?"

Aim: To think about the virtue of integrity. Jesus was a man of integrity, but it was not always easy for him.

Leader's Reflection: Jesus was a man of integrity. Integrity is a very particular virtue, but it is difficult to describe in a few words. It means wholeness, completeness, without a flaw, without anything missing. If we say a person has integrity we mean that who they are, what they believe, what they say and what they do are all the same thing. They are trustworthy and reliable and they stand by their word. Like the writing in a stick of rock, their values are written all through them and show up in everything they do.

2. We arrive

We sit in a circle ready to listen to the Gospel.

Focus

A lighted candle, green fabric for ordinary time, big word on a card – INTEGRITY.

Gospel: Mark 8:27-35

Read from the Lectionary or the Children's Lectionary.

3. We respond

What is the Gospel asking of us?

We think about how hard it was, sometimes, for Jesus to be God. Juniors should listen to the story with the young ones today, before starting their own work.

Young ones

Story

Peter was feeling pretty pleased with himself. Ever since he first met Jesus, he had been sure there was something special about him, and now he knew he had been right!

Jesus had asked them a few minutes ago who they thought he was. Everybody had gone very quiet and started mumbling things about Jesus being very nice and very kind, and being their best friend, and their leader and all that sort of thing.

But Peter could see that Jesus was waiting for them to say something extra, something a bit different, so he said it: "I think you are God," he said, and Jesus had turned to him with a solemn look on his face and said that he was right!

Oh yes, Peter was feeling very pleased with himself.

But Jesus was still talking ... what was he saying? "... and when we get to Jerusalem, the soldiers will arrest me, and beat me, and kill me by nailing me to a cross".

Absolutely not! No way José! Not if Peter had anything to do with it they wouldn't! Jesus was his best friend, and he was God. Those soldiers would have to get past Peter and his mates before they so much as laid a finger on Jesus. "I won't let them!" he bellowed angrily at Jesus.

Jesus turned to him sadly, "You are wrong, Peter," he said, "you of all people. You know that I am God but most people don't, and they won't like it very much when I tell them."

"So, don't tell them," muttered Peter crossly.

"Be quiet!" said Jesus very sharply. "I can't stop being God just because people don't like it, or because they beat me up for it, or even kill me. And if you want me to pretend that I am not God, then you are not my friend."

Poor old Peter. Top of the class one minute, and now being sent away in disgrace. Being friends with Jesus was sometimes very confusing. Peter had a lot of thinking to do.

Juniors

Story

Jesus was a man of integrity. Integrity is a virtue, a good thing to have, but it is difficult to describe in a few words. It means being whole or complete, without anything missing. If we say a person has integrity we mean that who they are, what they believe, what they say and what they do are all the same thing. A bit like the writing in a stick of rock, the things they believe are written all through them and show up in everything they do.

Jesus was a man of integrity. He knew who he was: he was God and man. He knew what he believed in; he believed God loved him. And he wanted to share that belief with other people, even if it made him unpopular and the people wanted to kill him. We often think of Jesus as just being good, as if that was easy for him, but there are at least three times in the Gospel when we are told how hard it was for him to choose to be good, to be God, to behave with integrity.

The first was when he spent 40 days in the desert and the devil tempted him to use "being God" to make his life easier. Jesus said that being God was not about having an easy life.

Today we read about the second time when Peter tried to persuade him that being God was too dangerous – he should play safe and try to protect himself so the people would not kill him. Jesus said that "playing safe" was not a thing God does.

The third was in the Garden of Gethsemane when Jesus wanted to run away from being crucified. In the end, Jesus said that being God meant that he loved people like God loved them, and he couldn't run away from them; if that meant he would be crucified, then that must be a part of being God as well.

Behaving with integrity takes a lot of courage, even for Jesus.

4. Activity

Young ones

Peter has made Jesus sad by saying that he should pretend not to be God so that the people will like him more. Help Peter to draw a card, or write a letter to Jesus to say "Sorry".

Juniors

Integrity is a virtue: a good way of behaving which is easily recognisable in the people around us. It is also one of the words we use to describe God. One of his titles in the Old Testament is "The Lord my Integrity".

Can all of the words we use to describe God be used to describe people as well?
Jesus had to find a way of being God – which meant being all the things that God is, whilst still being a man. On the chart on the template page, write down any words which you can use to describe God, and then, in the second column, words which can be used to describe people. Why was it so hard for Jesus to be God and man?

Tips for learning difficulties

Children can use pictures to illustrate God's characteristics – of people doing good things, beautiful scenery, magnificence etc.

5. We come together

Parents can be invited to join in at this stage.

Focus

Gather around the candle and the word.

Gospel

Jesus asked his friends who they thought he was. Peter said, "You are God."

Prayer

Dear Jesus, you are God, and you wanted to behave like God all the time, but sometimes that was very hard. Peter was your friend, and he wanted to behave like your friend all the time, but sometimes that was very hard for him as well. We are your friends, and we want to behave like your friends all the time, but sometimes that is very hard for us too. Help us when we find it hard. Amen.

Share

The children can show the work they have been doing today.

Sing

"Jesus is God"
"Jesus, you are Lord"

What are people like?

25th Sunday in Ordinary Time

Proper 20

1. Introduction to the theme of the day

Aim: It's easy to feel unimportant. It's easy to feel that no one notices you, and no one thinks much of you. We all want to be admired! But God isn't fooled by silly things. God wants us to understand what is important.

Leaders' Reflection: A core message of today's Gospel is that the first shall be last; that those who serve others modestly are the ones who do God's will. Those who seem important in the world may be much less important in God's eyes than people who are more modest.

2. We arrive

We sit in a circle ready to listen to the Gospel.

Focus

Three candles: one very big, one medium, one small.

Gospel: Mark 9:30-37

Read from the Lectionary or Children's Lectionary.

3. We respond

What is the Gospel asking of us?

Work in age groups if appropriate. Then come together as a community at the end of the session.

Young ones

Don't try to be the best, the cleverest, the most important one. All that matters to God is that we love and care for each other.

Story

Once upon a time there were three candles: a big one, a middle-sized one and a little one.

The biggest candle felt very important. He was very fat, and he was sure he was the best candle of all.

The middle-sized candle was very vain. He was so much bigger and better than the smallest candle! And who would want to be as fat as the biggest candle? The middle-sized candle was sure that he was the best.

The smallest candle thought the others were wonderful. They were so big! He was sure that they were the best. He was only a little candle.

One night, a mouse came to the candles, where they lived on the mantelpiece. "Help," said the mouse. "My home is so dark! I can't find my glasses, so I can't see to find the nuts and berries my babies need to eat. We're so hungry! Please, help me find my glasses." All the candles felt sorry for the mouse, and they agreed to help.

The biggest candle said he would be the best for the job, because he was the grandest. But when they got to the mouse's hole, he was too fat to get in. Oh dear! The mouse said: "You could shave off a bit of your wax, and make yourself thinner," but the biggest candle said "NO!" He didn't want to be thin.

The middle-sized candle said he would do it. But when he tried to get into the hole, he was too tall. "You could shave off the bottom of your wax, and make yourself shorter," said the mouse. But the middle-sized candle wouldn't: he didn't want to be short.

The smallest candle said: "I could fit in the hole just as I am." The other two candles laughed! "How could you make enough light?" they said. "Let's try," said the mouse. All the candles lit their flames – and what a surprise! The smallest candle burned just as bright as the others. So he went in and lit the mouse's hole, and she found her glasses.

The two big candles were cross, so they didn't say "well done". But the little candle didn't mind. He was just happy to help the mouse.

Juniors

God wants us to do the best we can in everything. Jesus tells us not to worry about being better or more important than other people. The best thing is to love and care for each other.

Story

Some time ago, there was a very funny cartoon on TV. It was called *Captain Pugwash*. Perhaps you've seen it. It was about pirates who lived on a ship and tried to capture treasure. Pugwash was the captain of the ship, and he thought he was a very fine fellow. His crew were all big and strong except for Tom, the cabin boy, who was only a lad.

Well, Pugwash had an enemy, another pirate called Black Jake, who played tricks on him and attacked his ship and stole his treasure. Poor Pugwash! Black Jake was much cleverer than Pugwash, and much more cunning, so he usually won. He'd capture Pugwash and all his crew and tie them up or lock them in a dungeon. But he didn't always bother to catch Tom – after all, he was only the cabin boy.

However, Tom was the cleverest of them all. Tom loved Pugwash and his crew, and he knew that they needed his help. It was always Tom who found a way to rescue the others. It was always Tom who found the secret passage out of the dungeon. It was always Tom who had the best plans, always Tom who thought of a way to beat Black Jake, and his plans always worked. So Pugwash and his crew always won in the end.

Pugwash and the crew never thanked Tom for saving them. After all, he was only the cabin boy, and they were pirates. But Tom didn't mind. He knew how much they needed him, and he knew he had saved the day. So he just smiled quietly to himself and waited till next time the pirates got into trouble!

4. Activity

Young ones

What can we do to help other people? Think of something you could do to make your friends, or your brother or sister, happy. Think about the little things (smiling) as well as the big things. Use the template to show the ways we can show God's love to other people.

Juniors

Think about times when we've tried to win, to be the best, to be the leader. Being important makes you feel big! But it doesn't always make other people feel good. Think about times when we've just wanted to help, wanted to make someone else feel special. How different that feels! Make a poster to show how or write on the template.

Tips for learning difficulties

Today's Gospel is particularly good for children with learning difficulties, who often feel (and are treated by others as) less than everyone else. Focus: whoever feels lowly is high in God's love.

5. We come together

Parents can be invited to join in at this stage.

Focus

The three candles and the products of the activities.

Gospel

Jesus says: "The smallest child is just as important as me! If you love me, you will look after everyone. Don't worry about being big and important. All that really matters is that you love and care for everyone."

Prayer

Lord Jesus, help us to see when we can serve and help others. Fill us with your spirit of love. Amen.

Share

Share the work from the activities.

Sing

"Here I am, Lord"

THIS IS HOW I CAN SHOW GOD'S LOVE

26th Sunday in Ordinary Time

Proper 21

1. Introduction to the theme of the day

Aim: Today we focus on asking: "Who are God's people? Who can the spirit of God work through?"

Leader's Reflection: The first reading and the Gospel for today ask us to accept and honour people who live as Jesus wants us to live even if they are not "one of us". Anyone who is not against us is for us: the spirit of God can work through anyone. God calls us to be humble, and not to seek to be more important than other people. We are called to serve others. Christians must recognise God in everyone, and not just in other Christians.

2. We arrive

We sit in a circle ready to listen to the Gospel.

Today we focus on readings that remind us that all people, even those who don't share our faith, can be part of God's harvest. The spirit of God may work in anyone.

Focus

Light a candle. Put a Bible next to it, the Qur'an, meditations by the Dalai Lama, and so on.

Gospel: Mark 9:38-43. 45. 47-48

Read from the Lectionary or Children's Lectionary.

3. We respond

What is the Gospel asking of us?

Work together in age groups if appropriate.

Then come together as a community at the end of the session.

Young ones

Where can we look for God? God can be everywhere. You can see God working in all sorts of people: whenever someone is good and kind and loving, there's a little bit of God working in them. God wants us to see him in those good people, and he wants us to show him to other people, by being good and kind and loving ourselves, too.

Story

There was a little duck called Jennifer. One day some boys caught her in a sack, and took her a long way away from her pond and her friends and family. She pecked and pecked at the sack, and finally she escaped and ran away into the dark.

Oh, she was sad and frightened. She didn't know which way to go, to find her home. She couldn't fly, because her wing was broken. She waddled along, and she said, "Please, God, help me find my way home."

By and by a sparrow found her. "What's the matter?" he asked. Jennifer told him everything. "Oh, I can help you," said the sparrow. "I can fly up high and see where your pond is." And he did just that, so Jennifer knew which way to go.

She walked towards her pond. But oh! She was tired! She wished God would come and help her get home quickly.

By and by a goat came along. "What's the matter?" he asked. Jennifer told him everything. "Oh, I can help you," said the goat. "You can sit on my horns and I can carry you home." And he did just that.

Jennifer was SO pleased to be home. But she was cross that God hadn't helped her. "You silly duck!" said her mother. "Every time you asked God for help, you got just what you needed. Don't you think God was working through that kind little sparrow, and that generous goat?" "Oh!" said Jennifer. And from that day on, she did her best to help other creatures, so that God would work through her, too.

Juniors

God's spirit is all around us in the world. We can see it in many of the people we meet. God wants us to notice his spirit in other people, and be glad. How can we recognise God's spirit working in someone else? And how can we help God's spirit work in us? What can we do, to bring God's spirit into the world?

Story

Now, this is a true story. It's about a man whose name was Roy. Roy wasn't a Christian, and he didn't believe in God. But that didn't mean that God didn't believe in him. It didn't mean that God could not work through him.

One day, Roy was going to a job interview. He really needed that job, because he had four children to look after, and he had no money. He was wearing his very best suit, which was made of wool and was very expensive. He was hurrying along, over the bridge, on his way to the interview when he heard someone shouting. There was someone in the river underneath the bridge – a young boy. That boy was drowning!

Roy jumped straight into the river, in his best suit, and he rescued the boy. Of course, he missed his interview and he didn't get the job. His suit was ruined – it shrank so much he had to throw it away.

Roy didn't tell anyone what he had done, or why he was so wet. But the boy whose life he saved told the newspapers about the "mystery stranger" who had saved his life.

Now, I think God was working very strongly in Roy that day, whatever he thought. He did exactly what Jesus would have wanted, even though that cost him a lot. If only we were all so good, so Godly!

4. Activity

Young ones

Use the template, which shows a rich man holding a basket out to a poor person. What could you put in the basket? Draw in some good things the poor person might need: the fruits of a harvest we can share with others. Colour in the people's clothes! When we do good, and when we are glad, we are God's harvest.

Juniors

God wants us to recognise his spirit wherever it works in the world, and whoever it works through. He wants us to rejoice in everyone who shows his spirit in the world. How can we recognise the spirit of God in someone we meet? God wants his spirit to work through us, too. How can we help the spirit of God to shine through our lives? How can we add to God's harvest of good things? Make a poster to show how.

Tips for learning difficulties

Focus on the contrast between the good, which comes from God, and the bad, which does not. Help the child to identify simple contrasts relevant to the readings: being helpful to others versus doing hurtful things; giving the good gifts of the harvest versus giving useless things; and so on.

5. We come together

Parents can be invited to join in at this stage. Tell the children that next week we will be talking about sharing with each other. Ask them to bring an item of fruit with them to share next week.

Focus:

The lighted candle. The fruits of our activities – the harvest of our thoughts.

Gospel

God says: "Don't think I speak only to you, or only work through people who are important in your church. I speak to you, but I work through many more people than that too!" God wants us to recognise his spirit, wherever we find it. He wants us to look out for him everywhere, and to rejoice in everyone who loves and looks after other people. He wants us to live good lives so that other people can see his spirit in us.

Prayer

Lord God, help us to see you, wherever you are in the world. Help us to give thanks for every good person. Help us to be good people, too. Help us to shine with your love, so that other people can see you in us. Amen.

Share

Share the products of our activities.

Sing

"Make me a channel of your peace."

27th Sunday in Ordinary Time

Proper 22

1. Introduction to the theme of the day

"The kingdom of God belongs to the children"

Aim: Jesus loved children. As children we have responsibilities towards each other, to share with each other and to care for each other. This is our world, and Jesus wants us to make it a better place.

Leader's Reflection: Oscar Romero wrote that teachers were "Prophets of a future not their own". Jesus loved children because they were open and ready to change. We need to prepare our young people to take their adult places in a constantly changing world, but we also need to encourage them to participate in that world now.

2. We arrive

We sit in a circle ready to listen to the Gospel.

Focus

A lighted candle and a basket of produce (ideally brought by the children – see share activity below); green fabric for ordinary time.

Gospel: Mark 10:2-16

Read from the Lectionary or Children's Lectionary.

3. We respond

What is the Gospel asking of us?

Work in age groups if appropriate. Alternatively, choose the discussion ideas and story most suitable for your group.

Young ones

Discussion: Jesus loves children. How does he show that he loves them? Who else loves children? How do they show it?

Story

Daphne was very flustered. The ducklings were playing up, and she was finding it difficult to get everything done. When she tried collecting worms for their tea, they sploshed about in the mud getting dirty. When she took them to the river with the washing, they splished and splashed until they were totally soaked, and then just when she had finished sweeping out the nest, they all came tramping back in with bits of twigs and leaves, making a mess again. Ducklings!

Daphne was just about to get cross and quack very loudly at them all, when she noticed something. There should be three ducklings, David, Dickie and Debbie. David and Debbie were standing in front of her looking very untidy and ashamed of themselves, but where was Dickie? David and Debbie did not know. "He was with us down by the river; we must have lost him on the way back."

Daphne was very worried. Dickie down by the river? He could not swim! She grabbed the other two ducklings, and hurried off down to the river.

When they got to the river, Dickie was nowhere to be seen. They could see his footprints on the muddy bank, but right at the edge they suddenly stopped.

"He must have fallen in!" wailed Daphne. The other two ducklings were getting really worried now. They looked everywhere but could find no other sign of Dickie.

"Oh dear!" they wept. "Oh dear!" wept Daphne.

Just then they heard a happy little quacking sound. There was a little duck swimming down the middle of the river. It was Dickie! "Look at me!" he called. "I've learned to swim."

Daphne was overjoyed to see him. "Ducklings might be a nuisance or a worry some of the time, but I love them so much, I don't ever want to lose one of them again. Thank you, God, for keeping my duckling safe."

Juniors

Children are more highly valued in some parts of the world than in others. In China, parents are only allowed to have one baby, so that one baby is very important to them. In other parts of the world families are bigger because children are needed to work. Sometimes children may be neglected because their parents cannot afford to look after them properly. But God loves all children.

Talk about our own society. Are children valued here? Is there a change from the past? What is good about the way we treat children? What could be better?

Story

It is a Catholic tradition that the month of October, in particular, is devoted to praying the rosary. When your parents were children, the rosary was a very common prayer, but it is said less frequently now. In it we join with Mary in remembering Jesus' childhood and his death and resurrection.

Where did the rosary come from? The rosary is the prayer of the worker, and in a way it comes from the Bible, from the book of Psalms. There are 150 psalms altogether, and since the early days of the Church, people have used them as prayers. We say one each Sunday at Mass. Monks and nuns had plenty of time for praying, and so they said all 150 psalms every day! Ordinary people working in the fields did not have so much time, but wanted to join in the prayers anyway, so each day they would collect 150 small pebbles and carry them in their pocket. When the church bells rang for prayer, they would take a pebble out, genuflect, and say a short prayer – usually the beginning of the Our Father or Hail Mary. Collecting 150 stones every day became a bit tedious, so people began to use ropes with knots instead – 150 knots, one for each psalm.

Eventually all these Our Fathers and Hail Marys were organised into groups called decades – one Our Father and ten Hail Marys followed by one Glory be. St Dominic was a saint who liked to pray the rosary, and he encouraged people to think about Jesus' life whilst they were doing it. Five decades to think about his childhood, five to think about his passion, and five to think about his resurrection and glory with God. Not long before his death, Pope John Paul II made five new decades, to think about Jesus' adult life and ministry. They are called the mysteries of light.

It is a good way to pray for the children of other countries who are working in the fields, because that is where it started hundreds of years ago.

4. Activity

Young ones and Juniors

This week's activity can be shared by all the children. There are suggestions as to how it might be developed further for older children.

Find pictures of children from developing countries (Cafod/Christian Aid/Traidcraft calendars or websites are usually good for these).

Talk about the harvest collected by children in other countries. Talk about how we help people in need.

Ask the children to colour in the template of the harvest basket, then "fill" it with produce using drawings or cut-outs, or sticking on rice or pulses.

Older children could fill it with produce from one specific country, e.g. India (tea, rice, spices, cotton); Brazil (coffee, chocolate, sugar, tropical fruits); England (apples, barley, carrots, potatoes) – a children's encyclopaedia or atlas should give sufficient information.

Tips for learning difficulties

Use a real basket and bring a selection of foods grown in different countries. Talk about the products. Use a globe or world map to help the discussion.

5. We come together

Parents can be invited to join in at this stage.

Focus

Gather around the candle and basket.

Gospel

Jesus was tired, and was sitting down by a well. Some people saw him and brought their children to see him. Jesus' friends tried to send the children away because they were making too much noise, but Jesus said, "Let the little children come to me; do not stop them." And he put his arms around them and blessed them.

Prayer

Jesus, we know that you loved children in a special way. Bless all of us, and bless all the children in the world. Bless the harvest and help us share fairly with people who are poor and hungry. Amen.

Share

Each child can select something from the produce basket which was filled as the children came in, and give it to another child.

Sing

"All things bright and beautiful"

28th Sunday in Ordinary Time

Proper 23

1. Introduction to the theme of the day

> "It is easier for a camel to pass through the eye of a needle than for a rich man to enter the kingdom of God"

Aim: There is nothing wrong with being rich except that it makes us think we can manage on our own. Jesus tells us today that it is better to trust God than to be rich.

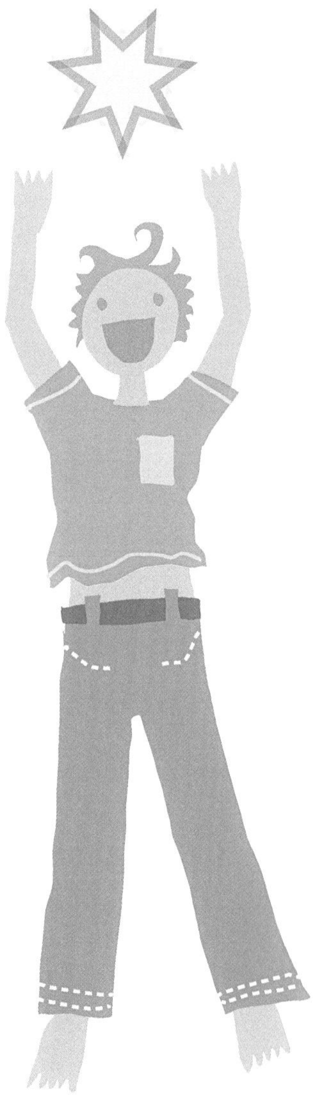

Leader's Reflection: The only way to be with God is by recognising our need for him. If we know that we need God, then we have already found him. If we surround ourselves with luxury and security, if we become totally self-dependent, it is very difficult to recognise that we need God, in this life as well as the next.

2. We arrive

We sit in a circle ready to listen to the Gospel.

Focus

A lighted candle, green fabric for ordinary time, a pile of coins (this might be the "collection money" of the adults present).

Gospel: Mark 10:17-30

Read from the Lectionary or the Children's Lectionary.

3. We respond

What is the Gospel asking of us?

Work in age groups if appropriate.

Young ones

Sometimes we care more about the things we have, than our friends. Can you think of any toys you like to play with on your own instead of with other children? Jesus tells us that our belongings are not so important as other people or God.

Story

Brian the badger was in a grumpy mood again. Nobody had been to see him for three whole days. "I don't care," he muttered. "I don't need friends, I've got my ball to play with." And he got out his ball, and began to play with it.

Just then, Michael the mole stuck his head out of the ground, "Hello Brian, can I play with you?" he called. Brian looked at Michael, then he looked at the ball. "I'm playing with my ball," growled Brian. "I don't need to play with you." And he wandered off pushing the ball in front of him. Michael was very sad.

Brian pushed the ball down to the river. Daphne was splashing around in the middle of it with her three ducklings. "Come and watch us," called Daphne. "We are having great fun!" Brian looked at Daphne, then he looked at the ball. "I'm having fun with my ball," grunted Brian, "I don't need to have fun with you." And he wandered off pushing the ball in front of him. Daphne was very sad.

Camilla the cow was eating her lunch when Brian arrived in her field. "Come and have lunch!" she called to him. Brian looked at Camilla, then he looked at the ball. A ball was good for playing with, but you couldn't eat it; and Camilla's lunch did look very tasty and it would be very nice to have a little chat with Camilla while they ate. Brian cheered up a bit. Maybe a friend was better than a ball after all, "Thank you, God, for all my friends," he muttered gruffly and sat down for lunch.

Juniors

Suggestion – build the camel (activity) before having this discussion.

Jesus doesn't tell us that it is difficult for rich people to enter the kingdom of heaven; he tells us that it is almost impossible. This is not because riches are bad, but because they make us feel safe, so we do not think we need God any more. We all have some riches. How do they make us secure? In what ways do we still need God?

Story

St Edward the Confessor was King of England in the eleventh century, and died in 1066, just before William the Conqueror invaded England.

In many ways St Edward was a very strange king. He was born in 1003 into an interesting family. King Edmund Ironside and King Hardicanute (son of King Canute, who tried to stop the tide from coming in) were his half-brothers. Edward was sent to France when he was ten because the Danes had invaded England. Whilst he was there he became very religious and prayerful, going to church whenever he could, and singing in the church choir.

In England King Canute died and there were a lot of squabbles over who should be the next king. In the end, it fell to Hardicanute, and it was not until his death in 1042 that Edward became king himself. Edward's reign was one of almost unbroken peace. He sorted out some of the big arguments in his kingdom without battles or wars, but through diplomacy. During the reign of the Danes when he was a child, the people of England had been made to pay very high taxes. Edward abolished this system, and gave many of his own riches to the poor as well. A court biographer wrote about him: "How great is the influence of a king who is truly father of his people. He is remarkable for his generosity to the poor, and never happier than when giving alms."

Edward had made a promise to God that he would make a pilgrimage to St Peter's tomb in Rome during his lifetime. Once he was king, however, he did not want to leave England for fear that the troubles might start again, so instead he built a new Minster (church) for London. This was not in the city itself, but just outside, to the west. That is why the church is called Westminster. Since that time, all the kings and queens of England have been crowned there.

For discussion: Edward was a rich man. How did he use his money? How did he show he still needed God by what he did? Did his money separate him from God?

4. Activity

Young ones

With a ball, ask the children to suggest games they could play on their own, then ask for games which they could play together. Which are better? Choose a game to play together. Or use the template of the treasure pile and colour, cut and share it out.

Juniors

A camel is one metre high and two to three metres long, sitting down. Use the furniture and people in the room to build a camel. Somebody can stand at the front to be the head. Camels are very fierce and often try to bite people that walk too close to them.

How big would a needle have to be for the camel to walk through?

If you have time, you can make one using rolls of newspaper and sellotape or staples.

Tips for learning difficulties

Have ready a selection of games and decide together which are good for sharing.

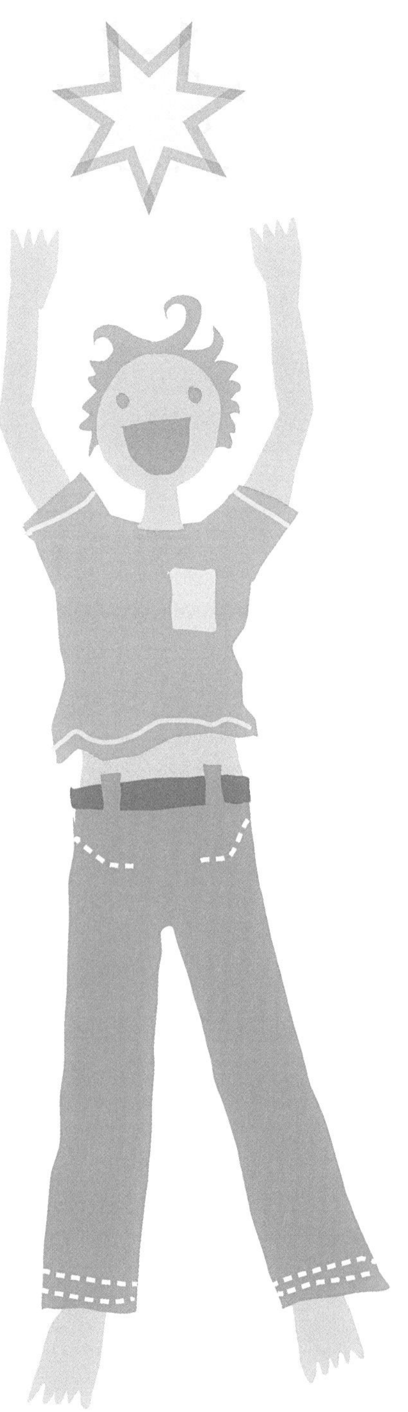

5. We come together

Parents can be invited to join in at this stage.

Focus

Gather around the candle.

Gospel

A rich young man asked Jesus, "What must I do to live with God for ever in heaven?" Jesus said, "You must sell everything, give the money to the poor, and then come with me." The man was very sad, "That is too difficult," he said, "I cannot do that." Jesus was sad too, because he liked the man. "You are right," he said. "It is easier for a camel to pass through the eye of a needle than for a rich man to enter the kingdom of God."

Prayer

Jesus, thank you for all the riches you have given us, our toys, our homes, our food, our pocket money. Help us to share these things with each other, and to remember that without you we would have nothing at all. Amen.

Share

Distribute the pile of coins amongst the children present. Either have a collection around the group, or let the children put it in the collection plate in the church.

Sing

"All that I am"

29th Sunday in Ordinary Time

Proper 24

1. Introduction to the theme of the day

"Serving other people is a sign of greatness"

Aim: Jesus tells us that if we can respect the greatness of other people, then we will become great ourselves.

Leader's Reflection: When we look at our greatest leaders, we find that their leadership is always focused on something beyond themselves – e.g. Gandhi, Martin Luther King. We quickly recognise as a sign of weakness the tendency of prominent people to put themselves first, or to focus on their own successes. Jesus goes further than this. He tells us that the truly great are so aware of the greatness and dignity of every person other than themselves, that all they want to do is to serve them.

2. We arrive

We sit in a circle ready to listen to the Gospel.

Focus

A lighted candle, green fabric for ordinary time.
Large cards with the words, "We're great!"

Gospel: Mark 10:35-45

Read from the Lectionary or the Children's Lectionary.

3. We respond

What is the Gospel asking of us?

Work in age groups if appropriate.

Young ones

What does "great" mean? Who do you see on the television that is great? How do you know they are great? Do you know any great people yourself? How do you know they are great?
The greatest person that any of us knows is Jesus.

Story

The animals were having a competition. They wanted to find out who was the greatest of them all. Each animal was given a slip of paper, and had to write down who they thought was the greatest, and why. Then the papers were collected in and sorted out, and the winner was announced. Who do you think it was?

Was it Owen the owl? He was certainly the cleverest and wisest animal in the meadow, and everybody respected him a lot.
Or was it Henry the honey bee? Everybody liked Henry, he was always cheerful, and could sort out everybody's arguments. That was very important.
Maybe it was Camilla the cow. She was the strongest of all the animals. She could carry all of them on her back at the same time.
Or could it be Daphne the duck? Everybody was very impressed by the way she kept all those ducklings in order, and she did have the loudest quack of anybody!

But no, it was none of those animals. Do you want to know who they chose? It was poor little Wendy the worm! Why do you think that was? It was because all the other animals were great and important and impressive during the daytime, but Wendy was a glow-worm, and only Wendy could give them light during the night-time. That made her the greatest of them all.

Who would you choose?

Juniors

Sometimes we use the word "great" to mean that we like somebody a lot, but a dictionary tells us that the word really means "important, high up, distinguished, grand". This is what Jesus meant when he used the word "great".
What do you think makes a person great in this way? How do we know they are great?
A great person might expect other people to serve them, but Jesus said that a person who is prepared to serve others is the greatest of all, because they recognise that other people are great too.
God has created them, and God is in them, and who could be greater than God?

Story

St John de Brébeuf (feast day 19 October) was born in 1593 in Normandy, France. From an early age he wanted to be a priest. He joined the Jesuits and was sent to Canada to work as a missionary amongst the Huron people. The society which he left behind regarded the native Americans as savages, less than human, but John taught that they were brothers and sisters with us in the sight of God. He said that it was his privilege to serve them and bring the word of God to them.

These are some of the instructions he gave to the other missionaries:

- You must love these Hurons as Jesus does, as brothers and sisters.
- You must never keep them waiting at the time of embarking.
- Carry a tinder-box or a piece of burning-glass, or both, to make fire for them during the day for smoking, and in the evening when it is necessary to camp; these little services win their hearts.
- Try to eat the little food they offer you, and eat all you can, for you may not eat again for hours.
- Eat as soon as day breaks, for native Americans, when on the road, eat only at the rising and the setting of the sun.
- Be prompt in embarking and disembarking and do not carry any water or sand into the canoe.
- Do not ask many questions; silence is golden.
- Always carry something during the portages.
- Do not begin to paddle unless you intend always to paddle.
- Always show any other native Americans you meet on the way a cheerful face and show that you readily accept the fatigues of the journey.

St John was martyred in Canada by another tribe of native Americans – the Iroquois – in 1649.

4. Activity

Young ones

Colour in the paper doll to look like someone you know. Colour in the clothes and the crown to make them look very grand and important, then dress the doll in them (use Blu-tack to attach them).

Juniors

Using magazines, cut out two sets of pictures. The first set should be of people that our society thinks are great; the second should be of people that show they are great by serving other people. Cut out the faces and make a collage of them all. Now look carefully at the faces of the people in the two groups. Which group looks happier and more involved in what they are doing? Why do you think that is?

Tips for learning difficulties

Have the clothes etc. ready cut out, or you could use a proper doll and dress it in grand clothes.

5. We come together

Parents can be invited to join in at this stage.

Focus

Gather around the candle and the work from the activities.

Gospel

James and John were Jesus' friends. One day they asked him if they could sit next to him in heaven when they got there. Jesus said, "I am saving those places for my greatest friends. If you want to be great, then you must serve each other and you must serve other people."

Prayer

Jesus, you are our great God, far greater than any of us, but you died on the cross for us because you thought we were worth it. Help us to see that the people around us are great too and worth serving like you did. Amen.

Share

Share the work of the session, praying for each "great" person in turn.

Sing

"How great is our God"
"O Lord my God"

30th Sunday in Ordinary Time

Proper 25

1. Introduction to the theme of the day

> "What do you want me to do for you?"

Aim: When we are having difficulties, God will help us to see the way forward again, if we ask him.

Leader's Reflection: What must it be like to suddenly see again after having been blind for years? It is difficult to imagine physical blindness, or the impact of sudden sight, but there are other "revelations" in our lives which we have experienced. Suddenly being able to read, ride a bike, solve that maths problem, work the video recorder, understand another person's point of view. God is revealed to us as we grow and develop in every way.

2. We arrive

We sit in a circle ready to listen to the Gospel.

Focus

A lighted candle, green fabric for ordinary time.
A card with a big eye (see template).

Gospel: Mark 10:46-52

Read from the Lectionary or Children's Lectionary.

3. We respond

What is the Gospel asking of us?

Work in age groups if appropriate.

Young ones

What do you think it is like to be blind? Shut your eyes for a few moments. Are there other people in the room? How can you tell? Feel around until you touch someone. Without opening your eyes, can you can work out who it is? The man in today's Gospel could not see at all, even if he opened his eyes. Sometimes at night we cannot see anything. This is what happened to Henry.

Story

Whoah! Henry the honey bee woke up suddenly. He could not see a thing. It was pitch black. All the lights in the hive had gone out. What had happened?

Henry got up very carefully. Feeling his way across the room, he found the door and opened it. The corridor outside was totally black. Henry could see nothing. He guessed that one of the light switches must have broken and decided to go and check. But which way to go? Henry knew that the switches were near the main entrance to the hive, past the nursery where all the baby bees slept, through the honey store, and then down to the main entrance.

Which way to the nursery? That was easy. Henry could hear the wailing of the baby bees just up the corridor. Keeping one hand on the wall, he fumbled his way up towards them. The wailing got louder and louder until, suddenly, there was a gap in the wall and the wailing got very loud. Where do you think Henry was?

Next stop was the honey store. Henry thought for a while and then sniffed. Sniff, sniff. What was he doing? Sniffing all the way, Henry went up one corridor and down another and then, very carefully, down a ramp. He didn't need to sniff any more; Henry knew where he was. Feeling his way along the sticky shelves, Henry managed to find the doorway out of the honey store. He gave his sticky feet a quick lick, then thought again.

How to get to the main entrance? Right down in the distance, Henry could see a faint light. Keeping his eye fixed on it, he inched his way forward. The light got brighter and brighter. It was the moon outside the hive. Somebody had left the main door open, so the moonlight could get in. Henry moved faster as the light got brighter. He was right! One of the light switches was broken. Henry fixed it quickly and switched it back on. The whole hive was lit up again. How wonderful!

Henry said a little prayer. "Thank you, God, that I can see again!"

Juniors

Today's Gospel tells us about a man who was blind; he could not see things with his eyes. Sometimes we use the word "see" to mean "understand" – "I can't see how to do that", "I can't see your point of view". When Jesus cured people of blindness, he was showing us that he can help us when we can't "see" or understand things with our minds as well as with our eyes.

Story

St Jude was a cousin of Jesus. His mother (also called Mary) was a cousin of Jesus' mother, Mary. His father, Cleophas, was the brother of St Joseph. Before Jesus called him to be an apostle, Jude was either a fisherman or a farmer.

After he became an apostle, Jude is hardly mentioned again in the Gospels, except in places where all twelve apostles are listed, and at the Last Supper when he asked Jesus, "Lord, why have you only shown yourself to us and not to the whole world?"

There is another story about him. King Abagar of Edessa wanted Jesus to cure him of leprosy. He could not travel, but he knew he only had to see Jesus to be cured, so he sent an artist to draw Jesus' face. Jesus was so impressed by King Abagar's faith that he pressed his face into a cloth and gave it to Jude to take to Abagar. The king was cured and became a Christian. In pictures, Jude is often shown carrying the cloth of Jesus' face.

After Pentecost, Jude travelled throughout Mesopotamia, converting many people. There is a letter written by him in the Bible. He is writing to the people of an Eastern Church, encouraging them to stay as Christians despite their difficulties. It is because of this letter that he is the patron saint of lost causes – when we find things difficult to understand, we can rely on St Jude to pray with us and ask God to help us.

4. Activity

Young ones

Ask the children to shut their eyes. Read through the story again, and let them act it out. Adults can help with the wailing; a spoonful of honey heated over a candle releases a wonderful aroma. Use the template of the eye. Draw in its vision something that Jesus wants you to help with.

Juniors

How many phrases can you think of which use the word "see" to mean something other than seeing with our eyes? Choose one, and design a poster which shows how Jesus can help us to see in that way as well.

Tips for learning difficulties

This activity is suitable if you have a visually impaired child in the group.
Using words, but without referring to anything which is sight dependent (e.g. colour), the children are to describe and identify various objects in the room.

5. We come together

Parents can be invited to join in at this stage.

Focus

Gather around the candle. Sit young ones separately from their parents (ref. share activity).

Gospel

Jesus was walking through a crowd with his friends in Jericho, when he heard a voice calling, "Jesus, have pity on me!" Jesus asked, "Who is that? Bring him to me!" So the crowds pushed the man forward. "Why are you calling to me?" asked Jesus. "What do you want?"
The man turned his face to Jesus. He was blind. "Master, I want to see again," he said. "Your faith has saved you," said Jesus, and suddenly the man was cured. He followed Jesus around all the rest of the day.

Prayer

Today we have two prayers. The young ones will pray the thanking prayer, and the juniors will pray the asking prayer. But we join in the Amen of both prayers.

Young ones

Jesus, thank you for all your gifts. Thank you especially that we can see the world around us, and all the people that we love. Amen.

Juniors

Jesus, sometimes things get very difficult and we cannot see what we should do. Help us to remember that you are with us at these times. Help us to get over our difficulties and to see things clearly again. Amen.

Share

Young ones – with their eyes shut again, can feel their way round the circle until they find their parents.
Juniors can share their posters.

Sing

"I watch the sunrise"

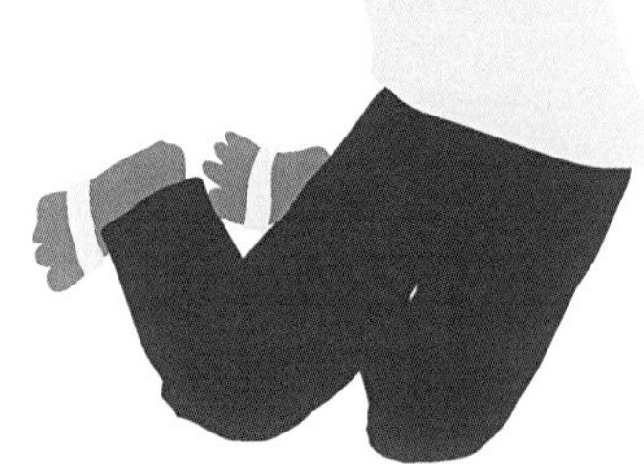

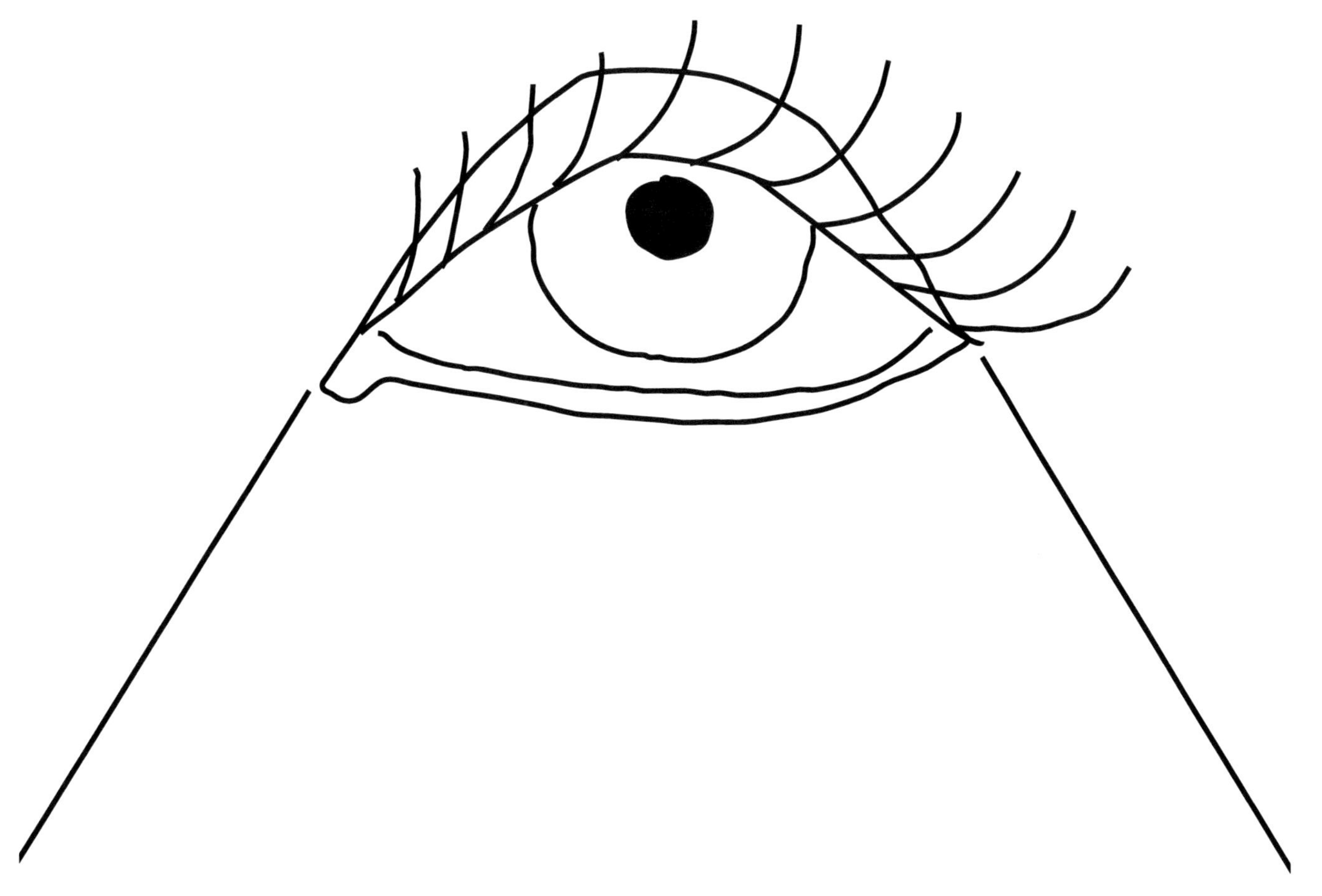

31st Sunday in Ordinary Time

The 4th Sunday before Advent

1. Introduction to the theme of the day

"The great commandments"

Aim: To remind the children of the greatest commandments upon which all others depend.

Leader's Reflection: It is very important for children to have boundaries and to be aware of the need for rules for living. However, rules on their own are not enough to ensure good order and a general sense of happiness. It is important that rules are underpinned by a sense of mutual respect and, for Christians, love.

When life seems complicated it is good to go back to something simple upon which the rest can be built. To ask oneself: "is this action loving towards God or my neighbour?" gives a straightforward way of judging whether an action or a word is good or not. Whatever the situation, the simple question of whether this is of love or otherwise is a sure guide for the way we should act or speak.

2. We arrive

We sit in a circle ready to listen to the Gospel.
Has anyone anything they would like to tell us about last week's Family Sheet?

Focus

Green cloth, Bible open at today's Gospel, flowers.

Gospel: Mark 12:28-34

Read from the Lectionary or Children's Lectionary.

3. We respond

What is the Gospel asking of us?

Today's story can be used with the whole group – or by each group separately. Use the activity ideas that best suit your group.

Young ones and Juniors

How can we show we love God? How can we show we love the people around us? Here is a story that will help us to think about that.

It was Sunday morning and the autumn sun was shining. Tom and Amy were excited as they were going to the country park. They hoped that they would be able to collect acorns and conkers and it was a perfect day.

They went downstairs and found Dad putting out all the bits for the picnic.
"Shall I do the soup, Dad?" Oliver asked.
"It's a bit early for that – it will get cold. Remember we have something else to do first. You can heat the soup when we get back."
(Get back from where? What does the family have to do first? How is that loving?)

When Amy had told Fr Stephen about their walk after church, he had been really interested and said he'd like to hear about it next time. Amy promised to bring him some conkers!
(Amy has done a few loving things here – what are they – and who was she loving?)

When the family got home from church, everyone mucked in and got the picnic ready.
(How is this loving? What things might the family be doing?)

When Amy mentioned that Fr Stephen had been interested in their visit, Dad wondered if he might like to join them – he knew Fr Stephen was a keen walker. Mum went to phone and Fr Stephen said he'd love to come but would need to bring the hospital bleep and might need a lift to the hospital if it went off. Mum said that was fine.
(What loving things are happening here? What might the family need to do to include Fr Stephen?)

There were quite a few people enjoying the sunshine. The country park had woods and a large lake and lots of interesting walks. The trees were beautiful with autumn colour and the blue sky reflected in the lake. Ducks and swans were swimming on the lake and they could hear birds still singing in the trees. Fr Stephen paused and smiled. "Isn't God's creation wonderful?" he said.
(What is loving here? Who is being loved?)

The family and Fr Stephen had found a picnic table in the sunshine and enjoyed their soup. They were just about to go into the woods to collect acorns and conkers when the hospital bleep went off. Fr Stephen phoned the hospital on his mobile and said he would have to go. Mum said she would give him a lift and would wait to give him a lift home afterwards. She would meet the family in the car park at 5 o'clock but Dad said not to worry, if she wasn't there they would get the bus back. Dad also said they would keep the person in their prayers.
(What is loving about what everyone is doing in this part of the story?)

Dad got a call on his mobile a couple of hours later to say Mum and Fr Stephen were on their way back. The family of the person in hospital had been really grateful to see him and the person was very peaceful after his visit. Fr Stephen was glad he had gone and had thanked the children's Mum for going with him. She'd made him have a cup of tea before they left the hospital.
(How is love being expressed here?)

They dropped Fr Stephen back at his house and went home to tuck into the piping hot casserole that Mum had put in the oven before they left.
Everything was checked for Monday morning and Oliver and Amy got ready for bed.
They came together for their bedtime cuddle and prayers and looked back on a lovely loving day.
(What might they have prayed – and where is the love?)

4. Activity

Young ones

Ask the children to think of something from the story where the family and Fr Stephen had shown love for God and for others – perhaps remind them of some of the things that happened. Invite them to colour in the bubble-writing "Love God! Love one another!" and then to draw their favourite bit of the story.

Juniors

Use the template. It might be helpful to have several print-outs of the story for the children to refer to. Invite the children to think about the story and decide which bits were loving God and which loving others. They can either write or draw each incident.

Help them to see that quite often they will overlap.

Tips for learning difficulties

This is quite a long story. For children with limited attention span it might be helpful for them to record their thoughts as they go along rather than at the end.

5. We come together

Parents can be invited to join in at this stage.

Focus

Light the candle. Invite those gathered to become still.

Gospel

In the Gospel, Jesus reminds the people around him of two great commandments in the Old Testament. The scribe is doing what many Jews like to do – talking about their faith and trying to understand it better. He is very pleased when Jesus quotes from the Book of Deuteronomy – one of the oldest books in the Bible.

"You will love the Lord, your God, with all your heart, with all your soul, with all your mind and with all your strength and love your neighbour as yourself."

Jesus sees that the scribe is beginning to understand what the kingdom of God is about.

Prayer

Lord Jesus, you give us two simple rules for living –
to love God and to love each other.
Help us to be faithful to these commandments
and build your kingdom of love. Amen.

Share

We listened to a story about a family and their parish priest and how they spent an autumn Sunday. We thought about how the ordinary things they did showed how love works. Here are a few of the things the children thought ...

Invite the children to share a few of their words and pictures.

"Lord of all hopefulness"
"A new commandment I give unto you"
"Brother, sister, let me serve you"

LOVE GOD

LOVE ONE ANOTHER

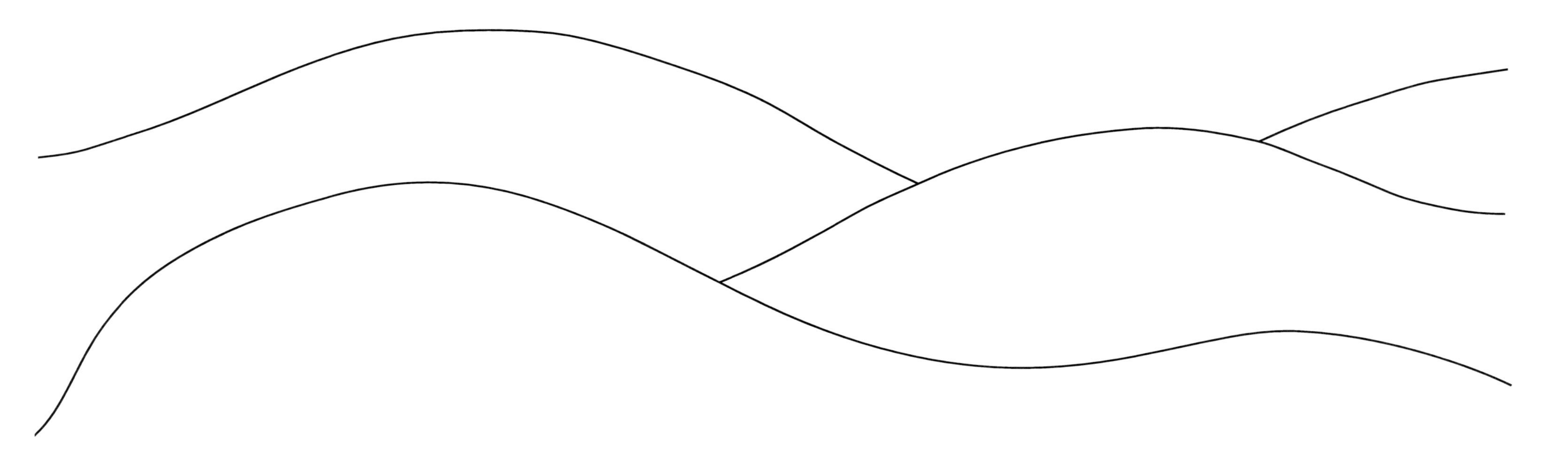

32nd Sunday in Ordinary Time

The 3rd Sunday before Advent

1. Introduction to the theme of the day

"The widow's penny"

Aim: To help the children to see that a small contribution can make a very big difference.

Leader's Reflection: We are constantly bombarded with images of need and it is hard sometimes to know how to respond. We feel that we have little to offer – that the small amount we have cannot possibly make a real difference to anyone. It can lead to a kind of paralysis.

For children, this can be an even stronger feeling – they often empathise with children they see on television and want to respond. This sense of human solidarity is something to encourage. By giving the last money she had, the widow was demonstrating her trust in God, but also pooling the little she had into the common good. By noticing it, Jesus assures us that he notices the small things we do and sees their worth far beyond their material value.

2. We arrive

We sit in a circle ready to listen to the Gospel.

Has anyone anything they would like to tell us about last week's Family Sheet?

Focus

Green cloth, Bible open at the Gospel, autumn flowers or leaves, an open purse with two small coins, a candle.

Gospel Mark 12:38-44

Read from the Lectionary or the Children's Lectionary.

3. We respond

What is the Gospel asking of us?

This week there is one story for all the children. Work in age groups for the activities, if appropriate.

Young ones and Juniors

Story

Liam and Grace had been watching the television news and had seen some things that had made them very sad. They were pictures of a great disaster like a __________

(Invite children to think about the things that people want to respond to with help.)

They wanted to do something to help but they knew their pocket money wouldn't help much. And their friends were not in any better a position. But they still felt they wanted to do something.

(What might they think of doing? What experience of fund-raising do the children have?)

Liam and Grace talked to their mum about their ideas and how they didn't think they could really make a difference. "I wonder if it would help if Auntie Debbie came and talked to you all." Auntie Debbie was really keen on helping CAFOD and her friend Kate was a great supporter of Christian Aid. It sounded like a good idea to talk to them about their problem.

Auntie Debbie and Kate came round to their house and Liam and Grace had invited some of their friends. They took them to the CAFOD website where it showed what they were already doing to help with the disaster. "When something like this happens," Auntie Debbie said, "CAFOD gets in touch with Caritas in that country and they get aid to people straight away and tell us what they need us to send money out for." They showed them the Christian Aid website and saw how different churches work together in partnership with local workers to help with a disaster or ongoing problems.

"But don't you send things out from here?" asked Jack, a friend of Liam. "I've seen people loading planes with medicine and things."

"Sometimes," replied Auntie Debbie, "but we always try to buy things in the country itself. It gets there quicker – it means money is going into the country to help them get over the disaster and it's a lot cheaper."

"Cheaper?" asked Grace.

"Yes," said Kate, "things cost less than they do here. For £10 you can buy enough seeds for a family to plant a kitchen garden which will feed them – and even have enough left over to sell. £5 could buy a couple of buckets."

"Buckets!" exclaimed Lucy.

"Buckets," laughed Kate. "Imagine you have managed to get clean water – and you need it to stay clean – a bucket with a good lid is perfect."

"So we don't need to send a lot of money to make a difference?"

"No, however little you can send, it can make a huge difference."

The children continued their chat with Auntie Debbie and Kate and decided to collect some of their good toys and books and do a table sale. They also did a "guess how many sweets in the jar competition" and a "name the teddy".

(Can the children think of other things they could try?)

Their families came and other friends from school and the neighbourhood and just about everything was sold.

At the end of the sale the children went in to have cake and lemonade and counted up their takings: £23.47.

"That's really good," said Auntie Debbie.

"That's lots of seeds and buckets and some left over!" said Kate.

Auntie Debbie agreed to send off the money, "You see, you had some fun – a lot of people gave a little bit – and you have made a big difference to someone's life ... several lives in fact!"

4. Activity

Young ones

Above the map of the world, draw in the children with their table sale in the space provided and colour in the children in Africa going to school, children in Bangladesh area planting seeds, children in South America with a water pump. As they work, talk about the links between them all and how we are all God's family.

Juniors

Talk to the children about how giving a little makes a big difference. Consider taking part in a fund-raising activity leading up to Christmas. Ideas might include: saving odd coins and asking families to do the same; baby boxes: children bring small items, toiletries/little toys/bibs, and then make up boxes that can be offered to the local "Life" Group; Christmas boxes: some charities collect items to distribute in Eastern Europe/Africa and other needy areas. Explore the possibilities locally. Is there a soup run or shelter who might appreciate tins or packets of soup?

Tips for learning difficulties

Encourage the children to see that everyone can make a difference. Do they have any ideas? Could they join in with the collections?

5. We come together

Parents can be invited to join in at this stage.

Focus

Light the candle. Invite those gathered to become still.

Gospel

In the Gospel, Jesus is watching as people come into the Temple. Some people are giving large amounts – and making sure that everyone notices. But Jesus spotted someone else: someone who was not fashionable or important and who was not noticed by anyone else – not even the disciples.

Jesus tells them that she has given more than anyone else. They are surprised but he says that she has given everything she had: a great gift given to help others who might be in need.

Prayer

Lord Jesus, you spot the kindness of everyone
and you see that even the smallest gift is of great value.
Help us never to forget that,
and to be generous in the little things we can do and give.
Amen.

Share.

We have been thinking about the work of CAFOD and Christian Aid, the aid agencies that work with their partners in developing countries to help people to build happier and healthier lives.

We thought about how money raised here could do a lot of good because things cost less in those countries, so money goes a long way.

The younger ones have looked at how children are linked around the world. (Children can be invited to show their pictures.)

The Juniors have been looking at things they could do to make a difference for people at Christmas. Here are some of the things they have thought of... Perhaps we could think about that over the coming week and make some decisions next time.

"Christ be our light"
"When I needed a neighbour"
"Plenty of bread at the feast of life"

33rd Sunday in Ordinary Time

The 2nd Sunday before Advent

1. Introduction to the theme of the day

Aim: To foster a sense of confidence that the words of Jesus can be trusted.

Leader's Reflection: The world can be a frightening place. War, natural disaster, the fear of terrorism, and things much closer to home: fear of crime and sadly, for some children, the lack even of a safe home. Fear can be crippling and can lead to mistrust. For children, the implications can be even greater because of their powerlessness – events happen around them and things happen to them they are unable to stop or even to understand.

Trust in the words of Jesus can be a source of great strength. He did not promise an easy ride – far from it – but he did promise to be in it with us until the end of the age. The liturgical year begins to draw to a close with an apocalyptic vision, looking to the end of the world. This could be frightening, especially in turbulent times when we can easily wonder if we are indeed in the end times. At these times, it is perhaps more important than ever to trust the words of Jesus and to help our children see that trust, so that, by our example, they grow in confidence in the enduring and unshakeable love of God.

2. We arrive

We sit in a circle ready to listen to the Gospel.

Has anyone anything they would like to tell us about last week's Family Sheet? Did anyone have any thoughts on what can be done to make a difference for other people at Christmas?

Focus

Green cloth, candle and open Bible or Lectionary.

Gospel: Mark: 13:24-32

Read from the Lectionary or Children's Lectionary.

3. We respond

What is the Gospel asking of us?

One long story this week – with a choice of discussion points and activities. Work in age groups if appropriate.

Story

Paul and Rosie couldn't wait to get back to school after the holidays. They had had an adventure and wanted to tell everyone about it!

Not that it had felt like an adventure at the time. It had been really scary, but now it was over they were very proud of themselves – and even more proud of their mum and their rescuers. Yes, their rescuers!

They had been on holiday and teamed up with another family to go for a walk in the hills. Paul and Rosie had done lots of long walks with their mum. She was what Granddad called a "walking fanatic" and she was bringing the children up to be the same. They loved it. They met lots of other people on the walks and were always made a fuss of by the older ramblers.

The family they went for this particular walk with had not done so many, but Mum was well equipped and they were not going too far this time. They had climbed to the top of the hill and had looked at the great view and had a picnic. The sun had been shining and it had been brilliant.

The problems started on the way down. It began to get misty, but Mum said they would be fine as she knew the route and they would come to a track in a few minutes and that would be very easy to follow.

Paul and Rosie knew Mum knew what she was doing and that all they had to do was to follow her instructions. Unfortunately, the other family did not think they needed to. "We'll push on ahead," they said. "Don't want to get caught up in fog, do we?" and, laughing, they'd rushed on ahead. "But..." said their mum. But it was too late – the other family were charging down the hill.

A few minutes later, they heard a terrified scream and shouting. Mum turned to her children – "We'll go and find them but you must stay close."

A few hundred yards away, they came across the family. Tom, the youngest boy, had skidded on some stones and his leg was gashed and at a funny angle.

The dad wanted to rush and get help – but Mum got firm and said, "No. The fog is going to get thicker, we must stay together." The man did not look so sure – but when Mum took off her rucksack and got out the First Aid kit and a mobile phone, he realised she did know what she was talking about. She dialled the rescue services and explained what had happened and gave them details of roughly where they were. She calmed Tom's mother down and got a space-blanket out to keep Tom warm. The fog got thicker and thicker and they could hardly see each other. It was cold, damp and very scary.

After a while they heard voices. Mum got out a whistle and gave it to Paul – who blew SOS on it. Rosie took the torch and flashed that too – while Mum kept an eye on Tom and his parents.

The rescuers soon found them. They made Tom comfortable and put him on a stretcher and led everyone to the track and down to the rescue vehicles where they gave them hot drinks. They also congratulated Mum, Paul and Rosie for keeping cool heads and knowing what to do. Paul and Rosie almost popped with pride – but they knew that it was all down to trusting that Mum knew what to do.

No wonder they could not wait to get back to school to tell everyone!

Young ones

How did Paul and Rosie feel when they were lost in the fog? What made them feel sure that things would be all right? Have the children ever been frightened like that? What made them feel safer?

Juniors

Have the children had similar experiences – maybe in Cubs or Brownies or other activity groups? Do they know someone who has? What did they learn from their experience?

4. Activity

Young ones

Act out the story with the children. Let them all be a Paul or Rosie and an adult, Mum. The other family could be played by adults or left to imagination. Be confident and fairly light-hearted – and maybe a little melodramatic. Encourage the children to say how they feel at various points in the story; allow them to be melodramatic too!

If space does not permit amateur dramatics, use the template page. As the children colour it in, ask them to describe what is happening and how people in the story might be feeling.

Juniors

Older children might like to act out the story but to take on the roles of Mum and the other family themselves. Remind them of the story where necessary.

Alternatively, allow the children to colour the template in and add speech bubbles.

Tips for learning difficulties

A simple acting out of the story with much emphasis on Mum keeping everything safe.

Alternatively, the children colour in the template with an adult alongside to chat with the children about what is happening in the story.

5. We come together

Parents can be invited to join in at this stage.

Focus

Light the candle. Invite those gathered to become still.

Gospel

In the Gospel, Jesus tells us about the time when he will come in glory and gather everyone together. It sounds as if it could all be quite frightening but Jesus promises that whatever else happens, we can trust his word.

Prayer

Jesus, the world can be a frightening place –
but you have given us your word that whatever happens you will be with us.
Help us to trust you even when things are very hard for us.
Amen.

Share

In the session, we had a story about two children who had an adventure. It was quite scary, but they listened to what their mum said and everything worked out safely in the end.

(If the template was used, the children can be encouraged to show it to their parents and tell them what happened.)

This is a bit like our relationship with Jesus. We might be in trouble but if we keep as calm as we can and try to listen for his voice, everything will be fine in the end, even if it takes a while.

Sing

"My God loves me"
"He's got the whole world in his hands"

Our Lord Jesus Christ, Universal King

Christ the King

1. Introduction to the theme of the day

"Jesus' kingdom"

Aim: To explore what Jesus means when he says that his kingdom is not of this world.

Leader's Reflection: If we say the words "king" or "kingdom", it is quite likely that an image of splendour and majesty will come to mind. The King we meet in today's Gospel could not be more different. Jesus is facing the might of the Roman Empire in the person of Pontius Pilate and yet, of the two, Jesus seems the more composed. He is aware of the fate that awaits him but the fear has passed and the dignity befitting a King has taken its place.

It is a paradox of our faith that our King ended his life as a convicted criminal on a cross. If Jesus' kingdom was of this world, he would undoubtedly have been able to call on vast armies to defend him, and yet his Kingship is manifest in apparent weakness and isolation with not even one subject or adviser to call on.

Our King is not one who lords it over his subjects but one who enters fully into their life experience, taking upon himself the worst that the world can do to them. He is a King who leads his people through the worst into an eternal best: a kingdom not of this world, where all are healed and made whole, for ever.

2. We arrive

We sit in a circle ready to listen to the Gospel.
Has anyone anything they would like to tell us about last week's Family Sheet?

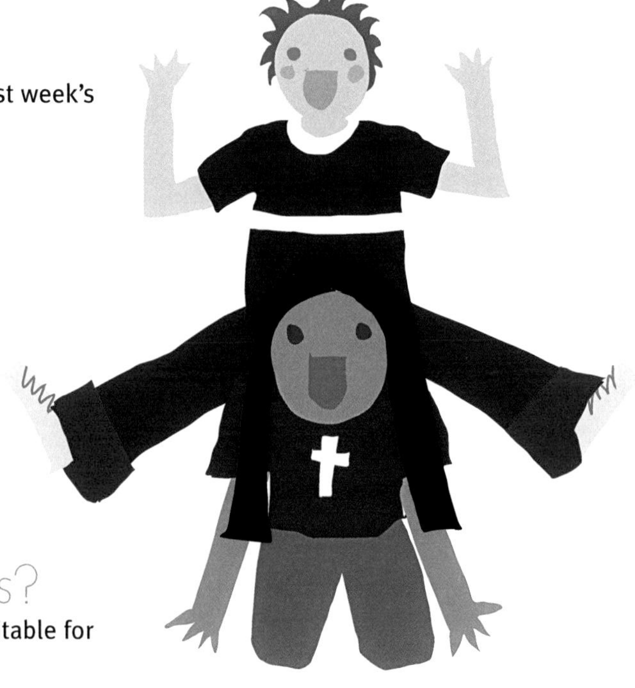

Focus

White cloth, candle, a calendar.

Gospel: John 18:33-37

Read from the Lectionary or Children's Lectionary.

3. We respond

What is the Gospel asking of us?

Choose the story, discussion ideas and activity most suitable for your group.

Young ones

A story about Muriel, the apprentice angel who helps the Angel Gabriel.

Story

Muriel was really getting into human history. Muriel was an angel who had had a great success with the mission with Gabriel to tell Mary about her baby. Since then, she had begun to take an interest in how humans lived: what they liked to do, what they liked to eat, where they went for their holidays, and so on.

Her best friend Nathaniel could not get over the sight of Muriel with her nose peering into human history, visiting different times and places. "Muriel, if you peer any further, you're going to land in human history, and you know we only go if we're sent by God!"

But Muriel's curiosity was just too strong. One thing that really puzzled her was that some places had kings and queens and some places didn't. No one could really explain why. One thing all the rulers had in common was that they were very powerful – and usually very wealthy. She looked into the time of King David. He had started life as a shepherd boy and ended up as a king in a great palace. And when she looked at King Solomon's time, the palaces were even bigger. And when she looked at King Herod's time, she nearly did fall into history – his palace was so amazingly decorated she could hardly believe it.

She looked further into history and saw that some kings and queens had lots of houses – and castles – and palaces! All of them were very beautiful and richly decorated, and all the rulers were very powerful. Some used their power wisely, but some of them used their power to hurt other people, sometimes even their own people.

This was really not like heaven. Jesus was their king, even if he was living on the earth at the moment. Jesus was always kind and looked out for everyone. When she had been a clumsy apprentice angel, he had reassured her that it would all work out. She even wondered sometimes whether it was Jesus who had arranged for her to go with Gabriel to visit Mary, she wouldn't be surprised.

She missed Jesus and looked forward to him coming home to heaven. She knew he had an important mission to do. She couldn't wait for him to come back to tell him about everything she had learnt about kings on the earth, and how glad she was that she had him as her king.

Juniors

Today might be a good time to allow the children to share their thoughts about world leaders of which they are aware and to clarify their understanding of what makes a good leader.

Who are the leaders of our country? What about in other countries? What about spiritual leaders? Are all the leaders good? What does a good leader do? Who is a good leader concerned about? Who is a bad leader concerned about? What example of kingship and leadership does Jesus give? What is Jesus' kingdom like?

Story

The feast of Christ the King was established by Pope Pius XI in 1925. He saw that the world had not recovered from the First World War and sensed that new dictators would use the situation to gain power. He wanted to have a feast every year to celebrate Christ as the Universal King. He was right. Very soon, Hitler came to power, then Stalin, and countless other dictators who have used power for evil purposes.

The feast reminds us that, though we are part of this world, we are also part of Christ's kingdom. This gives people the courage to stand up for what is right, even when they are afraid of the consequences: Jesus is our King.

4. Activity

As we are coming to the end of the liturgical year, this would be a good time to look back over the past months. Were there any favourite sessions? What do the children want to thank God especially for this year – either from the sessions or something that happened at home or school?

Young ones

Jewels in Jesus' crown. Use the crown template and cut out diamonds and circles in shiny paper. Invite the children to stick the jewels on the crown for special things that have happened to them this year, e.g. this jewel is my First Communion; this is my new baby brother. Talk to them about their special memories and help them to see that their joys are Jesus' joys too.

Juniors

Use the crown template and jewels as with the younger children, but invite the children to use their jewels to represent good news from this year, e.g. money sent to a charity; someone was rescued; babies were born; someone recovered from illness; someone died after a long illness and is now with Jesus, etc.

Tips for learning difficulties

Have crowns and jewels cut out. Explain that we are decorating Jesus' crown with things that make us happy. Invite the children to think of happy things as they stick the jewels on.

5. We come together

Parents can be invited to join in at this stage.

Focus

Light the candle. Invite those gathered to become still.

Gospel

In today's Gospel we heard about Jesus and Pilate. Pilate seems to have all the power but Jesus knows that he is the greater king, but that his kingdom is not of this world.

Prayer

Jesus, you are our King,
strong, kind and merciful.
We thank you for our times together over the last year –
for all you have given us
and all that we have learnt about you.
Amen.

Share

(Use these or your own words)
We have been on a Journey with the Gospel writer Mark.
Today, we come to the end of Year B.
There have been happy times when ...
(*N*...'s parent was received into the Church/*N*, *N* & *N* made their First Communion... etc.)
There have been sad times when ...
(*N*... died/ *N*... moved away from the area ... etc.)
We thank God for this year ... if you would like to thank God for something in particular, share it with us and we will all say: Thanks be to God

Sing

"Alleluia, alleluia, give thanks to the risen Lord"
"Sing it in the valleys, shout it from the mountaintops!"
"The King of Glory comes"

The Most Holy Trinity

1. Introduction to the theme of the day

"In the name of the Father,
and of the Son,
and of the Holy Spirit"

Aim: We are called into the family of the Trinity.

Leaders' Reflection: In his love for us, God has called us to be his adopted children. We are not God, but he calls us to enter into the relationship of love which exists in God. St Paul tells us that if we live in Christ we become like him; this includes sharing his love for the Father. But we can only become like Christ by sharing his Spirit.

Hymn singing is an excellent but simple example of this. By the inspiration of the Spirit, we sing words as Jesus' brothers and sisters, of love to the Father.

2. We arrive

We sit in a circle ready to listen to the Gospel.

Has anyone anything to say about last week's Family Sheet?

Focus

A lighted candle, white or gold fabric for Trinity Sunday.

Gospel: Matthew 28:16-20

Read from the Lectionary or Children's Lectionary.

3. We respond

What is the Gospel asking of us?

This week there is one story for all the children. Work in age groups, if appropriate, for the activities.

Young ones and Juniors

One way of explaining the Trinity in simple terms is as a family. God is a family, and he invites us to share in his family. When we join God's family, we have Jesus (who is God) for our brother, and we have Jesus' Father in heaven (who is God) as our father. The Father loves Jesus, and he loves us as well. That love is so important that we call it God's Spirit. Because we have been given God's Spirit, we can love each other, and love the Father as well.

This is a story about Jesus which isn't in the Bible at all, but I can imagine really happening.

One day, when Jesus and his friends were out walking, Peter came up to him and asked him a question, "Lord," he said, because he knew Jesus was really important, "Lord, how come you find it so easy to be good, and we don't?" Jesus looked surprised, "Well, to be honest, Peter, it isn't always that easy, but I probably find it easier than you because I am nearly always happy. It is easier to be good if you are happy." Peter went away again, and told his friends what Jesus had said.

Next day, Peter was back again, "Jesus, I can see that it must be easier to be good if you are happy, but why are you happy? You haven't got many clothes, and you haven't got a fast car, and you haven't got much money at all. Why are you happy?"

"Ah, that is easy," replied Jesus, "I'm happy because I sing all the time. If you are singing it's very difficult to be unhappy." And so Peter went away again and told his friends.

Next day, Peter and his friends decided they would try singing as well to see if it made them happy. First they sang "The wheels on the bus", which was fun at first, but after the fifty-fifth time of it, they got bored, then they sang the theme tune for (give an example of a soap opera) but that was a bit miserable, then they tried to sing pop songs but nobody could remember all the words. So Peter went back to Jesus.

"Your singing idea is all very well, Jesus," he complained, "but none of the songs we tried really made us happy – though 'The wheels on the bus' was quite fun."

"Ah," said Jesus, wisely. "It depends mostly on who you are singing to. Most of the time I sing to God, and I sing lots of different songs so I don't get bored."

"How do you know lots of different songs?" asked Peter, "We couldn't even remember the words for one pop song, never mind lots of different songs." Jesus smiled, "The Holy Spirit teaches the songs to me, and he teaches me the tunes as well. He will teach you as well one day if you like, but for now I will teach you myself."

Peter and his friends all sat in a circle around Jesus whilst he gave them a singing lesson. The first song he taught them was "Kum Bah Ya" ... at this point move into a singing session, use the structure and prayers overleaf if they are helpful.

4. Activity

When we sing a hymn, we are joining in the family of the Trinity in a special way.

Young ones

Borrow a selection of instruments or make some simple "shakers" from plastic bottles with dried pulses; hollow boxes/ tins; wooden spoons etc. Work out some actions to bring the hymns to life.

Juniors

Provide hymn books for each child. Practise finding the numbers from the selection below.

Find the name of the person who wrote the hymn. The Holy Spirit helped them to think up the words and music for the hymn. The Holy Spirit helps us to sing it. When we sing the hymn, we use our minds and our bodies. Jesus used his mind and body to sing hymns, so will we as his brothers and sisters. The hymn praises God the Father, so we are telling God that we love him as part of his family. Write the names of your favourite hymns in the template triangle.

Prayers before each hymn

- Thank you, Holy Spirit, for helping ... to write this hymn. Please help us to sing it.
- Jesus, we are part of your Christian family, please sing with us.
- Father, we sing this hymn to show you that we love you, that we are your children.

Choose hymns from the list below or use others that would be suitable.

Abba, Abba Father
Be still and know that I am God
Father I place into your hands
Glory to God
I will sing, I will sing
Our Father
Sing hallelujah to the Lord
All that I am
Bind us together
Give me joy in my heart
How great is our God
Kum ba yah
Rejoice in the Lord always
The love I have for you, my Lord

Tips for learning difficulties

Have a selection of cartons/boxes/foil and other materials to explore different sounds. Choose some to accompany the hymns.

5. We come together

Parents can be invited to join in at this stage.

Focus

Gather together around the candle.

Gospel

After the resurrection, Jesus met his friends on top of a mountain. Some of them were still a bit unsure about who he was, so he told them straight, "Because I have risen from the dead, I am in charge of everything now. Go and tell everybody about me, and about God my Father, and my Spirit. Because I have risen from the dead, God is your Father and your Spirit as well."

Prayer

Thank you, Holy Spirit, for inspiring the writers of the music and the lyrics for our hymns.
Jesus, we are part of your Christian family, please sing with us.
Father, we sing hymns to show that we love you, that we are your children. Amen.

Share

Discuss how the activities worked out. How did singing make the children feel?

Sing

Choose any of the hymns that you have talked about today.

These are my Favourite Hymns

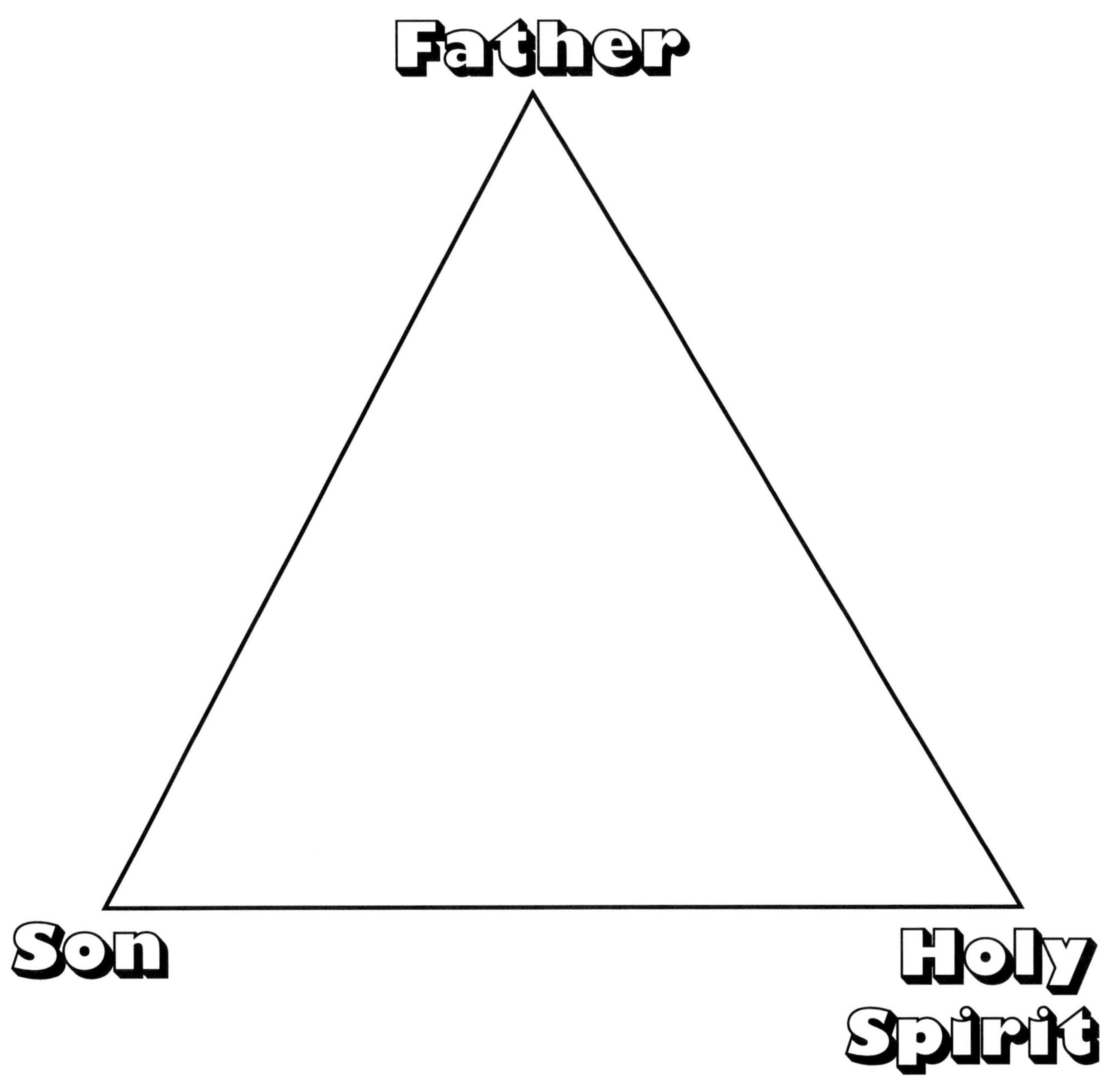

The Body and Blood of Christ (Corpus Christi)

1. Introduction to the theme of the day

"This is my body,
this is my blood"

Aim: To explore more deeply the mystery of the Eucharist

Leader's Reflection: An ambitious project today – we are going to teach the juniors the principles of transubstantiation. Young people can be surprisingly adept at picking up and using technical terms, so they are introduced at this early stage to help them to deepen their understanding of the Eucharist. It might be helpful to have flashcards ready prepared with the keywords: transubstantiation, accident, substance, and change.

2. We arrive

We sit in a circle ready to listen to the Gospel.
Has anyone anything they would like to tell us about last week's Family Sheet?

Focus

A lighted candle, white fabric for the feast day. A loaf and a bottle of wine.

Gospel: Mark 14:12-16. 22-26

Read from the Lectionary or Children's Lectionary.

3. We respond

What is the Gospel asking of us?

We think about what happens when we celebrate Mass together.
Work in age groups if appropriate.

Young ones

Story

Peter was lonely. Jesus had gone back to heaven, and Peter missed him. At first he had been really sad and upset, but then Jesus had sent his Holy Spirit to be with them, and that had made Peter feel a whole lot better. Even so, he still missed him; he just wanted Jesus to be with them again. Peter sighed. Oh well, it was his turn to make tea today – jam sandwiches – Jesus' favourite! He smiled to himself, remembering. Best get on.

It was whilst he was cutting the bread for the sandwiches that he suddenly remembered something else about Jesus. What was it that he had said at that Last Supper together, when he gave them the bread and the wine? (See if the children can remember.) "This is my body, this is my blood." Peter had an idea.

At teatime, when everybody was sitting around the table, Peter explained his idea to his friends, then he picked up the bread and said, "Jesus said, 'This is my body'", and he picked up the wine and said, "Jesus said, 'This is my blood'". And then, with a big smile on his face, he sat down again. Everybody else was looking at the bread and wine and smiling as well.

Peter knew that his idea had been right. When he said the things that Jesus had said, Jesus had come to be with them again. The bread and wine still looked like bread and wine, but somehow they had changed into Jesus. It was a miracle! No it wasn't, it was even better than a miracle!

Juniors

The juniors might like to listen to the story for the young ones before moving on to this more in-depth discussion.

Some time ago in this book, we did some very difficult work about Jesus being God and man at the same time. That sort of work is called **Theology** (which means, about God) and today we are going to do some more of it.

When we study theology, we often have to use long words. The theology we are going to do today is about something called transubstantiation, which is a very long word. It has 18 letters. We need to learn two other new words as well. They are substance and accident. You probably think you know what they mean already, but in theology, they mean something different.

When you buy medicines or pills from the chemist, some of them look very nice, a bit like sweets (that is why they come in childproof bottles – so that little children won't eat them by mistake). What they look like (like a sweet) is called the appearance or accident of the pill. What they really are (medicine) is called the substance.

For most things the accident and substance match up; so, a flower looks like a flower, and it really is a flower; a pencil looks like a pencil, and it really is a pencil. But sometimes, like with the medicine, it doesn't.

(The children might be able to think of other things e.g. video cases that look like books, etc.)

Transubstantiation is the word that we are really interested in today. What does it mean? It means changing (trans) the substance (substantiation) of something without changing the accident. So we are changing what something really is, without changing what it looks like. That is not very easy to do – in fact, we only know of one occasion when it happens. At the beginning of Mass, the bread and wine look like bread and wine, and they really are bread and wine. After the priest has said Jesus' words, "This is my body. This is my blood", the bread and wine still look like bread and wine, but they really are Jesus' body and blood.

When you receive Jesus at communion, you are receiving all of him, body and blood, God and man.

4. Activity

Young ones

When you are older, you will be given the bread and wine which has changed into Jesus during Mass. The first time you are given it is called your First Communion, and it is a very special day. Today you are going to eat ordinary bread together. To show that we are all one family, we will all share the same loaf. Whilst you are eating it you can think about Jesus, and thank him for all the food and drink which he gives you every day.

Show the children how to tear off a small piece of bread from the loaf, and pass it round in a circle. The children can say "Thank you, Jesus", or similar.

Juniors

Fill in the chart from the template page to help you to remember what happens at Mass.

Tips for learning difficulties

Share some bread and juice while talking about the Last Supper with Jesus and his friends. Look at some pictures of the scene. Talk about receiving Jesus in the form of bread at communion time at Mass.

5. We come together

Parents can be invited to join in at this stage.

Focus

Gather around the candle, the bread and the wine.

Gospel

When they were at table, Jesus held up the bread. He said, "This is my Body." Then he held up the wine, "This is my Blood."

Prayer

Jesus, thank you for changing the bread and wine into yourself. That way you are always with us, and we can always talk to you. Help us to remember how special and holy it is when we celebrate Mass together. Amen.

Share

Juniors can share the work they have done together. On this occasion it might be appropriate to point out that those who have made their First Communion will not eat any of the bread which the young ones have been sharing.
This is because the bread which they will eat during Mass is so holy, because it is Jesus, that they do not want to eat anything else before they receive it.

Sing

"This is my body"

	Before Consecration		After Consecration	
	Accident	Substance	Accident	Substance

Fill in the blank squares in the table – you can draw or write descriptions.
Remember! Accident is what it looks like, Substance is what it really is.

The Presentation of the Lord

1. Introduction to the theme of the day

> "I have seen your light with my own eyes"

Aim: Good news is not something to be kept secret. When Simeon and Anna see Jesus, the light of the world, they go and tell other people about him.

Leader's Reflection: This Gospel is one of the great links between the Old and New Testaments. Joseph and Mary obey the Law by offering two pigeons to thank God for the birth of Jesus. Then we see the Spirit at work in two Old Testament witnesses – a man and a woman – who recognise God's promise working itself out in Jesus. For Simeon this Good News is for all the world, though it will bring pain for Mary and many after her. A woman, Anna, is perhaps Jesus' first missionary, telling people about his birth, just as Mary Magdalene was the first to tell the news of his resurrection. Simeon's prayer is part of the traditional Night Prayer of the Church. We have seen the light. It burns in our hearts, we need not fear anything at all.

2. We arrive

We sit in a circle, ready to listen to the Gospel. Perhaps we want to talk about something from last week's sheet?
We are God's people, living in his light. Pray together, holding up a candle:
"The light of Jesus be in our hearts."

Focus

Today has, traditionally, been known as Candlemas, so make the candle the centrepiece. If the children do not have blessed candles already, give them one each now. Light them with a taper from the main candle. Set them in a sand tray around it. (You may wish to extinguish candles during the activity and relight them at the end.)

Gospel Luke 2:22-40

Read from the Lectionary or the Children's Lectionary.

3. We respond

What is the Gospel asking of us?

If appropriate, work in age groups, but join together as one community at the end of the session.
We are the children of light. God's light in Jesus shows us how to live in this world. Simeon's prayer reminds us that we have nothing to fear, which is why it is used for Night Prayer by the Church. Dreams or sudden death cannot hurt us! God's light is in our hearts, so we can shine out too. We can live as children of the light. We can overcome our fears and bring God's love to the people we meet.

Young ones

This is a story about saying "Thank you" and about how we can, with help, overcome our fears and live happily.

Story

Grandad had come to visit because it was Joe's birthday. He had parked his car round the corner and walked up to the house. He was in the kitchen talking to Mum before Joe knew he was there. On the table was a red shiny parcel. "Happy birthday," said Grandad.

Joe opened the present: a red cycling helmet. "But I haven't got a bike," he said, as his face fell.

"Bring that helmet here," said Grandad, and led Joe round the corner to his car. There on the rack was a red mountain bike.

This was the present Joe really wanted, but hardly dared hope for. The frame, the colour, the tyres, even the bell – just perfect. He gave Grandad a big squeeze, because he couldn't get the words out to say, "Thank you." But Grandad understood.

"Hop in," said Grandad, "and you can learn to ride the bike in the park." Joe felt a bit strange. "Don't worry," said Grandad, "you have got a helmet, and the grass is a soft landing. Of course you'll hurt yourself, but it will be worth it!"

Joe fell off a few times. He was muddy, scratched and bruised, but he rode that bike home at teatime. The only bit of his face clean enough for his mother to kiss was the end of his nose!

Juniors

Story

Have you ever lit a candle in the dark, or sat around a campfire? Somehow your eyes are drawn to the light. Light can touch your heart too.

Saul was riding to Damascus when he was struck blind. He had been going to arrest the Christians there. When he arrived he went straight to bed, with the words ringing in his ears, "Saul, this is Jesus. Why are you persecuting me?"

After a while God sent Ananias, a Christian, to restore Saul's sight. Saul had been thinking and praying. Not only did he get back the sight of his eyes, but the light of Jesus was in his heart. He knew that Jesus was the light of the world.

Paul, as he now called himself, lived quietly nearby for three years, learning what being a friend of Jesus meant, living as a member of the Church. Only after that did God send him to be Jesus' great messenger to the peoples of the Roman Empire.

Remember, Jesus lived very quietly for thirty years after the Presentation, and Paul was quite an ordinary Christian for three years. Keep your light shining – maybe someone will be looking for a light in the dark tomorrow, or in three years, or thirty, and they will see you.

You may never know who comes to Jesus because of your light, so keep it shining bright!

4. Activity

Talk about light. The candles, like our baptismal candles, remind us that the light of Jesus was given to us, usually when we were babies. When Jesus went to the Temple as a baby Simeon said that Jesus WAS the light. He still is. He always will be.

Young ones

Using the template picture of a burning candle, colour the flame brightly or stick on red/yellow foil. Write the child's name on the candle itself; talk about how we can shine for Jesus this week.

Juniors

Using the template as for the young ones, the children could write or draw on it some way in which they could shine with Jesus' light this week.

Tips for learning difficulties

Children can colour in the candle from the template page. As they do this, talk to them about Jesus being the light of the world.

5. We come together

Parents can be invited to join in at this stage.

Focus

The light from the big candle and all the little ones, which should be relit ready for the Gospel reading. Talk about how God's light was shining in the two stories.

Gospel

Simeon met Joseph and Mary when they brought baby Jesus to the Temple. He said, "This child is the light of all the nations." Anna went out to tell people that Jesus was the one they were waiting for.

Prayer

Thank you, God, for light, and eyes to see. Thank you for your light in our hearts, for your reflection that we see in each other.

We pray for those who cannot see; for eye doctors and opticians; thank you for their work.

Amen.

Share.

Talk about the candle pictures we have prepared. How will Jesus' light shine in us?

Sing

"This little light of mine"

"Children of the light"

The Birth of St John the Baptist

1. Introduction to the theme of the day

Aim: To talk to the children about the birth of John the Baptist and his great importance to the future ministry of Jesus.

Leader's Reflection: The birth of John the Baptist was greeted with joy by his family and neighbours – for it was a sign of God's favour. However, it is easy to forget that the circumstances were not as easy as they might seem. Elizabeth was fairly elderly, certainly beyond the usual age of child-bearing. Zechariah was also old and to make things worse had been struck dumb, with no indication if, or when, his speech would be restored. It reminds us that even where there is great joy, there can be suffering and difficulty. The scriptures are full of the reality of human life, its joys and sorrows, and the story today is an example of how life in all its fullness is found in the pages of the Bible.

2. We arrive

We sit in a circle ready to listen to the Gospel.
Has anyone anything they would like to tell us about last week's Family Sheet?

Focus

White cloth, candle, flowers, a bowl of water.

Gospel: Luke 1:57-66, 80

Read from the Lectionary or Children's Lectionary.

3. We respond

What is the Gospel asking of us?

Use the story and activities best suited to the children in your group.

Young ones

Muriel was worried. Actually, Muriel was very worried. A few months ago, she had gone on her first baby-announcing mission with Gabriel. She had been really nervous, which might explain her BIG mistake.

Gabriel had announced to a man called Zechariah that his wife was going to have a baby. Zechariah didn't believe him and turned round to Gabriel, an archangel, and said he was too old and so was his wife. Muriel had thought that this was really rude and said so, nearly. She was telling him that he couldn't speak to Gabriel like that, but she didn't finish the sentence, and only got as far as "You can't speak." And Zechariah couldn't!

Gabriel had said he would be all right when the baby was born but even though Muriel had had a successful baby-announcing mission since then, she was still worried. What if Zechariah didn't get his voice back? How could he tell the new baby he loved him?

So, Muriel was looking into history waiting to see what happened.

She heard all the bustle when Elizabeth said the baby was on the way. She saw Zechariah pacing up and down with other men from the village. Then she saw him going into the house and quietly went to look through the window. There was Elizabeth with a beautiful baby boy. Zechariah looked so proud, but, to Muriel's horror, he still wasn't speaking.

She went back a week later to watch the baby-naming ceremony. Zechariah still couldn't speak but when an argument broke out about the baby's name he picked up a writing tablet and wrote: His name is John. At that very moment, a huge smile came over Zechariah's face and he started – not to speak – but to sing!

"Blessed be the God of Israel," he sang. And in an angel voice that no one but the baby could hear, Muriel sang for joy with him.

Juniors

One of the things that John the Baptist said was that he must diminish, and Jesus must increase. At this time of year in the northern hemisphere, the days are at their longest and, sad though it seems, the nights will begin to lengthen as we move towards the end of the year.

Christians used the solar year to mark important feasts.

With a diary, find the longest and shortest days and the spring and autumn equinoxes. What feast do we celebrate on/ near the spring equinox? What is happening to the days at that time? (Becoming longer than night.) What about the longest day? And what begins to happen then? How does that match what John foretells about himself? What feast is on/ near the autumn equinox? Explain that Michael is a powerful angel, as the nights get longer, we pray for his protection. What about the shortest day? How does this tie in with Jesus being the Light of the World? (The days begin to lengthen, the dark days are gradually becoming brighter.)

4. Activity

Young ones

Use the template picture of Elizabeth, baby John and Zechariah and Muriel holding a banner with "His name is John" on. Can they identify the people? Can any of them write their names? (Special praise for those who manage Zechariah!)

Invite the children to colour the picture in. As they do, encourage them to talk about the characters and what happened in today's Gospel. What did John grow up to be? Who was John's cousin? Who was one of his aunts?

The children could also act out the story of today's Gospel: Elizabeth and Zechariah, the neighbours making suggestions about what John could be called, maybe even Muriel!

Juniors

Bible detective. Help the children to find clues about John's life using these references.

Who did the baby John grow up to be? What sort of life did John lead? (Mark 1:2-8) What special thing did he do with Jesus? (Matthew 3:13-17) What happened to John? (Mark 6:14-29)

Create a cartoon strip – either individual or one for the whole group. Use the strip to illustrate John's life, using some or all of the following: The announcement to Zechariah; John's birth/naming ceremony; John proclaiming his message; John baptising Jesus; John challenging Herod; John in prison; John in heaven. If done as a group, it would work as a collage using a variety of materials. Try to find something hairy for John's garment.

Tips for learning difficulties

The children colour the picture in, while talking about the Gospel story. Names of the characters can be written underneath each one.

5. We come together

Parents can be invited to join in at this stage.

Focus

Light the candle. Invite those gathered to become still.

Gospel

In the Gospel we hear about the birth of John the Baptist. Zechariah had been struck dumb when he would not believe that Elizabeth could have a child. But she did. All the neighbours were surprised when she wanted to call him John, but Zechariah took a writing tablet and wrote "His name is John." As soon as he did that, he could speak again.
Here is part of his prayer.

Prayer

Blessed be the Lord God of Israel,
for he has looked favourably on his people and redeemed them.
He has raised up for us a mighty saviour
in the house of his servant David,
as he promised through the mouth of his holy prophets from of old.

And you, little child, will be called the prophet of the Most High;
for you will go before the Lord to prepare his ways,
to give knowledge of salvation to his people
by the forgiveness of their sins. Amen.

Share

Talk about the things the children have done during the session. What have the children learnt about John the Baptist? What can they tell their families about what happened to John later in his life?

Sing

"Bless the Lord, my soul"
"Blest be the Lord God of Israel"

His name is John

Ss Peter and Paul, Apostles

1. Introduction to the theme of the day

"St Peter and St Paul, pray for us"

Aim: We thank God for St Peter and St Paul who were the leaders at the beginning of the Church.

Leader's Reflection: St Peter and St Paul were the first leaders of the Christian Church. Their track record did not suggest they would make good leaders – Peter was impulsive and a coward; Paul was cruel and argumentative. Even in today's "personality cult" society, it is surprising to note how many of our leaders succeed despite their personalities, rather than because of them. It is some relief to find that there is not a blueprint for leadership, or for any other role in life.

2. We arrive

We sit in a circle ready to listen to the Gospel.
We may have something to say about last week's Family Sheet.

Focus

A lighted candle, red fabric for Ss Peter and Paul. If possible, a mitre for Peter (pope) and a staff for Paul (missionary).

Gospel: Matthew 16:13-19

Read from the Lectionary or Children's Lectionary.

3. We respond

What is the Gospel asking of us?

Talk about leaders. Can the children name any leaders? How would they choose a leader? What sorts of people make good leaders? Use the story and activities best suited to the children in your group.

Young ones

Story

Close to the field where the animals lived, there was a big hill, and one day the animals decided that they wanted to climb it. First they collected everything they needed: Daphne brought along four duck eggs for their lunch, and Camilla brought four pints of milk to drink; Owen the owl had the map and Wendy the worm had covered herself in glow paint so that they could see if it got dark. Now all they needed was a leader. They looked round at each other; who would be best? "We need to think carefully about this," advised Owen, so they all went off home to think.

Henry was having a nice cup of tea when there was a knock at the door. There stood Daphne. "Henry," she quacked, "we want to climb the hill, but we haven't got a leader. We need someone who is sensible and won't do anything dangerous. Will you be our leader?"

"Oh no," said Henry, "I can't be a leader. I'm too small!"

Just then there was another knock at the door. There stood Camilla. "Henry," she mooed, "we want to climb the hill but we haven't got a leader. We need someone who won't get scared or panic if things go wrong. Will you be our leader?"

"Oh no," said Henry, "I can't be a leader. I'm not strong enough."

Just then there was another knock at the door. There stood Wendy. "Henry," she squeaked, "we want to climb the hill but we haven't got a leader. We need someone who will be able to find the way back down again. Will you be our leader?"

"Oh no," said Henry, "I can't be a leader. I haven't got a loud voice."

Just then there was another knock at the door. There stood Owen. "Henry," he hooted, "we want to climb the hill but we haven't got a leader. We need someone we can all trust. Will you be our leader?" Henry looked around at them all. "All right," he buzzed, "I'm not big, and I'm not strong, and I haven't got a loud voice, but if you all trust me then I will be your leader."

And a very good leader he was too.

Spend some time seeing the Gospel story through this story.

Juniors

Story

St Peter was one of Jesus' best friends. When Jesus ascended to heaven, he left Peter in charge. Peter was a Jew, and so he began by teaching other Jews about Jesus.

St Paul was a Jew as well. He never met Jesus but he had a vision which made him realise that Jesus was God. Paul told everyone he met about Jesus, it didn't matter if they were Jewish or not.

One day, Peter and Paul had a big argument. Peter said that because God had been talking to the Jewish people for thousands of years before Jesus was born (you can read everything God said to them in the Old Testament) only Jewish people could talk to him and understand him properly. St Paul said that was a load of nonsense. He said that although God had spoken to the Jewish people first, there was no reason why other people should be stopped from talking to him now. Jesus wanted everybody to talk to his Father, whether they were a Jew or not.

After nearly 20 years of thinking and praying about this, Paul and Peter finally met in Jerusalem. They invited some of the other apostles and leaders to join in the discussion. After a lot of discussion, they finally agreed that you did not have to be Jewish to talk to God.

Peter and Paul were the two most important people at the beginning of the Church. Peter was the first Pope, and Paul was the first missionary, so we celebrate their feast days together. We do not usually celebrate feast days of saints on a Sunday, because that is God's special day, but Peter and Paul are so important that we can celebrate their day, and praise God at the same time.

4. Activity

Young ones

St Peter and St Paul were leaders in the Church after Jesus went back to heaven. Draw a picture of Peter, Paul or Henry or someone you know who is a good leader. Label the picture to show how this character is a good leader.

Juniors

Refer to the New Testament stories (preferably from a children's Bible): Jesus walks on water (Matthew 14:22-33), Peter denies Jesus (Mark 14:66-72), stoning of Stephen (Acts 7:55-60; 8:1), Paul's conversion (Acts 9:1-19).

Use the template, and, working in pairs or all together, make a list of all the characteristics expected of a good leader. Write them down the left-hand column. For each one, put a tick or a cross under the apostle's name, or use some other symbol which illustrates that they do or do not have the characteristic. There are also two columns for you to write in your own name of a leader.

Jesus chose very strange people to be the leaders of his Church.

Tips for learning difficulties

Either of these activities could be done as a group activity using a flip chart and suggestions from the children instead of working individually. If the juniors' activity was done in this way, a leader could read the stories aloud, whilst others mark the flip charts.

5. We come together

Parents can be invited to join in at this stage.

Focus

Gather around the candle, mitre and staff.

Gospel

Jesus asks his friends, "Who do people think I am?" His friends tell him that people think he is important – a holy man or a prophet. Jesus then asks them, "Who do you think I am?" Nobody said anything for a while until, eventually, Peter spoke up, "I think you are God!"

Prayer

Jesus, you chose St Peter and St Paul to be the leaders at the beginning of your Church. They were unusual people to choose for leaders, but they did a very good job. Thank you for giving them to us. Amen.

Share

The work from the activities.

Sing

"Jesus, you are Lord"

Characteristics of a good leader	Peter	Paul	------------------------	------------------------

The Transfiguration of the Lord

1. Introduction to the theme of the day

"This is my Son, the Beloved"

Aim: To help the children to see the transfiguration as a glimpse of the glory that is in Jesus and to think about what listening to God's word means.

Leader's Reflection: The story of the transfiguration appears twice in the Church's year – on the Second Sunday of Lent and on the Feast of the Transfiguration on 6 August. In Lent, the transfiguration is overshadowed by the approach of Holy Week and the remembrance of the passion and death of Jesus. Even this far away from Good Friday, the shadow of the passion is still present in the reading. One of the features of Mark's Gospel is the "Messianic secret", where Jesus reveals things to his disciples but with the warning not to tell anyone else until after the resurrection, which, of course, they did not understand either.

In the transfiguration, we are given a glimpse of the power and glory that is in Jesus. All this will seem to have been destroyed through his torture and crucifixion when two thieves will take the places of Moses and Elijah at either side of him. But we have the advantage of living in the knowledge that this was not the end and can see in this feast an affirmation from God that despite all that will happen, when all seems to end in failure, Jesus is indeed his Son, his beloved, and the one to whom we should listen.

2. We arrive

As the feast occurs in the summer holidays, it is likely that many children will be away. There might also be young visitors to welcome; if so, ensure that you know their names and introduce them to the group.

We sit in a circle ready to listen to the Gospel.

Has anyone anything they would like to tell us about last week's Family Sheet?

Focus

White cloth, candle, flowers.

Gospel: Mark 9:2-10 (Catholic) Luke 9:28-36 (Anglican)

Read from the Lectionary or Children's Lectionary.

3. We respond

What is the Gospel asking of us?

As the group is likely to be smaller and perhaps more mixed in age than usual only one story is offered. Work in age groups for the activities, if appropriate, but join together as a community at the end of the session.

Young ones and Juniors

Story

Malcolm was not a boy most people noticed. He had joined St Chad's School at Christmas. After six months, most people would say "hello" to him but he did not seem to have many friends. He did not like football much, though he was really good at jumping and seemed very fit. When he was asked to join a football team that played on Saturday mornings he said he couldn't as he already had classes that day. He did not say what the classes were; he had made the mistake of doing that at his last school. Malcolm went to dance classes.

He loved the movements and the music and his teacher said he was very promising, but at his last school he had been teased by some of the other boys who thought dancing was for wimps. As Malcolm could jump higher than most of them, and could keep on running long after they had run out of breath, he could not see how they worked that one out, but decided to keep quiet about it at St Chad's.

In any case, he was far too busy to worry at the moment. Not only was he going to dance class on Saturdays, he was having extra practices during the week. A ballet company was coming from London to put on a performance and they needed a boy to act as a pageboy, and Malcolm had been chosen to play that part.

As the time for the performance drew nearer, Malcolm had to be measured for his costume and practise even harder.

Then something awful happened. Mr Josephs, the headteacher, announced that there was going to be a special performance of a ballet at the local theatre and schools could have cheaper tickets, and he was going to organise a trip.

Malcolm was horrified – his secret would be out! He almost wanted to give up the show, but realised he could not let the company down. Maybe people would not recognise him on the stage.

The Wednesday came around very quickly and by then Malcolm had done two performances and was feeling quite confident. The stage looked magnificent and he could hear the school children "oohing" and "aahing" as they came in. The first dancers went on and Malcolm waited for his cue. He walked onto the stage and felt the heat of the spotlight on him. He forgot all about who was there and performed his dance perfectly.

At the end the dancers all took their bows. Malcolm took his turn and could hear whoops and cheers from the audience: "Malcolm! (clap, clap, clap) Malcolm! (clap, clap, clap)."

The group from St Chad's had recognised him, and it seemed that they thought he'd been brilliant!

How did Malcolm feel as he took his bow? What did the people from his school think about his performance? How might they treat him when they next see him in school? How does this story help us to think about what happened with Jesus in today's Gospel? (Seeing someone in a very different and special way.)

4. Activity

Young ones

Have pictures of Jesus, Mary and some of the saints with halos around them. Saints whose feast days are around this time include: St Alphonsus Liguori (1 August), St John Vianney (4 August), St Dominic (8 August), St Teresa Benedicta (9 August), St Lawrence (10 August), St Clare (11 August).

Find out a little about them. They demonstrated different kinds of holiness which may help the children to see the wide variety of ways in which God works through people. Explain that a halo is the artist's way of showing someone's holiness, how their goodness seems to make them glow. Have the children ever seen someone glow with happiness and joy? Have there been times when they have felt that their own happiness has shone out? When did it happen?

God tells us to listen to Jesus. How can we do that? What helps us to listen well to what Jesus says? Do the children have any favourite things that Jesus says? Using the template picture of Jesus, invite the children to draw themselves in and write or draw one of their favourite things that Jesus says in the speech bubble.

Juniors

Bible Detective: Who were Moses and Elijah? Why did they appear with Jesus?

Have a few children's Bibles available and help the children to look up the references that give us clues about the importance of Moses and Elijah. Here are a few questions to start you off:

What was special about Moses' birth and childhood? (Exodus 2:1-10)

How did God give Moses his mission? (Exodus 3:1-12)

How did God convince the Egyptian Pharaoh that he had to let God's people go? (snippets from Exodus 7:14 – 12:32)

What happened at the Red Sea? (Exodus 14:1-31)

How did Moses find water in the desert? (Exodus 17:1-7)

What did God give to Moses on Mount Sinai? (Exodus 20:1-17)

How did Elijah help a widow during a long drought? (1 Kings 17:8-16)

How did Elijah show that God is stronger than Baal (a god people believed in at that time)? (1 Kings 18:20-39)

What happened at the end of Elijah's life? (2 Kings 2:1-11)

Tips for learning difficulties

The children can colour the picture of Jesus in from the template page. Talk to them about the Gospel story whilst they are doing this.

5. We come together

Parents can be invited to join in at this stage.

Focus

Light the candle. Invite those gathered to become still.

Gospel

In the Gospel we heard how Jesus' glory was suddenly revealed to the disciples. They were terrified to see Jesus radiant with power, standing with Moses and Elijah: a great leader and law-giver and a great prophet.

They hear God telling them that Jesus is his Son and that they should listen to him, but Jesus warned them not to tell anyone until after he had risen from the dead.

Prayer

Lord Jesus, you showed your glory to your disciples. Help us to remember the power of your love
and to listen faithfully to your words. Amen.

Share

Talk about the story and activity that you chose to use with the children. Invite the children to say what their favourite saying of Jesus is and/or tell their parents the results of their investigation into Moses and Elijah.

Sing

"The light of Christ"

The Assumption of the Blessed Virgin Mary

1. Introduction to the theme of the day

Aim: To see in the Feast of the Assumption our promise of eternal life and so help to overcome our natural fear of death.

Leader's reflection: It is absolutely natural for people to be afraid of death. We have little idea of what lies ahead. The ideas we have are often confused between harps and angelic singing and stern judgement of what we have done in our lifetimes.

The Feast of the Assumption is, therefore, a gift to us as it carries with it the great promise of Mary being carried into heaven body and soul. As the mother of Jesus, it is understandable that she should not face the corruption of death but should be taken direct to heaven. It is again something we cannot explain but, as an act of faith, something we sense to be deeply true. It is a hint of what lies ahead for us.

2. We arrive

We sit in a circle ready to listen to the Gospel.

Has anyone anything they would like to tell us about last week's Family Sheet?

Focus

White cloth, candle and open Bible or Lectionary. If you are unable to go into a church (see below) have a statue or picture of Mary and enough candles for the children to light one each.

Gospel: Luke 1:39-56

Read from the Lectionary or Children's Lectionary.

3. We respond

What is the Gospel asking of us?

This feast day has the same story for both young ones and juniors. Work in age groups, if appropriate, for the activities.

Young ones and Juniors

Story

Ciara had known Mrs Reynolds for ever. She had seen her every week since she was a baby and Mrs Reynolds had knitted some clothes for her and for her baby brother Christopher. Mrs Reynolds wasn't able to get out much, she was very old and had trouble walking.

Ciara loved to go round to Mrs Reynolds'. There were always chocolate biscuits, but before they had those, Ciara's mum gave Mrs Reynolds Communion. Because Mrs Reynolds could not go to Mass, Fr Michael had asked Ciara's mum to take Communion to her. Ciara's mum had said that she felt very lucky because she was taking Jesus himself to Mrs Reynolds.

Ciara had learnt to sit still and quiet and joined in the prayers. Christopher was still learning to be quiet, so sometimes Ciara rocked his pram or gave him things to play with.

One day, Ciara's mum got a phone call. It was Fr Michael. He was ringing to say that Mrs Reynolds had been taken into hospital. Ciara heard her mum say that she would pick up some things for Mrs Reynolds and call in later.

Mum went to see Mrs Reynolds every day. She took Communion with her and said how much Mrs Reynolds loved to see her and to receive Communion.

Then, very early one morning, the phone rang again. Ciara heard Mum getting dressed and going out, even though it was only just getting light. Mum was gone nearly all day. When she came in, she looked very tired. Dad had cooked the tea and went to warm Mum's up for her. Ciara wasn't sure what to say, so she played quietly with Christopher until Mum had had her tea.

Dad took Christopher up for his bath and Mum called Ciara to come and sit on her knee. Ciara guessed what had happened but when Mum told her that Mrs Reynolds had died she still felt a bit shocked and began to cry. Mum hugged her close and gave her some tissues, and used quite a few herself. They had loved Mrs Reynolds so much and knew they would miss her.

Mum and Dad thought Ciara was old enough to go to Mrs Reynolds' funeral. Ciara was a bit nervous, she hadn't been to a funeral before. Mum had helped her to choose some flowers and taken her into the church on the evening before when Fr Michael received Mrs Reynolds' body into the church. Ciara put her flowers on the coffin and had another little cry. But somehow she could tell that Mrs Reynolds wasn't really there and felt a bit better.

The next day, Ciara was amazed to see so many people; Mrs Reynolds' family and friends and lots of parishioners. The bit that Ciara liked best was when Fr Michael talked about Mrs Reynolds – and her! He told people about how Ciara had visited Mrs Reynolds and how Ciara's mum had taken Communion to her. He said that Mrs Reynolds was looking forward to meeting Jesus because, as he had promised, anyone who eats the bread of life will live for ever. Fr Michael said that, though it was right to be sad, they could also be happy that Mrs Reynolds and Jesus were together for ever, and that she would be ready to meet them when they went to heaven too.

As Ciara went with Mum to get the food ready for people after the funeral, she was pleased to get the job of putting out the chocolate biscuits – they would always remind her of Mrs Reynolds. "Mum," she said, "do you think Mrs Reynolds will have chocolate biscuits waiting for us?"

Mum smiled, "Well, if there are chocolate biscuits in heaven, it wouldn't surprise me one bit!"

4. Activity

Young ones

Invite the children to think about what made Ciara sad. What made her happy when she thought about Mrs Reynolds?
Talk about how Mary, the mother of Jesus, went straight to heaven. The children can colour in the template of Mary, or use fabrics to dress her.

Juniors

Have the children experienced the death of someone close to them? How did they feel?
Do they know anyone who gets Communion at home? If possible, show them the vessel used to carry the host.
Talk to the children about the Assumption of Mary. Because she was Jesus' mother, she was taken to heaven, body and soul at the same time. We have to leave our bodies behind but Jesus promises that, one day, we too will have resurrection bodies in heaven.
Invite the children to draw a picture of Mary arriving in heaven to be met by her Son.

Tips for learning difficulties

Help the children to talk about the story and to tell you about anyone they know who has died.
Talk about how Mary is in heaven with Jesus and how we will go there too.
The children can colour in her picture or use ready cut-out fabric to dress her.

5. We come together

Parents can be invited to join in at this stage.

Focus

Light the main candle. Invite those gathered to become still.

Gospel

In the Gospel we hear about Mary's visit to her cousin Elizabeth. Both of them are expecting special children but Elizabeth realises that Mary's is even more special than her own. In response, Mary sang a wonderful song called the "Magnificat".

Prayer

Jesus, Mary was your mother, and you loved her so much that when she died you took her straight away to be with you in heaven; body and soul. We know that you love us as well. When we die, bring us and all our families and friends to be with you in heaven so that we can be happy there, for ever, with you. Amen.

Share

We have listened to a story about someone who died and went to heaven. It reminded us that Jesus has promised eternal life and asked Mary to be our heavenly Mother who cares for us on earth too.

Sing

A hymn to Mary

The Triumph of the Cross

Holy Cross Day

1. Introduction to the theme of the day

"The power of the cross"

Aim: Today is the Feast of the Triumph of the Cross. We focus on Jesus' sacrifice for our salvation, and for the salvation of the whole world.

Leader's Reflection: Through his sacrifice, Jesus has made the cross his symbol for victory over the power of evil. Today we thank Jesus for that sacrifice, and for our salvation. We remind ourselves of the meaning of the cross, and we commit ourselves to doing our part to make the world a better place for everyone: for justice and salvation for all the people on earth.

2. We arrive

We sit in a circle ready to listen to the Gospel.

Around this time we celebrate Racial Justice Day, and we remember God's call to share his love with everyone, whatever their creed or race. Through the readings, we celebrate God's great gift of love to us, his sacrifice on the cross. God wants us to remember Jesus' cross, so we know how much he loves us.

Focus

The cross, a candle.

Gospel: John 3:13-17

Read from the Lectionary or Children's Lectionary.

3. We respond

What is the Gospel asking of us?

Work in age groups if appropriate. Then come together as a community at the end of the session.

Young ones

Jesus died on the cross so that we can be saved. We thank him for doing that for us, and we try to do the things he wants us to do. The cross is there to remind us to love everyone.

Story

Maria had a little crucifix, on a little golden chain. She wore it round her neck. It made her feel special, because it reminded her that God loves her. And it reminded her to be kind to other people.

That summer, Maria went on holiday to another country. It was a lovely holiday, in a big hotel on a beach. But Maria noticed a boy who sat begging, outside the hotel. He had no nice clothes, and if he tried to go on the beach the hotel porter chased him away. He was very thin and sad.

One afternoon Maria saw the boy sitting under a tree, crying. She felt her little crucifix, all hot against her skin. She wanted to be kind. So she went and put her arm round the little beggar boy. He was so surprised that he jumped! But by and by, they began to talk. They became friends, and Maria saved the rolls from breakfast to give him, and showed him her toys.

The day came to go home. Maria went to say goodbye to her new friend. He was so very sad! Who would help him and look after him now? Maria felt terrible. Suddenly she knew what to do! She took off her crucifix and gave it to him. "Jesus will look after you," she said. "And this little crucifix is here to remind you of that, every day."

Juniors

The cross is a powerful symbol. What does it mean to us? Why do we make the sign of the cross when we pray? What do we mean, when we say that Jesus' death on the cross showed that evil can be beaten and that the cross stands for salvation for everyone? God wants us to help everyone from every country in the world to feel his love. How can we do that?

Story

A man set out to sail across the Atlantic Ocean from Africa to America, in a tiny boat. On that boat was a horrible little dustbin. Its lid didn't work properly, and it pinched the man's fingers. It was hard to clean, and it smelt bad. It often fell out of its holder and threw rubbish everywhere, when the sea was rough. How the man hated that bin! But he needed it. He had to have somewhere for the rubbish.

Well, his boat sank one night. Perhaps it was hit by a whale. One minute he was safely asleep in his bunk, and the next minute he was covered in water. All he had time to do was to launch his life-raft and jump in.

Next day he was in an awful state. He had no clothes, no food, no water. Nothing but a little fishing line – and (you've guessed) the horrible little bin, which had floated into the life-raft. "At least I can be rid of YOU!" he said, and threw it away. But it kept floating back. In the end, he kept it. Just as well, because he was stuck in that life-raft for ten weeks, and the little bin was the only thing he had that could collect fresh rainwater to drink. It saved his life. Suddenly, he saw that it was the most beautiful thing in the world. Instead of making him think of rubbish and dirt, it reminded him of life.

This story reminds us that things can carry important messages, like the cross. It's difficult for you or I to really understand the triumph of the cross. For all of our lives, we've only known the cross as a sign of God's love. We've never hated it, or been afraid of it as people were in Roman times, because Jesus changed the cross from something terrible to something wonderful, all those years ago. The cross is our sign of life, of God's love and of everything wonderful in the world. How can we share that feeling, and help everyone, from every part of the world, feel God's love?

4. Activity

Young ones

The template for this week is a line drawing of five children holding hands. Colour them to show that they are from different races: Caucasian, Middle Eastern, Asian, Black, Oriental. Colour their clothes, make them smart to celebrate the triumph of Jesus' cross and Jesus' love.

Juniors

How can we show God how happy we are, that he sent Jesus to save us, and how proud we are of the cross, which Jesus has turned into a powerful symbol of life? How can we help everyone to feel God's love and the power of the cross? Make a poster, including cuttings from newspapers and pictures from magazines.

Tips for learning difficulties

The notion of a symbol is hard for a child with learning difficulties. The idea of reminders is easier to get over. We love the cross because it reminds us of Jesus, and how much he loves us, and how much he wants us to love others.

5. We come together

Parents can be invited to join in at this stage.

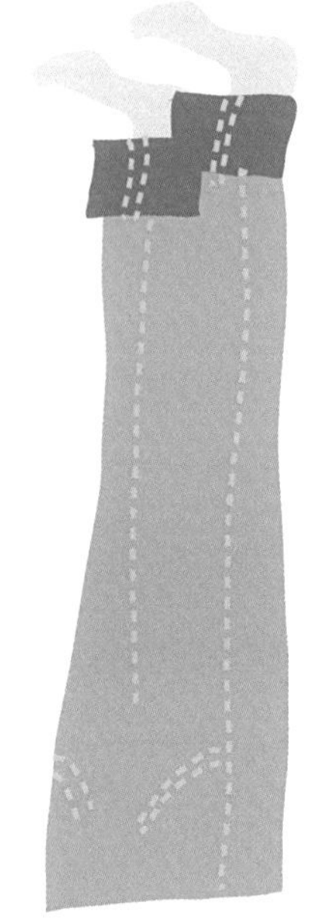

Focus

The cross, and the things made in the activities.

Gospel

Jesus died on the cross so that the power of evil in the world could be broken.
If we believe in him, he will save us from evil.
If we believe in him, we will help him fight evil.

Prayer

Lord Jesus, we thank you for loving us so much.
We thank you for saving us through the cross.
Help us to share your love and your salvation with everyone.
Amen.

Share

Share the work from the activities.

Sing

"At the name of Jesus, every knee shall bow"

All Saints

1. Introduction to the theme of the day

"I want to be in that number"

Aim: To encourage a sense of anticipation about the joy that awaits us in heaven.

Leader's Reflection: Few of us view death as something to look forward to. There is a natural fear of what lies beyond – an awareness of unfinished business and, perhaps, a sense of unworthiness for heaven. When we compare our lives with those of the great saints, that sense is heightened. Today's feast offers us great reassurance for this is not just about the canonised saints but all the saints – some of whom we have known.

These are the people who lived lives just like ours – sometimes good and holy but also prone to the vagaries of human nature – just like us. What comes after death we do not exactly know, but church tradition offers an image of "Purgatory". This is, perhaps, a state during which we are purified and made ready for eternal happiness. Over the years, purgatory developed a bad name and people were as afraid of that as of hell. However, if we identify ourselves with the Prodigal Son arriving home and facing the prospect of a banquet with family and friends, unwashed and with matted hair, we catch a glimpse of what that purification could be like. He would have bathed, washed and cut his hair, discarded filthy clothes and then felt ready to face the banquet. In the same way we will be spiritually washed, and, with the last vestiges of sin laid aside, we will feel ready to enter the eternal banquet – to be greeted by Our Lord and family and friends and take our place in heaven.

It is our belief that one day this will be our feast day – when we become one of all the saints.

2. We arrive

We sit in a circle ready to listen to the Gospel.

Focus

White cloth, candle. If your parish has a Book of the Dead, display that with honour. If not, prepare a "scroll" using parchment or thick paper with the names of people who have died recently – or perhaps family members and friends of the children.

Gospel: Matthew 5:1-12

Read from the Lectionary or Children's Lectionary.

3. We respond

What is the Gospel asking of us?

This week's story is particularly appropriate for the young ones. Detailed discussion ideas are provided for the juniors. Work in age groups, if appropriate. Join together as a community at the end of the session.

Story

It was three months since Mrs Reynolds, their neighbour and friend, died. Ciara was still sad but did not cry about it any more. Mrs Reynolds' house had been sold to a young couple with a baby about Christopher's age. Mum had said Mrs Reynolds would be pleased to think that Christopher had a new friend living in her house.

Mrs Reynolds had left gifts for everyone. Mum got a beautiful brooch – and a letter which made her cry. As she said, "Why did she thank me so much for taking Communion to her? It was a lovely thing to be able to do." And then she blew her nose again!

Ciara had been given a special card saying how happy Mrs Reynolds had been to have a little girl to buy chocolate biscuits for. And that made Ciara cry! Mrs Reynolds had also left her a musical jewellery box and her bird table and bird bath. Ciara had fed the birds when Mrs Reynolds wasn't well enough – so she knew exactly what to do.

Christopher, the baby, got some animal carvings and bells that Mrs Reynolds had brought back from Africa. Ciara wasn't quite sure what Christopher made of them as he tried to eat the elephant and jangled the bells but she loved the idea that Mrs Reynolds had bought them in Africa and then carried them all across the sea and now they were in their house.

Mrs Reynolds had also left money to their church – Fr Michael said they could get the new hymnbooks now and looked really pleased. In fact, Mrs Reynolds was making a lot of people happy and lots of them said, "She was a saint, that woman!"

Ciara thought about this a lot and decided to ask Mum about it.

"Mum," she began, "you know how everyone says Mrs Reynolds was a saint?"

Her mum nodded.

"Well," Ciara continued, "I thought saints had to do great things – you know like Mother Teresa going to live in India. But Mrs Reynolds didn't do anything like that."

Mum smiled, "No – maybe not. But she was very kind – very holy and loved God so much that she is sure to be in heaven. You don't have to be superhuman to be a saint; just someone who loves God and other people, and that's just what Mrs Reynolds did really well."

Ciara had to agree.

"And," said Mum, "she has a feast day – a day when we can remember her and celebrate her being in heaven. We call it 'All Saints'. There are so many saints in heaven that we could never get through the whole list even in a year, so we have a special day for all the saints, especially the ones we know."

Ciara was very impressed that Mrs Reynolds had a feast day. And then thought,

"So Mr Reynolds would have it too ... and Grandma Jane ... and Jack's Uncle Tom... "

"Probably," said Mum.

"I bet it's a really big party in heaven on that day... And Mum ... could we celebrate Mrs Reynolds' feast day with a few ..."

"Chocolate biscuits?" asked Mum.

Young ones

Invite the children to respond to the story – do they know anyone in heaven? What good things did they do? What sort of person were they?

Juniors

Do the children know the names of any saints? Talk to the children about All Saints as the day when we celebrate all the people in heaven whose names most people do not know. Can they think of people who might be saints?

Talk, too, about the companion feast of All Souls. You may like to use the analogy of the Prodigal Son – turning up unkempt and not at all ready for a banquet – and how his father kindly let him get sorted out before he had to go and face everyone. Explain that most of us die with things we regret: things we did and should not have done, and things we did not do. God gives us time to put this right so that we are ready for heaven. This is why we set November aside as a month for praying for people who have died. We don't know who is in heaven and who is on the way – but we can all pray that, if not this year, then next year we will be celebrating even more saints who have marched in to be among that number.

4. Activity

Young ones

Have a selection of flowers ready for the children to tie into small posies. Moisten some cotton wool or kitchen paper and wrap it around the base of the stems. Wrap an elastic band around them and then a ribbon.
What is the tradition of flowers for the dead?

Juniors

Using the template page, read the Beatitudes and the rewards. The children listen to the Gospel again – and then join each Beatitude to its reward.

Tips for learning difficulties

Have paper plates ready to use as faces. Have facial features cut out and ready for the children to stick on: eyes, noses, mouths, ears, big smiles. As they work, talk about God wanting people to be happy with him in heaven – and this is what they will look like when they get there.

5. We come together

Parents can be invited to join in at this stage.

Focus

Light the candle. Invite those gathered to become still – to look at the candle and think about the time of year.

Gospel

Today, we have been thinking about saints and about what it takes to be a saint.
Jesus says that saints are happy. They are poor in spirit but have the kingdom. They are gentle; they mourn but shall be comforted. They want what is right; they are merciful and pure in heart. They are peacemakers and sometimes are persecuted for what is right.
But for all of them their reward is great in heaven.

Prayer

Thank you, Jesus, for showing us how to be saints.
Help us to live good and holy lives
so that we can join that great number of people
who live in everlasting happiness in heaven.
Amen.

Share

In today's story, we heard about Mrs Reynolds – an elderly friend of Ciara. Mrs Reynolds had died – but Ciara learned that she was quite likely to be a saint in heaven and that "All Saints" is her feast day. The older children thought about how God gives us time to get ready for heaven if we need it.
We don't know who in this "Book of the Dead" (or scroll) is a saint or still on the way – but we can pray for them all during November.
Invite the younger children to place their flowers close to the book/scroll. When we take the book back into the church we will leave the flowers with it – unless any of the children would like to take them away to put somewhere special.

Sing

"Oh when the saints go marching in!"

Blessed are the poor in spirit
Blessed are those who mourn
Blessed are the meek
Blessed are those who hunger and thirst for righteousness
Blessed are the peacemakers
Blessed are the pure in heart
Blessed are the merciful
Blessed are those who are persecuted for righteousness' sake

...for they will be comforted
...for they will inherit the earth
...for theirs is the kingdom of heaven
...for they will be filled
...for they will be called children of God
...for they will receive mercy
...for they will see God
...for theirs is the kingdom of heaven

The Commemoration of All the Faithful Departed (All Souls)

1. Introduction to the theme of the day

"Gateway to heaven"

Aim: To help children to see death as the way to eternal life and to offer them ways to pray for those who have died.

Leader's Reflection: Helping children to understand death can be quite difficult and much depends on the age and emotional development of the child. Some children will have experienced death within their circle of family and friends, others will only have heard of it on television.

As Christians we have a great gift in our belief in the resurrection. Though humanly speaking we fear death and what lies beyond, we bring to it our faith that Jesus' death has opened the way to eternal life. As suggested in the Preface for the Dead: "for your faithful people life is changed not ended". This is the message we can try to live by and pass on to the children in our charge.

2. We arrive

We sit in a circle ready to listen to the Gospel.

Has anyone anything they would like to tell us about last week's Family Sheet?

Focus

Purple cloth, candle, open Bible, basket with flowers in.

Gospel: Mark 15:33-39; 16:1-6

Read from the Lectionary or Children's Lectionary.

3. We respond

What is the Gospel asking of us?

What do we call the day when we remember that Jesus died?

What do we call the day when the women found the empty tomb?

Work in age groups if appropriate.

Young ones

Story

Julie and John's Auntie Ruth had been ill for a long time. But even though she was quite thin and weak she carried on doing her garden. Mum used to tell her off – and sometimes, Julie and John heard her saying to Gran, "She should save her energy! She's tiring herself out and she probably won't even see the things she's planting." And then she used to sniffle a bit as if she was crying. John and Julie didn't know what was happening, but felt the house getting sadder and sadder until one day they heard that Auntie Ruth had died. Everyone was very unhappy and at her funeral the church was packed with people who wanted to say goodbye to Auntie Ruth.

A few months later, Julie and John went round to Gran's. It felt odd to be going there with no Auntie Ruth and everyone was a bit quiet and not talking much. "Why don't you two run outside and play for a while?" said Gran. She had put a swing and climbing frame in the garden for when the children came, but they didn't feel like playing with them. Instead they decided to go for a walk round the garden and looked at the last bit of garden they had seen Auntie Ruth doing. They couldn't believe their eyes! They rushed in to Gran and Mum. "Come and see! Come and see!"

Everyone went out to the garden. There, coming up through the ground were strong little shoots and when Gran and Mum looked closer they saw why the children were so excited because Auntie Ruth had planted the seeds so that they spelt out "I love you!"

"Well I never," said Gran, "our Ruth knew she wouldn't see these grow but she knew we would! Isn't that just like her!"

And everyone agreed it was!

Juniors

Story

What hope does the Gospel offer to us? What hope does it give us for people who have died?

One of India's greatest people was a man called Mahatma Gandhi. He was born at the end of the 19th century and became an icon of the 20th century. He was a lawyer in South Africa and fought for human rights there. He returned to India and set about working for Indian independence; at that time it was part of the British Empire. Gandhi's technique was not to use terror tactics but to use prayer and fasting and peaceful protest to encourage change. Most Indians revered him and gave him the title mahatma which means "great soul". As often happens with great people, there were others who disagreed violently with him. One of these people forced his way up to Gandhi as he was on his way to evening prayer. He shot Gandhi three times. Gandhi had said a short while before, that even many bodyguards could not protect him and that God was his protector. As he fell unconscious, his last words were a prayer: "O God Rama".

The whole world mourned the loss of this great man but his influence still bears fruit to this day. His peaceful ways of seeking justice were taken up by Martin Luther King in the USA and in South Africa by Nelson Mandela. His great soul continues to bring blessing to people on earth.

Have the children heard of Gandhi? What peaceful means of working for justice can they think of?

4. Activity

Choose the activities most suitable for your group.

Young ones

Use the template of stalks and leaves. Invite the children to add flowers and colour them in, making the whole picture look like Auntie Ruth's garden.

Juniors

Most people are not quite ready for heaven when they die. They need our prayers and may need to grow in love before they feel ready to meet God. Teach the children the prayer:

> "Eternal rest grant unto them
> and let perpetual light shine upon them.
> May they rest in peace. Amen."

Explain the words to them – e.g. perpetual means everlasting/continuing with no interruption.

Have the children write the prayer and decorate it – perhaps with pictures of people they have loved who have died.

Thinking about the good things people did when they were alive is a good way of praying for them. It reminds us of the love they showed when they were with us and may help them to grow in love on their way to heaven.

Talk to the children about some of these good things and invite them to write them down and decorate or draw them. Make a display of the children's work.

Tips for learning difficulties

Children with learning difficulties can find it hard to understand death but feel the loss nonetheless. Talk to them about people going to heaven where they are happy with God and still love us. Use the flowers idea above to illustrate that being in heaven is like becoming a flower in God's garden.

5. We come together

Parents can be invited to join in at this stage.

Focus

Light the candle. Invite those gathered to become still.

Gospel

In the Gospel, we hear how Jesus died. Many people mocked him as he was dying but, as he died, a Roman centurion standing by suddenly realised that Jesus really was the Son of God.

As soon as they could after the Sabbath, Mary of Magdala, Mary, the mother of James and Salome went to the tomb to anoint Jesus' body with spices. They were worried about who would roll away the huge stone in front of the tomb. But when they got there it had already been rolled back, and they saw a young man sitting there. They were amazed, but he said to them, "Do not be afraid. Jesus is risen. He is not here."

Prayer

Lord Jesus, you died and were buried and your family and friends were sad.
But you rose from the dead and so you opened up the gateway to heaven.
Bless our loved ones who have died.
Help them to grow in love so that they can live with you for ever. Amen.

Share

We have been thinking about people who have died but who still love us. We thought about how we could help them by praying for them and remembering the good things they did. While the music plays, the children will place flowers by the cross to remember people who have died and the things they did that made life better.

Sing or play Taizé chants:

"Jesus, remember me"
"Bless the Lord, my soul"

I

Love

You

The Dedication of the Lateran Basilica

Dedication Festival

1. Introduction to the theme of the day

Aim: To celebrate our freedom to worship – and to remember those who do not share this freedom.

Leader's Reflection: Why should a church in far-away Rome have a feast important enough to break the flow of our journey through Mark's Gospel? As most of us know, the early Church suffered persecution and most Christian worship took place in secrecy. When Constantine converted to Christianity in the fourth century, he gave Christians the freedom to worship publicly. He gave Pope Sylvester I property belonging to the Lateran family and on 9 November 324, the first Christian basilica in history was dedicated.

St John Lateran (dedicated to Christ the Saviour, St John the Baptist and St John the Evangelist) is the cathedral church of Rome – not St Peter's. This is where the Pope, as Bishop of Rome, has his Chair and, as the Pope is head of the worldwide Church, St John Lateran can be seen as the cathedral of the world and is sometimes called the Mother and Head of all Churches of the City and the World.

Today's feast reminds us of a time when Christians were not free to worship publicly, and of what a privilege it is to be able to, in our day. We might reflect on those in the world who continue to have to keep their worship secret.

2. We arrive

We sit in a circle ready to listen to the Gospel.

Has anyone anything they would like to tell us about last week's Family Sheet?

Focus

White cloth, lighted candle and, if possible, some photographs of the Basilica of St John Lateran (ask people who may have been to Rome – or look on the Internet).

Gospel: John 2:13-22

Read from the Lectionary or Children's Lectionary.

3. We respond

What is the Gospel asking of us?

Work in age groups if appropriate. Alternatively, choose the story and activity most suitable for your group.

Young ones

Story

Marcus was a Christian – but his mum and dad said he must keep this a secret. Marcus had heard stories about some Christians who had been put in prison – and some had even been killed – so he knew it was very important not to tell anyone that his family were Christians.

Every Lord's Day, what we would call Sunday, Marcus and his family went round to Phoebe's house and shared a meal with the other Christians in their neighbourhood. They would sing songs, someone would tell the children stories, people who were preparing to become Christians learned about God and Jesus, and the adults would celebrate the Breaking of Bread.

Marcus had learnt to keep his eyes and ears open for anyone following them and to tell Dad at once if he thought someone was watching where they were going. It had not happened yet, but Dad reminded the whole family each week that this was the only way to keep safe.

Then, one Lord's Day, Phoebe ushered them into her house. She was very excited – there was to be an announcement! When everyone had gathered, Dominicus the leader stood up and said that the emperor had become a Christian. There was a stunned silence. All the emperors since Peter's time had hated the Christians.

Dominicus said that he had heard that Emperor Constantine had had a vision of a cross before a battle and, when he won, had become a Christian. Even more wonderfully, he had said that Christians were free to worship in public – they were not to be harmed.

Everyone clapped and cheered – this was the best news ever.

Some years later, Marcus had his own family and Constantine had kept his word – he did not have to tell his children to watch out for people following them. They still met at Phoebe's house, but on the Lord's Day, he would take his family to the Pope's church dedicated to Christ the Saviour and St John the Baptist. It was a huge, impressive building. But the most important bit for Marcus was seeing hundreds of other Christians all gathered to do what he and his family had come to do: to give praise and worship to God – together.

Juniors

Story

Constantine was born around AD 280. His mother, Helena, was a Christian and his father, Constantus Chlorus, a pagan – but a very powerful man.

Much of Constantine's early life was taken up with training as a soldier and fighting battles around the Roman Empire. He even came to Britain to serve in York where, with the death of the emperor, his soldiers proclaimed Constantine as emperor.

Not everyone agreed with this, of course, and Constantine had many battles to prove himself.

The most significant one for Christians was one against a man called Maxentius whose army was about four times larger than Constantine's. Years later, Constantine said that he had had a vision and had seen a cross in the sky and heard the words, "in this sign you shall have victory". He ordered all his soldiers to paint the sign on their shields and the next day they defeated the army of Maxentius.

Constantine realised that the Christian God was very powerful and so proclaimed that now he was emperor, all persecution was to stop and Christians could have their lands and churches back.

He was very generous to Christians, giving them land and building churches. He gave property to the Pope to build a basilica – a great church. This was to be dedicated to Christ the Saviour and St John the Baptist and the family who had the land was called Lateran, so we call that church "St John Lateran". Constantine gave 250 kg of gold to go on the ceiling – about £60 million nowadays.

Although he became a Christian, Constantine remained a catechumen (someone preparing to be baptised) for most of his life. When he realised he was dying, he called Bishop Eusebius to him and asked to be baptised. For the last few weeks of his life, he put aside his rich purple clothes and wore only his white baptismal ones.

4. Activity

Young ones

Use the template of the church – perhaps with the name of your parish already written on it. Fold along the solid lines to form three sides of a church. With the church "closed", talk first about how we think of the church just being a building. "Open" the church and ask the children what is missing. Talk about the things – but also about the people. The children can then draw themselves, their families and friends on the inside of the church.

Juniors

If you have found pictures of St John Lateran, look through them with the children. Why do they think the basilica is so ornate? Do they like it? What shows that it is a place where people worship? Can they find things that are in their own church? How are they the same – and how are they different?

Tips for learning difficulties

Use the church template and explain that this is your church. Open it up and ask what is missing. Draw out – the people. Who especially is missing? Invite them to draw themselves and other special people who come to your church.

5. We come together

Parents can be invited to join in at this stage.

Focus

Light the candle. Invite those gathered to become still.

Gospel

In the Gospel, Jesus goes to the Temple to pray. When he gets there, he finds that he has to go past stalls and people selling things, getting in the way of people who want to use the Temple for what it was built for – prayer and worship. He becomes angry and knocks over the stalls and reminds people that God's house is a house of prayer not a market.

Prayer

Lord Jesus, you loved your Father's house and want all our churches to be places where we can gather to pray and worship him.
We thank you for the gift of our church/churches (*N...*) and pray for those who still have to worship in secret because they are afraid of persecution.
Amen.

Share

Today the children have learnt that not everyone can just go to church as we can. We have particularly looked at the early days of the Church when Christians had to worship in secret because they were being persecuted and how Constantine changed that when he became emperor.

We realise how lucky we are to have our church, but also how it is not just the building, but us coming together to pray and worship.

Sing

"We see the Lord"
"I will sing, I will sing unto the Lord"

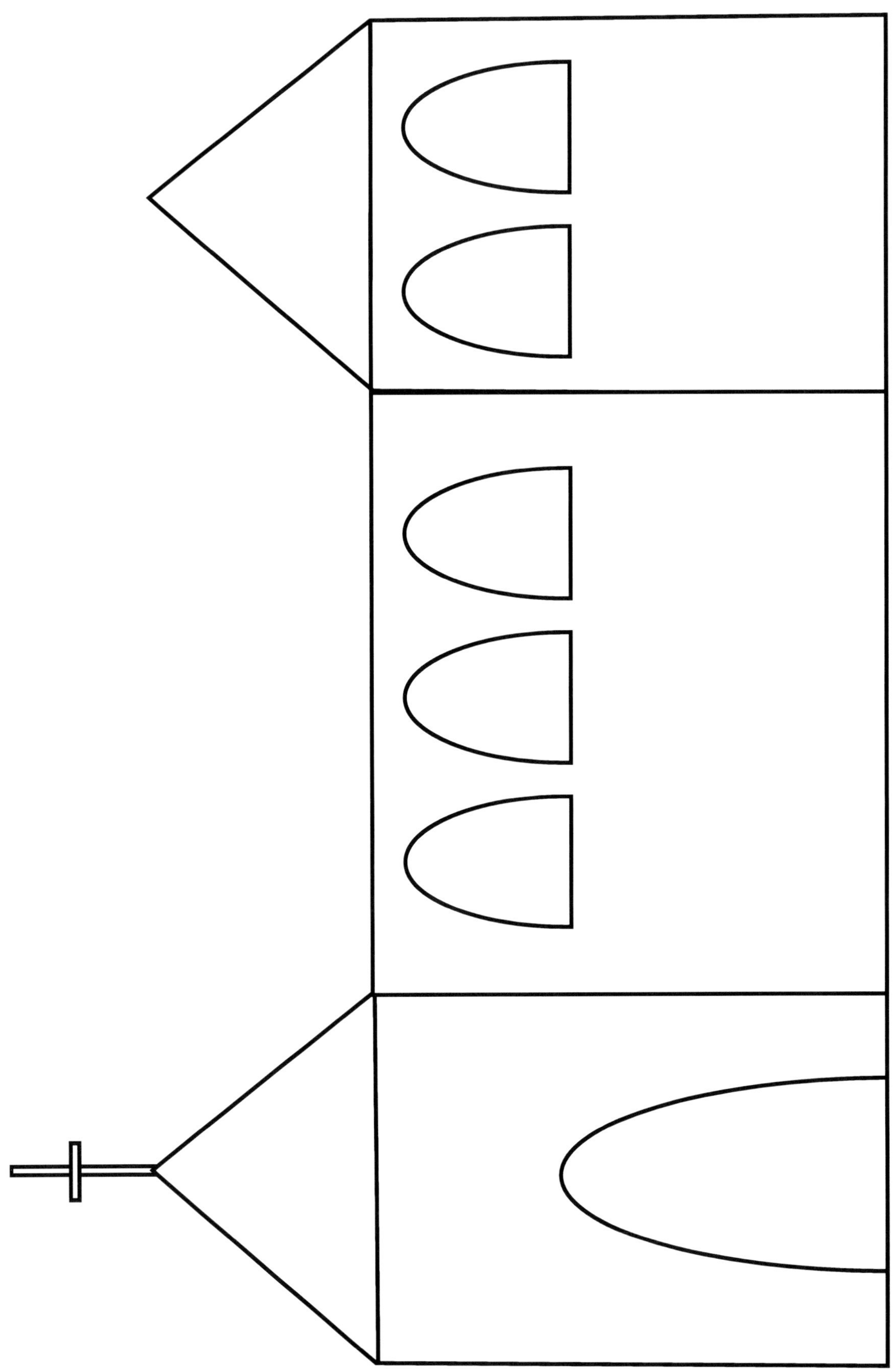

St David, Bishop

1. Introduction to the theme of the day

> "Happy St David's day
> Dydd gwyl Dewi hapus"

Aim: To celebrate St David's Day and Welsh culture.

Leader's Reflection: All over the world, Welsh people will be celebrating the feast of their patron saint, David. Little is known about the life of the saint though great deeds are attributed to him. National feast days give people an opportunity to celebrate their heritage especially when they are living far from their homeland. Putting a country under the patronage of a saint reminds us of the importance of Christianity in the history of the British Isles and the confidence that 1500 years after his death, St David is still praying for the land of his birth and its people.

2. We arrive

We sit in a circle ready to listen to the Gospel.
Has anyone anything they would like to tell us about last week's Family Sheet?

Focus

White cloth; Bible open at today's Gospel; daffodils and/or leeks.

Gospel: Matthew 5:13-16

Read from the Lectionary or Children's Lectionary.

3. We respond

What is the Gospel asking of us?

This week there is one story for all. Work in age groups, if appropriate, for the activities but join together as a community at the end of the session.

Young ones and Juniors

Story

Myfanwy (Mu – van – wi) and Iestin (ee – est – in) had just moved to a new school. They had left the school in their village in North Wales because their father had got a new job in England. Their old school had been small and they knew the names of everyone there. Now, their school seemed to be as big as their whole village. Their mum said that they were exaggerating, but sometimes that was how they felt. The hardest thing, though, was having to think in English all the time. The children could speak English, they had learnt it at school, but at home and in their old school, they spoke Welsh. And people couldn't say their names – well, they could, but they got teased about them. "My fan why" one girl kept calling Myfanwy and poor Iestin had to put up with "I stin" and people laughed sometimes when they answered in Welsh or said something in their Welsh accent.

Their parents told them that it would stop but it wasn't very nice while it was happening.

On St David's Day, the children went to school. They had got cards from their grandparents and Uncle Rhys but did not expect it to be a good day.

Imagine their surprise when they arrived and went into assembly and saw a flag with a red dragon on it. Then, Mr Meredith, the headteacher, stood in front of everyone and said "Bore da" (Boreh da) and without thinking, Myfanwy and Iestin replied, "Bore da, Mr Meredith." Mr Meredith smiled broadly. "Of course," he said, "you come from my homeland too! Today is a special day for us. I left Wales a long time ago but every year, my family still celebrates St David's Day."

He called Myfanwy and Iestin forward and asked them to teach the other children how to say "Bore da" which means "Good morning" and to tell the children what they would be doing to celebrate. They were a bit shy but talked about how Mum had bought lots of daffodils and that Dad had threatened to wear a huge leek to work, but Mum had made him wear a small leek badge instead. Everyone had laughed, but it was happy laughter. At the end, Mr Meredith had shaken their hands and said, "Diolch yn fawr" (Dee-olch un vowr) and asked everyone else to do the same. It sounded very funny to hear everyone speaking Welsh, but lovely to hear them saying, "Thank you very much."

St David was a Celtic saint who lived in the 6th century. He was one of many people who lived a very austere life of prayer and work. We do not know much about the people of the time simply because they did not write about themselves. If they wrote it was to write of the wonders of Creation and the power of God.

What do the children know about the Celtic saints of Wales?

Talk about the holy places where they live, by springs, in woods, taking the traditional sacred places and making them holy by their prayer. Legends grew up around them: wonderful healings and raising people from the dead. One such legend is that a blind man was healed by water splashing from David's baptism. The legends may not be true but they try to convey something of the specialness of the person.

How do the children think that David was a good example of being "salt for the earth" and "light for the world"?

4. Activity

Young ones

Using the template of a "St David's Day" card, make a card to celebrate the feast of St David and give it to a Welsh friend. Write "Happy St David's Day" or "Dydd gwyl Dewi hapus".

Juniors

Celebrating a feast!

We have, in many cases, forgotten that a church "Feast" is often the opportunity to get together and feast – to bring out special foods, sing old songs and tell old stories. This is particularly appropriate for the Feast of St David with the Welsh love of story and poetry.

Have available simplified traditional Welsh stories, e.g. the story of Beddgelert, Elidyr's Sojourn in Fairy Land, St Tegla's Well and give some of the children time to read them through and prepare to tell or read them.

Encourage others to lay out a celebratory "meal" using traditional Welsh foods, e.g. bara brith, crumpets (many more recipes/ideas available online).

Create a "Welsh" atmosphere using red and green (from the Welsh flag) and daffodils in vases.

Tips for learning difficulties

Use the gifts of the children as appropriate: some will be welcomers and hosts or hostesses for the celebration meal, others will enjoy the more artistic option.

Ensure all the children recognise that they are contributing to the success of your celebration.

5. We come together

Parents can be invited to join in at this stage.

Focus

Light the candle. Invite those gathered to become still.

Gospel

In the Gospel, Jesus says that his disciples are to be salt of the earth and light for the world. He wants their light to shine out so people recognise the glory of God working through them.

Prayer

God, Creator of everything,
help us to follow the example of St David
who tried to find you in everything and everyone.
Amen.

Share

We have thought about some of the heritage of Welsh people and, though we don't know much about St David's life, we see how, 1500 years after his death, we still entrust Wales and its people to his prayer.

We celebrate his concern for us and the richness of Welsh culture and enjoy a "feast" in honour of his Feast!

Sing

Welsh hymns and folk songs (in Welsh where known).

"Guide me, O thou great Redeemer"

"All through the night"

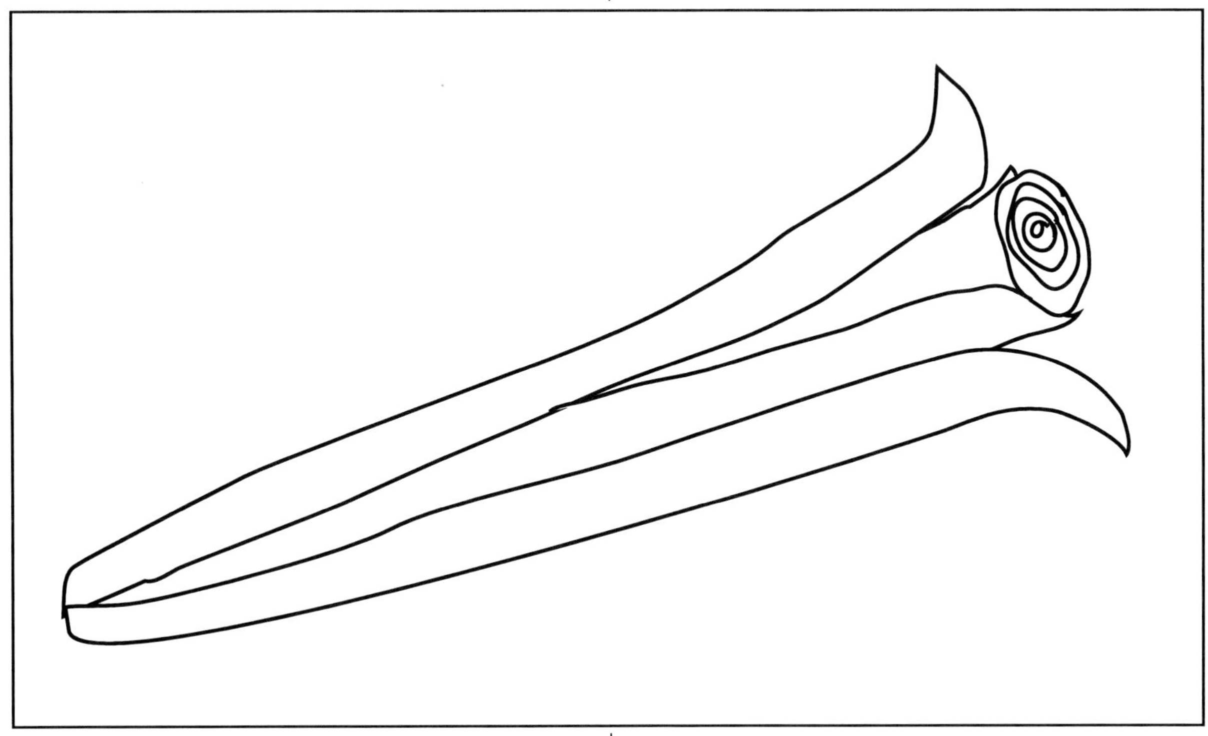

St Patrick, Bishop

1. Introduction to the theme of the day

Aim: To honour the feast of the patron saint of Ireland and to celebrate some aspects of Irish culture.

Leader's Reflection: Although St Patrick lived over 1500 years ago, his feast is celebrated with great enthusiasm in countries all around the world. The St Patrick's Day parade in New York is a great celebration for Irish Americans and other New Yorkers. There is even a St Patrick's Day parade in Tokyo. One of St Patrick's greatest achievements was to bring the Good News to the Celtic peoples of Ireland in their own language. His captivity as a young man had made him fluent and so, unlike other missionaries sent before him, he knew both the language and druidic customs and was able to communicate directly with people who heard the power and hope of the words he spoke. He also used signs and symbols to help his teaching – the most famous being his use of the shamrock to illustrate the mystery of the Trinity. We continue that work: opening God's Word in ways that people can understand and using sign and symbol to deepen people's understanding of it.

2. We arrive

We sit in a circle ready to listen to the Gospel.
Has anyone anything they would like to tell us about last week's Family Sheet?

Focus

White cloth; Bible open at the Gospel reading (or first or second reading if chosen); shamrock if available; Celtic cross.

Gospel: Luke 10:1-12. 17-20

Read from the Lectionary or Children's Lectionary. The first reading (Jeremiah 1:4-9) or second reading (Acts 13:46-49) are also helpful in giving a scriptural context to St Patrick's life.

3. We respond

What is the Gospel asking of us?

Work in age groups if appropriate. This week, a short story is provided for the young ones and detailed discussion ideas are offered for the juniors.

Young ones
Story

St Patrick was not born in Ireland, he was born in Wales. When he was sixteen he was kidnapped and taken over the sea to Ireland where he was sold as a slave and lived in what is now Antrim in the north of Ireland. He worked for six years and during the long hours of loneliness watching his master's sheep, learned to pray, lots of short prayers so that sometimes he thought he must have said over a thousand in one day!

One day he was lucky enough to escape and went to France where he learned more and more about God and realised he wanted to be a priest.

Years later, he thought he heard a voice calling him to go back to Ireland. He was not happy about this as it had been a hard and unhappy part of his life. But he sensed that God wanted him to go back and so he trusted that God would be with him and would protect him.

St Patrick did have problems – the powerful chiefs and druids (the pagan religious leaders) tried to stop him, but God always came to his help. One example was when a chief had said that all fires had to be put out until his own fire was relit. The problem for St Patrick was that this happened just before the Easter Vigil when he needed to light a fire to prepare to celebrate the resurrection. He went ahead and lit the fire and though his life was threatened and people tried to put it out, he was kept safe and the fire continued to burn. St Patrick told the crowds that this was a sign from God that the Christian faith would continue to burn in Ireland whatever happened in the future.

For many people, 1500 years later, his words are still true.

Juniors

Think about the reading you have chosen and invite the children to respond. How is St Patrick like Jeremiah – or Paul and Barnabas – or the people Jesus sent out to the villages? How do their problems mirror those of St Patrick? Think about his time in slavery, the opposition he met from Irish chiefs and druids, the miracles he worked and the power of his words changing people's lives.

What does his example encourage us to do? How can we learn to be strong in faith? How can we share our Good News with other people and help them to come to know Jesus?

4. Activity

Young ones

Use the template to cut out a shamrock. Invite the children to decorate their shamrock – not necessarily just green! With sticky tape fix a safety pin on the back and put it on the child as a badge.

Juniors

Invite the children to write and decorate part of St Patrick's breastplate. Explain that he used the idea of putting on spiritual armour to protect him when he was facing the Irish chiefs and druids who opposed him.

I bind to myself today
God's Power to guide me,
God's Might to uphold me,
God's Wisdom to teach me,
God's Eye to watch over me,
God's Ear to hear me,
God's Word to give me speech,
God's Hand to guide me,
God's Way to lie before me,
God's Shield to protect me,
Against everyone who would injure me,
Whether far or near,
Whether few or with many.

If you are having a party, older children could prepare a "feast" of traditional Irish food. Use shamrock and Celtic designs to decorate the tables. White cloths with green ribbon/streamers would also look good. Ask one or two children to prepare to read traditional folk tales from Ireland – have them practise in readiness for the party. If paints/felt tips are available, other children might like to do illustrations for the stories. Celebrate the Irish love of poetry and song.

Tips for learning difficulties

Choose the activity which best suits the gifts of the children in the group. Some children will be natural welcomers and hosts – others might prefer a more artistic activity.

5. We come together

Parents can be invited to join in at this stage.

Focus

Light the candle. Invite those gathered to become still. If shamrock is available, people might like to pin some on their clothes.

Gospel

In our reading today, we heard about how God chooses people to take his Good News to the world. Quite often they do not feel very confident, like St Patrick. However, God is on their side and protects them from harm and gives them strength and power to fulfil their mission.

Prayer

Here is another part of St Patrick's Breastplate prayer. He used to imagine that he was putting on spiritual armour when he knew he was facing threats and difficulties. This gave him the courage and strength to carry on with his mission:

Christ with me, Christ before me,
Christ behind me, Christ within me,
Christ beneath me, Christ above me,
Christ at my right, Christ at my left,
Christ in the heart of everyone who thinks of me,
Christ in the mouth of everyone who speaks to me,
Christ in every eye that sees me,
Christ in every ear that hears me. Amen.

Share

We have been thinking about St Patrick and how he brought the Good News to Ireland. It was a difficult job but he spoke to the Celtic people in their own language and many were happy to hear about God's love for them. He used symbols like shamrock to explain difficult ideas like the Trinity. (Invite those who made the shamrock badges to indicate how they show God, Jesus and Spirit as three leaves on one plant.)

We thought it would be good to celebrate the feast day by having a small party. Some of the children have prepared some stories for us as well.

Sing

"Hail glorious St Patrick"
"St Patrick's Breastplate"
Any Irish hymn

GOD
JESUS
HOLY
SPIRIT

1st Sunday of Advent

Family Sheet

To do at home with your family

For parents: Weekly Thought

Advent is a special time of year which can remind us of the greatness of our faith. We look way back into history to the prophets – and forward to the coming of Christ. As the busyness of preparing for Christmas increases, take time to gaze at the stars with your child and celebrate the wonder of being loved by the God who knows each one by name.

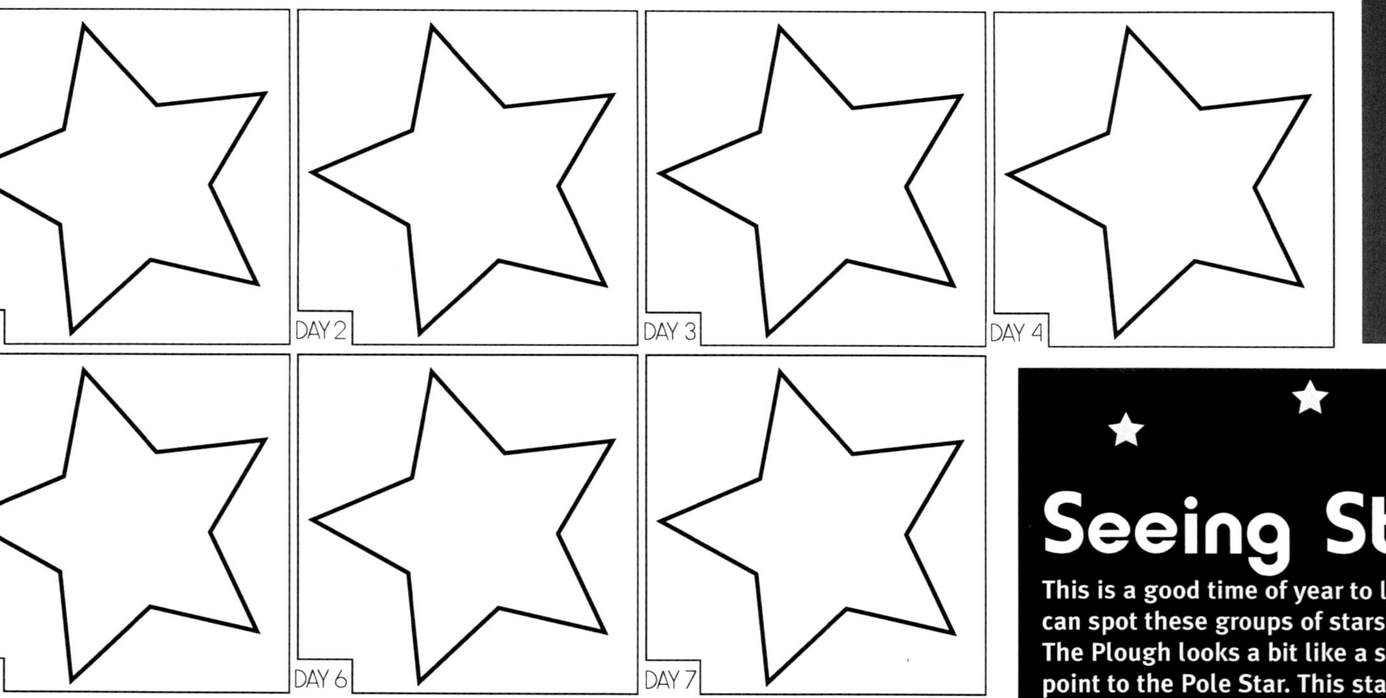

Watch out for people making others happy this week. Colour in or make a star smile each day.

This sheet has been completed by ....

FAMILY PRAYER

Lord Jesus, help us to prepare for Christmas with joy.
Help us to live this Advent well so that our Christmas presents to you are hearts ready to welcome you and invite you to make your home in them for ever.
Amen.

Seeing Stars

This is a good time of year to look at the stars. Wrap up warm and see if you can spot these groups of stars called constellations.Tick the ones you spot.
The Plough looks a bit like a saucepan! The two stars at the side of the pan point to the Pole Star. This star is overhead at the North Pole so people sometimes use it to navigate. The Pole Star is the first star in the "pan handle" of a constellation called the Little Plough. Can you see it?
Cassiopeia – looks like a giant W in the sky on the other side of the Pole Star.
Orion – the star at the top left-hand side is red and is called Betelgeuse (pronounced beetle juice!). Orion was a hunter. Follow Orion's belt down and you come to Sirius the Dog Star. This is the brightest star in the sky.

2nd Sunday of Advent

Family Sheet

To do at home with your family

For parents: Weekly Thought

John the Baptist was an extreme prophet and few could match his example. However, we are all called to a similar kind of witness even though ours happens through our acts of kindness, our standing up for what is right and standing against what is wrong, our example of trying daily to grow more like Jesus. Encourage your children to be confident in their faith. Help them to understand that you do not always find it easy to be a Christian and that you worry about standing out from the crowd but that Jesus understands this and will offer his love and support to them as you do too.

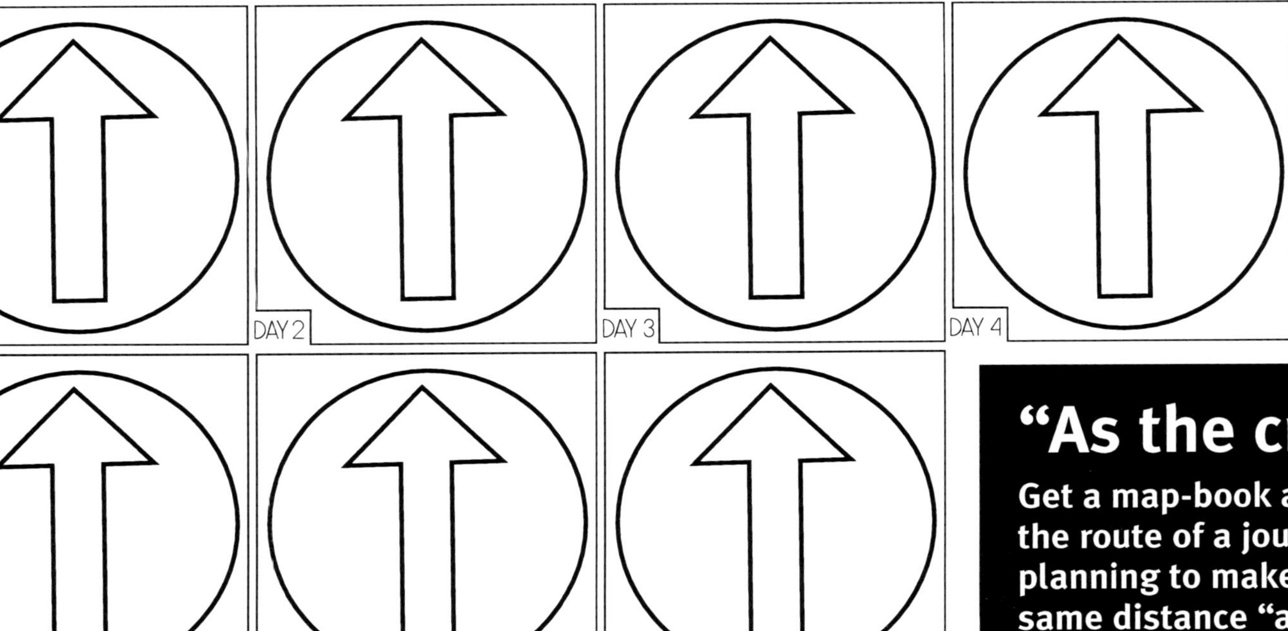

Colour in a road-sign each day. Write on it something that is making a way for Jesus.

This sheet has been completed by ....

FAMILY PRAYER

Lord Jesus, bless our family this week as we try to grow more like you.
Help us to be strong and brave – especially if people make fun of us for being Christians.
Amen.

"As the crow flies"

Get a map-book and use a piece of string to measure the route of a journey, perhaps one that you are planning to make over Christmas. Now measure the same distance "as the crow flies" (i.e. direct from point A to point B). You might like to do the same thing taking going up and down hills into account. No wonder people thought making a straight path for Jesus was such a good idea!

3rd Sunday of Advent

Family Sheet

To do at home with your family

For parents: Weekly Thought

The nights are at their longest and darkest now. Are your children afraid of the dark? How do you help them to cope? If they are not afraid of the dark, talk to them about how they might help someone else to overcome the fear. Help them to be grateful for the gift of light, especially at this time of year.

DAY 1 DAY 2 DAY 3 DAY 4 DAY 5 DAY 6 DAY 7

Switch on a light by colouring these lampshades brightly every time you have a good idea or do something that brings a little light into someone's life.

This sheet has been completed by ....

FAMILY PRAYER

Lord Jesus, we ask you to be the light in our family. We thank you for the light in N… who … For N… who …

(Use each child's name and invite other family members to say what that person's "light" is.)

Longest night, shortest day

We are getting close to the longest night of the year, the winter solstice. Try to find a diary that shows you the times of sunrises and sunsets. What time does the sun rise and set on the solstice? What about on the summer solstice on 21 June? About what time does the sun rise and set on your birthday?

The solstice was a festival time long before Jesus was born. People celebrated the "turning of the year" when the sun started to get stronger and they knew that the days would get lighter. We do not know when Jesus' actual birthday was but remembering his birth at the darkest time of year makes us think about how he has made the world a brighter place.

4th Sunday of Advent

Family Sheet

To do at home with your family

For parents: Weekly Thought

Obedience means more than doing what one is told. It means listening and acting accordingly. Mary listened and reflected on her answer. She recognised what was being asked as being the will of God and not her own selfish desire, and so was freely able to agree. Encourage your children to listen by listening to them. Help them to learn that listening and thinking about what they hear will help them to make wise choices.

You will have lots of opportunities to bring Good News to people this week. Colour in an angel each day that you cheer someone up or make someone smile.

This sheet has been completed by ....

FAMILY PRAYER

Jesus, we celebrate your coming into the world. We thank you for the example of your mother who shows us how to respond to God's love. Help us to listen to each other – and to have a blessed and happy Christmas. Amen.

Christmas Jokes

What is the favourite carol for parents?
Silent Night

Which Christmas candle burns longer – a silver candle or a gold candle?
Neither – all candles burn shorter.

What did one angel say to the other?
Halo there!

What's Tarzan's favourite Christmas song?
Jungle bells.
But what about his chimp?
King Kong merrily on high, of course!

Knock, Knock.
Who's there?
Our Wayne.
Our Wayne who?
Our Wayne in a manger!

Knock, Knock.
Who's there?
Doughnut.
Doughnut who?
Doughnut open till Christmas!

The Nativity of Our Lord (Christmas Day)

Family Sheet

To do at home with your family

For parents: Weekly Thought

Christmas is a lovely time of the year – though often we come to it exhausted by the sheer effort of preparing for it. It can also be a time when tensions run high as weariness and over-excited and over-tired children meet! Being prepared is half the battle. A game, or video or DVD that you can all enjoy mid-afternoon might just save everyone's sanity! Christian family life includes our parish and church activities; but God can also be found in the cuddles and shared "slobbing out" of the post-Christmas dinner.

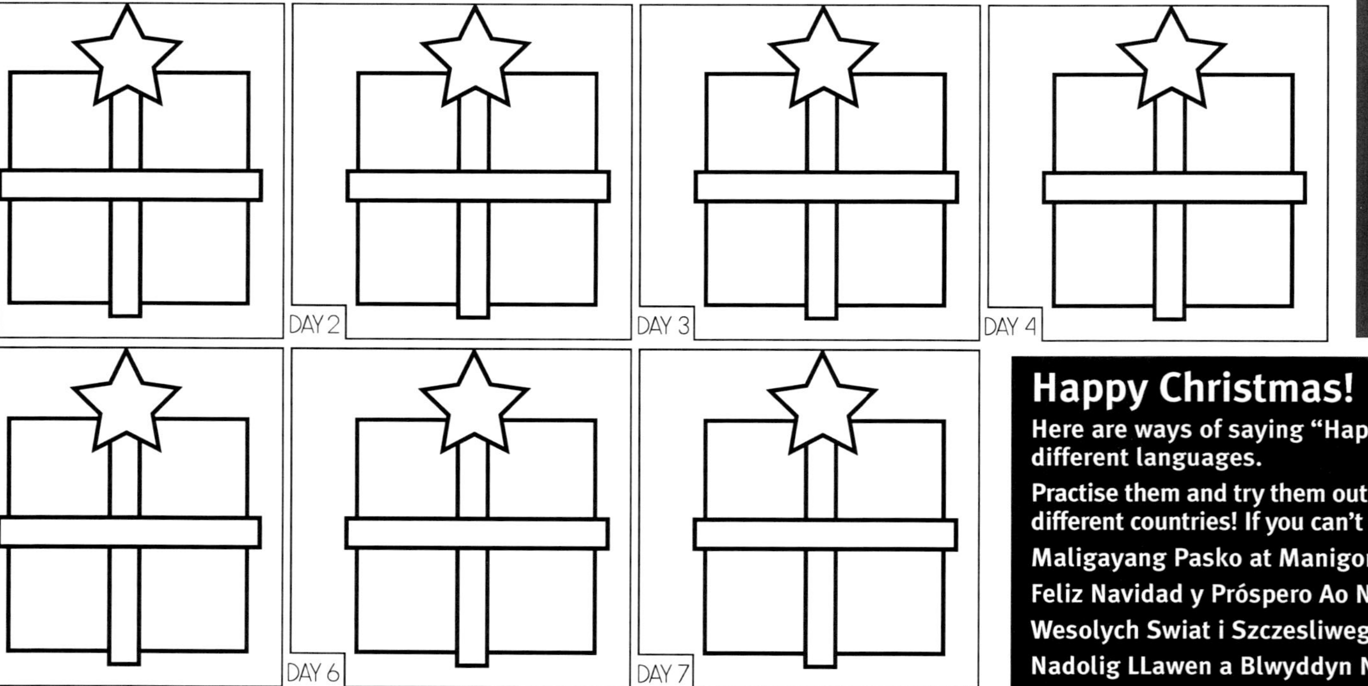

Christmas is a time for presents. But some of our presents can be things we do rather than things we give. Colour in a present when you have done something kind to make this Christmas happy for someone else.

This sheet has been completed by ....

FAMILY PRAYER

Lord Jesus, when you were born you, your mother Mary, and Joseph made a Holy Family.
Bless our family – N... N... N...
Keep us safe in your love – and help our love for one another grow day by day.
Amen.

Happy Christmas!

Here are ways of saying "Happy Christmas" and "Happy New Year" in different languages.

Practise them and try them out on people in your parish who may come from different countries! If you can't work out how to say them, ask someone who can!

Maligayang Pasko at Manigong Bagong Taon (Tagalog, Philippines)

Feliz Navidad y Próspero Ao Nuevo (Spanish)

Wesolych Swiat i Szczesliwego Nowego Roku (Polish)

Nadolig LLawen a Blwyddyn Newydd Dda (Welsh)

Nollaig Shona Dhuit (Gaelic)

Joyeux Noël et Bonne Année! (French)

Fröhliche Weihnachten und ein glückliches Neues Jahr! (German)

Wilujeng Natal Sareng Warsa Enggal (Sudanese)

If you have the internet, see if you can find out how to say "Happy Christmas" in even more languages. See if you can find some that we have not thought of!

The Holy Family of Jesus, Mary and Joseph

Family Sheet

To do at home with your family

For parents: Weekly Thought

The relationship between children and their grandparents can be a great blessing to them all. Grandparents often have more time to enjoy being with grandchildren than they had when they had their own children. Think about ways in which you can foster that relationship and encourage your children to develop loving relationships with elderly people in your parish and community.

DAY 1

DAY 2

DAY 3

DAY 4

DAY 5

DAY 6

DAY 7

Christmas is a time for presents. Colour in a box for each day that you give someone a gift. Remember some gifts, like a hug, don't come wrapped up!

This sheet has been completed by ....

FAMILY PRAYER

Loving Father,
thank you for the gift of our family.
Thank you for N… and N…
We ask you
especially to bless N… and N…
(grandparents).

A family tree

Look at the picture and talk about why our family history can be like a tree.
Look at all those roots!

Solemnity of Mary, Mother of God — The 1st Sunday of Christmas

Family Sheet

To do at home with your family

For parents: Weekly Thought

Theotokos: Mary, the God-bearer. This is a deceptively simple title, in which is embedded the whole mystery of our faith. It moves us on from the naivety of the crib and the stable, to the full honour which is due to Mary as Mother of God. In the same way as Mary was a vehicle for Christ's incarnation in first-century Palestine, so now in this title she becomes a vehicle for his revelation to us: Mary, Mother of Jesus – true God and true man.

DAY 1 | DAY 2 | DAY 3 | DAY 4

DAY 5 | DAY 6 | DAY 7

Babies are born every day, and given all sorts of names by the people who love them. Each day, choose a favourite name, and write it underneath one of the babies in the chart. Pray for all the babies born that day who have been given that name.

This sheet has been completed by ....

FAMILY PRAYER

Mary, when your son Jesus was born, you knew that he was the Son of God. You thought about him, and about what that might mean for the whole of your life. Think about us now, and help us to be good people like Jesus wanted. Amen.

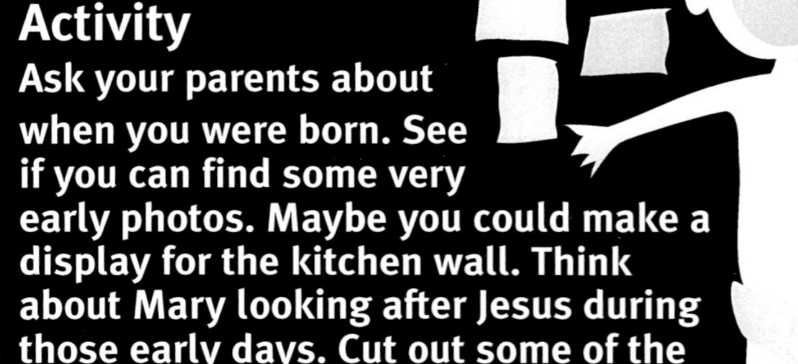

Activity

Ask your parents about when you were born. See if you can find some very early photos. Maybe you could make a display for the kitchen wall. Think about Mary looking after Jesus during those early days. Cut out some of the pictures of Mary and the baby Jesus from your Christmas cards. Add them to the display.

2nd Sunday after Christmas

Family Sheet

To do at home with your family

For parents: Weekly Thought

We celebrate Jesus being revealed or shown to mankind. Throughout the Old Testament and in St Matthew's Gospel in particular, we find family trees which locate the people of Israel, and ultimately Jesus, very firmly in history. It is as if the writers cannot emphasise enough that Jesus really was born at a certain time and place, into a particular family, with all the history and traditions of that family.

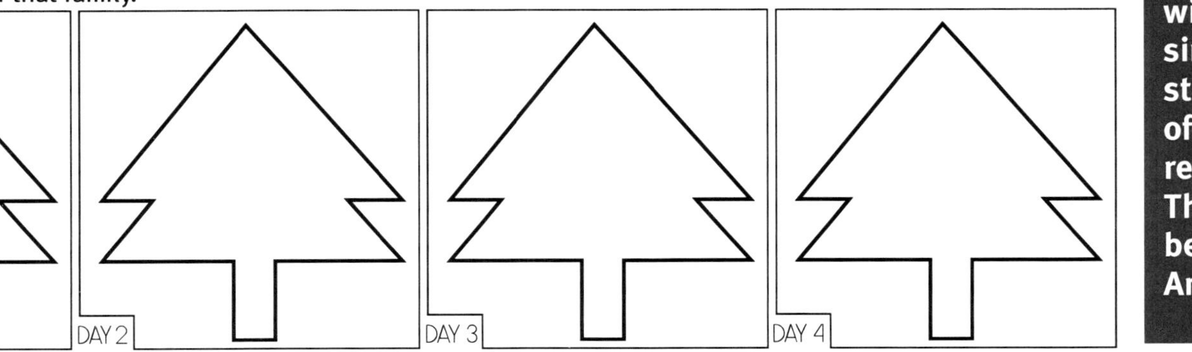

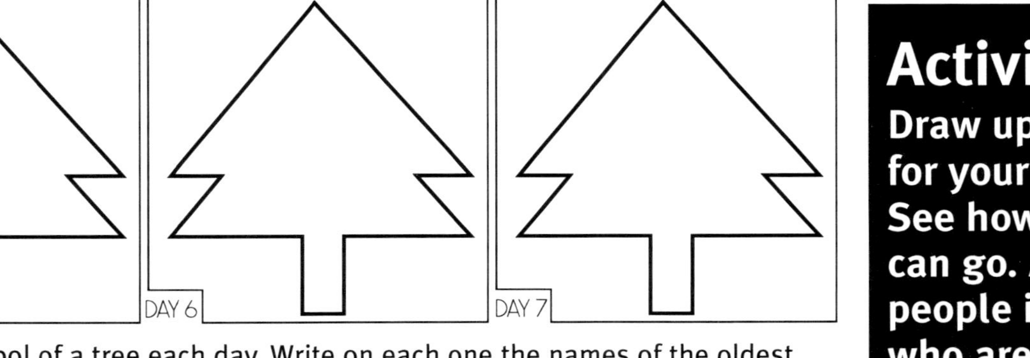

Colour in a symbol of a tree each day. Write on each one the names of the oldest people in your family tree, and pray for them during the family prayers each day.

This sheet has been completed by ....

FAMILY PRAYER

Dear Jesus, since the beginning of time, you have been with God. You have been with our family since the very start, before any of us can ever remember. Thank you for being with us. Amen.

Activity

Draw up a family tree for your own family. See how far back you can go. Ask the oldest people in your family who are still alive to help you.

The Epiphany of the Lord

Family Sheet

To do at home with your family

For parents: Weekly Thought

Jesus was the greatest gift that God could give to the world. The wise men responded by giving him lavish gifts. We continue to receive Jesus as a gift from God – in God's Word, in Holy Communion and in each other. Our Christian life is our response to that ongoing giving by God. We may not be able to give gifts of gold, frankincense and myrrh but each week we offer bread and wine and an offering of money to represent the words and actions of our daily lives. Encourage your children to see that they can offer the "gifts" of their words and actions in the offertory at the Eucharist.

DAY 1
To:
From:

DAY 2
To:
From:

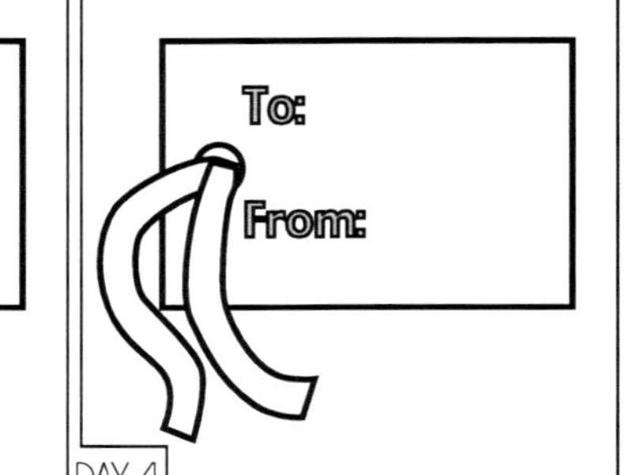

DAY 3

DAY 4
To:
From:

DAY 5
To:
From:

DAY 6
To:
From:

DAY 7
To:
From:

Colour in the gift tag each day. Think about something that you have said or done that you know God would be happy to receive as a present.

This sheet has been completed by ....

FAMILY PRAYER

Loving Father, thank you for the gift of your only Son, Jesus.
Help us to grow more like him – and like you –
by being generous in our giving and sharing with one another and with other people.
Amen.

Lights in the sky

People in the ancient world were fascinated by the stars and planets. They did not know that they were millions of miles away but thought that they were part of a dome over the world. Some civilisations thought that their gods lived there and, until quite recently, Christians thought that God lived in the sky too. We now know that the stars are suns – some of them much bigger and hotter than our sun. We know that they are born and that suns can die too. See if you can find pictures of stars from the Hubble telescope and try to imagine what an ancient astronomer would make of them.

The Baptism of the Lord

Family Sheet

To do at home with your family

For parents: Weekly Thought

When you made the decision that your children should be baptised, you were giving them one of the greatest gifts you ever could. You gave your children life – and in baptism, you allowed them to receive new life in Christ. With the gift came the responsibility to play your part as your children's first educators in faith. This is not done by formal teaching but in the day-to-day unfolding of your lives together. Encourage your children to be proud of their dignity as Christians and wisely to use the gifts they have received from God.

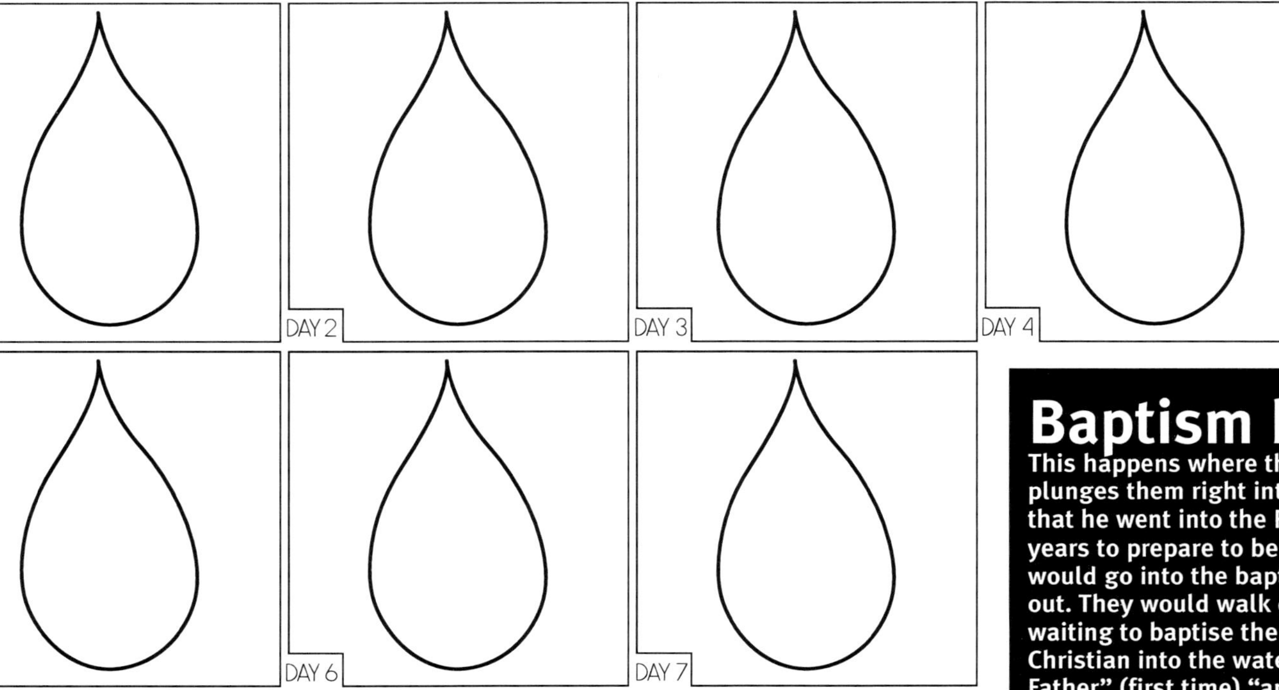

Colour in a drop each day to show that you are living as a baptised Christian.

This sheet has been completed by ....

FAMILY PRAYER

**Loving Father, you have chosen us to be your beloved sons and daughters.
Help us to be loving and kind and show your love to the world through the love we have for each other.
We ask this in the name of your beloved Son, Jesus Christ. Amen.**

Baptism by full immersion

This happens where the person to be baptised gets into a pool and the priest plunges them right into the water. This is what happened to Jesus – except that he went into the River Jordan. In the early Church, people took several years to prepare to be Christians. When they did, it was a great event. They would go into the baptistery, which was a room in which a pool had been dug out. They would walk down the steps into the deep pool where the person waiting to baptise them would be waiting. The baptiser would plunge the new Christian into the water three times, saying "I baptise you in the name of the Father" (first time) "and of the Son" (second time) "and of the Holy Spirit" (third time). The new Christian would be gasping for breath by this time and this was seen as a sign that they had died with Christ and were now breathing in the breath of new life.

They would walk up steps at the opposite end of the pool and would be clothed in a white garment and taken to meet the bishop who would anoint them and welcome them into the community of the Church.

1st Sunday of Lent

Family Sheet

To do at home with your family

For parents: Weekly Thought
God's kingdom is happening all around us. We can read of it in the newspapers, see it on the television, experience it in our family lives; but we will only see it if we look for it.

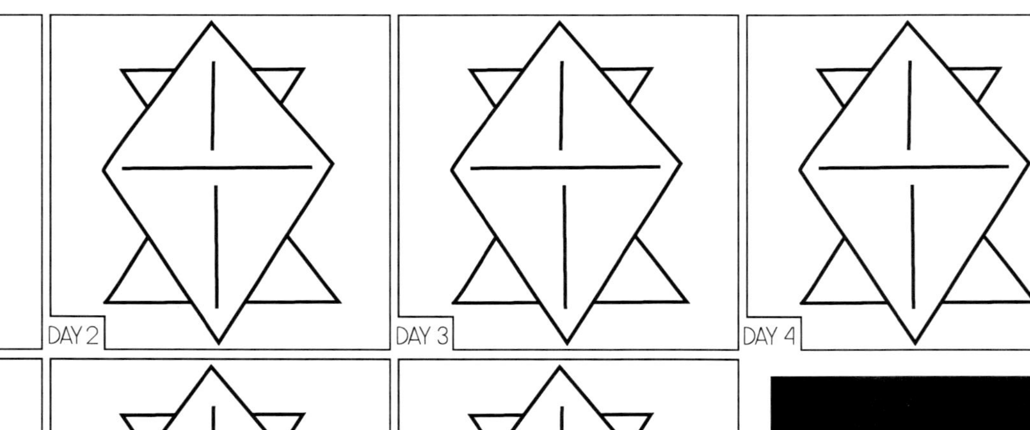

Fill in the jewels each day to make Jesus' kingdom come.

This sheet has been completed by ....

FAMILY PRAYER

Jesus, we want to live in your kingdom. In your kingdom, we will be kind to each other even when we are tired; we will be cheerful even if we are a bit fed up; we will love each other even if we don't always like each other. Help us to live in your kingdom now. Amen.

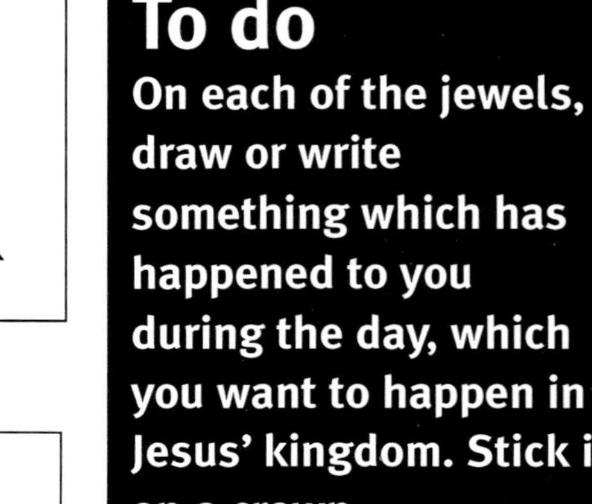

To do

On each of the jewels, draw or write something which has happened to you during the day, which you want to happen in Jesus' kingdom. Stick it on a crown.

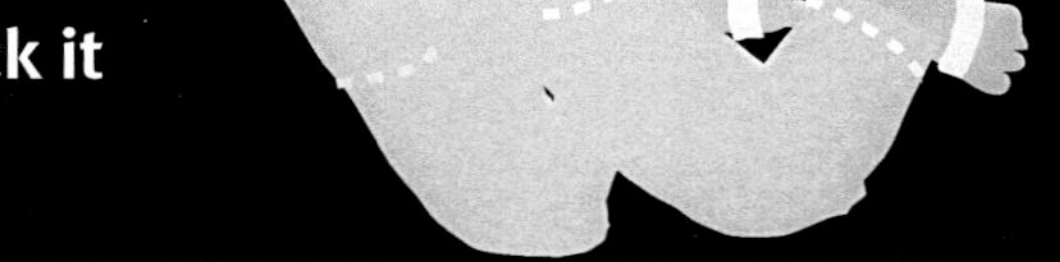

2nd Sunday of Lent

Family Sheet

To do at home with your family

For parents: Weekly Thought

No matter how well we think we know God, he is always full of mystery and surprise. Some questions will never be answered until we meet him face to face.

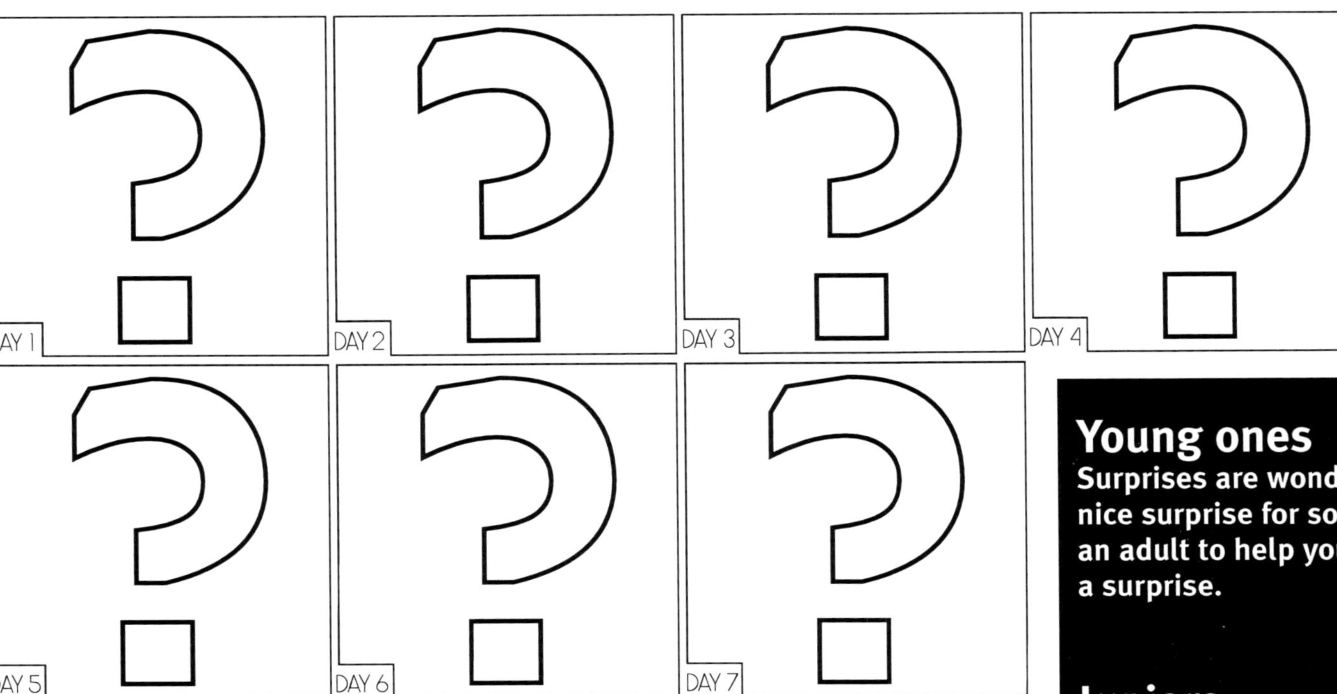

Colour each question mark or write around the question mark with something new you have learnt each day.

This sheet has been completed by ....

FAMILY PRAYER

Jesus, you came to the earth to tell us about God, but there is still so much we don't understand. Thank you for all the questions we have, and all the surprises you give us. Amen.

Young ones

Surprises are wonderful things. This week see if you can plan a nice surprise for somebody in the family. You might need to ask an adult to help you. Remember to keep it a secret, or it won't be a surprise.

Juniors

Try to find out the answers to the questions you thought up on Sunday – ask your friends, teachers, parents. The questions which no one can answer are the real mysteries!

3rd Sunday of Lent

Family Sheet

To do at home with your family

For parents: Weekly Thought

Jesus tells us how to behave in church. It is a time to think about God and to talk to God. We can practise this during our prayer time at home when we spend time quietly together, thanking God for everything he has given us, and asking him to bless us.

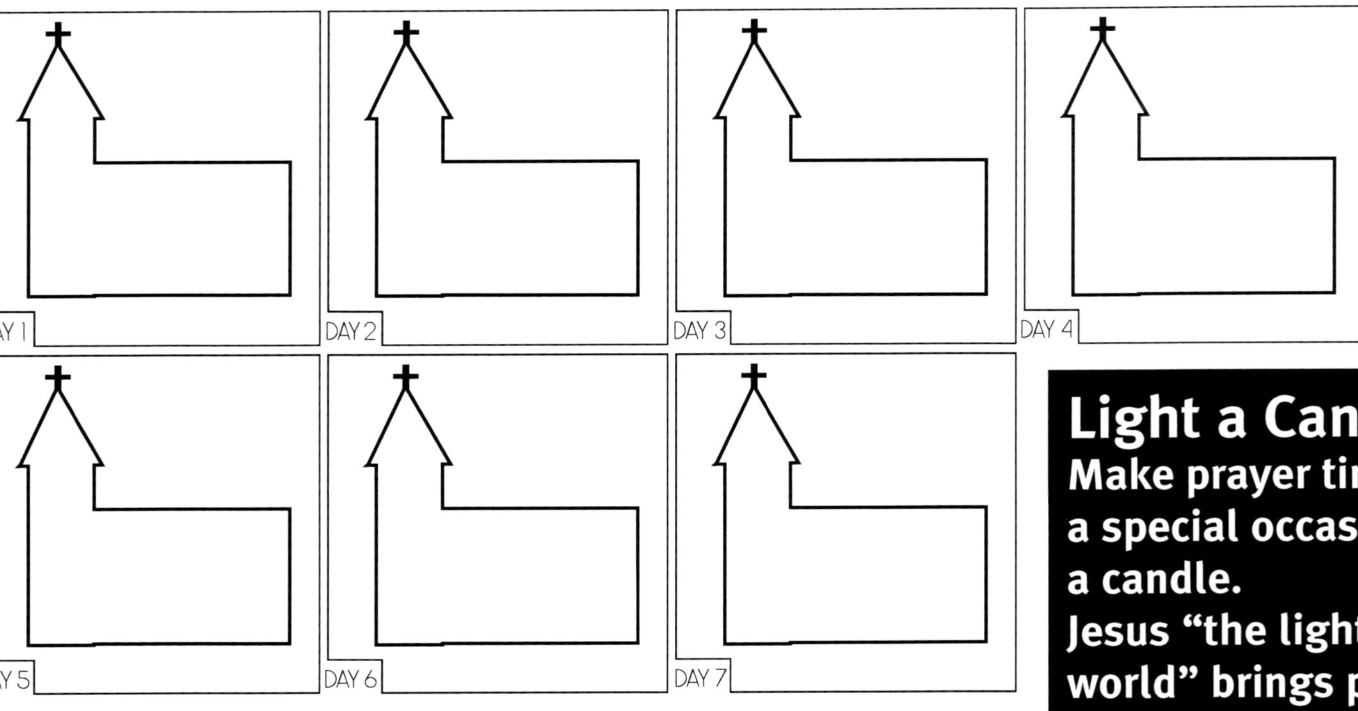

Fill in the churches day by day and make them come alive with your prayers.

This sheet has been completed by ....

FAMILY PRAYER

Jesus, we come to your house on Sunday to be with you and to talk to you. Come to our house now, bless us all and look after us. Amen.

Light a Candle

Make prayer time together a special occasion and light a candle. Jesus "the light of the world" brings peace and hope to the whole world.

4th Sunday of Lent

Family Sheet

To do at home with your family

For parents: Weekly Thought

The Church teaches us that we are a "pilgrim people", the end of our pilgrimage being with God in heaven. In effect we are refugees from heaven, longing to return there. It is worth remembering at times that our lives, our homes and our possessions are only transitory. We can only truly be at home with God.

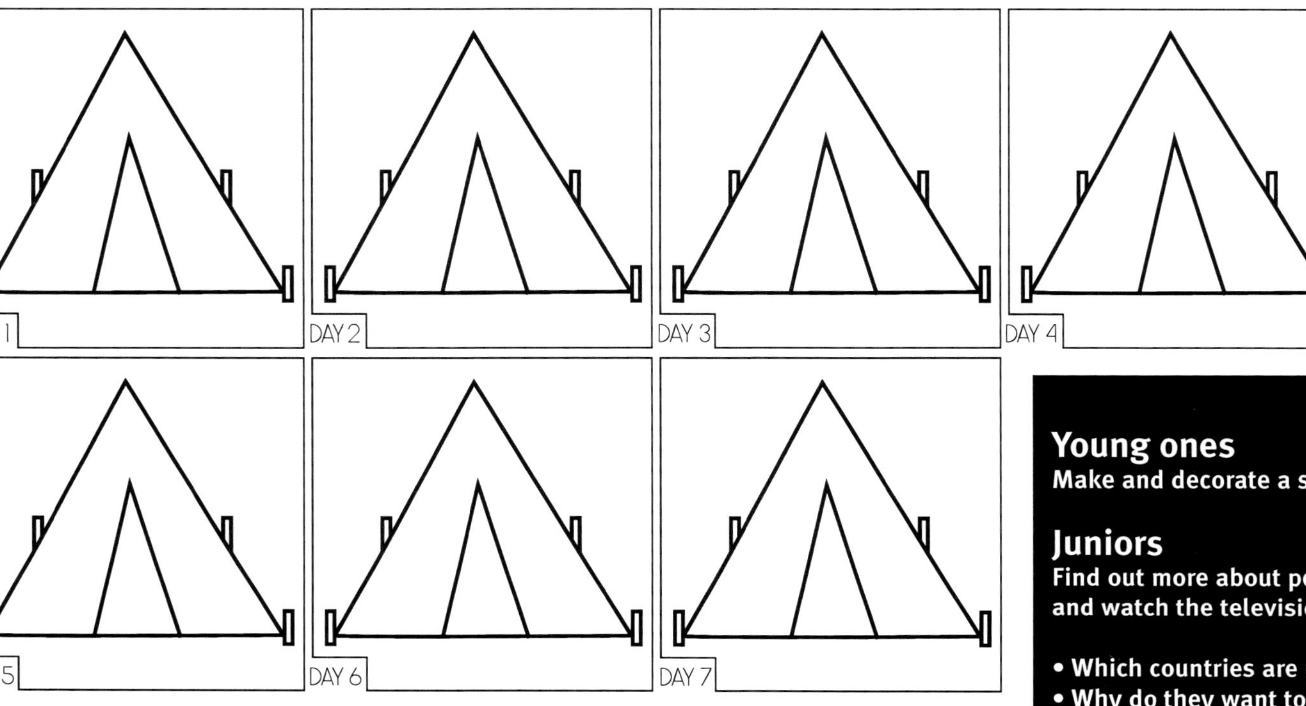

Colour the tent each day as you pray for refugees.

This sheet has been completed by ....

FAMILY PRAYER

Jesus, many people cannot live in their own homes and countries because of disaster or war or violence or threat. Thank you for the home you have given to our family. Help us to make it a place where we all want to be. Amen.

Young ones

Make and decorate a small tent to remind you of the refugees.

Juniors

Find out more about people who are refugees today. Look in the newspapers and watch the television news. Try to answer these questions.

- **Which countries are people trying to escape from?**
- **Why do they want to leave their own country?**
- **Why do they want to come to our country?**
- **How do they get here?**
- **What difficulties do they face on the journey?**
- **What difficulties will they face when they arrive here?**
- **What will they need to do to settle into your neighbourhood?**

5th Sunday of Lent

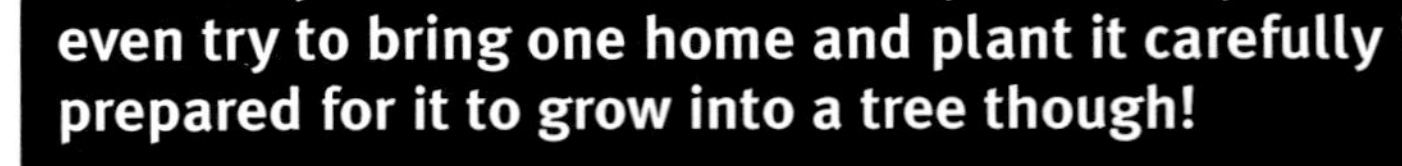

Family Sheet

To do at home with your family

For parents: Weekly Thought

As parents, we often have to make sacrifices for our children – it is part of the deal! Sometimes, we can feel resentful at having to put our own interests second. Hopefully, though, there are other occasions when we catch a warm glow and see something in our child that would not have been there without those sacrifices. The day they read in church – possible because we gave time to hearing the first stumbling attempts. This is the life-giving sacrifice of which Jesus speaks, that bears fruit in our families.

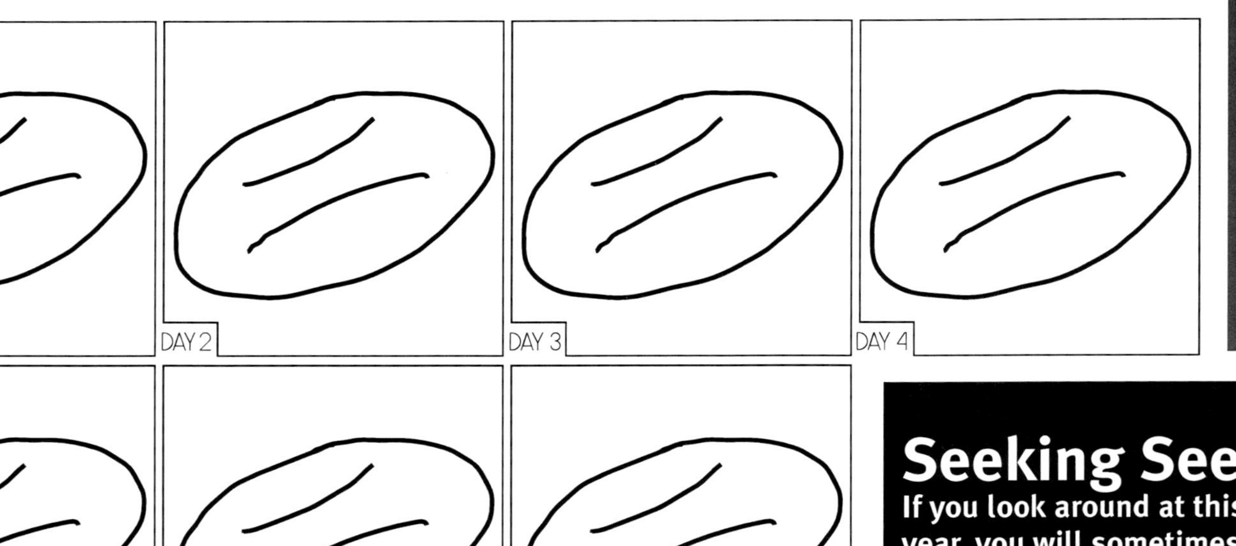

Add a small root and two little leaves to each seed. Think of something that you gave up to make someone else happy.

This sheet has been completed by ....

FAMILY PRAYER

**Lord, help us to remember your promise – that everything we seem to give up actually gives your life to the world.
Help us to be generous in our giving.
Amen.**

Seeking Seeds

**If you look around at this time of year, you will sometimes see signs of seeds which fell to the ground last autumn beginning to stir to new life. Some grow in very strange places – even in walls.
See whether you can spot old conkers or sycamore "helicopters" which are splitting open to show tiny leaves. Show them to your family and friends. Perhaps even try to bring one home and plant it carefully in a pot. Be prepared for it to grow into a tree though!**

Passion Sunday (Palm Sunday)

Family Sheet

To do at home with your family

For parents: Weekly Thought

Passion, or Palm, Sunday marks the beginning of the most solemn week of our Christian year – Holy Week. Allowing our children to experience this as fully as possible in the liturgy of this week introduces them to the central and majestic truth at the heart of our faith: that Jesus lived, died and was buried ... but that he has overcome sin and sorrow in his glorious resurrection.

Each day in Holy Week we remember a special event. Find out what each symbol on this page means in the days of Holy Week. Colour the symbols as you go through the week.

This sheet has been completed by ....

FAMILY PRAYER

Lord Jesus, we love you.
We are sad that you died,
but glad that you call us
your friends.
Help us to know how much
you love N... N... N...
and help us to love each
other as much as you love
us.
Amen.

The Days of Holy Week

Holy Week is very special. It is a solemn week which means that we are thinking about very important things. Some of it is very sad – but Christians do not stay sad for long because we know what happened on Easter Sunday. For this week, though, let's think about the last week of Jesus' earthly life.

PALM SUNDAY – we remember Jesus going into Jerusalem

MONDAY – the Gospel is about Mary pouring expensive oil over Jesus. Jesus says it is as if she is anointing him for his burial.

TUESDAY – Jesus warns Peter that before a cock crows twice Peter will have denied him three times.

WEDNESDAY – Judas betrays Jesus for thirty pieces of silver.

HOLY THURSDAY – Jesus celebrates Passover and gives us bread and wine as his Body and Blood.

GOOD FRIDAY – Jesus dies on the cross to save God's People.

HOLY SATURDAY – we wait in darkness for the coming of the new Light of the World... at Easter.

Easter Sunday

Family Sheet

To do at home with your family

For parents: Weekly Thought

For children, Christmas outranks Easter as a feast – not least because of the presents. It is good for us to be reminded that the events we celebrate are powerful and life-changing. We are moved by the birth of the baby in a stable but his rebirth in resurrection empowers us and our children to bear witness to a God of infinite power and tender mercy.

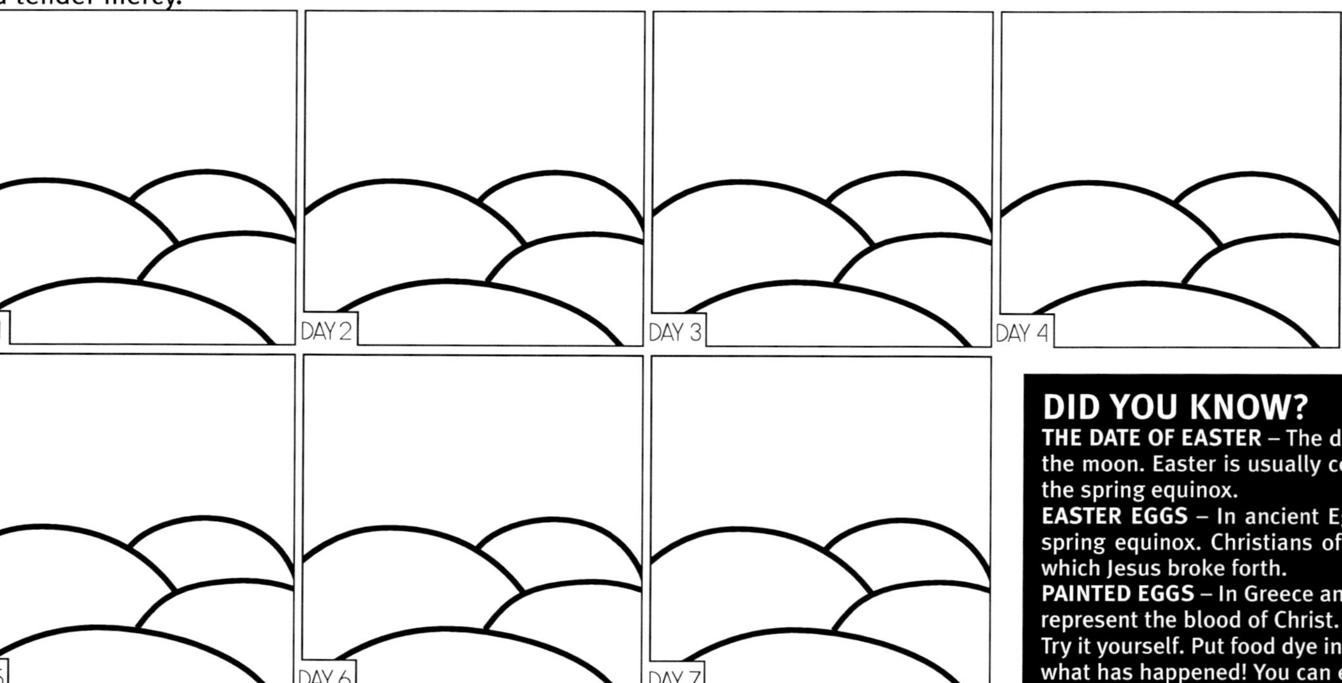

Draw a sun rising over the countryside and decorate the picture. As you do, say thank you for the beautiful world God has created for us.

This sheet has been completed by ....

FAMILY PRAYER

Lord Jesus,
we live as part of your family
at (address...)

Help us to make our home a
place where you are welcome
and where other people meet
you through us.
Amen.

DID YOU KNOW?

THE DATE OF EASTER – The day we celebrate changes every year because it is based on the moon. Easter is usually celebrated on the Sunday following the first full moon after the spring equinox.

EASTER EGGS – In ancient Egypt and Persia friends exchanged decorated eggs at the spring equinox. Christians of the Near East used the egg to symbolise the tomb from which Jesus broke forth.

PAINTED EGGS – In Greece and other European countries, eggs are often coloured red to represent the blood of Christ. Many countries have the custom of decorating eggs.

Try it yourself. Put food dye into a pan of water and boil your egg. When you open it – see what has happened! You can eat these eggs.

Hard boil your egg and let it cool. Decorate it with felt tips. You cannot eat these eggs.

EGG ROLLING – In some places, people have the custom of rolling hard-boiled eggs down a slope. The one whose egg goes furthest is the winner. Perhaps your family or friends could organise a competition.

EGG HUNTS – Some free-range hens like to lay their eggs where they are hard to find and their owners have to look hard for them. Some families and churches have Easter egg hunts where children search for the eggs that have been hidden. This might be fun to do during the holiday.

2nd Sunday of Easter

Family Sheet

To do at home with your family

For parents: Weekly Thought

We pass on a faith in someone our children cannot experience physically and yet they have an innate sense of belief. This is fostered in part by experience of life with us. When they hear of Jesus healing someone, they recognise that it is like our caring for them when they are ill. When Jesus hugs the children in the Gospels, our children know that it is like us hugging them. In simple everyday things, we help our children to make real their encounters with Jesus in the Gospels and prepare them to meet him in the sacraments.

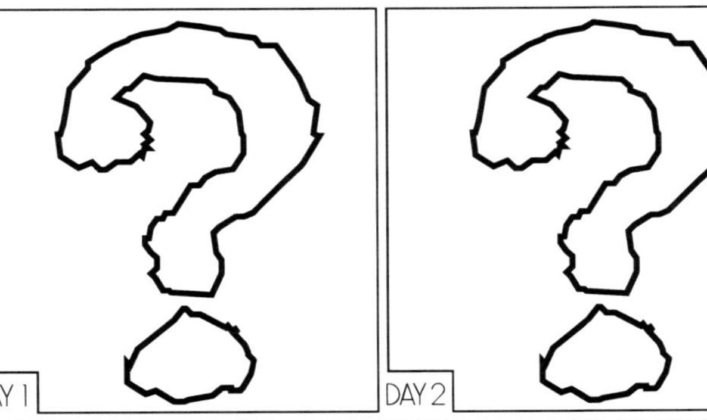

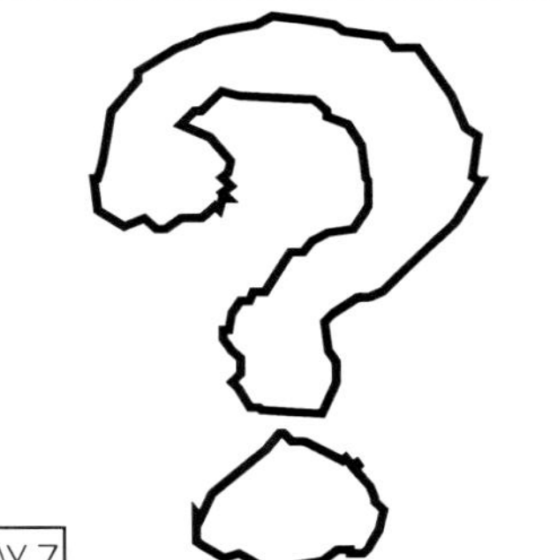

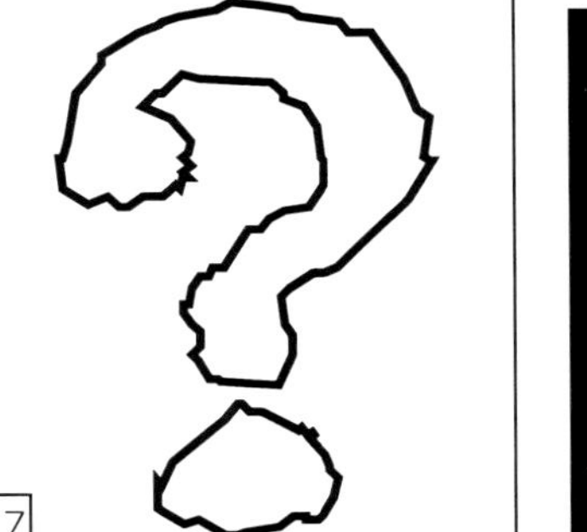

DAY 1 DAY 2 DAY 3 DAY 4

DAY 5 DAY 6 DAY 7

Colour in the question mark each day to show that you have thought about something before acting and not just gone along with everyone else.

This sheet has been completed by ....

FAMILY PRAYER

Lord Jesus, let us not be afraid to ask questions about you even when we may not understand the answers.
Help us to grow in love and trust in you.
Amen.

St Catherine of Siena

At the end of April we celebrate the feast of St Catherine of Siena. Catherine was born in 1347 and knew from a very early age that she wanted to dedicate her life to God. Her parents tried hard to discourage her but eventually, when she was about sixteen years old, Catherine was allowed to become a Dominican. Even though she did not learn to write until near the end of her life, she dictated her letters and thoughts and insights about God – sometimes reciting three documents to three secretaries at the same time. She wrote letters to popes when she felt that they were not obeying God's will – she even told one who was hiding in Avignon to stop being like a frightened child and to go back to Rome to lead the people.
Catherine was deeply in love with God and during a vision received the marks of Jesus' wounds on her own body. She died when she was only 33 years old but her writing was so powerful that Pope Paul VI named her as a Doctor or teacher of the Church.

3rd Sunday of Easter

Family Sheet

To do at home with your family

For parents: Weekly Thought

So often we can be afraid to talk to our children about death because it is something we ourselves do not fully understand. However, we need to embrace death and see it as a beautiful opportunity to remember our loved ones, just as Jesus himself asks us to do ... to remember him always and to do all things in memory of him. Only then can we see the beauty of dying as the chance to remember and thus be able to prepare our children for this most natural event in life.

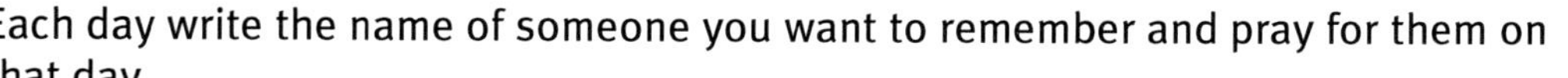

Each day write the name of someone you want to remember and pray for them on that day.

This sheet has been completed by ....

FAMILY PRAYER

Dear Lord, we thank you for all the people that we know and remember, and we thank you for all those who know and remember us.
We pray also for those that no one remembers: those who feel alone, abandoned, unloved, that they may find friends who will remember and love them.
And that we too may be people who help those who are most forgotten in our world today. Amen.

4th Sunday of Easter

Family Sheet

To do at home with your family

For parents: Weekly Thought

Jesus uses many examples from nature to explain things about God and his kingdom. In order to help parents and children alike to understand these parables, take some time to visit a forest, farm, zoo or even just to go for a walk in a park. Then when you watch the trees, birds and animals, you will be able to see and understand better what Jesus talked of when he spoke about God, using the environment as a rich illustration.

Colour or write in a house each day when you can see how the kingdom of God is in your daily life.

This sheet has been completed by ....

FAMILY PRAYER

**Dear Lord,
you used the trees, birds, animals and seas to tell us about God and his goodness. These days, however, we are destroying these symbols of God around us. How will we know you if there are no plants or trees? How will we see you if there is no clean air or fresh water around us?
Lord, teach us to use the environment in harmony with your will, so that we will always be able to see you present in our midst. Amen.**

Remember

Jesus tells us that the kingdom of God is like a man who sows seeds, like a woman making bread, like a shepherd looking after sheep and like a mustard seed that grows.

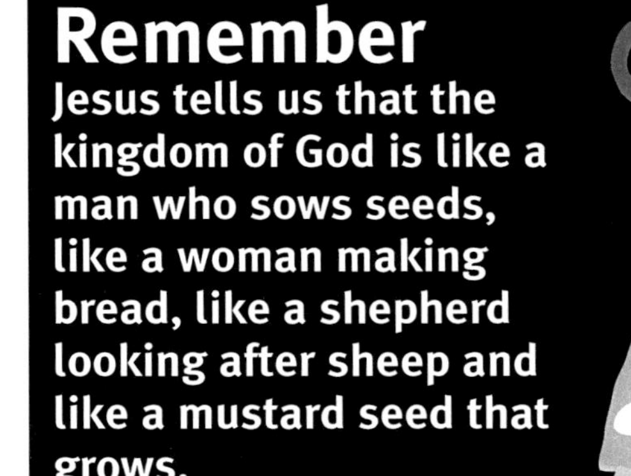

5th Sunday of Easter

Family Sheet

To do at home with your family

For parents: Weekly Thought

Jesus reminds us of the importance of staying close to him through prayer. Like a plant that every day needs a drop of water in order to grow, we too need a drop of prayer every day in order to live. As God provides the sun and nutrients and shade for all plants, he will also provide the other things that we need to live. Read Matthew 6:25-34. "So do not worry... seek first the kingdom of God and all these things will be given to you."

Colour the leaves every day when you have prayed for someone who hasn't got everything they need to grow strong.

This sheet has been completed by ....

FAMILY PRAYER

Dear God, today we want to thank you for all that we forget to thank you for.
We thank you for the water we drink today.
We thank you for the house we live in today.
We thank you for the clothes we are wearing today.
We thank you for the weather that we have today.
We thank you for the air we breathe today.
We thank you for... (everyone to say something that they would like to thank God for today)
We thank you, God, for everything. Amen.

Activity

Do we need it or can we do without?
Try to see today if you really need the following things...
Do you need TV?
Do you need chocolate?
Do you need to wash?
Do you need to use your hands?
Do you need sweets?
Do you need to talk?
Do you need to wear shoes?

6th Sunday of Easter

Family Sheet

To do at home with your family

For parents: Weekly Thought

Love can grow or fade as time passes. What was romantic love between man and woman becomes commitment and faithful love between husband and wife. This love can then bring forth new life and new love between mother and father. All these loves are different yet complementary and cannot fully exist without each other. Do we try to keep these loves alive and let those loves go that need to die?

DAY 1

DAY 2

DAY 3

DAY 4

DAY 5

DAY 6

DAY 7

Colour in a heart each day when you have done a loving action for someone.

This sheet has been completed by ....

FAMILY PRAYER

Lord, when I am hungry, give me somebody who needs food.
When I am thirsty, send me somebody who needs a drink.
When I feel cold, send me somebody to warm up.
When I am in trouble, offer me somebody to console.
When my cross becomes heavy, grant me to share the cross of others.
When I am poor, guide me to somebody in need.
When I am busy, give me somebody to help for some moments.
When I am humiliated, give me somebody to praise.
When I am discouraged, send me somebody to encourage.
When I need understanding from others, give me somebody who needs mine.
When I need somebody to care for me, send me somebody to care for.
When I think only of myself, draw my attention towards another person.
Amen.

The Ascension of the Lord

Family Sheet

To do at home with your family

For parents: Weekly Thought

At the Ascension we are usually left standing with the apostles as Jesus disappears from sight. Among the many different forms of prayer which are available to us, there is one in which we take on the role of some person in a biblical story and re-enact the story in our mind. With young children we can take this a step further and re-enact the story through role play. Maybe the child could take on the role of Jesus. The insights gained might be bizarre or somewhat startling – but it can be a rewarding way of praying together.

Stick some cotton wool or tissue paper onto a cloud each day as you think about somebody whom you do not see very often. Say a prayer for them.

This sheet has been completed by ....

FAMILY PRAYER

Jesus, you have gone back to heaven. We miss you and want you to come back. Help us to remember that you are always with us. Amen.

When Jesus disappeared in a cloud, everybody assumed that he went upwards, and that heaven was somewhere up above the clouds. Now that we have explored space with probes and satellites, we know that heaven is not a place we will be able to find on a map. Visit your local library or log onto the web and find out more about space exploration. Whilst you are doing that, think about the question: If heaven can't be located inside the universe or space, then where can it be?

7th Sunday of Easter

Family Sheet

To do at home with your family

For parents: Weekly Thought

These few days between the Ascension and Pentecost are a time of waiting for the Holy Spirit. We are not used to thinking of waiting as being a good thing, but it is part of the process of getting to know God, and we cannot rush that: we will spend all our lives doing it. We must learn to wait happily for him.

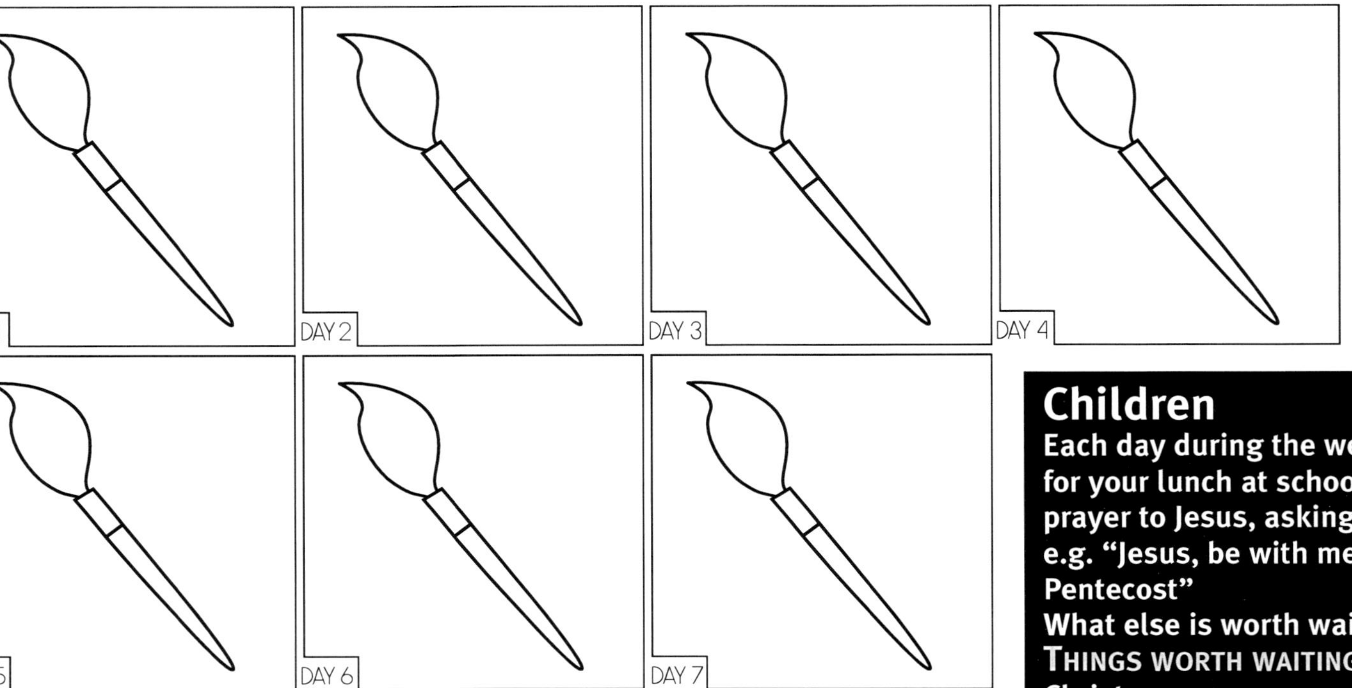

We have to wait for lots of things, and it is good if we can wait patiently. Colour in a paintbrush each day when you have had to wait patiently for something.

This sheet has been completed by ....

FAMILY PRAYER

**Dear Jesus, you are in heaven, you have promised to send us your Holy Spirit.
Please send him quickly, but help us not to be impatient as we wait for him. Amen.**

Children

Each day during the week, when you are waiting for something – for your lunch at school, for a bus, in a shop etc. – say a short prayer to Jesus, asking him to wait with you for the Holy Spirit, e.g. "Jesus, be with me as I wait for your Holy Spirit to come at Pentecost"

What else is worth waiting for? Add your own ideas.

THINGS WORTH WAITING FOR:	WAITING TIMES:
Christmas	A year
A new-born baby	9 months
Summer holidays	11 months
A nice cup of tea	3 minutes

Prayer of Waiting: Give me patience O Lord, but hurry!

Pentecost Sunday

Family Sheet

To do at home with your family

For parents: Weekly Thought

Fire changes things, that is why it is such a good symbol for the Holy Spirit. When we allow God's Spirit to work in us, we can expect to change as well. The Holy Spirit gives us gifts to help us to change to be more like Jesus. There are seven special gifts which he gives to us all at Pentecost, and again in a special way when we receive the sacrament of Confirmation when we are older. The fruits of the Spirit are love, joy, peace, patience, kindness, goodness, trustfulness, gentleness and self-control.

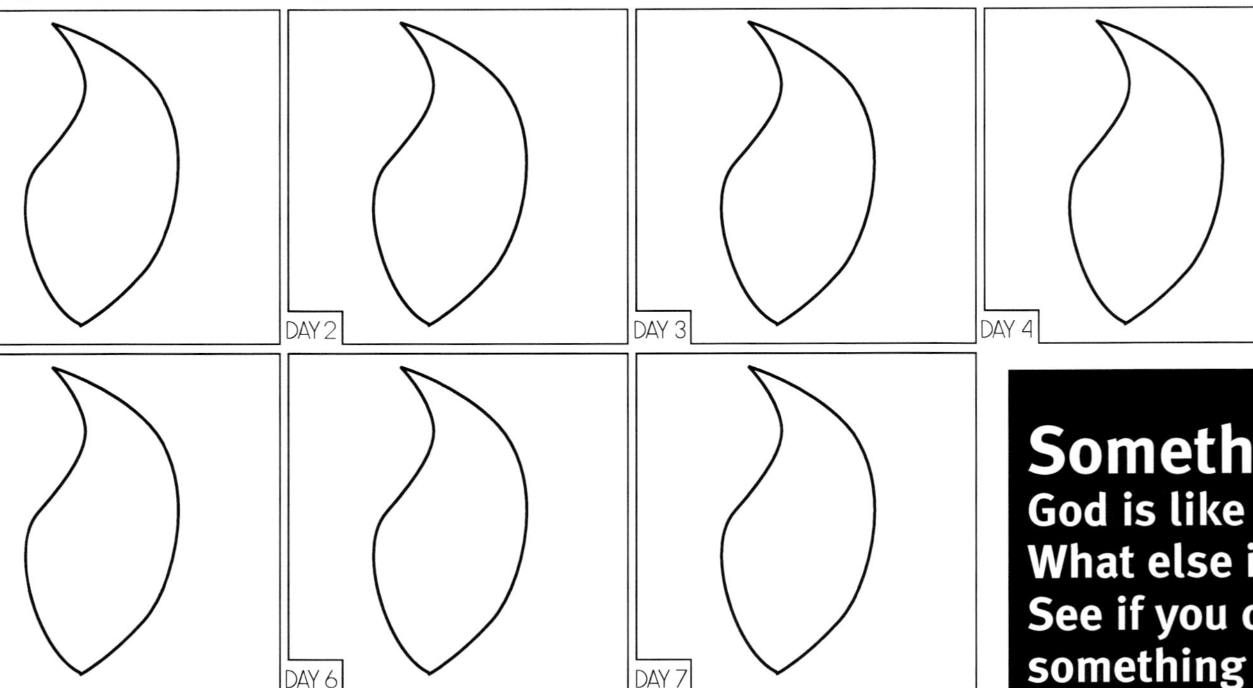

Colour in a flame each day, or write in the flame outline as you use one of your gifts of the Holy Spirit.

This sheet has been completed by ....

FAMILY PRAYER

Holy Spirit, come and live with our family, help us to change to be more like Jesus. Amen.

Something to do

**God is like fire.
What else is like fire?
See if you can find something each day which is like fire (e.g. heat, light, bright colour ...)**

2nd Sunday in Ordinary Time — The 2nd Sunday of Epiphany

Family Sheet

To do at home with your family

For parents: Weekly Thought

We often hear the Christian life referred to as a journey. This is an important thing for you to convey to your children – that you and they are on a shared part of the journey. You may know more than they do but you are still getting to know Jesus just as they are. One of your greatest roles is to introduce your children to Jesus and to set them firmly on the path to eternal life.

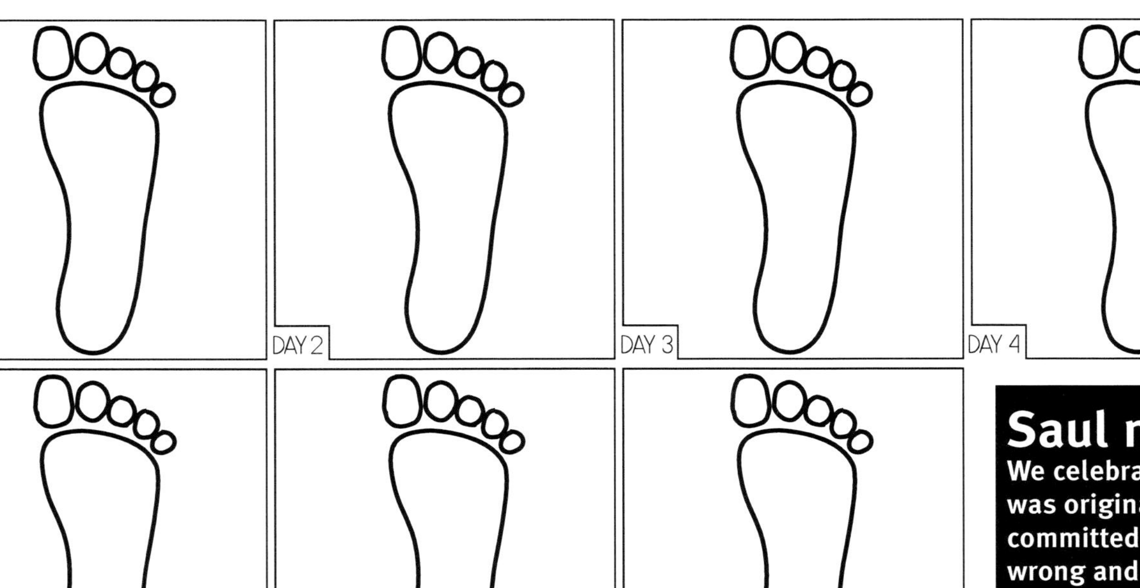

Colour in a footprint each day to show that you are following Jesus.

This sheet has been completed by ....

FAMILY PRAYER

Everyone: Lord Jesus, we are sharing our journey of getting to know you.
Adults: Bless N... and N... (names of children) as they learn to know and love you more and more.
Children: Bless N... and N... (names of parents/carers) as they help us to grow up in your love.
Everyone: Thank you for loving us and calling us to be your friends.

Saul meets Jesus in the Spirit

We celebrate the feast of the conversion of St Paul on 25 January. He was originally called Saul and he was a very devout Jew. He was so committed to being a Jew that he thought the early Christians were wrong and persecuted them.

One day, he was setting out to deal with Christians in Damascus when he saw a flash of light which blinded him and heard a voice which said, "Saul, Saul, why are you persecuting me?" He realised that the voice was the voice of Jesus. Unlike Andrew and Peter, who met Jesus face to face, Saul met him in spirit. Even so, he knew he had met a real person and from that moment he became Paul and spent the rest of his life helping others to meet Jesus in spirit too.

We meet Jesus in the Spirit too. We cannot see or hear or touch him yet – that has to wait until we get to heaven.

Family Sheet

To do at home with your family

For parents: Weekly Thought

The call of Peter and his colleagues to leave their nets behind and take up the new work of fishing for people was a key moment in the Gospel. As the Church grew, and especially when non-Jews were allowed to become Christians, the issue of the diversity within the Church became increasingly important. We are a universal Church with people of all races, colours, languages and backgrounds: Peter's net has spread very wide. For some, the differences are alarming but the diversity is a source of great enrichment to the Church. Encourage your child to grow to delight in knowing all sorts of people and to celebrate diversity.

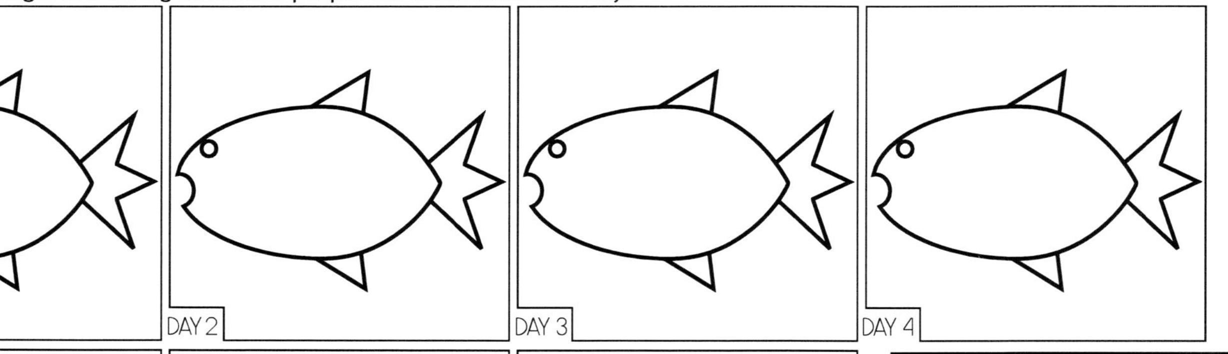

Colour in a fish each day. Try to make each one different from its friends.

This sheet has been completed by ....

FAMILY PRAYER

Lord Jesus, help us to enjoy people who are different from us.
Remind us that God does not want everyone to be the same. We thank you for *N*... who ... (name a member of the family and a unique attribute or talent they bring to the family – and then do the same for each person)
Lord, keep us happy and united in love.
Amen.

Fishy Jokes

What did Jiminy Cricket sing to Pinocchio the pike?
When You Fish Upon A Star

What is the most musical sea creature?
The tune-a fish!

Why are fish cleverer than mice?
Because they live in schools.

Why is it so easy to weigh fish?
They have their own scales.

What do you call a fish with no eye?
FSH!

What is the fastest fish in the sea?
Go-carp.

What lives under the sea and carries a lot of people?
An octobus

What did the boy octopus say to the girl octopus?
I want to hold your hand hand hand hand hand hand hand hand.

Where do fish keep their money?
In the river bank.

What is the best fish on ice?
A skate.

What did one rock pool say to the other rock pool?
Show me your mussels.

Family Sheet

To do at home with your family

For parents: Weekly Thought

We hold authority over our children until they grow. Giving up our authority can be as hard.

This week colour in one of the symbols each day you remember that God is in charge.

This sheet has been completed by ....

FAMILY PRAYER

Take time this week to be quiet – to remember that God is present. Close the quiet time by saying the closing doxology of the Lord's Prayer.

"For the kingdom, the power..."

Draw a picture of Jesus the king, surrounded by his faithful people in glory. Can you remember to bring your picture to next week's meeting?

5th Sunday in Ordinary Time

Proper 1

Family Sheet

To do at home with your family

For parents: Weekly Thought

When she was healed the response of Peter's mother-in-law – we don't even know her name – was to serve Jesus. We have all been healed, too. Baptism, the Eucharist, Reconciliation, the love of spouse, family and friends, all touch our heart with God's love.
How then can we serve him? How can we create opportunities for our children to serve him? Can they help with household tasks? Do we show them we appreciate the help they give? Do we praise good behaviour? Would they like to serve, sing, or play music in church?

Peter's mother-in-law served Jesus a meal when she was healed. Colour a mug in each day when you have served or helped someone.

This sheet has been completed by ....

FAMILY PRAYER

**Lord, you have given us each other as a family.
We ask you to care for us as you cared for Peter's family.
Help us to look after each other as Peter's mother-in-law looked after you.
Amen.**

**Jesus is involved in family life. For thirty years he had a humdrum existence, working with his hands to earn a living. He was the sort of man you'd invite round to lunch or supper.
For most Christians, like Peter's mother-in-law, it is in our family life that God comes to us. How can we invite Jesus into our homes? What problems would we bring to him for his healing touch?**

Family Sheet

To do at home with your family

For parents: Weekly Thought

Paul urges us, "Whatever you eat, whatever you drink, whatever you do at all, do it for the glory of God." Jesus' gesture of touching and healing the leper proclaims God's glory in a way beyond our power. Yet, day by day, we are called to share our meals and family life as if God were present – as indeed he is! A special effort to say grace before meals, perhaps holding hands together, might be appropriate this week.

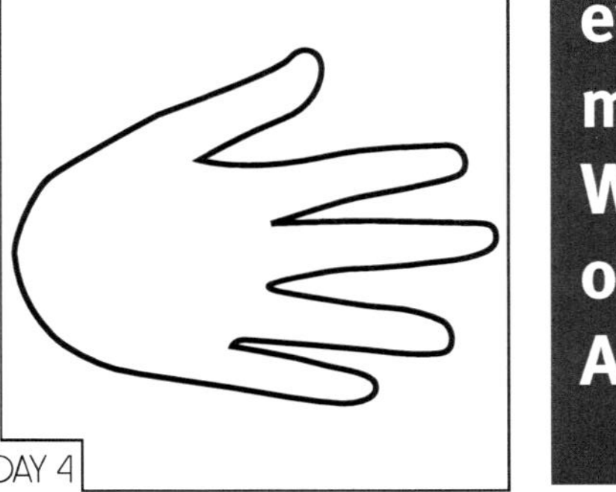
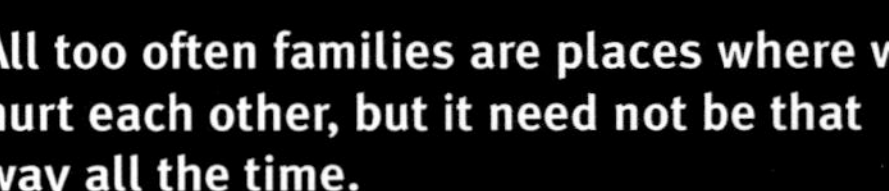

Colour in the hand when you have brought the touch of Jesus' love to someone this week.

This sheet has been completed by ....

FAMILY PRAYER

Dear Lord, be in our hearts and our hands.
May your love flow out to everyone we touch or meet this week.
We ask this through Jesus, our Lord and our brother.
Amen.

All too often families are places where we hurt each other, but it need not be that way all the time.

Parents may need the wisdom of Solomon to know just how to forgive, to heal, to reconcile. But we should remember that Solomon was wise because he asked God for wisdom. We are not alone.

Children, too, can learn to forgive, heal, reconcile. There is much wisdom in "Kiss and make up", or "Let me kiss it better." No need to be an expert masseur to bring healing with a touch, a stroke, a cuddle.

7th Sunday in Ordinary Time Proper 3

Family Sheet

To do at home with your family

For parents: Weekly Thought

Jesus wants us to bring each other to him: spouses, children, friends. This can be mighty difficult as adults and children can resist love. There will always be a hole in the roof for our prayer to reach God, even if the one we are praying for seems to fight against us all the way.

Colour a heart when you have done or said something to bring God's love to someone.

This sheet has been completed by ....

FAMILY PRAYER

Hold hands out, palms uppermost.
Dear Jesus, we bring to you people who need your help.
We ask you to bless them and heal them
in body, mind and spirit.
We bring you .... (Names and intentions can follow).

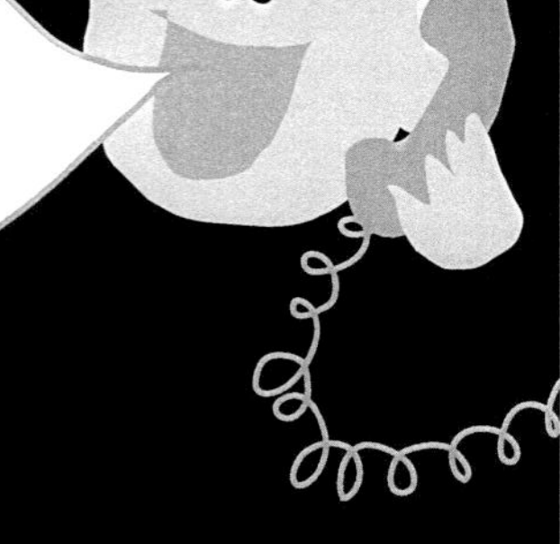

Who are we going to bring to Jesus?
What do we want for them?
In today's Gospel the man's friends wanted him restored to health – and he was – but more was given than asked for.
Let us look out for anyone who needs our help.
Let us remember our older relatives and friends, whom we could cheer up by sending a letter or making a telephone call.

8th Sunday in Ordinary Time

Family Sheet

To do at home with your family

For parents: Weekly Thought

How do we see others and how do others see us? Take time to think a little about our attitude to other people and how this can affect them. Maybe some of our attitudes need changing, but first of all we have to be aware of what our attitudes are.

Colour in the face each day when you have thought something nice about someone else.

This sheet has been completed by ....

FAMILY PRAYER

Jesus, the way we think and feel helps us to decide how we will behave and the things that we will do. Help us to think in the same way that you think, and to feel in the same way that you feel. Amen.

Young ones

At the end of each day, try to remember how you felt during the day. Draw a picture of yourself and say a prayer to Jesus asking him to bless you.

Juniors

During the week, watch your favourite soap on television. Pay particular attention to the attitudes of the different people. How does the way they think affect the decisions they make and the way they behave? Can you find just one or two words to describe their attitude? Does the rest of the family agree with you?

Family Sheet

To do at home with your family

For parents: Weekly Thought

Our rules are usually negative: "Don't..." For ourselves and our children we need to make them positive: "Do... try to make other people happy. Do... enjoy the achievements of your friends..."

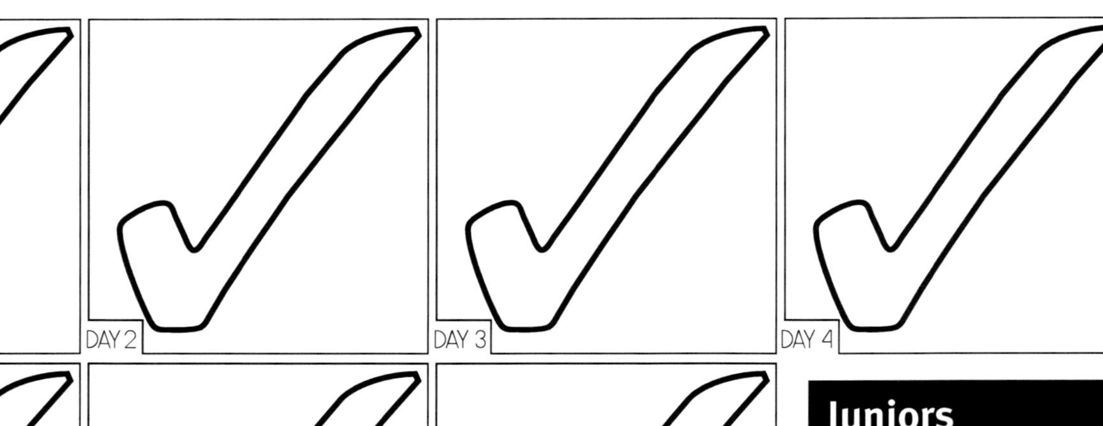

Each day this week colour in a tick when you try to keep Jesus' law of love.

This sheet has been completed by ....

FAMILY PRAYER

Help us to look out for chances to make other people happy. Amen.

Juniors

Can you find out what the Bible says about keeping the Sabbath day special? Why did God make this one of his 10 commandments? Which number commandment was it? Look in the Bible, in the Book of Exodus, chapter 20.

Younger ones

Colour in this bouquet of flowers. Who could you give flowers to, to say I love you?

10th Sunday in Ordinary Time — Proper 5

Family Sheet

To do at home with your family

For parents: Weekly Thought

We belong to a family in which we are not the responsible adults.

DAY 1 DAY 2 DAY 3 DAY 4

DAY 5 DAY 6 DAY 7

Colour in a helping hand on the days you remember that other people need you to smile at them, need you to praise them, need you to help them...

This sheet has been completed by ....

FAMILY PRAYER

Dear Lord, help our family to reach out to other people, especially those who are lonely. Help us to remember that we belong to your family of loving kindness. Amen.

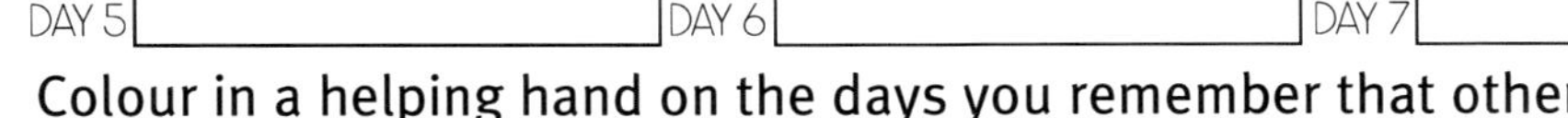

Juniors

Find out the names of all Jesus' first friends, his disciples. They were all members of God's family. You may need to look them up in a Bible. Can you find out some facts about any of them to tell everyone next week?

Younger ones

Draw your family (the very important members) in one circle, draw another family (your friend's perhaps) in another.

Join the families together – they are part of God's family.

It would be difficult to draw all the families which are a part of God's family.

Family Sheet

To do at home with your family

For parents: Weekly Thought

Jesus used the things around him to tell us about God. Unfortunately for us he did not live in twenty-first-century Britain, so he would have no experience of many of the things around us today. Each day, during family prayer, choose some familiar object and use it to tell a "parable" about God.

Each day draw the object which you use in your family prayer on one of the leaves.

This sheet has been completed by ....

FAMILY PRAYER

Jesus, you used the things around you to try and teach us about God. When we look at the things around us, help us to see what they tell us about God as well. Amen.

Activity

Sow some mustard seeds on potting compost, in supermarket trays. Once they have sprouted, transplant some into larger pots. Keep it indoors on a sunny windowsill until the warmer weather arrives, then stand it outside or plant into the garden. In a good Mediterranean climate it could reach up to 3-4 metres, but even in our climate it is likely to form a sizeable shrub a metre or more tall.

Family Sheet

To do at home with your family

For parents: Weekly Thought

It is debatable whether Jesus was talking only to the wind and the sea, or to the apostles in the boat with him as well when he told them, “Quiet now! Be calm!” Note that the apostles were prepared for Jesus to take charge in an environment in which their authority normally held sway – he was after all only a carpenter, they were the sailors and fishermen. There may be occasions in our own lives when our expertise and authority tell us we ought to be able to cope, but we can’t and blunder around ineffectively, perhaps making things worse. “Quiet now! Be calm!” is good advice; even the winds and the sea obey him.

Each day draw a circle around the weather for that day. Say a prayer thanking Jesus for the weather.

This sheet has been completed by ....

FAMILY PRAYER

Dear Jesus,
today the weather has been ... Say a prayer here, either thanking Jesus for the weather, or asking for patience and for his help if it has prevented some planned activity from happening.

Activity

If you have access to the internet, keep a daily weather journal over the next week, comparing the weather where you live with the weather in the Holy Land. A good weather site is http://weather.yahoo.com – select Middle East, Israel, and then Nazareth or Tiberius.

13th Sunday in Ordinary Time

Proper 8

Family Sheet

To do at home with your family

FAMILY PRAYER

Jesus, sometimes we really need help, but we don't know how to get it, or we don't want other people to know, or maybe we just can't be bothered. Help us to remember to ask you for help, and help us to help each other as well. Today we thank you for ... who helped ... with ...

Amen.

For parents: Weekly Thought

There can be a sort of elitist attitude, which says that prayers of crisis are somehow of less value than those which are sustained through both bad times and good. In today's Gospel we read of two people in despair, and Jesus' response is immediate and effective, despite their apparent lack of any previous devotion to him. God does not appear to be elitist when it comes to helping those in need. Maybe our mistake lies in our failure to recognise our state of crisis and despair more frequently. Our home-grown security and complacency are the real barriers to effective prayer. Before God we are nothing, and we have nothing. Only God can save us.

Colour in a cloak each day that you help someone, like Jesus did.

This sheet has been completed by ....

To think about

Think of the things that sometimes get in the way of us asking for help when we need it. Maybe we don't want our friends to know, or maybe we put it off by watching the television instead, or maybe we find something easier to do, or maybe we are just too tired. This week, make a point of asking for help if you need it. Keep a lookout for people who might want your help as well.

Family Sheet

To do at home with your family

For parents: Weekly Thought

Our children need encouragement to be brave enough to be different. They may be the only child in their class to go to church – or have an active faith life. Help them to be proud of their heritage – part of a group of people who seek to change the world for the better.

Write or draw something that you said or did each day that showed you are a Christian.

This sheet has been completed by ....

FAMILY PRAYER

Lord Jesus, you have called our family to show the world what your Good News means.
Help us speak and act in ways that show your love for the world.
Amen.

St Benedict Feast day: 11 July

He was born into a wealthy family and was well educated. He realised that having too much money and time was not always a good thing – people were using both badly.

Benedict left Rome and lived by himself for a long time while he worked out what God wanted him to do. Eventually, he set up monasteries – the first person to have the idea of people living in a community dedicated to prayer, work and study. He loved scripture, especially the psalms, and instructed his monks to pray them at set times each day. We call this the Divine Office – and though it has changed over the years, monks, nuns, priests and many lay people use this even today.

Europe was beginning to descend into the Dark Ages. Benedict's idea meant that small lights were kept burning as books were treasured in the Benedictine houses he founded.

Family Sheet

To do at home with your family

For parents: Weekly Thought

Throughout the world there are people doing just what you are doing with your children – helping them to come to know and love God, to follow Jesus, to help them to develop under the guidance of the Spirit. Some people are called to leave home and family behind and be missionaries far away. We though are called to be missionaries here – to make our homes a place where the Word can take root, grow, and bear fruit in the lives of our children.

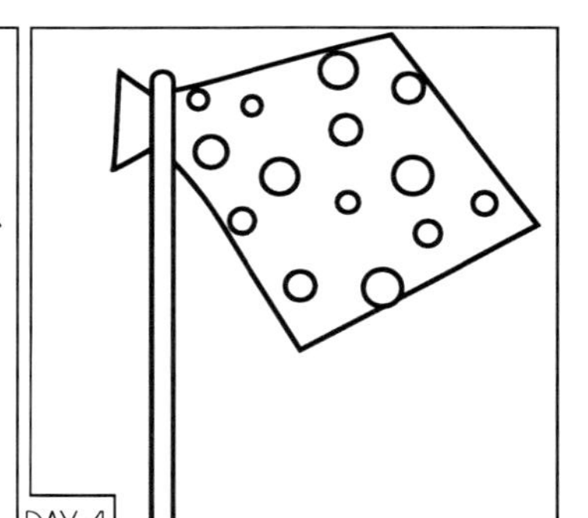

Colour in a hankie tied to a pole each day. Remember the people who travelled to your country so that you could hear God's Good News... say thank you to God for them. Think about the people who are doing just the same thing now – and pray for them.

This sheet has been completed by ....

FAMILY PRAYER

**Lord Jesus, thank you for sending your disciples into the world.
We pray for the people you are sending into the world today.
We send our love and support for them
especially those in (choose a country – perhaps a different one each day). Amen.**

Watch the weather on 15 July!

If it rains on St Swithun's Day there is a saying that it will rain for 40 days afterwards.

Here is the rhyme that someone wrote to tell us...

**"St Swithun's day, if thou dost rain, For forty days it will remain;
St Swithun's day, if thou be fair, For forty days 'twill rain na mair."**

St Swithun lived a long time ago – in the mid-800s – and was one of the cleverest men of his day. He was even tutor to two kings, one of whom was King Alfred the Great. When he died, he wanted to be buried in the churchyard where the rain could fall on his grave. Unfortunately, some of his monks thought he should have a much grander resting place and tried to take his body inside. When they tried, there was a great clap of thunder and it rained day and night for 40 days. A hundred years later, St Swithun's body was taken into Winchester Cathedral.

16th Sunday in Ordinary Time

Proper 11

Family Sheet

To do at home with your family

For parents: Weekly Thought

As the summer holidays approach, it is quite likely that your thoughts are of holiday activities for your children – holidays away, play-schemes and so on. You may, yourself, be desperately in need of rest – though afraid to admit it in case you never get started again.

Colour in the deckchair for each day you spend a few minutes of peace and quiet.

This sheet has been completed by ....

FAMILY PRAYER

Lord Jesus, you made your
disciples have time to themselves
to rest and to be restored.
Give us time this summer to rest
and be restored –
help us to share the chores and
the joys
so that you can renew us
and make us strong for your work.
Amen.

Biblical Aromatherapy!

On 22 July, we celebrate the feast of St Mary Magdalene. She loved Jesus so much that she was one of only three people who dared to stand at the foot of the cross as he died – a very brave thing to do.

So what about aromatherapy? Jesus made sure that people knew that he appreciated the gift of the woman who poured out a jar of aromatherapy oil over him – even though it cost so much – and the fragrance filled the whole house! He knew that it was a gift of love. Some people make aromatherapy a bit like a religion, but it is actually something people have used for thousands of years – a part of being human and, often, a way of helping people to be at peace when they are under stress.

You might like to take a bath with some oils – and a good book or tape – and relax...

Let God give you rest and re-creation!

Family Sheet

To do at home with your family

For parents: Weekly Thought

In a world of great need and distress, we can feel overwhelmed and unable to make a difference. If we feel like that, it is likely that our children feel it even more so. As the Gospel suggests, though, we are not necessarily called to do marvellous things – but to offer what we have with generosity and trust.

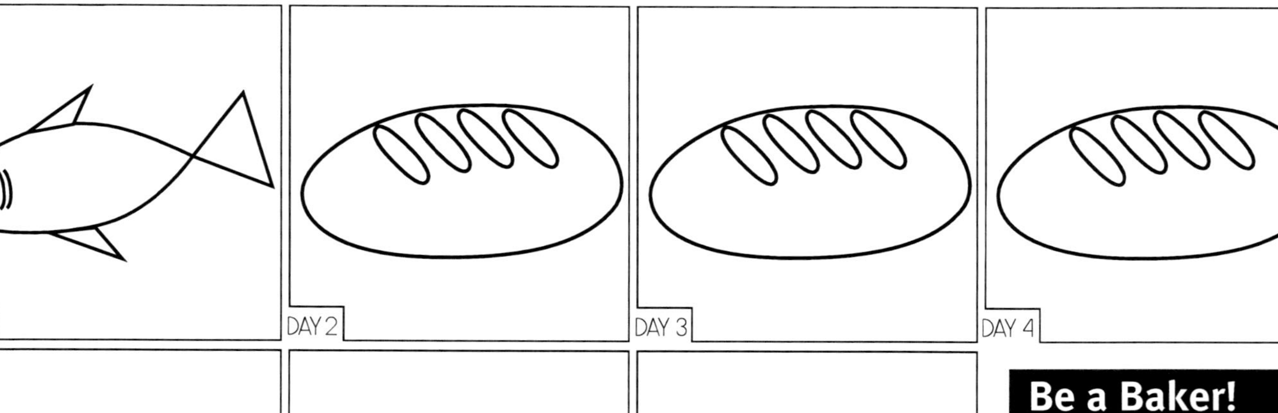

Colour in a loaf or fish each day. As you colour it in think of one thing from that day that you can offer to God.

This sheet has been completed by ....

FAMILY PRAYER

Lord Jesus, you have given us different talents.
***N*... is good at ... *N*... is good at ... etc.**
Help us all to offer our talents, and all we do, to you, Lord.
Help us to use them to make the world a better place.
Amen.

Be a Baker!

We are going to hear a lot about bread over the next few weeks. Try making some! You will need 700g strong white flour, 1 level teaspoon salt, 1 level teaspoon dried yeast, 1 level teaspoon caster sugar and about 425ml warm water. Mix into the flour, the salt, yeast and sugar. Make a well in the mixture and add the water – just enough to make a soft dough. Put your dough onto a flat surface and knead it until the dough becomes really springy and smooth. This can take 5 minutes or more. Pop the dough into a bowl and cover with oiled cling-film and leave it somewhere warm. Now go off to play until the dough has doubled in size and springs back when you press it (1-2 hours). Take it out of the bowl and start punching it and kneading it for 1-2 mins.

Put the dough into oiled bread tins – or experiment with different shapes.

Leave to rise (prove) for 20 mins. Bake: 200ºC/400ºF/No7 Time: 30-40 mins. To test your bread, ask an adult to take it out of its tin and tap the bottom of your loaf. It should sound hollow. (Small 100g rolls will only take 15-20 mins.)

Now the really hard part – wait for it to cool before cutting your first slice!

Family Sheet

To do at home with your family

For parents: Weekly Thought

Children usually love to be active and the summer holidays offer a wonderful opportunity for them to get out into the fresh air. However, it is also good to help them to develop the ability to be still and to enjoy simply "being". They learn how to make space where God can get in. Try to find time each day just being still with your child. Perhaps light a candle and give them a cuddle and rest content in the shared silence.

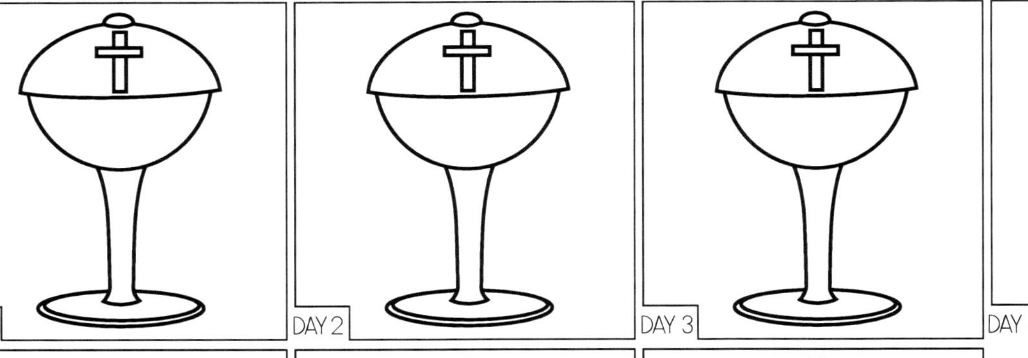
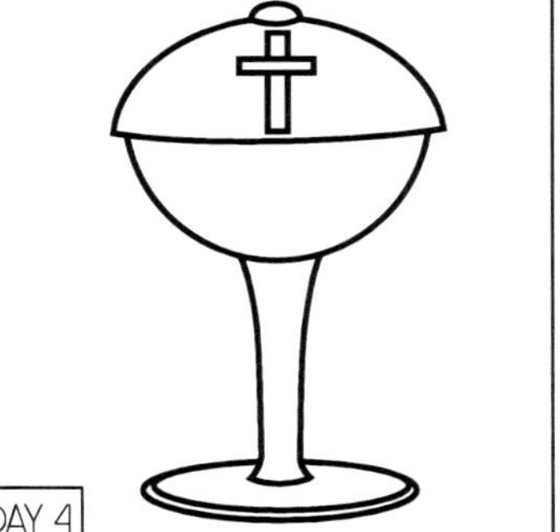
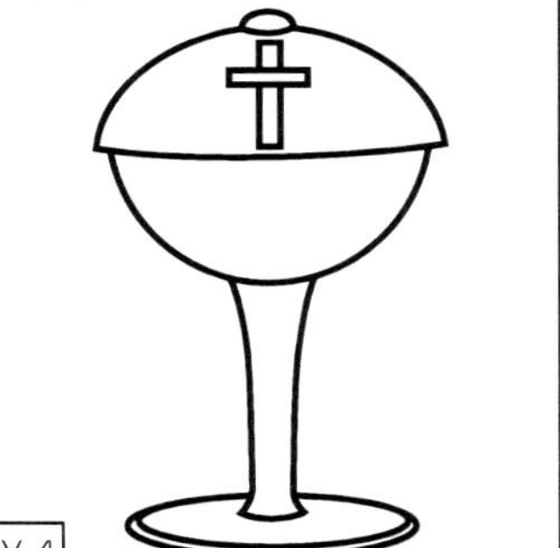

Colour in – or stick kitchen foil onto the ciborium each day. As you do remember Jesus and say thank you for being with you always.

This sheet has been completed by ....

FAMILY PRAYER

Lord Jesus,
thank you for being with us –
for loving our family.
Help us to grow closer to you and to share your love with everyone we meet.
Amen.

BAKERY INVESTIGATOR

Did you make bread last week? If you did, did you enjoy it?
If you go to the shops this week look in the baker's or bakery section of the supermarket.
How many different kinds of bread can you find?
What shapes can you see?
Do any of them have unusual ingredients?
Is any of the bread based on bread from another country? Which?
Draw some of the different breads and name them.

Family Sheet

To do at home with your family

For parents: Weekly Thought

We have no pictures of Jesus – no way of knowing what he actually looked like. We develop our images of him – and of God – from the stories in the Gospels and through other people telling us about them. Sadly, many adults have a negative image of God and this stifles their spiritual growth. Help your child to develop a positive image of Jesus – as one who loves them as much as you do.

Jesus DAY 1

Jesus DAY 2

Jesus DAY 3

Jesus DAY 4

Jesus DAY 5

Jesus DAY 6

Jesus DAY 7

Draw a picture of Jesus each day. Try to make each one different.

This sheet has been completed by ....

FAMILY PRAYER

Lord Jesus, thank you for helping us to see you.
Help us to see each other in good ways –
***N*... could be like a...**
***N*... could be ...**

(Invite the members of your family to offer a positive image of each other)

Some seaside jokes

Why don't bananas like to sunbathe?
Because they've a tendency to peel!

Why is a man wearing sunglasses like a bad teacher?
Because he keeps his pupils in the dark

Knock knock
Who's there?
Ann
Ann who?
Ann-emone

Knock knock
Who's there?
Seamus
Seamus who?
Seamus time to go home!

Family Sheet

To do at home with your family

For parents: Weekly Thought

Many children have little experience of death and bereavement. There is a natural tendency to want to protect them from the sadness and perhaps also the fear that death evokes. However, our faith offers us great hope in the promise of Jesus that we will inherit eternal life. Helping your child to talk about their feelings and sharing with them some of the traditional ways of dealing with mourning and bereavement will prepare them for their inevitable encounters with death in later life.

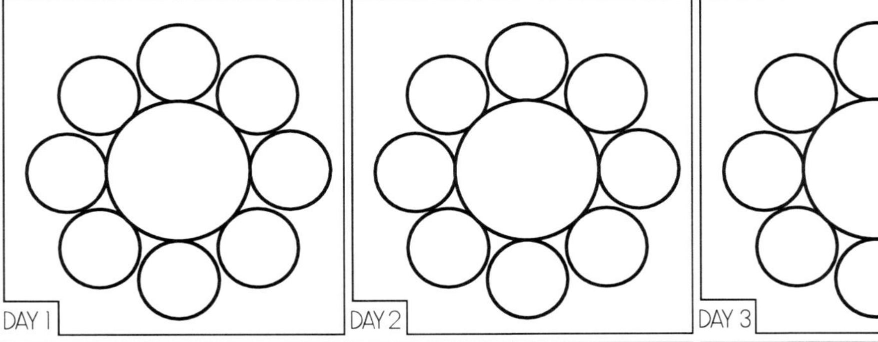

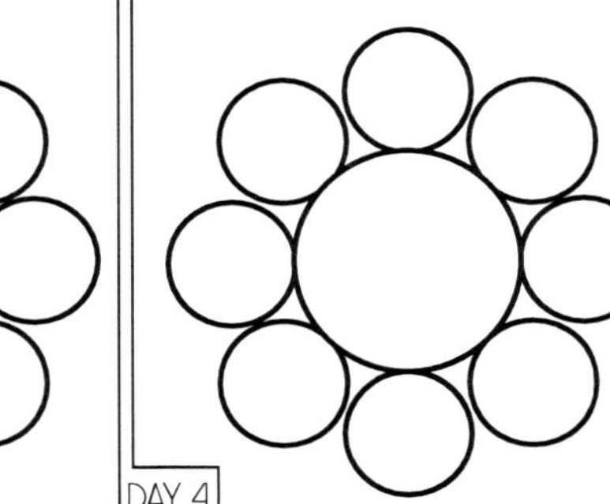

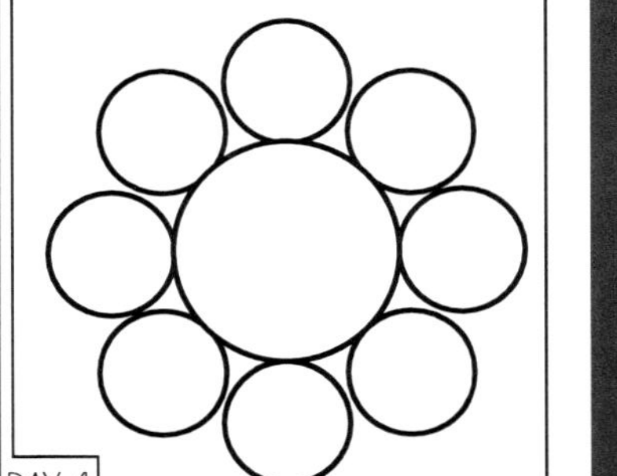

DAY 1 DAY 2 DAY 3 DAY 4 DAY 5 DAY 6 DAY 7

Colour in a flower each day. Think about the people you love and ask God to bless them.

This sheet has been completed by ....

FAMILY PRAYER

We pray for people who receive Communion at home
(include any names you know of).
We pray for the Eucharistic Ministers who take it to them
(include any names here).
We pray for people we love who have died
(include names here).
Bless everyone we love –
and bless us too.
Amen.

Be alert to God's gifts on earth

Heaven is about everything being the best we can imagine. During this week, try to keep all your senses alert and jot down all the things that make you happy.

- Things I saw
- Things I heard
- Things I touched
- Things I smelled
- Things I tasted

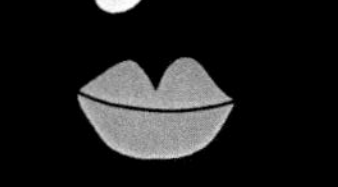

These are God's gifts to you now – even better things are waiting for you in heaven.

Family Sheet

To do at home with your family

For parents: Weekly Thought

Celebration is part of our lives as Christians. Though we know sorrow and sadness, we also know how to enjoy the good things in life. With the end of the holidays in sight, you may be feeling a mixture of relief and perhaps sadness – especially if your child is taking a crucial step to another school. This weekend could be the one in which to give yourselves permission to do something special – something that you can look back on and smile at over the weeks ahead.

Draw a big smile on each face to remember some fun that you and your family have had this week.

This sheet has been completed by ....

FAMILY PRAYER

**Lord Jesus, you loved to be with people –
you healed them –
and challenged some of them –
but you also knew how to have fun and to relax with your family and friends.
Help us to share good times –
and to know that you are sharing them with us. Amen.**

Interesting fact

Did you know that the word holiday comes from the Old English words for Holy Day – halig (holy) + dæg (day)?
These were days set aside to be like Sundays in the week – days for people to go to church and to rest.

Here are Holy Days – or holidays that Christians celebrate

Epiphany – 6 January
Ascension – 40 days after Easter (the Thursday of the Sixth Week of Easter)
The Body and Blood of Christ – the Thursday after Trinity Sunday
St Peter and St Paul – 29 June
Christmas Day – 25 December
Notice how most of them are in the middle of weeks in the summer!
The Church knows that people can work hard – but that they need times to rest and enjoy being alive.

Family Sheet

To do at home with your family

For parents: Weekly Thought

Our children are living in an age when outward appearances matter – they are aware of designer labels and brand names in a way that older generations were spared from. It is, however, the world in which they live and our job is, perhaps, to help them to discern between the outward appearances and the real thing. We can help them to learn to look at things more closely – and to decide for themselves.

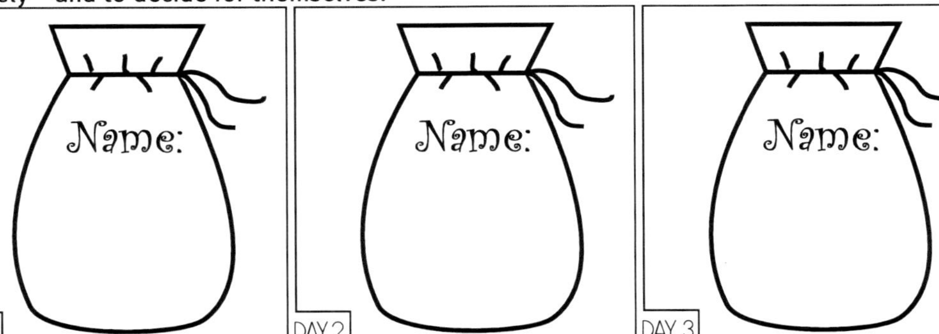

Colour in a PE bag for each time you help someone as they settle into their new class or school.

This sheet has been completed by ....

FAMILY PRAYER

Lord Jesus,
we are beginning a new school year.
Some people will be joining us for the first time –
help us to help them to settle in well;
help us to make new pupils to feel at home. Amen.

A New School Year

Many people are starting new terms – some of them new schools! Talk to your family about your hopes and dreams for the year ahead.
What are your New School Year Resolutions?
Write or draw them here.

23rd Sunday in Ordinary Time — Proper 18

Family Sheet

To do at home with your family

For parents: Weekly Thought

This week is about listening, and hearing God around us. Listening is actually very difficult. We all have so much to say! But standing back and paying attention, really listening (or looking), creates a stillness in which we may see God in others, and hear his will.

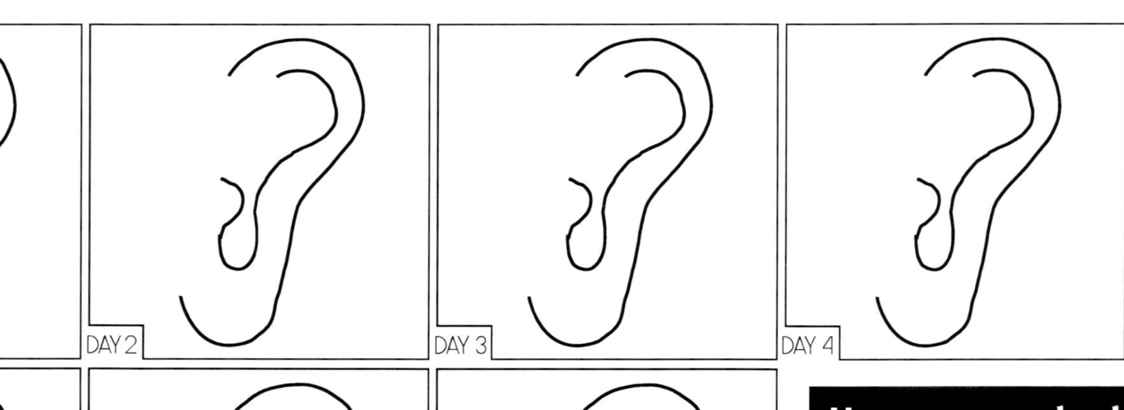

Colour an ear each day when you have really listened to someone else or to God, and discovered something new.

This sheet has been completed by ....

FAMILY PRAYER

Lord, be in my ears, and in my hearing. Be in my eyes, and in my seeing. Be in my mind, and in my understanding. Be in my heart, and in my caring. Lord, make me open to your word and to your world. And, Lord, be on my lips, and in my speaking.

How can we be better listeners?

Listen with your mind: what does what you hear really mean?

Listen with your heart: what do other people really feel?

Can we hear God in what other people say?

Can we reflect God's love to them, in what we do and say?

Family Sheet

To do at home with your family

For parents: Weekly Thought

One of the titles for God in the Old Testament is "The Lord my Integrity". We cannot be people of integrity by focusing on ourselves. God is our integrity, unchanging, whole, complete.

This week, Peter upset Jesus because he didn't really want to tell people that Jesus was God. You can help to make Jesus and Peter feel better by telling somebody you know that JESUS IS GOD! Each day, when you have done it then you can put a smile on their faces.

This sheet has been completed by ....

FAMILY PRAYER

Dear Jesus, you are God, and you wanted to behave like God all the time, but sometimes that was very hard. Peter was your friend, and he wanted to behave like your friend all the time, but sometimes that was very hard for him as well. We are your friends, and we want to behave like your friends all the time, but sometimes that is very hard for us too. Help us when we find it hard. Amen.

Keep an eye out this week for people acting with integrity – at home, at school, on the news, in the soaps. Discuss with your family how you know they are acting with integrity. If you spot anyone who is not acting with integrity, then think about what they could have done differently.

25th Sunday in Ordinary Time — Proper 20

Family Sheet

To do at home with your family

For parents: Weekly Thought

This week is about being a servant, not the boss. How easy it is to "pull rank"! To feel that being bigger and stronger gives one rights too valuable to forgo. How easy it is for children to pick up that message, instead of the message of humility and service Christ offers us. Can we set the right example for our children?

Colour a set of candles each day when you have been God's "secret agent".

This sheet has been completed by ....

FAMILY PRAYER

Lord Jesus, be with me whenever there is a need I can serve. Help me to see what needs doing, and to do it. Help me to find my reward in serving you, whether anyone else notices or not. Amen.

God's secret agents

Do you know what a secret agent is? James Bond is a secret agent. No one is supposed to know who he is. He goes about, fighting the baddies, and no one ever knows. God wants all of us to be his secret agents! He wants us to quietly step in and do the right thing, the loving thing, and step quietly away.

Family Sheet

To do at home with your family

For parents: Weekly Thought

This week is about seeing God in others. Recognising God in others is always hard, doubly so, when the “other” is very different, maybe from a different race or religion. But God is not limited by our preconceptions. Jesus exhorts us to see him in the most unlikely people.

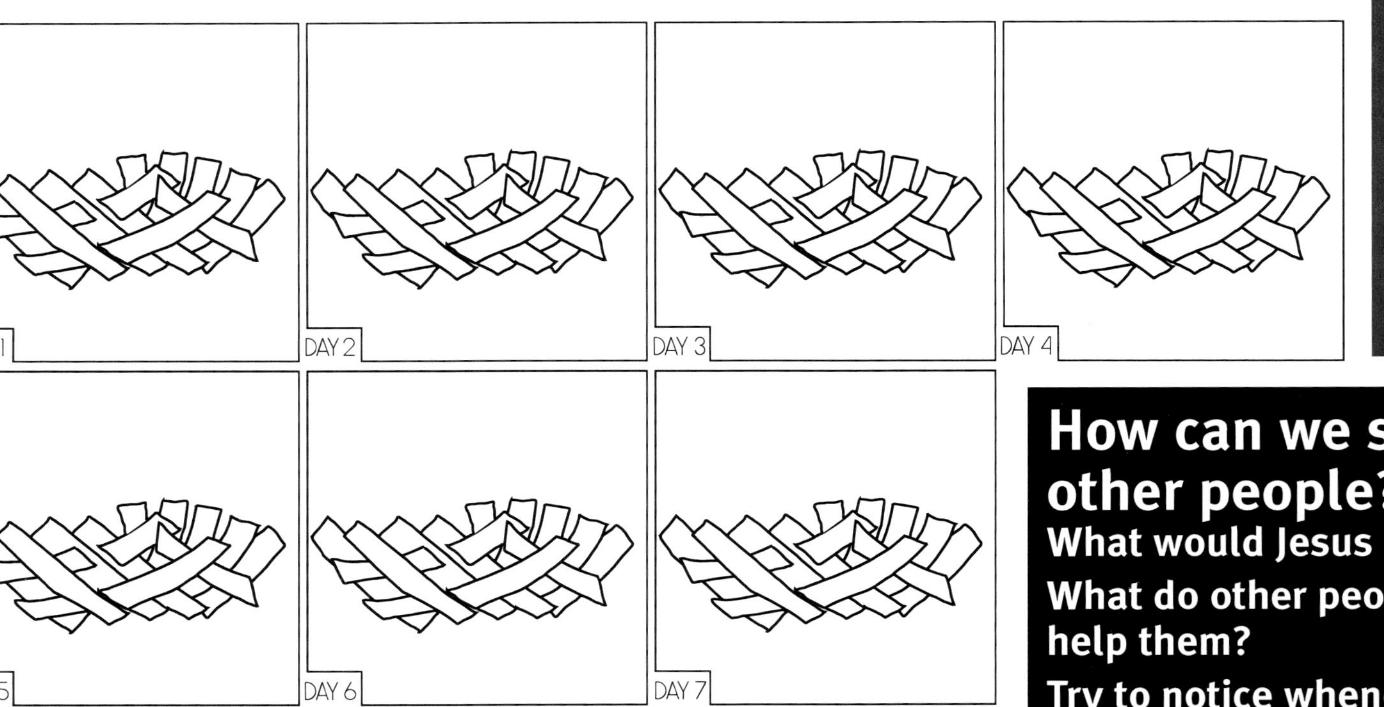

Colour a basket each day when you have done something loving and kind for someone, when you have shared God’s harvest.

This sheet has been completed by ....

FAMILY PRAYER

Lord Jesus, I know that you are everywhere in my world. Help me to see you, and your love for us all, in the people I meet. Help me to be you, and share your love with the people I meet. Amen.

How can we spot God working in other people?

What would Jesus do, if he were in this situation?

What do other people need someone to do, to help them?

Try to notice whenever someone does something loving and kind.

Try to find ways to be loving and kind, and to share God’s love.

Family Sheet

To do at home with your family

For parents: Weekly Thought

Our children are our future. We are often anxious that they are growing up too quickly in our post-modern society, becoming cynical and jaded before their time. One way to counteract that tendency is to encourage them to explore their roles and responsibilities towards other children in the world. What can they learn from those of the developing world who often have to share family responsibilities? How can this influence our family life?

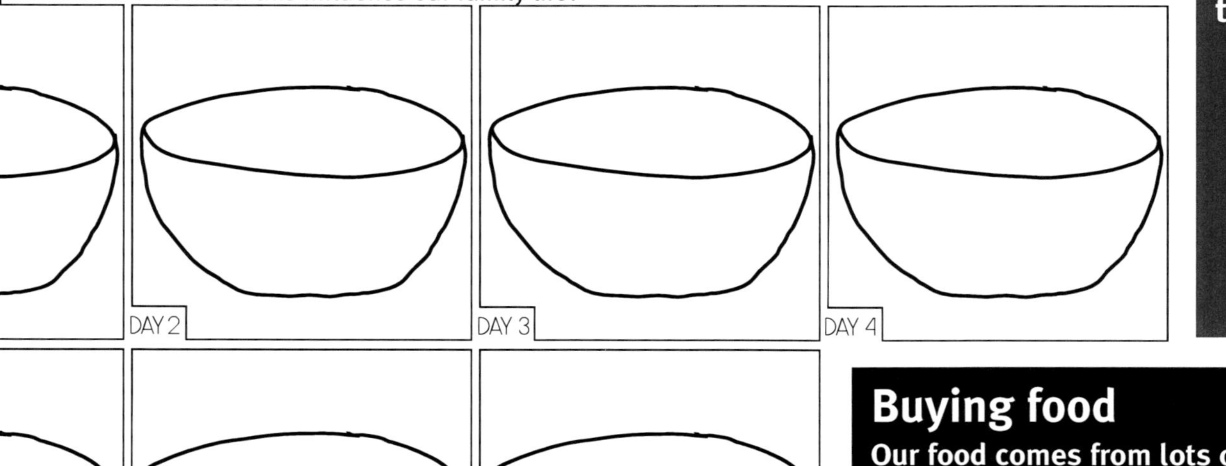

Draw something you have eaten, and write the name of the country it came from on each bowl this week.

This sheet has been completed by ....

FAMILY PRAYER

Dear Lord, thank you for the children in our family. Thank you for *N...*, *N...* (name the children). Thank you for all we have done together today.

Buying food

Our food comes from lots of different countries. In some countries the children work on the farms as well as grown-ups. When you go to the supermarket this week, ask your Mum or Dad to read the labels on the food so you know where it has all come from.

Find out about the Fairtrade organisation. They have a special logo. Go to a supermarket and find out which products you can buy with the Fairtrade logo on them. What does that tell you about these products? How will it help the children in these countries if you buy these things?

Family Sheet

To do at home with your family

For parents: Weekly Thought

Money can be the root of all evil, but only if it makes us take our eyes off God. This week we pray that we will use the riches God has given us wisely and prudently, remembering always that they come from God – and for God everything is possible.

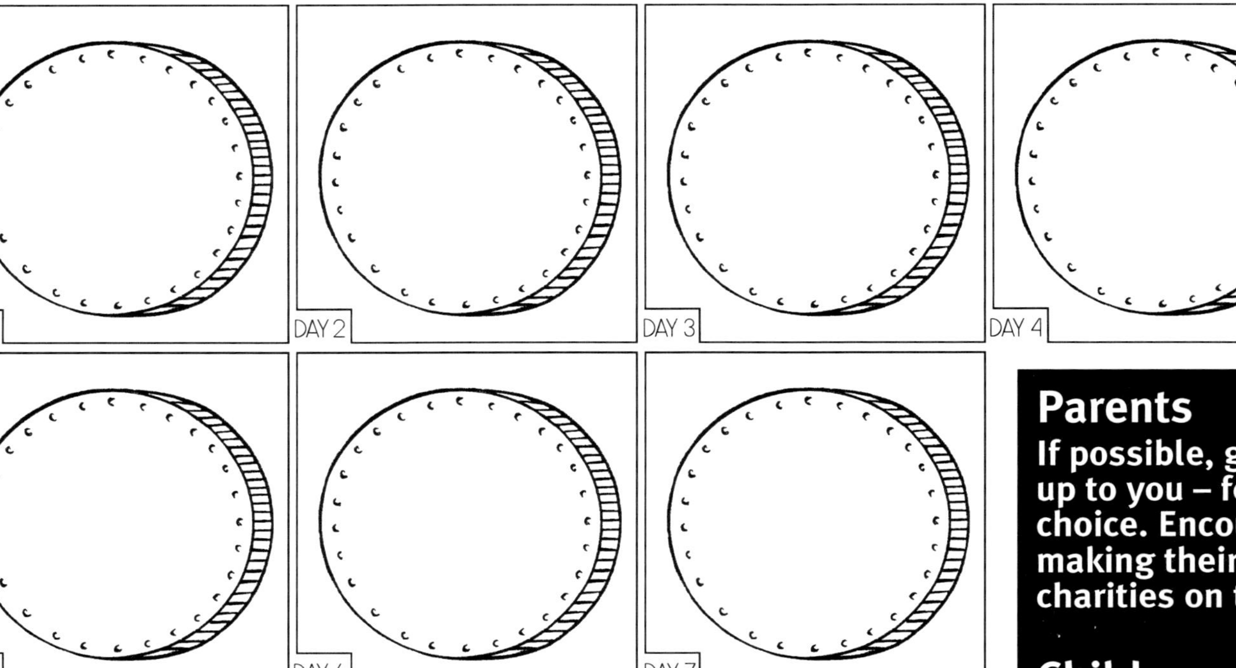

Write the names of the charities of your choice on the coins.

This sheet has been completed by ....

FAMILY PRAYER

God in heaven, we thank you for all the riches you give us. We want to use them to come closer to you, not to separate us from you. Help us to share them with other people. Amen.

Parents

If possible, give each child some money – the amount is up to you – for them to give to the charities of their choice. Encourage them to do a bit of research before making their choice. They can write the names of the charities on the coin symbols in this week's calendar.

Children

Each time you spend any money this week – pocket money, school dinners etc. – say a quiet prayer to God, thanking him for taking care of you. You might want to give a bit of your pocket money to a charity as well.

Family Sheet

To do at home with your family

For parents: Weekly Thought

Jesus does not ask us to serve each other as a way of humiliating us. He asks us to do it as a way of recognising the greatness of every person. Some of the greatest saints – St Catherine, St Teresa, St John, St Francis – all delighted in serving the people around them, because they recognised in every other person a great and wonderful and beautiful expression of God.

DAY 1 ------------ is great!

DAY 2 ------------ is great!

DAY 3 ------------ is great!

DAY 4 ------------ is great!

DAY 5 ------------ is great!

DAY 6 ------------ is great!

DAY 7 ------------ is great!

Write in the name of a person you think is great each day of this week.

This sheet has been completed by ....

FAMILY PRAYER

Dear God, I know that I am great, because you made me that way. Help me to see that the people around me are great as well. Thank you for all the great people you have given to me to live with. Amen.

World Mission

Today, we remember especially Jesus' words "Go and tell all nations, teaching them all that I have taught you." Jesus taught his apostles by living with them simply, serving them, and showing them God's greatness in his life and in their own lives. After he ascended to heaven, the apostles taught other people in the same way. We read that St Paul lived and worked with the people he was teaching, and refused to accept any food from them unless he had earned it first by serving them in some way.

This week you can take part in World Mission by doing the same thing. Make somebody feel really great each day this week, by working with them or serving or helping them in some way.

Family Sheet

To do at home with your family

For parents: Weekly Thought

Very often we see what we want to see, and we often get caught in the trap of seeing things in only one way. In the film *Dead Poets Society*, the teacher, played by Robin Williams, encourages the children to stand on their desks so as to see their world (the classroom) from a different perspective. Jesus wants to heal our sight so that we see things rightly and fully.

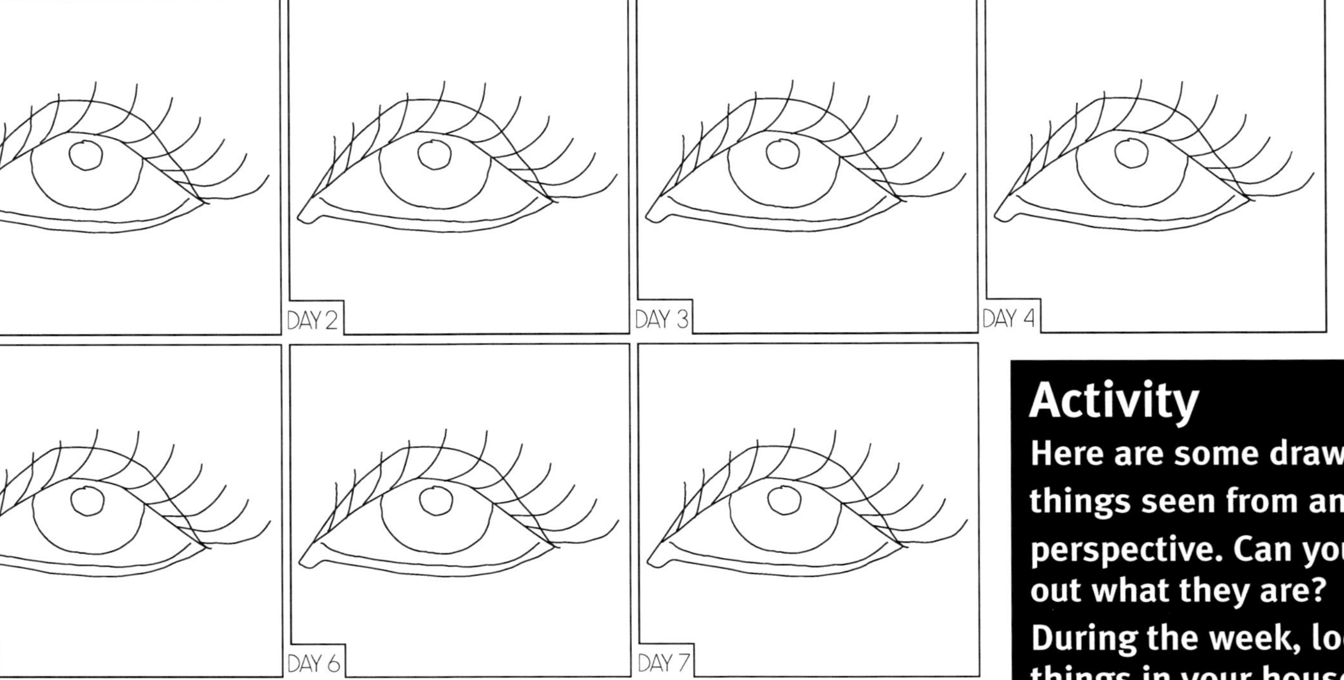

Colour in an eye each day that you have seen a thing or an idea in a different way.

This sheet has been completed by ....

FAMILY PRAYER

Dear Jesus, thank you for giving us the gift of sight. Help us to see the wonder of your world and all the beautiful people in it. Help us to see things and other people in the way you do. Amen.

mirror

bottle

Activity

Here are some drawings of things seen from an unusual perspective. Can you work out what they are?

During the week, look at the things in your house in a different way e.g. from underneath, or through a glass bottle etc. Draw some of them and see if your family can work out what they are.

Family Sheet

To do at home with your family

For parents: Weekly Thought

It is easy to forget how much ordinary family life has to teach us about love. It is less about the grand gesture than the simple putting others first. By your example of love – cuddling your child, caring for them when they are ill, listening to their woes and helping them to grow through them – they absorb what it means to be a loving person.

By noticing and praising their loving actions you can reinforce their growing up to be people who love and can be loved.

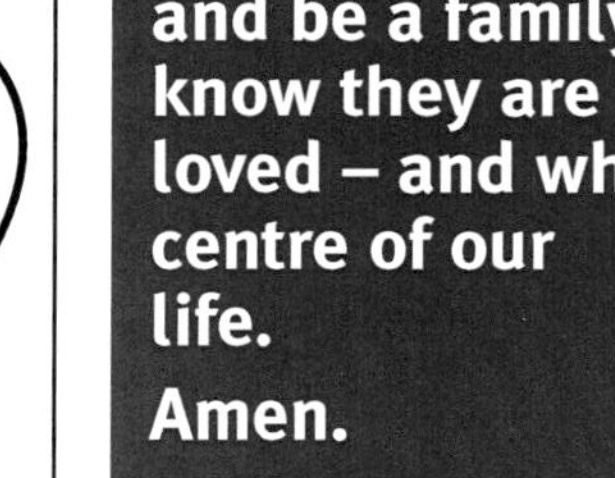

DAY 1 DAY 2 DAY 3 DAY 4

DAY 5 DAY 6 DAY 7

Lots of people use hearts to symbolise love. Colour in a heart each day and think about how people have loved you and how you have loved God and other people.

This sheet has been completed by ……………………………………………

FAMILY PRAYER

Lord Jesus, you remind us that the way to please you and to be happy is to love God and to love each other.

Help us to love each other

and be a family where people know they are welcomed and loved – and where you are at the centre of our life.

Amen.

Walking into Autumn

Oliver and Amy went to a country park to collect acorns and conkers. There are lots of things to see in parks and in the countryside at this time of the year.

See if you can find a sunny day when you can wrap up warm – take some soup in a flask and go on a walk into autumn.

Can you still find conkers and acorns – or helicopters? Collect some of the different leaves that have fallen. Use them to create a picture when you get home.

Family Sheet

To do at home with your family

For parents: Weekly Thought

The Church has a strong tradition of social teaching and holds the common good in high regard. The Church also has an option for the poor – seeing the care of the vulnerable as a vital part of its mission. The Gospel of the widow's mite reminds us that we don't have to be able to give a huge amount to make a difference. In a world of great disparity of wealth, it is even more important to help our children to develop a sense of solidarity with their brothers and sisters around the world.

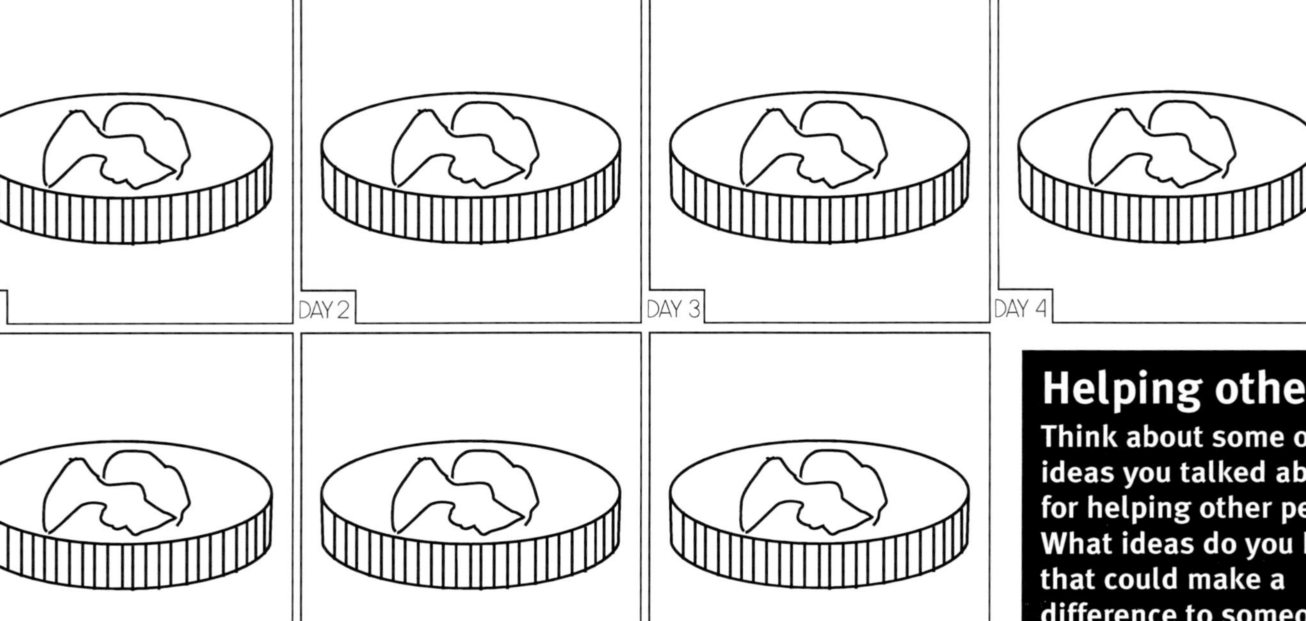

Decorate a coin for each day. Think about people who are generous with the little they have and of people who are in need of help to make a good life.

This sheet has been completed by ....

FAMILY PRAYER

Lord Jesus,
we are very blessed in our family.
We have ... (name some of the good things that your family has).
Thank you for all these gifts – help us to use them wisely and generously. Amen.

Helping others

Think about some of the ideas you talked about for helping other people. What ideas do you have that could make a difference to someone this Christmas?

Look around your church and see what people are already doing – do they give you any ideas?

Visit some websites to find out what is going on:

www.cafod.org.uk or www.christianaid.org.uk are good places to start.

Family Sheet

To do at home with your family

For parents: Weekly Thought

Trust can be a liberating quality in a person's life – just as mistrust can be debilitating. If our experience teaches us that, on the whole, people are decent and will treat us with respect, we grow in confidence in ourselves and in others. If our experience is the opposite, the results may be catastrophic: someone may appear confident but inside they are constantly afraid. As parents, we hope to help our children to develop trust and confidence in us – a responsibility all the more important as this will enable them to have trust and confidence in their heavenly Father too.

Colour in a picture of Jesus each day and remind yourself that you can trust Jesus in everything. You might like to tell him about something that went wrong and imagine him reminding you that he's with you and loves you.

This sheet has been completed by ....

FAMILY PRAYER

Jesus, you ask us to trust you always.

Help us to be a family that other people can trust.

Help us to be trustworthy to each other –

so that we can all grow in love and confidence in you.

Amen.

Praying for prisoners and their families

When people are sent to prison, it is easy to forget about them, to think that it is all their own fault – and sometimes it is. We pray that they learn their lesson and come out of prison ready to lead a better life.

Usually, though, their families had nothing to do with the crime – but they suffer too. They may be lonely; the children might be teased. They feel as if they are being punished for something that they did not do.

And some people are in prison who are innocent or waiting for trial. This can be a very hard and worrying time for them and for their families.

If you can, light a candle in church this week and say a prayer in your own words for prisoners and their families. Or ask a grown-up to light one with you and say the prayer at home.

Our Lord Jesus Christ, Universal King

Christ the King

Family Sheet

To do at home with your family

For parents: Weekly Thought

Most years see their share of conflict, famine, illnesses, refugees and more. It is likely that your children have seen news bulletins that have frightened them – or heard things at school. Part of our role as parents is to create a safe place where children can confide their fears and find reassurance – even if we share their worries. We can help them to learn that, however powerful they seem, earthly kingdoms and tyrannies pass away – but the kingdom of God endures for ever.

DAY 1 DAY 2 DAY 3 DAY 4 DAY 5 DAY 6 DAY 7

Colour in a crown each day. Try to do something that Jesus would be proud of and make it a jewel in his crown.

This sheet has been completed by ....

FAMILY PRAYER

Lord Jesus, you are our King.

Thank you for everything good that has come our way this year like ...

We thank you for being with us in the bad things too like...

Bless us always and help us to be ready to come to live in your kingdom for ever.

Amen.

End of the Year Quiz

See how much you can remember.

1. Who were the man and woman who met the baby Jesus and his parents in the Temple? _ _ _ _ _ _ and _ _ _ _
2. Lent begins on _ _ _ _ _ _ _ _ _ _ _ _
3. We remember Jesus' death on _ _ _ _ _ _ _ _ _ _
4. We remember Jesus' resurrection on _ _ _ _ _ _ _ _ _ _ _
5. Forty days after Easter we celebrate _ _ _ _ _ _ _ _ _ _ _ _
6. And ten days after that, we remember the Coming of the Holy Spirit at _ _ _ _ _ _ _ _ _
7. We have a feast with a Latin name that means the Body of Christ. It is _ _ _ _ _ _ _ _ _ _ _ _ _
8. On 29 June, we remembered Saints _ _ _ _ _ and _ _ _ _
9. The Feast of the Assumption is on _ _ _ _ _ _ _ _
10. 1 November is the feast of _ _ _ _ _ _ _ _

The Most Holy Trinity

Family Sheet

To do at home with your family

For parents: Weekly Thought

God is three persons in one, the Father, the Son and the Spirit of love between them. We too have God's Spirit of love, and so, with the Son, we love the Father. We can show our love for God by singing him songs.

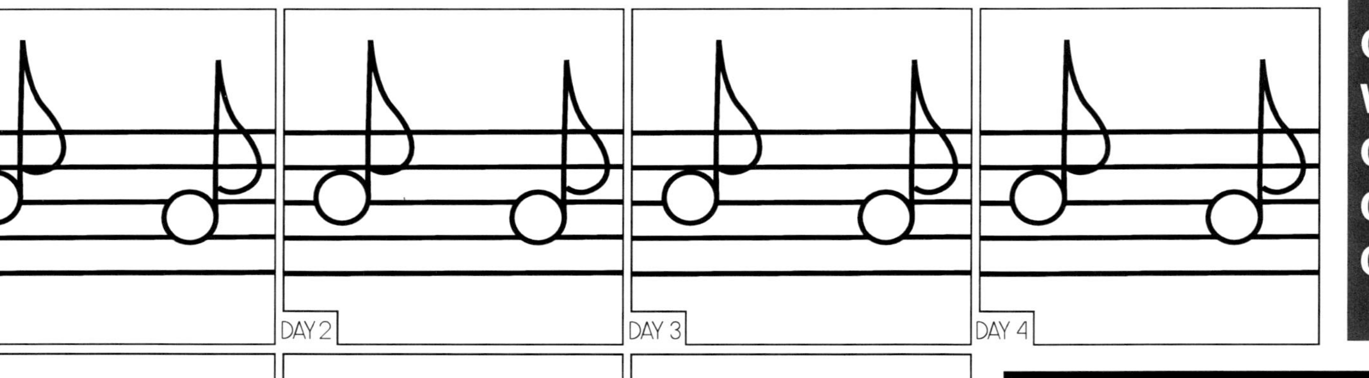

Colour in a song sheet each day when you sing your prayers to Jesus.

This sheet has been completed by ....

FAMILY PRAYER

"He who sings, prays twice"

"O Lord, hear my prayer
O Lord, hear my prayer
When I call, answer me,
O Lord, hear my prayer
O Lord, hear my prayer
Come and listen to me."

(Taizé)

It's difficult to sing if you're unhappy; so have a talk about the good and bad things that have happened in your day. Listen to each other and say sorry, if you need to. Each night, choose a different song to sing to God during your prayer time. Don't forget to ask God's Spirit to help you sing, and remember to ask Jesus to sing with you. Mum or Dad might want to join in as well. Use actions to make your hymn come alive.

The Body and Blood of Christ (Corpus Christi)

Family Sheet

To do at home with your family

For parents: Weekly Thought

Today the juniors have been learning about the principles of transubstantiation. Young people can be surprisingly adept at picking up and using technical terms. You (might) remember the terms "substance" and "accident" from your schooldays. A good dictionary will give a quick reminder if you look up transubstantiation. Encourage the children this week to describe the substance and accidents of things around them to help them familiarise themselves with these words.

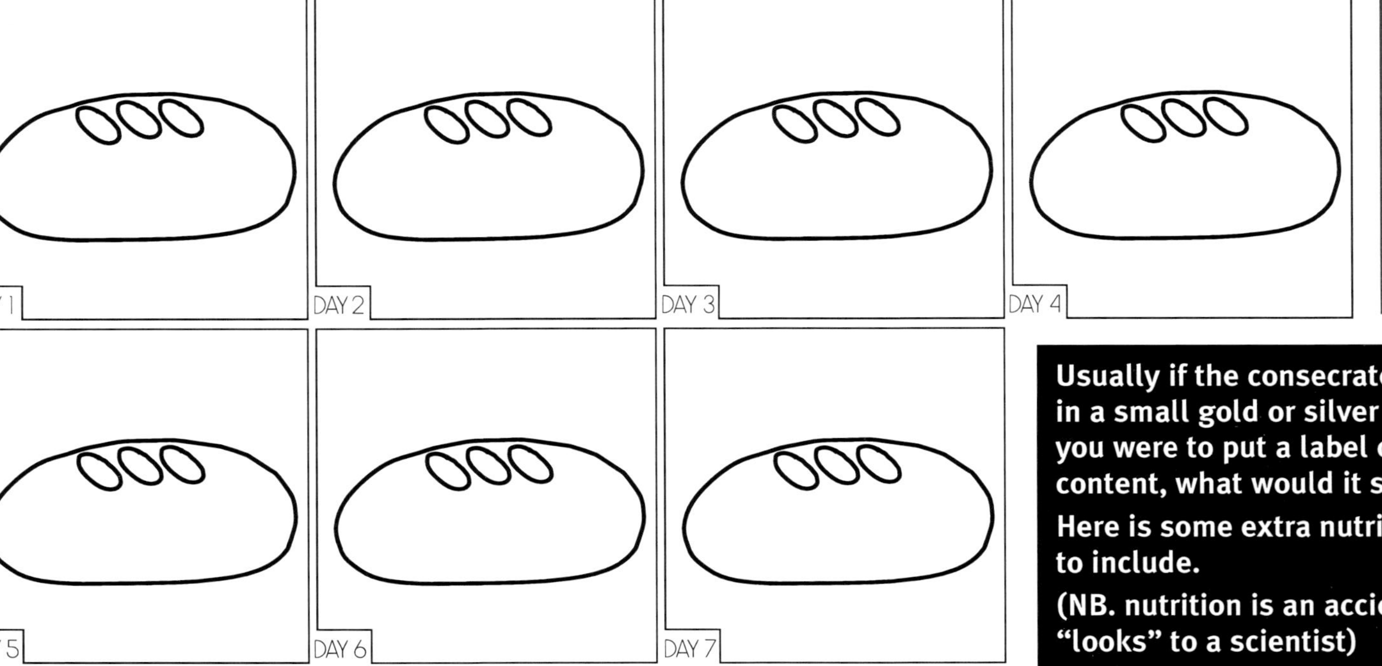

Young ones can be responsible for giving out the bread at mealtimes this week. Each day they can colour in a loaf to show they have done the job well.

This sheet has been completed by ....

FAMILY PRAYER

Dear Jesus, thank you for the bread you have given us. Thank you for giving yourself to us. Please bless all those people who do not have enough bread to eat. Amen.

Usually if the consecrated host is taken out of church, it is carried in a small gold or silver case to remind us of how precious it is. If you were to put a label on the case describing the nutritional content, what would it say?

Here is some extra nutritional information which you might want to include.

(NB. nutrition is an accident as well – as it is the way the food "looks" to a scientist)

In 1 large consecrated host,

Nutrition (Accidents): Energy 6Kcal, Protein 0.1g, Sugar 0.1g, Trace elements 10mg

Substance: 100% Jesus, 100% Holy!

The Presentation of the Lord

Family Sheet

To do at home with your family

For parents: Weekly Thought

Simeon told Mary that her heart would be pierced with sorrow. At Calvary she saw her son hurt and killed, but what of the years before that. Remember how Jesus got left behind in Jerusalem when he was twelve? How did she feel? Worried? Angry?
Children can be a worry! By entrusting them to God through the sacraments and fellowship of our church family, we give them a good start. May God's kindly light lead them on!

Here are seven candles with big flames. Colour one in when you have brought God's light into somebody's life this week.

This sheet has been completed by ....

FAMILY PRAYER

**Father, may your light shine in our hearts tonight and every night.
Amen.
Glory be to the Father, and to the Son, and to the Holy Spirit; as it was in the beginning, is now, and ever shall be, world without end. Amen.**

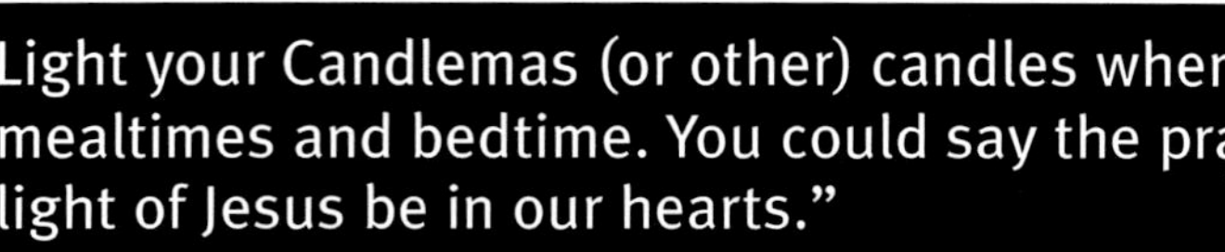

- ★ Light your Candlemas (or other) candles when you pray at mealtimes and bedtime. You could say the prayer: "The light of Jesus be in our hearts."
- ★ Talk about the way the days are growing longer. This is God's world. He uses it to talk to us, to remind us that he loves us. It isn't just little children who give us wild flowers, God does too!
- ★ Ask your children who brings light into their lives each day. Share such a moment from your day. It could be "Your smile when I picked you up from school", but they may like to hear about a moment of grace at work or home or the shops.

The Birth of St John the Baptist

Family Sheet

To do at home with your family

For parents: Weekly Thought

The decision about what name to give a child is one that can fill the whole pregnancy, especially when both boys' and girls' names have to be considered. How does it sound with the surname? Should we name them after a beloved relation? What happens if one partner loves one name and the other hates it? The name we give to our child will be part of its identity for the rest of its life. Still more powerful is the image offered in Isaiah chapter 49, that God has written that name on the palm of his hand.

DAY 1 DAY 2 DAY 3 DAY 4

DAY 5 DAY 6 DAY 7

This is the time when the days are at their longest in the northern hemisphere. Praise God for sunshine and summer. Colour in a sun and give thanks for a different part of Creation each day.

This sheet has been completed by ....

FAMILY PRAYER

Lord God, we thank you for our family.

For *N* ... and *N*...

Help us to grow in love for each other as Zechariah, Elizabeth and John did.

Amen.

Summer stroll for the senses

This is a lovely time of year to get out and about. The weather is usually warm and the evenings are long.

Take time to take a stroll. Take a notebook or sketch pad and jot down what you see – or hear – or touch – or smell – or even taste!

Even in a city you will be surprised how much you can find.

As you find each thing, say a prayer in your heart to thank God for it – and for the fact that it is there for you to find.

Ss Peter and Paul, Apostles

Family Sheet

To do at home with your family

For parents: Weekly Thought

Although we think that good leaders all have a certain type of personality, when we look closely, we find that many seem to succeed despite their personalities rather than because of them. Everybody can have a leadership role in some aspect of life.

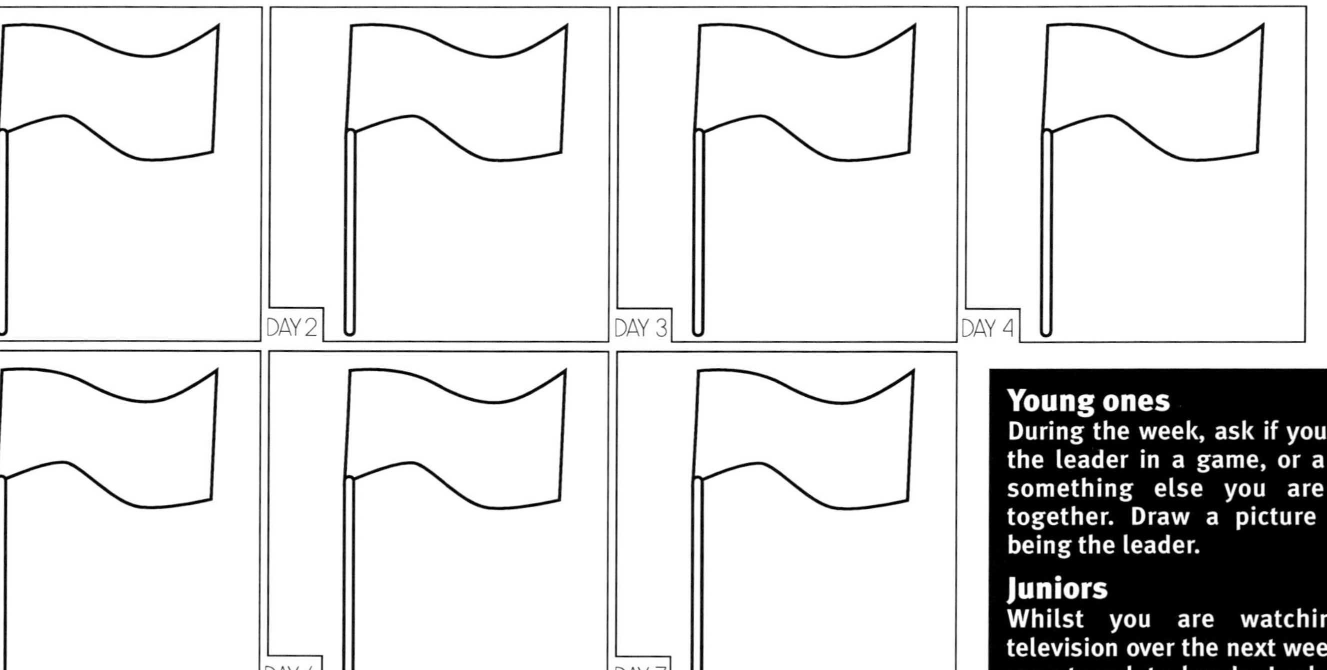

Colour a flag each day when you have either followed a leader, or been a leader yourself. You may like to write in words instead.

This sheet has been completed by ....

FAMILY PRAYER

St Peter and St Paul, you were the leaders in the Church when Jesus went back to heaven. That was not very easy. Thank you for all your work. Please pray for us when we find things difficult. Amen.

Young ones

During the week, ask if you can be the leader in a game, or a job, or something else you are doing together. Draw a picture of you being the leader.

Juniors

Whilst you are watching the television over the next week, keep your template handy. Look out for people who are leaders – on the news, in the soaps, children's presenters etc. Do they have the characteristics you would expect from a leader? If they don't, what do you think it is that makes them successful?

Poem - "The Leader" by Roger McGough

I wanna be the leader.
I wanna be the leader.
Can I be the leader?
Can I? I can?
Promise? Promise?
Yippee, I'm the leader
I'm the leader
OK what shall we do?

The Transfiguration of the Lord

Family Sheet

To do at home with your family

For parents: Weekly Thought

Many of us have had moments when we have held or looked at our child and been a little awe-struck by them. Often this can happen when they are born as we marvel at their tininess, the size of their fingernails. Sometimes, it is something they do that is beyond our expectations. Our hearts swell with love and pride. This parental love is something that is part of our being made in the image and likeness of God, our love reflecting on a small scale the great love God has for all his children.

Write or draw in your speech bubble, words or actions that have made you or others feel like glowing with happiness.

This sheet has been completed by ....

FAMILY PRAYER

PARENT:

Lord Jesus, your Father was proud of you and pleased to call you his Son.

I am proud to have *N*... as my son/ daughter and thank you for giving him/ her to me.

Bless him/ her and keep him/ her safe always. Amen.

CHILD:

Lord Jesus, thank you for my family.

Help me to do what is right so that they are always proud of me. Amen.

A word puzzle

How many words can you make from the letters of

TRANSFIGURATION?

20 – good 30 – very good 40 – excellent 50 – you are a genius!

The Assumption of the Blessed Virgin Mary

Family Sheet

To do at home with your family

For parents: Weekly Thought

Our instinct is to shield children from death but many will know someone – even of their own age – who has died or who is terminally ill. Our faith gives us a way to help our children to come to terms with these realities and ways to deal with them when they happen. Consider having a family candle to light at sad or happy times. Encourage your child to light candles in church at the end of Mass.

Colour in a flame on the candle each day and think about someone you especially want to pray for as you do.

This sheet has been completed by ....

FAMILY PRAYER

Pray the Hail Mary together. Or perhaps pray the Glorious Mysteries – one Mystery each day. There are books with beautiful illustrations which you could use with your child.

The Feast of the Assumption of the Blessed Virgin Mary: 15 August

It is an important day because it reminds us that God took Mary to heaven and promises to do the same for us one day.

We do not know much about Mary's death but in AD 451 a man called St Juvenal said that Mary had died in the presence of all the apostles. When St Thomas later opened her tomb, it was found to be empty. The apostles believed that this proved that her body had not been allowed to decay but had been taken up into heaven by God. Some people said that the tomb was not empty but filled with roses and lilies.

The Triumph of the Cross

Holy Cross Day

Family Sheet

To do at home with your family

For parents: Weekly Thought

This week is all about sharing the triumph of the cross with everyone. We take the cross so much for granted. It's easy to assume that our children understand the awe and glory of this symbol of life, and the dramatic struggle involved in making such a sign of evil into good. But they need our help! Share the power of the feelings released by the cross.

Colour a cross each day when you have shared God's love with someone.

This sheet has been completed by ....

FAMILY PRAYER

Lord Jesus, help us always and everywhere to remember your cross, the sign of your love for us, and to share that love with everyone we meet. Help us always to remember your love is for everyone. Amen.

How can we share God's love with other people?

- How do you feel when someone loves you?
- What makes you feel that someone cares about you?
- Can we find a way to show Jesus how happy we are that he loves us?
- Can we find a way to make someone feel special, every day?

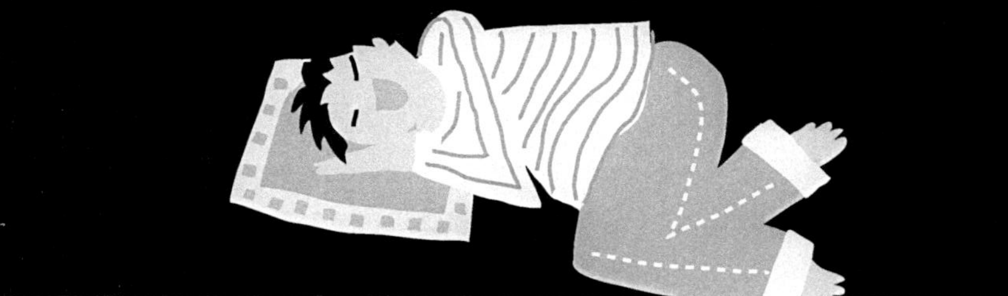

All Saints

Family Sheet

To do at home with your family

For parents: Weekly Thought

November is the month during which we traditionally remember those who have died. For many children, death is something they see on television but are otherwise sheltered from. The Church's teaching can help during bereavement or in dealing with your child's response to something they have seen or heard. We are promised heaven and, if it takes a while to get there, the prayers of those left behind can help on that journey.

DAY 1 DAY 2 DAY 3 DAY 4

DAY 5 DAY 6 DAY 7

Draw a halo on the smiley face each day. Think of something you have done that is helping you to get ready to be a saint.

This sheet has been completed by ....

FAMILY PRAYER

Jesus, thank you for opening heaven up to us.

We look forward to the day when we can be with you for ever.

We pray for *N*... and *N* ... (name people you know who have died).

If they are already saints, ask them to pray for us.

If they are still on the journey, use our prayers to help them on their way.

Amen.

Interesting fact

In Mexico, people celebrate the Feast of All Saints by going to their cemeteries. They call this the Feast of the Dead. People go to their families' graves and tidy them up – clear away old flowers and put bright marigolds and other flowers on them and on the crosses there. People take special meals and have picnics and chat with the other families. Sweets in the shape of skulls are exchanged – some even have the people's names on them!

The Commemoration of All the Faithful Departed (All Souls)

Family Sheet

To do at home with your family

For parents: Weekly Thought

Talking to children about death is not easy but having the tradition of holding November as a month of remembrance helps us to put it into a safe context. Doing the same things as other people is very reassuring for children. Light candles in church or during a quiet time at home and pray for people who have died.

If someone close to you has died recently, take your child to the cemetery or garden of remembrance. If it helps, look at photographs and remember happy times. Even if there are a few tears do not worry, learning about grief is an important part of growing up.

DAY 1 DAY 2 DAY 3 DAY 4

DAY 5 DAY 6 DAY 7

Colour in a flower each day. Say a prayer for someone who has died and ask God to take care of them.

This sheet has been completed by ....

FAMILY PRAYER

Lord Jesus, you passed through death into new life and opened heaven up to us.

We ask you to bless our family and friends who have died.

Keep them safe until we all meet again in heaven. Amen.

To think about

What do you think heaven will look like? What do you think it will sound like? What would you like it to smell like?

Think about all the things that make you happy and imagine them being even better...

Draw a picture, or write a poem about heaven and being with people you love for ever.

Family Sheet

To do at home with your family

For parents: Weekly Thought

It is very easy to take being able to go to church for granted. Throughout the history of the Church, worship has been suppressed. In Eastern Europe, police and secret service agents watched church buildings to see who went in and out. In China, Christians struggle to worship and their careers are blighted. And yet the Spirit moves people to persevere in their faith. Help your child to see how privileged we are and to make the most of the gift of freedom to worship.

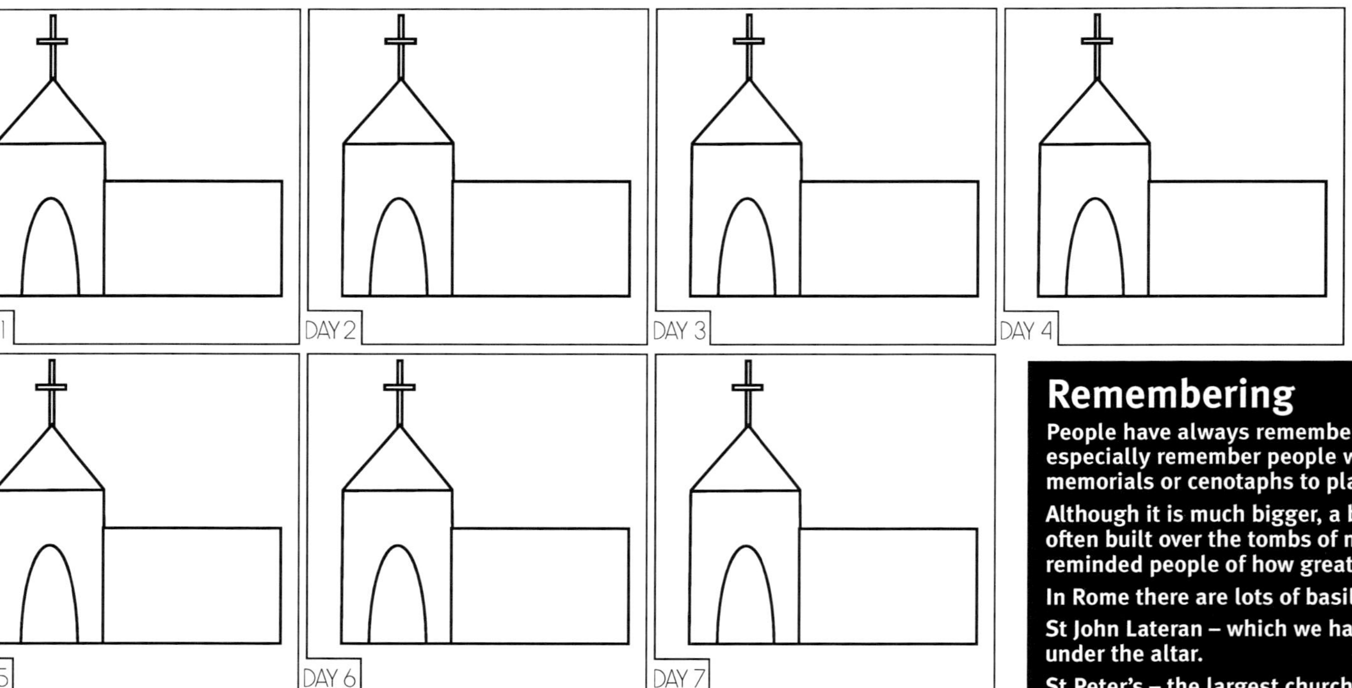

Colour in a church to remind yourself of people who are not as lucky as you because they cannot go to church. Draw a big smiley sun on the days that you actually go into church, even if it is just to pop in and say "hello" to God.

This sheet has been completed by ....

FAMILY PRAYER

Lord Jesus, thank you for the gift of our church (*N*...) and the hard work and fund-raising that went into building it.

Thank you for all the people who work to keep it looking beautiful – for our priest (*N*...) and for all the people who join us to praise and worship you.

Amen.

Remembering

People have always remembered people who have died. On Remembrance Sunday we especially remember people who have died in wars. Many people will go to special war memorials or cenotaphs to place poppies as a sign of remembrance.

Although it is much bigger, a basilica is also partly a memorial. In Rome, basilicas were often built over the tombs of martyrs with the altar directly over the tomb itself. This reminded people of how great a sacrifice some people had made for their faith.

In Rome there are lots of basilicas but there are four main ones:

St John Lateran – which we have heard about this week – which does not have a tomb under the altar.

St Peter's – the largest church in the world (186.35 metres long and 97.5 metres wide), built over the tomb of St Peter.

St Mary Major – where St Matthew is buried. The basilica is the main church in Rome dedicated to Mary.

St Paul's without the walls – this does not mean it does not have any walls! It was built outside the old Roman walls on the site where St Paul was buried.

See what more you can find out about buildings used for remembering people.

St David, Bishop

Family Sheet

To do at home with your family

For parents: Weekly Thought

Celebrating a feast like that of St David is a way of helping our children to reach into their heritage. We live in a world where many people feel "lost" and make things up as they go along, but our Christian tradition encourages us to look back to the richness of experience and wisdom that has gone before us. By knowing where we have come from we can perhaps be more confident about going forward into the future.

DAY 1 DAY 2 DAY 3 DAY 4

DAY 5 DAY 6 DAY 7

Colour in a daffodil each day as you try to follow St David's example of being a light for the world.

This sheet has been completed by ....

FAMILY PRAYER

Lord Jesus, thank you for the gift of St David to our Church.

Help us to be proud of our heritage and to live out his example of being someone who brought light to the world.

Amen.

A Welsh Treat

Did you have Bara Brith to celebrate St David's Day? Did you enjoy it? It is not hard to make.

450g (1lb) mixed dried fruit.
300ml (1/2 pint) tea. 2 tbsp marmalade. 1 egg, beaten. 6 tbsp soft brown sugar. 1 tsp mixed spice. 450g (1lb) self-raising flour.

1. Soak the fruit overnight in the tea.
2. Next day, mix in remaining ingredients. Spoon into a greased 900g (1lb) loaf tin and bake in a warm oven (gas 3, 160 C) for 1 hour or until the centre is cooked. Cover with foil if top is browning too much.
3. Once cooked, leave the Bara Brith to stand for 5 minutes, then tip out onto a cooling tray. Using a pastry brush glaze the top with honey.
4. Serve sliced with salted butter and farmhouse Cheddar. Store in an airtight tin.

St Patrick, Bishop

Family Sheet

To do at home with your family

For parents: Weekly Thought

The Irish people have given the world a great deal of their Christian heritage. As they travelled to all parts of the world, whether as a result of famine or the search for work, they took their faith and, even today, they are among the foremost missionary countries.

Our children are blessed that people have passed on the light of faith. In a way you are a missionary to your child, passing on the faith you have inherited in words and ways they can understand. Even today, the spirit of St Patrick lives on through us.

Colour in a shamrock each day. Think about St Patrick telling people about the Good News of Jesus. Try to find a way of showing people that being a Christian makes you happy.

This sheet has been completed by ....

FAMILY PRAYER

God of all creation,

thank you for sending St Patrick to us – and for all the people who have passed on the Good News about Jesus.

Help us to be the kind of people who continue to spread that Good News.

Amen.

A celebration cake to make
Apple Cake from the county of Kerry

150g/ 6oz butter. 150g/ 6oz castor sugar. 2 eggs, beaten. 200g/ 8oz self-raising flour. 2 medium cooking apples, peeled, and chopped.
1tsp lemon rind. 2tbsp demerara sugar, pinch cinnamon and nutmeg. Mix together.

1. Preheat oven to gas mark 4/ 180 C/ 350 F
2. Grease and line a 900g/2lb loaf tin.
3. Cream together the butter and sugar and gradually add eggs and flour.
4. Stir in the apples and lemon rind.
5. Pour into the tin and sprinkle the top with sugar and spices.
6. Put it in the oven and bake for 1- $1^1/_2$ hours.